THE POEMS AND FABLES OF
ROBERT HENRYSON

THE MORALL FABILLIS OF ESOPE THE

Phrygiã, Compylit in Eloquẽt, & Ornate Scottis mé-
ter, be M. Robert Henrisõe, scolmaiter of Dũfermlig.
Newlie correctit, and Vendicat, fra mony Errouris,
quhilkis war ouer sene in the last prenting, quhair baith
Lyntis, and haill Versis war left owt. VIII 21

ESOPVS

EDINBVRGH.

Inprinted att Edinburgh be me Thomas Bassandyne, dwelland at the nether Bow Anno. 1571.

THE POEMS AND FABLES OF
ROBERT HENRYSON

SCHOOLMASTER OF DUNFERMLINE

EDITED FROM THE EARLIEST
MANUSCRIPTS AND PRINTED TEXTS
BY

H. HARVEY WOOD

OLIVER & BOYD
EDINBURGH
LONDON

BARNES & NOBLE
NEW YORK
1968

FIRST PUBLISHED 1933
SECOND EDITION, REVISED .. 1958
REPRINTED 1965
REPRINTED 1968

First published in the United States of America
by Barnes & Noble, Inc. 1968

PRINTED IN GREAT BRITAIN BY
JOHN DICKENS AND CO LTD
NORTHAMPTON

'They do not care for Scottish bookes,—
    They list not looke that way :
But if they would but cast their lookes
    Some time when they do play,
Somewhat to see perhaps they might
    That then would like them wel,
To teach them treade thair way aright,
    To blisse, from paines of hel.'
'Farewel, good Phrygian Poet, now,
    I may no more sojourne.'
'If not,' sayth Esope, 'then adew,
    Into Scotland I'le returne.'

    The Argument between Esope and the Translatour,
    The Fables of . . . Master Robert Henryson . . .
    Englished.
                 RICHARD SMITH, *Anno* 1577.

PREFACE

It would be ungenerous to introduce a new edition of Henryson without a free and grateful acknowledgment of the admirable work done by David Laing and George Gregory Smith. David Laing owed more than a little to George Chalmers, and the late Professor Gregory Smith paid tribute to Laing: it is now my turn to confess my indebtedness to all three. Henryson has, in the past, been lucky in his editors, but it has been my good fortune to have the handling of material that was unknown or inaccessible to them. In the case of one text in particular, the 1577 Englishing of the *Fables* by Richard Smith, the volume was known to Chalmers in 1824, to Laing in 1865, and to Gregory Smith in 1914, but has never before, in upwards of a hundred years, been accessible to an editor of Henryson. The St John's College manuscript and the 1663 print of the *Testament of Cresseid*, though known, have not been used before, and the 1571 Bassandyne text of the *Fables*, upon which my text is based, was neither known nor used. Further, the valuable Asloan manuscript collection, which was withheld from previous editors, has been made available, edited, photographed, and the prints deposited in the National Library of Scotland. It is obvious, therefore, that a new text of Henryson is both possible and necessary; and I hope that in the Commentary and Textual Introduction I have been able to contribute to the better understanding of the poet.

My acknowledgments must be brief and comprehensive. To my friend, Professor Bruce Dickins, of Leeds University, I owe more than I can acknowledge in detail; his enthusiasm first kindled mine, and his scholarship has always been at my service. I wish to thank the Staff of the National Library of Scotland; Dr H. W. Meikle, the Librarian, who, by the purchase of the Bassandyne Henryson, not only accommodated me but enriched the Library; Mr William Beattie, the Keeper of Printed Books, who has kept neither books nor counsel from me; and

Mr M. R. Dobie, the Keeper of Manuscripts, for advice on many occasions. Dr Lauriston Sharp, Keeper of Manuscripts in the Library of Edinburgh University, has searched in the Laing papers for Henryson items, and has put his knowledge of the University MSS. at my disposal. Sir W. A. Craigie, of the University of Chicago, has answered questions relating to obscurities in the text; and the Duke of Rutland, Dr A. W. Pollard, Lieut.-Col. Frank Isaac, Mr A. F. Johnson, Mr J. C. Ewing, and Mr F. S. Ferguson have kindly replied to enquiries made on my behalf by Mr Beattie. Dr E. G. Millar, Deputy Keeper of Manuscripts in the British Museum, and the librarians of York Minster, by their kindness to me, lightened my labours in these libraries; while the generosity of the Trustees of the Moray Bequest made them possible. Mr H. M. Adams, Librarian of Trinity College, Cambridge, deposited the unique 1663 *Testament of Cresseid* in the National Library of Scotland for my use. Mr Angus Macdonald, Lecturer in English Language in this University, assisted me in the preparation of the introductory list of linguistic characteristics. And, in conclusion, my publishers, Messrs Oliver and Boyd, have treated me with rare toleration and generosity. The faults of the book are all my own.

EDINBURGH, 26*th May* 1933.

PREFACE TO SECOND EDITION

Two corrections in the text and commentary derive from D. Hamer's review of the first edition of this work, in *The Modern Language Review*, vol. xxix, No. 3, July 1934.

I am deeply indebted to my brother-in-law, Dr William Beattie, Librarian of the National Library of Scotland, for his enthusiastic help and fruitful suggestions in the preparation of this second edition.

EDINBURGH, 17*th January* 1958

CONTENTS

INTRODUCTION

LIFE

Of the life of Robert Henryson little is known but that he lived in the latter half of the fifteenth century, wrote a certain number of poems with which his name, in certain early manuscript and printed texts, is associated, and died sometime before 1508, when Chepman & Myllar printed Dunbar's *Lament for the Makaris*,[1] where his death is lamented—

> 'In Dunfermelyne he hes done roune
> With Maister Robert Henrisoun.'   (ll. 81-2)

And as this Lament groups the names of poets of an older school, together with that of 'Gud Maister Walter Kennedy,' for example, who at the time of writing 'in poynt of dede lyis veraly,' we cannot even infer from its evidence the exact date of Henryson's death.

If we give any credence to the late narrative of Sir Francis Kinaston we shall be confirmed in the belief that Henryson died 'very old,' and so, putting his death any time between 1500 and 1508, we may guess his date of birth at some time early in the second quarter of the fifteenth century. The narrative in question is contained in Kinaston's manuscript Latin translation of Chaucer's *Troilus and Cresseid*, made in 1639. After having rendered the five books of Chaucer's 'tragedie,' he added a version of Henryson's *Testament of Cresseid*, which, in William Thynne's edition of 1532, was printed as a continuation or sixth book. Thynne does not distinguish between the authorship of the two poems, and in later editions the confusion was continued. *Francis* Thynne, animadverting on the corruption of the Chaucer text, especially in Speght's edition (1599), writes: 'yt would be good that Chaucers proper woorkes were distinguyshed from the adulterat and such as were not his, as the Testamente of Cressyde.' Kinaston,

---

[1] In the *Porteous of Noblenes and ten other rare tracts*, Chepman & Myllar, 1508 (National Library of Scotland). Actually, the *Lament* is undated.

however, was better informed than most of the editors, and his ascription of the poem is accompanied by an account of Henryson's last moments, which, even if apocryphal, is the only anecdote at his biographer's disposal.

(I take the text of the note from Gregory Smith's edition, I. ciii.).

'For the Author of this supplement called the Testament of Creseid, which may passe for the sixt & last booke of this story I have very sufficiently bin informed by Sr Tho: Eriskin late earle of Kelly & divers aged schollers of the Scottish nation, that it was made & written by one Mr Robert Henderson sometimes cheife schoolemaster in Dunfermling much about the time that Chaucer was first printed & dedicated to king Henry the 8th by Mr Thinne which was neere the end of his raigne: This Mr Henderson wittily observing, that Chaucer in his 5th booke had related the death of Troilus, but made no mention what became of Creseid, he learnedly takes uppon him in a fine poeticall way to expres the punishment & end due to a false unconstant whore, which commonly terminates in extreme misery, about, or a litle after his time the most famous of the Scottish poets Gawen Douglas made his learned & excellent translation of Virgils Æneids, who was bishop of Dunkeld, & made excellent prefaces to every one of the twelve bookes: For this Mr Robert Henderson he was questionles a learned & a witty man, & it is pitty we have no more of his works being very old he dyed of a diarrhea or fluxe, of whome there goes this merry, though somewhat unsavory tale, that all phisitians having given him over & he lying drawing his last breath there came an old woman unto him, who was held a witch, & asked him whether he would be cured, to whome he sayed very willingly. ti en quod she there is a whikey tree in the lower end of your orchard, & if you will goe and walke but thrice about it, & thrice repeate theis wordes whikey tree whikey tree take away this fluxe from me you shall be presently cured, he told her that beside he was extreme faint & weake it was extreme frost & snowe & that it was impossible for him to go: She told him that unles he did so it was impossible he should recover. Mr Henderson then lifting upp himselfe, & pointing to an Oken table that was in the roome, asked her & seied gude dame I pray ye tell me, if it would not do as well if I repeated thrice theis words oken burd oken burd garre me shit a hard turde. the woman seing herselfe derided & scorned ran out of the house in a great passion & Mr Henderson within halfe a quarter of an houre departed this life.'

An account so far out in Henryson's *floruit* can be of no great authority on any other matter, so it is fortunate that the only other item of importance—'sometimes cheife schoolemaster in Dunfermling'—is confirmed by the testimony of early title-pages. George Chalmers' suggestion that the poet was one of the Henrysons, or Hendersons, of Fordel, in Fife, was dismissed by David Laing in 1865; and there is no good reason for believing that the John Henryson, Master of the grammar school in the Abbey of Dunfermline, who addressed a complaint to the Privy Council in 1573, was related to the poet by any bond, other than that of office. Attempts have been made to identify the poet with two other Henrysons. Laing identified him with a certain 'venerablis vir Magister Robertus Henrisone in Artibus Licentiatus et in Decretis Bachalarius,' incorporated in the newly founded University of Glasgow in 1462; and Chalmers, in 1824, recognised the poet in a 'Robert Henrison, notarius publicus,' who witnessed certain deeds in the Chartulary of Dunfermline (1477-8). But Laing himself, from whom all Henryson studies derive, provided a sufficient reason for rejecting these insubstantial figures by citing a list of over thirty contemporary and local Henrysons (six of them Robert Henrysons)—a list which could not hope, and did not pretend, to be complete.

There are two other references to our poet in the poetry of his own time. Gavin Douglas, in a holograph gloss to the word 'Muse' in his translation of the Æneid (*c.* 1522), *Camb. MS. Gale* 03.12, writes—

'Musa in Grew signifeis an inventryce or invention in our langgage. And of the ix Musis sum thing in my palys of honour and be Mastir robert hendirson in new orpheus' (*Orpheus and Euridyce*, ll. 29-60).

And Sir David Lyndesay, in his Testament and Complaynt of our Soverane Lordis Papyngo (*c.* 1530), writes of Henryson and other dead poets—

'Thocht thay be deed, thar libells bene levand, Quhilk to reheirs makeith redaris to rejoise.'

In the poems themselves there is little or nothing for the biographer. From *Orpheus and Eurydice* we learn that he had no ear for music (*CM* l. 125):

'For in my lyf I coud nevir syng a note;'

The *Abbay Walk* may suggest the great Benedictine Abbey of Dunfermline, in the Grammar and Song School of which the poet taught. The lost poem, *On fut by Forth*, also suggests local allusion, as does the phrase 'fra lawdian to lundin' [Lundin in Fife, not London] in the extravagant *Practysis of Medecyne*. When we have said this, we have given all the materials that exist for a life of Henryson.

THE POEMS

Henryson is known to the ordinary reader, if at all, as the poet of *Robene and Makyne* and the *Testament of Cresseid*. These two poems were frequently reprinted in the latter half of the eighteenth century, especially *Robene and Makyne*, which was included by Allan Ramsay in the *Ever Green*, in 1724, after which it was printed by the editor of the 1748 *Poems in the Scottish Dialect*, Percy, Lord Hailes, Pinkerton, etc. If it must be conceded that there are among the minor poems (and it should be remembered that the canon is by no means definite) some which have no title to immortality, it is right that the poet of the *Fables*, of *Orpheus and Eurydice*, *The Bludy Serk*, *The Annunciation*, and others, should be remembered and read. Indeed, in offering this edition to the public, the editor ventures a claim for Henryson, which, he is confident, the poems will sustain, that he is, without equal, the greatest of the Scots makars. The comparison with Dunbar immediately intrudes itself, for it is obvious that Dunbar is the only other with a right to contest the title. Dunbar, I am prepared to admit, is a greater virtuoso, a more accomplished technician, one of the greatest metrists, not only in Scots, but in all English literature. Not that the technical equipment of Henryson is in any way deficient. It is always adequate to his requirements, but it is never, as often with Dunbar, obtrusive. He is seldom, if ever, betrayed into mere virtuosity; but, on the other hand, he is, in the essentials

❧ The Prolog.

Thocht feinzeit fabils of auld poetrie,
Be not al grunded vpon truth, zit than,
Thair polite termes of sweit rhetore
Richt plesand ar vnto the eir of man,
And als the caus yat thay first began
Wes to repreif the haill misleuing,
Off man be figure of ane vther thing.

In lyke maner as throw the bustious eird,
(Swa it be laubourit with grit diligence)
Springis the flouris, and the corne abreird,
Hailsum and gude to mannis sustenence,
Sa dois spring ane morall sweit sentence,
Oute of the subtell dyte of poetrie,
To gude purpois, quha culd it weill apply.

The nuttis schell, thocht it be hard, and teuch,
haldis the kirnell, and is delectabill.
Salyis thair ane doctrine wyse aneuch,
And full of frute, vnder ane fenzeit fabill.
And clerkis sayis, it is richt profitabill,
Amangis ernist to ming ane merie sport,
To light the spreit, and gar the tyme be schort.

Forther mair, ane bow that is ay bent,
Worthis vnsmart, and dullis on the string,

of poetry, a more original artist than Dunbar or any other of the Chaucerians. His originality is of that kind which places a poet in the main current of poetic tradition; the more obvious originality of Dunbar is often one of mere technical eccentricity.

The greatest, and the most original, of Henryson's works is that one which would appear least likely to have that quality—his translation of the *Moral Fables* of Æsop. In this rehandling of popular and traditional material, the reader has the best opportunity of assessing the classical nature of Henryson's originality—the originality that makes all things its own, the originality of Chaucer, and of Shakespeare. Not only in tales for which no original is known (like *The Fox, the Wolf and the Cadger*), but in well-worn pieces like *The Town-mouse and the Country-mouse*, the story is told as though it had never been told before, with a wealth of personal observation, simple pathos, and lively humour. The dead bones are made to live. Æsop, the slow-pacing moralist of medieval tradition, is barely recognisable. Like the cadger of the fable, 'As he had hard ane pyper play, he gais'; and the moralising, which is admittedly dull, is confined to the postscript. Henryson's most Chaucerian gift, though it should be recognised as one distinctively Scottish, is his power of turning from pathos to humour, from the sublime to the ridiculous, in a line or phrase which breaks in upon the narrative like a spoken comment in the voice of the poet. When the two mice, seated at their alderman's feast, and singing, 'Hail, Yule, hail!' for very joy, are startled by the entrance of the steward with his keys, how is their scuttling to safety described?—

'Thay taryit not to wesche, as I suppose!'

It is perfect art, of the same kind as Chaucer's chat with the eagle in the *Hous of Fame*. The cadger, stepping out as to a piper's tune, and singing, 'Huntis up, up, upon hie,' belongs to the same realm of art as Dame Pertelote and Chanteclere singing

'In sweete accord, "My lief is faren in londe."'

And when the cadger finds the wolf stretched out on the highway before him, hoping to beguile him with the fox's wiles, and steps down cautiously, saying,

'"Softlie, . . . I was begylit anis;
Be I begylit twyis, I schrew us baith . . . ."'

we are, whether we recognise it or not, on the pinnacle of verse narrative. Henryson's sense of humour is ever in evidence, and it has a quality that is recognisable in Scottish humour to this day. In the fable of the *Fox and the Wolf*, the fox, having been forbidden all meat but fish by his ghostly confessor, the wolf, kills a kid and plunges it in the stream—

> 'He doukit him and till him can he sayne,
> "Ga doun schir Kid, cum up schir salmond agane!"
> Quhill he wes deid; syne to the land him drewch,
> And of that new maid salmond eit enewch.'

Then he stretched himself out under a bush, to warm his 'wame' in the sun's heat, and, in reckless vainglory, he reflected that a distended belly like his needed only an arrow in it, to complete the picture. With that, the keeper of the herd came past, and, with his bow, pinned him to the ground—

> '"Now," quod the fox, "alace and welloway!
> Gorrit I am, and may no forther gane;
> Methink no man may speke a word in play
> Bot now on dayis in ernist it is tane!"'

Or when the fox and wolf return from their embassy to the contumacious mare, the wolf with the top of his head kicked off and the blood running over his heels, the fox, in answer to the lion's questioning, says,

> '"My Lord, speir not at me!
> Speir at your Doctour off Divinitie,
> With his reid Cap can tell yow weill aneuch."
> With that the Lyoun and all the laif thay leuch.'

And we cannot but laugh with them. How irresistible is the dignified scorn of the burgess mouse, when faced with the homely cheer of her country sister—

> '"My fair sister" (quod scho), "have me excusit,
> This rude dyat and I can not accord;
> To tender meit my stomok is ay usit,
> For quhylis I fair alsweill as ony Lord;
> Thir wydderit peis, and nuttis, or thay be bord,
> Wil brek my teith, & mak my wame fful sklender,
> Quhilk wes before usit to meitis tender."'

She bids her come to town, where, says she, 'My dische weschingis is worth your haill expence,' and to town they run. Faced with the splendour and plenty of the city establishment what is the comment of the country sister?—

'"Yea, dame," quod scho, "bot how lang will this lest?"'

These are the commonplaces of life, recorded by one who observed them with a keen, kindly eye. In his treatment of the commonplaces of literature, he is equally skilful. Whether it is the *Ubi sunt* motive, as in the *Testament*,

'Quhair is thy Chalmer wantounlie besene?'

or the pastoral *estrif*, as in the incomparable *Robene and Makyne*, with the old refrain,

'The man that will nocht quhen he may
Sall haif nocht quhen he wald . . .'

or the hour-glass motive, as in the *Aige and Yowth*, or the death's head, as in the *Thre Deid Pollis*, these commonplaces, in Henryson's hands, become personal and sincere.

In the Trial of the Fox, for instance, he introduces one of the dullest and most familiar of medieval poetic devices, the beast-catalogue, the usual gathering of beasts real and imaginary, familiar and fantastic. But in his hands, even this takes on the interest of things seen and noted—

'The marmisset the Mowdewart couth leid,
Because that Nature denyit had hir sicht;
Thus dressit thay all ffurth ffor dreid off deid;
The musk, the lytill Mous with all hir micht
With haist scho haikit unto that hill of hicht.'

What will rejoice Scottish readers more than anything, I believe, will be to find in this fifteenth century Dunfermline schoolmaster the same distinguishing features that mark out the Scotsman, in any company, to-day. In the *moralitas* sections, for instance, he is more than disposed to address his Maker in an admonitory and chastening tone. The sheep cries out,

'"Lord God, quhy sleipis thow sa lang?
Walk, and discerne my cause, groundit on richt;"'

b

and elsewhere this peremptory note, reminiscent of the north-country pulpit, is to be heard. And, when the poet is visited in a dream by his master Æsop, listen to their conversation:

> '(He) said, "God speid, my sone"; and I wes fane
> Of that couth word, and off his cumpany;
> With reverence I salusit him agane:
> "Welcome, Father"; and he sat doun me by.
> "Displeis you not, my gude maister, thocht I
> Demand your birth, your facultye, and name,
> Quhy ye come heir, or quhair ye dwell at hame."'

Anyone who has travelled by train in the Kingdom of Fife, in the same compartment as one of the natives of that kingdom, knows that last line by experience—

> 'Why ye come heir, and whaur ye dwell at hame?'

And, in the reading of Henryson, the Scots reader's heart will be warmed again and again by such "couth words" and undeniable bonds of kinship.

Only once or twice in the poems is the narrative manner discarded for a few lines to make way for a personal comment, and one of these utterances has all the freshness and delight of Chaucer's best asides. When, in his account of Orpheus' flight through the outer heavens, he has become thoroughly involved in a long, pedantic description of the planets and the music of the spheres, Henryson extricates himself with an ease that is typically Chaucerian, and remarks,

> 'Off sik musik to wryte I do bot dote,
> Tharfor at this mater a stra I lay,
> For in my lyf I coud nevir syng a note.'

So Chaucer breaks free from the discussion of predestination in which Chanteclere and Pertelote are embroiled, with

> 'I wil not han to do of swich mateere,
> My tale is of a cok. . . .'

But in two of the poems there are passages that rise to real heights of tragic feeling and expression. Forsaken Orpheus, crying in vain for his Eurydice,

> '"Quhar art thow gane, my luf Erudices?"'

and

'"My lady Quene and luf, Erudices,"'

strikes a note of real feeling in the heart of that rather frigid poem, besides anticipating a rhetorical device that was to stand Marlowe in good stead when he wrote—

'Now walk the angels on the walles of heaven,
As Centinels to warne th' immortall soules,
To entertaine devine *Zenocrate*.'

And the epitaph on the marble tomb of Cresseid is one of the most moving things in literature—

'Lo fair Ladyis, Cresseid, of Troyis Toun,
Sumtyme countit the flour of Womanheid,
Under this stane, lait Lipper, lyis deid.'

THE TEXT

THE MORALL FABILLIS OF ESOPE·

Printed Texts.

1. There are four early printed texts of the *Fables*, two of which have not been used by any previous editor of Henryson. Previous editions have been based only on the manuscripts and the text printed by Robert Lekpreuik for Henry Charteris, Edinburgh, 1570 (small quarto, black letter), of which a single copy survives. This quarto, formerly in the Britwell Court Library, is now preserved in the British Museum. In 1865, David Laing, Henryson's first responsible editor, stated that a copy of the Charteris print was included in the sale of the library of Sir Andrew Balfour, M.D. (Catalogue, p. 113), which took place by public auction in Edinburgh in 1695. The book is described as : *Aesop's Fables, Englished by Mr Robert Henrison :* Edinb. 1570, 8vo, and was perhaps a copy of the Charteris print. Laing also claimed to have seen a copy in private hands in Edinburgh, 'not many years since.' It is more than possible that the copy seen by Laing was that sold in 1695;

but no other man has ever seen it since. Should it ever reappear, it is not certain that it will prove to be another copy of Charteris.

2. In the following year, another text was printed in Edinburgh, by Thomas Bassandyne, at the Nether Bow, and of this text, too, a single copy is all that survives (or is known to survive). No previous editor of Henryson has known of its existence, although until recently it has been in the Library of York Minster. The present editor owes his knowledge of the book to a marginal note made by the late Dr J. F. Kellas Johnstone in the late Dr Erskine Beveridge's *Bibliography of Dunfermline*. Under the description of the Charteris print of the *Fables*, he has noted: 'There is another copy (printed by Bassandyne) Edin^r., 1571, in York Minster.' A first enquiry at York Minster Library failed to discover the book, but, in reply to a more particular and importunate query, the Librarian, Canon F. Harrison, replied that the *Fables* had been in the Minster Library, but that the copy had been sold some two years ago to Dr Rosenbach, of New York. A search among Dr Rosenbach's printed catalogues revealed the book in question:

AESOP. The morall Fables of Esope, compylit in eloquēt, & ornate Scottis meter, be M. Robert Henrisoe. 1571.

At this stage of the hunt, the present editor enlisted the aid of the National Library of Scotland. Dr H. W. Meikle, the Librarian, entered into negotiations with Dr Rosenbach, and, as a result, the Fables returned to Scotland, to a more suitable and permanent home in the National Library. Upon the text as found in this copy, the present edition is based. A full description of the book is given in the Appendix, page 217.[1]

3. The third surviving printed text is less important from a textual point than either of the others, but, like the Bassandyne print, its actual history is of some interest. It was known to

---

[1] This edition *may* be the book recorded in the Inventory of Thomas Bassandyne (1579) [*Dickson & Edmond*, p. 292 ff. " Item, thrie Fabule Esopi, the pece xxx d.—summa vii s. vi d."]

David Laing about a hundred years ago, and in 1865 he described it minutely. The title runs as follows:

The Fabulous tales of | Esope the Phrygian, Compiled | *moste eloquently in Scottishe* | Metre by Master Robert | Henrison, & *now lately* | *Englished.* | *Every tale Moralized most aptly to* | *this present time, worthy* | *to be read.* [*Ornament ; with motto*—Occulta Veritas Tempora patet. (*McKerrow* : No. 186.)] | Imprinted at London by | Richard Smith | Anno 1577.

David Laing saw a copy of this edition in the Library of Sion College[1] (Press mark EB ix 40), but when in his preparation of his edition of 1865 he went to consult the volume, he found that it had disappeared. It reappeared some thirty years later in a London saleroom, where W. Carew Hazlitt bought and described it, and noted that it finally passed into the possession of the Rosebery Family.

'. . . I saw in a catalogue of miscellaneous books sold at Sotheby's in 1890 a lot which fixed my attention as a bibliographer. It was the English or Anglicised version of Henryson's Aesop, printed at London in 1577, and of which David Laing, in his edition of the old Scottish poet (1865), speaks as having been seen by him in the library of Sion College when he visited that institution about 1830. He mentions that he wished to verify something at a later date, and that the volume had disappeared. I found on inspection that this was the identical book, no other being known anywhere; and I bought it under the hammer for £6, and let Jarvis & Son have it for £12, 12s. They sold it to Lord Rosebery. It had probably been a wanderer above half a century, since it quitted the College in the pocket of some divine of elastic conscience or short memory.' (*The Confessions of a Collector*, pp. 126-7. London, 1897.)

The volume remained in the late Lord Rosebery's possession until 1927, when his valuable collection of Scottish tracts and early printed books became the property of the National Library of Scotland. Lord Rosebery offered to place the book at the

---

[1] The title of the work, and its location, were known to George Chalmers in 1824, when he published his reprint of the *Testament of Cresseid* and *Robene and Makyne* (Bannatyne Club).

disposal of the late Professor G. Gregory Smith when his S.T.S. edition of Henryson was in the press, but as his Lordship's books were stored in packing cases for the duration of the war, the opportunity was lost, and Gregory Smith had to be content to write:

'When the time comes for the return of the volumes to their old places, the Editor, or another, will have an opportunity of giving an account of this sixteenth century "Englishing" of the *Fables*. It is useless to speculate on its value, beyond suggesting that the effort of an appreciative Elizabethan to interpret Henryson's text may, even by its errors, help us to a better understanding of some of the more obscure readings. It is not likely that any biographical or bibliographical evidence escaped David Laing when he made his careful summary of its contents.' (*Henryson*, S.T.S. vol. i., p. clxiv.)

Errors and misunderstandings of the text, as the writer anticipated, are abundant in Richard Smith's translation, but his rendering is sufficiently interesting to justify a collation of the 1577 edition with those of 1570 and 1571. A fuller account of the book appears in the Appendix, page 222, where, too, the question of its relation to the *Harleian MS.*, which it closely resembles, is considered.

A fourth printed text has been used in the preparation of this edition—that printed by Andro Hart in Edinburgh, 1621. This text (like 1, 2 and 3) is an apparently unique copy, and (like 2 and 3) is in the National Library of Scotland. Although it is a late, and to some extent a corrupt text, displaying a considerable degree of Anglicisation, and a growing inability to understand older Scottish forms, it is capable of offering variant readings that are often interesting and sometimes almost plausible. This edition was reprinted by the Maitland Club in 1832, with a preface (unsigned) by David Irving, Keeper of the Library of the Faculty of Advocates, author of a *History of Scottish Poetry* (1861) and contributor of an article on Henryson to the *Encyclopædica Britannica*, 7th ed. (1836). The Prologue and the ninth Fable (The Tale of the Fox, the Wolf and the Cadger) were printed in the *Scots Magazine* 1813, p. 505, from Hart's edition. The unique copy, which is extremely defective,[1] was formerly

---

[1] Full title supplied from *Bagford's Coll. Sloane MS.* 885.

the property of Mr Archibald Constable, and later became the property of the Advocates' Library, now the National Library of Scotland.

Lost Printed Texts.

Fabillis of Isope, printed by Robert Smith, Edinburgh.

In 1599, Smith was granted a privilege to print the *Fables* and, in the inventory of his stock, made after his death in 1602, there were 743 copies (*Dickson & Edmond*, p. 483).

Manuscripts.

1. The most perfect and complete manuscript of the *Fables* is the Harleian MS. 3865, British Museum. (Described in S.T.S. edition, ii., p. 9.) *Title-page* (fol. 1b) : The morall fabillis of Esope compylit be maister Robert Henrisoun Scolmaister of Dun-fermling: 1571.

It is a manuscript of 75 folios, and contains 2968 lines. On ff. 3b and 43b are illustrations, crudely coloured. These illustrations reappear in printed form in the Bassandyne print (1571). A discussion of the relation between the Harleian and Bassandyne texts will be found in the Appendix, pages 221-2.

2. The Bannatyne MS. (1568) in the National Library of Scotland (Press mark: 1.1.6.), the 'fyift pairt . . . contenyng the fabillis of Esop with diverss uthir fabillis and poeticall workis maid & Compyld be divers lernit men 1568.' It contains 2296 lines. The Bannatyne MS. has been reprinted by the Hunterian Club (1873-1902) and the *Fables* are included in Vol. IV. (1896). More recently, the manuscript has been reprinted for the Scottish Text Society, by W. Tod Ritchie (1928-30). A full description of the manuscript is given by the editors.

3. The Prologue and the Fable of the Cock and the Jewel are contained in the Makculloch MS. in the Library of the University of Edinburgh (Laing MSS. 149). This is a volume of logic notes written in Latin by Magnus Makculloch (or Johannis de Tayn), a Scots student at Louvain, in 1477. The name of one I. Purde also appears on the volume, and it is possible that he may be the scribe of the poetical extracts on the blank pages. The lines from the *Fables* are written on the

front fly-leaves. David Laing acquired the MS. in 1854, and bequeathed it to Edinburgh University Library.

4. The Asloan MS.: When previous editors worked on the text of the *Fables*, they did so under the disability that the valuable *Asloan* MS. was withheld from examination; and only the 'Chalmers transcripts' were available. This early sixteenth century manuscript passed, in 1882, from the Auchinleck collection into the possession of Lord Talbot de Malahide, who saw fit to deny scholars access to it. There was, fortunately, the transcript made by William Gibb for George Chalmers in 1810, and preserved in the Laing MSS. in the Library of the University of Edinburgh; and with this former editors have had to be content. But permission to edit the manuscript was granted in 1917, and the Scottish Text Society issued a careful transcript, edited by W. A. Craigie (now Sir William Craigie) in 1923-25. For the purpose of the edition, the MS. was photographed, and the photographs were lodged in The National Library of Scotland. From these photographs the present editor has worked.[1]

Of these sources, printed and manuscript, there are four of outstanding importance :—the Charteris (1570) and Bassandyne (1571) printed texts; the Harleian (1570) and Bannatyne (1568) manuscripts; and upon these the present text is based, although readings from all the texts cited are included in the footnotes. The purpose of these footnotes is not the mere enumeration of all variants, but a significant selection of such variants as are interesting, either textually or philologically: for a better understanding of the text, or a wider understanding of the corruptions which have crept into even the best of our versions.

---

[1] There is an untraced manuscript, which Laing cited from the *Bibliotheca Arch. Pitcarnii, M.D.*, p. 11, No. 304, the last of "Libri in folio"—"Aesop's Fables, compiled in Scottish verse by Robert Henrisoun, Schoolmaster at Dunfermling."

THE TESTAMENT OF CRESSEID

The earliest printed text of the *Testament* is not the best. It is to be found in the edition of Chaucer printed in 1532 by William Thynne. It follows on the fifth book of Chaucer's *Troilus and Cresseide*, and is entitled the *Pyteful & Dolorous Testament of Fayre Cresseyde*. Thynne probably printed from a printed original, but, if so, it has not survived. In 1593, Henry Charteris issued a text of the poem, of which a single copy is known to exist, and is preserved in the British Museum.[1] In 1599, Charteris had in stock no less than 545 copies of the *Testament*.[2] It is more than possible that Charteris, too, printed from a printed original. Robert Gourlaw, or Gourlay, had in 1585 three copies of the *Testament*, at fourpence each.[3] The *Catalogus Bibliothecæ Harleianæ* reveals the fact that two other editions have been lost. In vol. iv., p. 644, No. 13734, there is an entry : 'Henrison's Testament of Cresseid, *black letter*—1605.' (There is no mention of Edinburgh in the entry, though Laing assumes one.) And there is another entry, in vol. v., p. 378, No. 12728 'Testament of Cresseid, *black letter—Edinb.* 1611.' A copy of the poem was apparently issued by Robert Smyth, an Edinburgh printer, some time before 1604[4]; and Thomas Finlason, also of Edinburgh, had, between 1602 and 1622, a privilege to print the *Testament* and the Fables of Esope (not necessarily Henryson's), which privilege he may or may not have exercised.[5]

A late print of the *Testament* has been preserved, which Laing (p. 259) attributes, on the evidence of the type ornaments used, to A. Anderson (Glasgow). It is preserved in the Library of Trinity College, Cambridge. The title reads : THE | TESTAMENT | OF | CRESSEID | [*Rule*] | Compyled by Master | Robert Henrison, Schoole- | master of Dunfermeling | [*Rule*] | [*Ornament*] | [*Rule*] | Printed in the Year, 1663.

[1] *A small quarto, of ten leaves, in black letter.* (*Press mark* : C. 21, c. 14.)

[2] *Bannatyne Miscellany*, ii. p. 224.

[3] *Bannatyne Miscellany*, ii. p. 214.

[4] *Inventory of Robert Smyth, 17th Feb.* 1604: *printed by Dickson & Edmund from the Bannatyne Miscellany*, vol. ii.

[5] '*Thomas Finlason*,' *by H. G. Aldis.* (*Publications of the Edinburgh Bibliographical Society*, vol. i., No. 20.)

There are no early manuscripts of the *Testament*. In St John's College, Cambridge, at the end of a fifteenth century copy of Chaucer's *Troilus and Cresseide*, there is a MS. copy of the poem, described by M. R. James (*Catalogue*, 1913, p. 274), as in a 'hand of cent. xvi.' Sir Francis Kinaston, about 1640, wrote a Latin version of the poem, annotated the text, and added the only story we have concerning Henryson's life.[1] (See Introduction, p. xi.) This translation is accompanied by a text of the poem, similar, but superior, to that of Thynne. Kinaston's improvements on Thynne are rather those of a logical emendator (which, as a translator, he was likely to be) than the contributions of a more authoritative text. His corrections have found their place in the text, and other of his divergences from Charteris in the footnotes. The Charteris edition is undoubtedly the most authoritative text at present known, and upon it the present text is based.

ORPHEUS AND EURYDICE

Orpheus and Eurydice is contained in three early texts, one printed and two manuscript:

1. The collection of tracts in prose and poetry printed in black letter by W. Chepman and A. Myllar, in Edinburgh, 1508. This, the first known production of the Scottish press, is described as *The Porteous of Noblenes*, and is preserved in a defective but unique copy in the National Library of Scotland. The collection was reprinted in black letter by David Laing in 1827, and has lately been edited for the Scottish Text Society by the late George Stevenson. The Chepman & Myllar print, unfortunately, is very incomplete. In it the poem runs to 461 lines, and lacks the passage contained in 11. 59-175 of the other two texts. It bears no ascription, but, as far as it goes, is a good text.

2. The Asloan MS. (c. 1515) ff. 247a *et seq.* (See Introduction, p. xxiv.)

3. The Bannatyne MS. (1568) ff. 317b *et seq.* (See Introduction, p. xxiii.)

The Asloan MS. contains 578 lines, and the Bannatyne, which is more prolix in the Moralitas sections, 633 lines. There is no attribution in Asloan, but Bannatyne provides one: 'ffinis:

[1] *Bodleian MS. Add. C. 287: Reprinted by G. Gregory Smith, S.T.S. ed.*, vol. i., pp. xcvii.-clxii.

quod mr. R.H.' That this solitary testimony might not be suspect, we have a manuscript gloss, in the hand of Gavin Douglas on the manuscript of *Aen.* I. cap. i. l. 13 to the word 'Muse' (Cambridge MS. Gale 03.12). (See *Introduction (Life)*, p. xiii. *supra.*)

The Bannatyne MS. is the longest of the three, by reason of the additions to the Moralitas. It is unlikely that these additions are Henryson's work, and it is possible that they may be by Bannatyne himself.

ROBENE AND MAKYNE

There is only one authority for the text of this poem, the Bannatyne MS., fol. 365a. The entry in the table of contents to the Asloan MS., 'Ane ballat of making of . . .' can be dismissed as having no probable reference to our poet or this poem. Fortunately, Bannatyne, who is often careless in the matter of attribution, ascribes the poem to Henryson. It has long been the anthology piece chosen by every editor since Allan Ramsay, who included it in his *Ever Green* (1724). An account of the possible origins of the poem will be found in the Notes, p. 266.

SUM PRACTYSIS OF MEDECYNE

This poem appears only in the Bannatyne MS., ff. 141b *et seq.*, where Henryson is named as the author.

ANE PRAYER FOR THE PEST

The Bannatyne MS., both the draft and the final version, contains this poem, and at the end of the copy in the latter is added, in another hand, 'quod Henrysone.' This is the only authority for the text and ascription, but there is no contradictory claim elsewhere, or difficulty in the text for accepting the ascription.

THE GARMONT OF GUD LADEIS

The Bannatyne MS. contains the only text of this poem, (fol. 228b) and ascribes it to Henryson. The first print of the poem seems to have been in Allan Ramsay's *Ever Green*, in 1724. Possible sources of the poem, and one imitation of it, are discussed in the Notes.

THE BLUDY SERK

The only text of this poem is that found in the Bannatyne MS., ff. 325a *et seq.* It appears in the section described as 'Fables' which also contains some of the *Morall Fabillis* and *Orpheus*. It is ascribed to Henryson, and the title by which the poem is now known is added in a later hand.

THE RESSONING BETUIX AIGE AND YOWTH

This poem is preserved in four MS. copies—the Makculloch MS., fol. 181b, the Bannatyne draft, the Bannatyne MS., and the Maitland Folio (*c.* 1580). The ascription to Henryson appears in the Bannatyne text.

THE PRAIS OF AIGE

This poem appears in the MS. of Magnus Makculloch (after 1477), fol. 87a in the 1508 *Porteous of Noblenes*, printed by Chepman & Myllar, and in the Bannatyne MS., both sections. Both the Bannatyne texts ascribe it to Henryson.

THE WANT OF WYSE MEN

This poem is given by Bannatyne, in a poor text, and in Chepman & Myllar, 1508, where its collocation with Orpheus in a single tract with a run-on title has suggested Henryson as the author. In Bannatyne, the poem bears no ascription.

THE ABBAY WALK

This poem is contained in the Bannatyne MS., both the draft and the complete copy, and in the latter is ascribed to Henryson. It appears also in the Maitland Folio MS., 'authore incerto.' Laing records (Henryson, p. 240) the existence of a MS. copy transcribed by Alexander Riddell of Bowland in 1636, in which the poem is entitled 'Ane Sonnet,' and, along with several other entries, claimed for his own by the scribe. This manuscript Laing found in the library of Mr Chalmers of Aldbar, but it has since been lost sight of. Laing's edition contains another reference to this poem which has long tantalised scholars and bibliographers. He stated, in a rather vague fashion, that John Forbes of Aberdeen had issued it in 1686, in a modernised form, with other popular verses, under the title, 'An ancient Dittie, entituled, *Obey and thank thy God of all*' (Henryson, p. 241).

A collection of Laing Papers lately came into the possession of the Library of the University of Edinburgh, and at my request Dr Lauriston Sharp hunted through them for some clue to this publication. It was found in a MS. note in Laing's hand, written on the back of an envelope, date-stamped 14th July 1862, and addressed to David Laing, Esq., Signet Library :—

'Mr Young[1] Glasgow/ has an unbound tract, 4 leaves, no/ title or pages but marked A₁ con-/taining/ The Last Good-night/ 14 stanzas of 8 lines/

> A Proper new Ballad, intituled/
> *Obey and thank thy God of all/*

7 stanzas of 8 lines, begins/
Alone as I walk'd up and down/ (See Henryson's Poems p.)/ also/ (*other side*)

A Pleasant Song/ begins/

> For earthly chance, for joy, for pain,
> I neither hope nor do despair/

7 stanzas of six lines/
concluding with two quatrains/

Flee anger, keep then (or *thou*) Gods/ commandement &
O Lord thou me defend.'

The title *The Abbay Walk* was first given to the poem by Lord Hailes in imitation of *The cheapel valk*, in the anonymous *Complaynte of Scotlande*. Henryson's poem seems to be a recast of a poem which appears in several earlier MSS.—in the Vernon MS. (Bodl.) of the fourteenth century, in the Simeon MS., Brit. Mus. Addit. MS. 22283, fol. 130v., and B.M. Cott. MSS. Calig. A. ii. fol. 68v. The relation between our poem and its original is fully discussed in the S.T.S. edition, vol i., p. lxviii.

THE ANNUNCIATION

The only text of this beautiful poem is in the Gray MS. (National Library of Scotland), ff. 70b *et seq.*, where Henryson is named as the author. In Laing's edition (1865), where the poem was first printed, the title was 'The Salutation of the Virgin.'

---

[1] Mr J. C. Ewing of Glasgow suggests that Laing's 'Mr Young' was Alexander Young, a well-known Glasgow book-collector, and has consulted the sale-catalogues of Young's books (1873, 1884, 1891) in the hope of identifying the tract described by Laing, but without success.

THE THRE DEID POLLIS

This poem appears in two different MSS. with different ascriptions. In the Bannatyne MS., fol. 57b *et seq.*, it is ascribed to Patrick Johnstoun; in the Maitland Folio MS. to Henryson. Hailes, who used only the Bannatyne MS., attributed the poem to the 'obscure versifier' Johnstoun; Laing, in 1865, attributed it confidently to Henryson. There is no reason why one ascription should carry more weight than another, except that we have a body of Henryson's work to compare with the poem, and that the poem, in subject and handling, conforms to the type suggested by the rest. In a musical MS. of Sir William Mure, in the Library of the University of Edinburgh, part of the poem appears set to music.

THE RESSONING BETWIXT DETH AND MAN

This poem appears only in the Bannatyne MS., both draft and final version; in the former, it is unascribed, but in the latter it is ascribed to 'hendersone.'

AGANIS HAISTY CREDENCE OF TITLARIS

This poem occurs both in the Bannatyne MS. and in the Maitland Folio MS.; and in both copies the authorship is given to Henryson. The present title appears to have been given by Lord Hailes (Ancient Scottish Poems: Edinburgh, 1770).

LOST AND SUPPOSITITIOUS PIECES

In the table of contents to the Asloan MS., appears 'Master Robert Hendersonis dreme, On fut by forth,' and in the *Complaynt of Scotlande*, in a list of good tales or fables, we come across what may be the first line of the poem:

'On fut by fortht as i coud found.'

But the portion of the Asloan MS. in which the poem should appear has been lost, and the poem does not appear elsewhere.

Dr Diebler, in his examination of the Fables (see Bibliography), made a vague claim for Henryson of several unidentified religious poems in the Makculloch MS. He did not advance any evidence in support of the claim (he did not even particularise the poems), and, indeed, there is no evidence to advance.

LANGUAGE.

In his introduction to the *Ballads of Scotland* (vol. i., p. lx.), Professor Aytoun says of Henryson : 'Although his phraseology is peculiarly Scottish, it is evident that he had studied the writings of Chaucer as well as of King James I., and had moulded his versification accordingly.' Of the peculiarly Scottish art of startling understatement it would be difficult to find a more perfect example. For while it is certainly possible to maintain the essential originality of Henryson's genius (and still more that of Dunbar) it is quite impossible to over-estimate their debt, in poetic form and doctrine, to Chaucer, their master and great original. If Chaucer had not been, they had not been. Chaucer had followers and pupils in England as well as in Scotland; but it is because the Scottish Chaucerians proved more apt and intelligent pupils than their English contemporaries, Lydgate, Hoccleve and the others, that they are of interest to us to-day.

It is possible, without perversity, to attack Aytoun's statement even where it concerns the phraseology of Henryson and his contemporaries; for it is *not* 'peculiarly Scottish.' It is not a spoken, historical dialect of the Scottish language at any period; but an artificial, created, 'literary' language, used, for almost a century, by writers of very different locality and degree, with an astonishing measure of uniformity. And Henryson would probably have designated it *Inglis* rather than *Scots*, for *Scots*, until at least the early sixteenth century, was the speech of the Celtic settlers, north of the Forth and Clyde. Even where 'Scottis' describes the nationality, 'Inglis' is the speech. Thus, the lines in the *Wallace*, describing Thomas de Longueville, read :

> 'Lykly he was, manlik of contenance,
> Lik to the Scottis be mekill governance,
> Saiff off his Tong, for Inglis had he nane.'

But, properly speaking, 'Scottis' originally described the nationality of the Celt, north of the Forth and Clyde, or in Ireland. Thus, in the Anglo-Saxon Chronicle for 891 A.D., it is recorded that King Alfred received 'three Scottas from Ireland.'

This spoken tongue was carried into Dalriada in the fifth century, and was the speech of the Dalriad Scots, whose King, Kenneth Macalpine, by his defeat of the Picts in 846, became

King of Alban, and invaded 'Saxony' (Lothian). In the south-west the spoken tongue was *Welsh* ; in Lothian, Tweeddale, and part of Northumbria, *English* : in Shetland and Orkney, and (after the ninth century) Caithness, Sutherland and the Hebrides, *Scandinavian*. And down to the fifteenth century at least, *Scots* meant the language of the north Celts, as distinct from the Welsh of the south-west, and the English of the south-east.

But in the sixteenth century the language of the north is described as *Ersch* or *Irish*, for patriotic feeling, in a burst of retrospective enthusiasm, had rejected *Inglis* in favour of *Scots* as the name of the Lowland tongue, and the distinction between north and south must still be maintained. Gavin Douglas in the Prologue to the first book of his translation of the *Æneid* (*c.* 1525) was the first to call the speech of the Lowlands 'Scots,' and to differentiate between that speech and that of the 'Inglis natioun.' Scots appears for the first time as the 'language of (the) Scottis natioun '—

> 'Kepand na sudroun bot our awin langage,
> And speikis as I lerit quhen I was page.
> Nor yit sa clene all sudroun I refuse,
> Bot sum word I pronunce as nychtbour doise ;
> So me behavit quhilum, or than be dum,
> Sum bastard latyne, frensch, or inglis oiss (use),
> Quhar scant war Scottis I had na uther choiss.'

So Lyndesay, in his *Defence of the Vernacular*, writes :—

> 'Had Sanct Jerome bene borne in tyll Argyle,
> In to Yrische toung his bukis had done compyle.'

Dunbar, in the *Goldyn Targe*, l. 259, asks (of Chaucer) :

> 'Was thou noucht of oure Inglisch all the lycht . . .?

and in the *Flyting of Dunbar and Kennedy*, ll. 107-112 —

> 'Sic eloquence as thay in Erschay use,
> In sic is sett thy thraward appetyte :
> Thow hes full littill feill of fair indyte :
> I tak on me ane pair of Lowthiane hippis
> Sall fairar Inglis mak, and mair parfyte,
> Than thow can blabber with thy Carrik lippis.'

Kennedy, being a Carrick man, from the south-west, has no 'fair Inglis,' and, on his tongue as on his boots, 'bringis the Carrik clay to Edinburgh Cors.'

Actually, there is no reason to believe that the language of Henryson and the Scots makars bore any closer a resemblance to the spoken Scots of their day, than the English of Lyly or Sir Thomas Browne bore to the spoken tongue of Elizabethan or Restoration England. For a full and scholarly account of the growth and structure of the language, I cannot do better than refer the reader to G. Gregory Smith's introduction to *Specimens of Middle Scots* (Blackwood, 1902). The account of the language which follows does not pretend to do more than give the barest of outlines. But it is a sketch which, I hope, will give the ordinary reader an idea of the construction of the language and enable him to read it with ease. Orthographical and typographical peculiarities conspire to give the language a look of unfamiliarity and strangeness—to make it seem the 'distressingly quaint and crabbed' dialect that W. E. Henley found it. In the short account of the language which follows, my aim is to enable the reader to discount these peculiarities, and to read rather by sound than by sight. Once 'quhissill' is transliterated into 'whissill,' there is little difficulty left.

Until the fifteenth century the language spoken in the region north of the Ribble and the Aire and south of the Forth and Clyde was one dialect, exhibiting few differences throughout that area—fewer, certainly, than in much more recent times and more restricted areas. It was *not* 'Scottish' speech at all; it was a dialect of Old and Early Middle English, the Northumbrian and later Northern dialect. This was the speech of Teutonic Scotland.

North of the Forth and Clyde, the spoken tongue was 'Scots,' for this term described the speech of the Celtic peoples (of the Goidelic branch) settled in Alban, and was subsequently extended to the prevailing speech of the entire northern area. This language was always distinguished from the southern or lowland tongue, and, as I have indicated, when the term Scots was appropriated for the lowland dialect, the Celtic speech was described as Yrische. With the northern tongue, Middle Scots literature has nothing to do. It was out of the Northumbrian dialect of English, or rather the Northern, in which the Northumbrian features were continued into the middle period that literary Scots developed. It was in this dialect that Richard Rolle of Hampole wrote in the neighbourhood of Doncaster; and it was in the same dialect that John Barbour, Archdeacon of Aberdeen, wrote. So that, if we wish to speak of the early alliterative poems or of the work of Barbour as being in early Scots, we must do so in full consciousness that the distinction is geographical and political rather than philological: and that we are actually breaking down a distinction which these poets themselves were at some trouble to maintain. Scots they might be, but their speech was Inglis, not to be confused in name with the Highland, the Yrische tongue.

Middle Scots, then, as we have said, was a product of the Court and essentially a literary language. So it happened that the language, in the time of the Reformation, came to be identified with the Court interest and the Catholic party. England and Protestantism were one, and so we find a studious cultivation of Anglicisms in the reformers. Copies of the Scriptures were imported from England before 1569. John Knox's Psalms were printed frequently in English, and only twice in Scots. For this and other reasons, English forms began to replace Scots ones— 'who' for 'quha,' 'from' for 'fra,' etc. And all this made it possible for the Catholic controversialists to stigmatise leaders of the Church reforming party as traitors. By the end of the sixteenth and the beginning of the seventeenth century the progressive penetration of Scots by English forms had developed so far that it only wanted the Union of the Crowns in 1603 to sign the death-warrant of literary Scots. There were poets in Scotland in the seventeenth century, but not Scots poets.

If, as Gregory Smith points out, it is advisable to study Middle Scots as a development and modification of early Northern English, it is not every reader who is capable of doing so, and it is not impossible for the reader with only a knowledge of modern Scots as his basis to acquaint himself with the main differences which he must expect to find between the modern spoken dialect and the older, written, artificial language. In the necessarily bare outline which I give, I shall try to use illustrations which may be equally intelligible to either sort of reader.

Some Characteristics of Middle Scots Phonology, Orthography, Accidence, and Syntax, as illustrated in Henryson's poems.

PHONOLOGY AND ORTHOGRAPHY

Vowels—

Long vowels are indicated by added *i* or *y* : e.g., *braid, glaid, rois, boir, foirsit, fuyll, suyith*, etc.

a and *ā* are represented by *ǭ* : e.g., *auld, tauld*, etc.

a for *e* and *i* in borrowed words : e.g., *expart, pansing, sampill* (=simple), etc., and in others : e.g., *than=then*, etc.

Orthographical *i* and *y* for *u*, and *vice versa* : e.g., *this, thys= thus*, and *thus=this*.

ā and *ō* are fronted, as is evidenced by rhyme forms : e.g., *nanis, stanis; similitude, gude.*

Consonants—

The combination *mb* represented as *m, mm* : e.g., *chalmer, hummle*, etc. [Cp. Lat. *camera, humilis*, etc.)

Initial *c* soft in foreign words : e.g., *celsitude.*

ch for *gh* : e.g., *dicht, troich, pleuch*, etc.

Final *ch* represented by *k* : e.g., *busk, streik, cluik*, etc.

'd for *'t* after a vowel : e.g., *dudᵉ* (=do't), *seid* (=see't), *albeid* (=albeit).

Occasional intrusive *d* : e.g., *barrand, suddandlie* (? on analogy with *-and= -ing*).

d occasionally in foreign words for *t* : e.g., *marchandis*, etc.

d, dd for *th* before *r* : e.g., *fadir, udir, weddir, erd*, etc.

d elided in combination with *l* and *n* : e.g., *moll* for *mold; sen* for *send.*

Initial *h* dropped in some cases, e.g. *armony*, and intruded in others, e.g. *haboundance.*

l often vocalised as in *row* for *roll, how* for *hollow*, hence 'invested spellings,' as *chalmir, waltir*, etc.

liquid *l* represented by *lʒ* : e.g., *failʒe, spuilʒe*, etc. (Cp. Mod. Scots *capercailzie, Dalzell*, etc.)

liquid *n* represented by *nʒ* : e.g., *fenʒeit, seinʒeis, pleinʒie*, etc. (Cp. Mod. Scots *Menzies, gaberlunzie, Cockenzie*, etc.)

ng represented by *n* : e.g., *strenth* for *strength*, etc.

quh=wh, in all parts of speech : e.g., *quhisling, quhyll* (=till), *quhyle* (=while).

quha (=who). Cp. Mod. Scots *Balquhidder, umquhile*, etc. This form is retained along with the Anglicisms of later M.Sc., and leads to hybrid forms like *quhome, quho, quhiche*, etc.

Initial and final *sh* represented by *s* in unaccented syllables : e.g., *sal, suld, wis* (=wish).

s and *sh* represented by *sch* : e.g., *schir, schemit, scheill, schort*, etc.

s and *sh* followed by a consonant sometimes give an *sk* sound : e.g., *sklender, skelfis*, etc. (Cp. the proper name *Sclater*.)

t for final *d* (*-it, -yt* endings), (*a*) in preterite and past participle of verbs ; (*b*) in *adj., adv.*, and other forms : e.g., *frawart, upwart*, etc.

Superfluous final *t :* e.g., *relict, thocht* (=though), *sicht* (=sigh), etc.

t occasionally lost after consonants : e.g., *correk, infek, precep*, etc.

t occasionally lost medially : e.g., between *s* and *l*—*thrissill, quhissill.*

v medial, between two vowels, disappears in pronunciation, and sometimes in writing : e.g., *euir, deuyll, euil ; cure* (=cover), etc.

Final *v, ve*, represented by *f, ff* : e.g., *haif, persaif, laif*, etc.

w occasionally vocalised : e.g., *oulk* (=week).

METATHESIS

Metathesis of *r*, and *gn*, is extremely common : e.g., *brast, gerss*, etc., and *ding, ring, benyng, conding*, etc.

ACCIDENCE

Nouns—

-is, -ys ending for plural, and singular and plural possessive of nouns (Mod. Eng. *-s, -es, 's, s'*) : e.g., *as cukis can devyne ; By goddis grace*, etc. But this form is gradually disappearing before modern *-s*. Cp. *Fables*, l. 1, *fabils*. Nouns ending in a sibilant usually take the *-is* ending, as *housis, causis*, etc., but a certain number of nouns have the same form for singular and plural : e.g., *as* (ash, ashes).

Adjectives and Pronouns—

Occasional plural form in adjectives and relative pronouns in agreement with plural noun : e.g., *the saidis, quhilkis*, etc. The pronoun *ane* takes the plural form, *anis*.

Ane is used as the indefinite article and numeral=*an, a, one.*
Thir is used as usual plural form of *this*; and *tha* (=those)
plural of *that;* but *thir* is frequently used in both cases, and
tha and *thai, thay* (=they) are frequently confused.

Verbs—

Infinitive suffix lost (normally present in Chaucer as *-en* or *-ë*):
e.g., *mak*=Chaucerian *maken.*

-and ending for present participle (Mod. Eng. *-ing*): e.g.,
scraipand, passand, etc.

-ing, -yng, gerundial ending. (But these distinctions in actual
practice are not strictly observed.)

Occasional aphetic forms of the verb: e.g., *servis, vaillis,* etc.

-it, -yt, ending for preterite and past participle of strong verbs
(Mod. Eng. *-ed, -d*): e.g., *widderit, blasnit, passit,* etc. The
i is frequently elided: e.g., *salust* for *salusit.*

-in, ending for preterite plural and past participle of strong
verbs: e.g., *haldin,* etc. Occasionally, however, strong verbs
are represented by weak forms, as in *cummit* (*Fables,* 627).

-is, -ys, ending for 2nd singular present (Mod. Eng. *-est*) and
3rd singular present (Mod. Eng. *-s*): e.g., *thow ganis, thy
stule standis,* etc., and the same ending generally when the
verb is separated from the pronoun, or when the pronoun is
indefinite, relative, or interrogative: e.g., *nathing of lufe I
knaw, Bot keipis . . ., Thinkis the morne . . . to hald ane
Parliament,* etc.

Occasional shortened verbal forms: e.g. *tais* (=takes), *ma*
(=make), etc.

The adverbial *na, nor*=*than* in comparative constructions: e.g., in
Fables, 2917 Bann., (*bettir*) . . . *Na be machit with a wicket
marrow.*

till=*to,* as preposition, and in infinitive forms: e.g., *Till mercury
but tary is he gone, hir till oppress,* etc.

and and *gif* used indifferently in the sense of *if:* e.g., *And we
wald play us in this plane, Thay wald . . ., Gif thow will
do na mair,* etc.

SYNTAX

Adjectives and nouns are occasionally used adverbially: e.g., *sair*
(=sorely), *wondir* (=exceedingly).

Occasionally the adjective follows its noun: e.g., *bludit cheikis
reid, misdeid wrangous,* etc.

Adjective used occasionally as substantive: e.g., *that myld, that
gay, the bricht.*

The adjectival phrase *of ane*, following an adjective of positive degree, is intensive in effect : e.g., *A fowll gyane of ane*.

Alkin, alkynd (=every kind of) : e.g., *Off alkin thingis*, etc.

Do is used as periphrastic auxiliary with all parts of the verb : e.g., *Thy cullour dois bot confort . . .*, etc.

Can (with its parts *couth, cowth, cowd, culd*, etc.)=*does, did*, as auxiliary : e.g., *Sweitlie can sing, he couth lour*, etc.

French and Latin Influences on Middle Scots

For a full and clear account of the present state of competent opinion upon this vexed question, the reader cannot do better than consult Gregory Smith, *Specimens (Introd.*, pp. l.-lxv.), where the importance of these and other foreign strands in Middle Scots is discussed. Debatable French and Latin forms are less common in Henryson than in other writers of the period, and are to be found most often in the poems which make use of the jargon of Scots Law (*The Trial of the Fox, The Sheep and the Dog*, etc.) or the hardly less stereotyped forms of devotional address (*The Annunciation, The Prayer for the Pest*, etc.). And as French and Latin influences were paramount in these matters, not only from the philological point of view, such usages cannot be taken as fair instances of linguistic modifications.

English Influences

As the original inspiration in poetic form and diction was derived from the south, from Chaucer and perhaps even more from his English followers, it is natural that a considerable number of southern forms should be found in the texts of the makars. The English influence steadily increased from the first quarter of the fifteenth century, and explains such forms as *stone* alongside Scots *stane*, and the present infinitive ending *-ing* alongside *-and*. In Henryson the degree of Anglicisation varies according to the text used, as is obvious from a study of the footnotes.

NOTES TO THE SECOND EDITION

IN my notes on this poem, commenting on line 61, *ane uther quair*, I wrote (p. 253) : ' This " other quair," if it ever existed, is not known to exist now.' This is still true, but shortly after my edition was published I happened on an extract, ' How The Good Knight Reasoned With His Son,' in Miss Eleanor Brougham's *News Out of Scotland* (Heinemann, 1926, p. 19) in which, in a catalogue of the ' many great evils and misfortunes that has come, and daily comes, to men, through that foul delectation of women, which thou callest love,' there is a reference to the fate of Cressida—' Or how quit Cresseid her true lover Troilous, and forgot his long service in love, when she forsook him for Dyomid ; and thereafter went common among the Greeks, and died in great misery and pain.' The extract is described by Miss Brougham as *Translated from the Latin in the City of St Andrews, in July*, 1492, *by ' ane clerk who had been into Venus' Court for the space of more than twenty years.'*

I wrote at once to Miss Brougham, asking her if she could indicate more precisely the source of the passage, but her reply was disappointing ' . . . full of regret that I am unable to give you any information. *News Out of Scotland* was done in a hurry when my father was very ill. With his death the old home with library complete disappeared and alas ! I cannot tell you the source of that note.' A little later, in the first volume of the Asloan Manuscript (Scottish Text Society, ed. W. A. Craigie, 1923) I found the reference, where I should have found it before. In *The Modern Language Review*, January 1945, B. J. Whiting, in ' A Probable Allusion to Henryson's *Testament of Cresseid*,' drew attention to this passage and suggested, on the strength of it, that the *Testament* ' was written before 10 July 1492, or at least eight years prior to the accepted end of Henryson's hazy *floruit*.'

This assumes that the Asloan entry, ' *The Spektakle of luf Or delectatiouñ of luf of wemen quhilk Is devydit in viij partis* . . . translatit out of latyñ in to our wulgar and maternall toung at The cyte of Sandris The x. day of Iulij The 3er of god ane thowsand four hundreth nyntye and twa 3eris be ane clerk quhilk had bene In to venus court mair yan ye space of xx 3eris,' derives from Henryson's tragedy, or from a Latin version based on Henryson. In support of this assumption, Mr Whiting points to the use of the word ' common ' in both versions, which is admittedly striking. It is perhaps equally remarkable that the St Andrews clerk, one MG. Myll, makes no mention of what appears to us most striking in Henryson's narrative, the judgment and vengeance of the offended gods, and the final encounter between Cressida and Troilus at the end of the poem. A Latin version of the *Testament* would surely have reproduced these episodes, so that they would not have been unknown to Master G. Myll. Mr Whiting considers both possibilities—that the *Spektakle of luf* derives from Henryson, or that it derives from an other and presumably earlier work (Henryson's ' uther quair ')—and comes down in favour of the former possibility. The evidence is inconclusive either way, but perhaps this is one case in which the medieval love of authority did not lead to the invention of an authority, ' fenyeit of the new Be sum Poeit, throw his Inventioun.' Perhaps Henryson *did* take down ' ane uther quair.'

In letters to the *Times Literary Supplement*, James Kinsley (14th November 1952) and James Gray (13th March 1953) refer to the *Spektakle of luf* and touch on the same possibility.

THE TAILL OF THE WOLF THAT GAT THE NEKHERĨG THROW
THE WRĨKIS OF THE FOXE THAT BEGYLIT THE CADGEAR

In my notes to this fable (p. 245), I wrote :—'. . . the source . . . is yet unknown, but Professor Bruce Dickins suggests that it may be an elaboration of the Bestiary story of the Fox feigning death in order to catch carrion-crows or ravens.' In the *Review of English Studies*, Vol X (1934), p. 319, Gavin Bone draws attention to the closer resemblance of the story as told in Caxton's version of ' Reynard '.

Henryson's fable unites in a composite whole the two episodes in the *Roman de Renart*, ' Comment Renart fit rencontre des marchands de poisson et comment il eut sa part des harengs et des anguilles ' (Huitième Aventure) and ' Comment Renart déçut le vilan et comment Ysengrin emporta le bacon qu'il ne voulut partager ' (Vingtquatrième Aventure).

In Méon's edition of the *Roman* (1826) the ' jambon ' episode is to be found in lines 7807-7970, tom. 1. The ' anguilles ' episode is to be found in the same volume, pp. 29-35 : ' Si coume Renart manja le poisson aus charretiers,' and again, in tom. 4 of Méon, pp. 257-259, ' Einsi conme Renart se coucha où chemin conme mort, et un convers de Citiaux qui avoit un hairon troussé darriers lui, descendi et prist Renart et le lia avec le hairon.'

Mr Bone's note had, I fear, escaped my notice until my attention was drawn to the passages in the *Roman de Renart* by my daughter, whose assistance I gratefully acknowledge.

BOWRANBANE : THE FABLES, I. 914

My note on *Bowranbane* (p. 237) was an unconvincing, and unconvinced, shot in the dark. My friend and colleague, Dr Neil Mackay, has what seems to be a more plausible suggestion to make, and I quote his note as he sent it to me. In such poems as Montgomerie's *Anser to ane Helandmanis Invectiue*, *The Buke of the Howlat*, etc., there is fragmentary evidence (as I attempted to show in my edition of *The Cherrie and the Slae*, Porpoise Press, Faber & Faber, 1937, with the necessary aid of the late Professor J. Carmichael Watson) that the Scots makars were not entirely cut off from, or ignorant of, " such language as thay in Erschrie use.' Dr Mackay's note reads as follows :

Line 914 : *bowranbane*. The sound and shape of this word, evidently a compound, suggest a Gaelic origin. As it stands, it should represent *bobhran bàn*.

The second, adjectival, element presents no difficulty. Bane ' or, more commonly, ' bain ' has long been a conventional rendering of the Gaelic *bàn*, meaning ' fair ' or ' light coloured ' (*cf.* Donald Bane, Malcolm Canmore's brother ; also the sur-name Bain, variously written Bayne, Bane, etc. in the sixteenth century). The modern pronunciation of ' bane ' or ' bain ' no longer corresponds to the Gaelic vowel sound : in this respect the *S* variant—*bourabant*—is closer to the original, although the final *t* is intrusive (probably a mis-reading).

There is no word *bobhran* in Gaelic, but *dobhran*, meaning
' a water dog ' or ' otter ' is so similar, and so appropriate to
the context, as to suggest a scribal error in transcription.

If we assume that *dowranbane* is the correct reading, we
still have to identify the animal. The name *dobhran bàn*
apparently is not used in modern Gaelic nor can it be traced
in any of the usual books of reference, but it may be significant
that the common otter is frequently referred to as *an dobhran
donn* (' the brown *dobhran* ') and not simply as *an dobhran*.
It might be held that this specific mention of colour establishes
a presumption, though not the certainty, that a distinction was
made at some time or in some place between the ordinary brown
otter and another animal which was also a *dobhran* and which
may have been the *dobhran bàn*. Otherwise there would be no
need to use the word *donn*.

If the word *dobhran* was used of an animal other than the
otter, our first and natural assumption is that it would apply to
a water animal of some kind since *dobhran* is a hypocoristic
form of *dobhar-chù* (' water-dog ').   But the only other water
animal to which the name *dobhran* is given is the beaver, *an
dobhran leas- leathan*, the colour of which would hardly justify
dobhran bàn as a local variant.   In any case, Henryson has
already mentioned the beaver twice in his list.

One Gaelic dictionary (MacLeod and Dewar) asserts that
dobhran is commonly applied to dogs of all kinds but gives no
supporting evidence. If the name was in fact transferred to a
land animal the usage must have been local and not general,
and it may have been established simply because the land
animal was so rare in the locality that its general name became
forgotten or misunderstood.   Could it have been the badger ?
It belongs to the same family (*Mustelidae*) as the otter, and its
white head could have caused some people to call it *an dobhran
bàn* although it has an ancient and widely-known name of its
own (*broc*).

THOMAS BASSANDYNE'S CIVILITÉ TYPE

It is now necessary to supplement the account of *civilité*
type on pages 219-222 and in particular to qualify a sentence
on page 221 relating to its use in Scotland : ' If Thomas

Bassandyne had this type in Edinburgh in 1571, it is at least surprising that no other example of its use has come down to us '.

In 1941 the National Library of Scotland received by the bequest of Thomas Yule, W.S. an apparently unique broadside printed with the same *civilité* as that used by Bassandyne in the *Fables*. It is a letter from the Scottish Privy Council, dated 8th March 1575 and charging each parish to advance to Alexander Arbuthnet five pounds Scots for the work of printing the Bible, the sum to be delivered before 1st July. No printer or place of printing is given, but clearly the sheet came from the press of Bassandyne, who had undertaken the printing of the Bible with Arbuthnet.

The text of the letter was printed with slight variants in Robert Wodrow, *Collections upon the Lives of the Reformers* (vol. I, page 214, Maitland Club, Glasgow, 1834) and reprinted from that source by Dickson and Edmond (*Annals of Scottish Printing*, pages 278-280). When Wodrow writes, ' I have before me an originall Act of Council made upon this application . . . in a very fair hand, which comes very near print', it is possible that what he was admiring was not secretary hand but the *civilité* type derived from it, as used in the broadsheet.

EDITIONS AND TEXTS OF
HENRYSON SINCE 1800

CHALMERS, GEORGE, *Robene and Makyne*, and *The Testament of Cresseid*, Bannatyne Club, Edinburgh, 1824.

HART, ANDRO (Edinburgh, 1621), Maitland Club reprint of *Fables*, Edinburgh, 1832.

LAING, DAVID, *The Poems and Fables of Robert Henryson*, Edinburgh, 1865.

DIEBLER, A. R., *Henrisone's Fabeldichtungen*, Holle, 1885 ; and Anglia, ix. (1886), 337, *et seq.*

SKEAT, W. W., *Chaucerian and other Pieces*, Oxford, 1897.

SMITH, G. GREGORY, *The Poems of Robert Henryson*, 3 vols. S.T.S., Edinburgh, 1906-14.

DICKINS, BRUCE, *The Testament of Cresseid*, Edinburgh, 1925, and London, 1943.

STEARNS, MARSHALL W., *A Modernization of Robert Henryson's Testament of Cresseid*, Indiana University Publications Humanities series, No. 13, Bloomington, Indiana, 1945.

WHITING, B. J., *The Testament of Cresseid* (modernized). Reproduced from typescript for private circulation. Cambridge, Mass., 1950. Copy in the National Library of Scotland.

MURISON, DAVID, *Selections from the poems of Robert Henryson*, Saltire Society, Edinburgh, 1952.

BISKBECK, J. A., *Robin and Makyne, a Scots pastoral*, Edinburgh, 1955.

STUDIES AND REVIEWS OF HENRYSON
SINCE 1933

BONE, GAVIN, ' The Source of Henryson's " Fox, Wolf and Cadger " '. *Review of English Studies*, July 1934.

ELLIOT, C., ' Two notes on Henryson's " Testament of Cresseid " '. *Journal of English and Germanic Philology*, April 1955.

GRIERSON, H. J. C. (Study), *Aberdeen University Review*, July 1934.

JONES, POWELL W., ' A Source for Henryson's *Robene and Makyne* '. *Modern Language Notes*, vol. 46, 1931.

MCINTOSH, A., Review in *Speculum*, July 1949 of *Robert Henryson*, by M. W. Stearns.

MOORE, ARTHUR K., ' Robene and Makyne '. *Modern Language Review*, July 1948.

MUDGE, E. LEIGH, ' A Fifteenth-century Critic '. *College English*, Dec. 1943.

MUIR, EDWIN, *Essays on Literature and Society*, London, 1949. Contains an essay on Robert Henryson.

PARR, JOHNSTONE, ' Cresseid's Leprosy Again '. *Modern Language Notes*, Nov. 1945.

ROSSI, SERGIO, ' L'Annunciazione ' di Robert Henryson. *Aevum*, anno XXIX, fasc. 1, Feb. 1955.

ROSSI, SERGIO, *Robert Henryson*. Milano, 1955.

ROY, JAMES A., ' Of the Makaris. A Causerie (devoted mainly to Henryson and Dunbar) '. *University of Toronto Quarterly*, vol. 16, 1946.

STEARNS, MARSHALL W., ' Robert Henryson and the Fulgentian Horse '. *Modern Language Notes*, April 1939.

STEARNS, MARSHALL W., ' Henryson and the Aristotelian tradition of psychology '. *Studies in Philology*, July 1943.

STEARNS, MARSHALL W., ' Henryson and the political scene '. *Studies in Philology*, July 1943.

STEARNS, MARSHALL W., ' Robert Henryson and the socio-economic scene '. *English Literary History*, Dec. 1943.

STEARNS, MARSHALL W., ' Henryson's allusions to religion and law ' and ' Henryson and the leper Cresseid '. *Modern Language Notes*, April 1944.

STEARNS, MARSHALL W., ' The Planet portraits of Robert Henryson (Description of the seven planets in *The Testament of Cresseid*) '. P.M.L.A., Dec. 1944.

STEARNS, MARSHALL W., ' A Note on Henryson and Lydgate '. *Modern Language Notes*, Feb. 1945.

STEARNS, MARSHALL W., ' Henryson and Chaucer '. *Modern Language Quarterly*, Sept. 1945.

STEARNS, MARSHALL W., *Robert Henryson*, New York, 1949.

TILLYARD, EUSTACE M. W., ' Five Poems, 1470-1870 '. London, 1948 (Another edition, 1955.) The first of the five poems is *The Testament of Cresseid*.

TROILUS, *The Story of Troilus, as told by Benoit de Sainte-Maure, Giovanni Boccaccio, translated into English prose, Geoffrey Chaucer and Robert Henryson*. Translations and introductions by R. K. Gordon, London, 1934.

WHITING, B. J., ' A Probable Allusion to Henryson's *Testament of Cresseid* '. *Modern Language Review*, Jan. 1945.

WILLIAMS, GWYN, *The Burning Tree : Poems from the first thousand years of Welsh verse, selected and translated by G. W.* London : Faber, 1956. Contains a translation of the second act of the Welsh *Troelus a Chresyd*, and on p. 226 mentions the influence of Henryson.

Reviews of *The Poems and Fables of Robert Henryson, edited by H. Harvey Wood*, 1933 :—*Times Literary Supplement*, 3rd August 1933 ; *The Spectator*, by Edwin Muir, 2nd Sept. 1933 ; *Modern Language Review*, by D. Hamer, July 1934.

ABBREVIATIONS USED IN THE TEXT

FABLES

Manuscripts					*Printed Texts*			
Asloan .	.	.	.	*A.*	Bassandyne .	.	.	*Bass.*
Bannatyne .	.	.	.	*B.*	Charteris	.	.	.	*C.*
Harleian	.	.	.	*H.*	Andro Hart	.	.	*Ht.*
Makculloch .	.	.	*M.*	Richard Smith	.	.	*S.*

OTHER POEMS

Bannatyne draft .	.	*Bd.*	A. Anderson (?)	.	*A.*
Maitland Folio	.	.	*MF.*	Chepman & Myllar .	*C.*
St John's Coll.	.	.	*SJ.*	Thynne .	.	.	*T.*
Kinaston	.	.	.	*K.*
Gray .	.	.	.	*G.*

NORMALISATIONS

i *for* j ; j *for* i : u *for* v ; v *for* u

th *for* þ : y *for* ȝ

The Morall Fabillis of Esope the Phrygian

Thomas Bassandyne, Edinburgh

1571

A

The Prolog

1 Thocht feinyeit fabils of ald poetre
  Be not al grunded upon truth, yit than
  Thair polite termes of sweit Rhetore
  Richt plesand ar Unto the eir of man;
  And als the caus that thay first began
  Wes to repreif the haill misleving
  Off man be figure of ane uther thing.

2 In lyke maner as throw the bustious eird,
  (Swa it be laubourit with grit diligence)
  Springis the flouris, and the corne abreird,   10
  Hailsum and gude to mannis sustenence,
  Sa dois spring ane Morall sweit sentence,
  Oute of the subtell dyte of poetry:
  To gude purpois quha culd it weill apply.

3 The nuttes schell, thocht it be hard and teuch,
  Haldis the kirnill, and is delectabill.
  Sa lyis thair ane doctrine wyse aneuch,
  And full of fruit, under ane fenyeit Fabill.
  And Clerkis sayis it is richt profitabill
  Amangis ernist to ming ane merie sport,   20
  To light the spreit, and gar the tyme be schort.

4 Forther mair, ane Bow that is ay bent
  Worthis unsmart, and dullis on the string;
  Sa dois the mynd that is ay diligent,
  In ernistfull thochtis, and in studying:
  With sad materis sum merines to ming,
  Accordis weill: thus Esope said I wis,
  Dulcius arrident seria picta Iocis.

    16 and is delectabill) sueit & delectabill *MB*
    21 light) blyth *MB* ; recreat *S*
    22 Forther mair) For as we se *B* ; For as a bow *M*
    24 Sa dois the mynd) Sa gais the man *C*

5 Of this Authour, my Maisteris, with your leif,
Submitting me in your correctioun,   30
In Mother toung of Latyng I wald preif
To mak ane maner of Translatioun;
Nocht of my self, for vane presumptioun,
Bot be requeist and precept of ane Lord,
Of quhome the Name it neidis not record.

6 In hamelie language and in termes rude
Me neidis wryte, for quhy of Eloquence
Nor Rethorike, I never Understude.
Thairfoir meiklie I pray your reverence,
Gif that ye find it throw my negligence,   40
Be deminute, or yit superfluous,
Correct it at your willis gratious.

7 My Author in his Fabillis tellis how
That brutal beistis spak, and Understude,
In to gude purpois dispute, and argow,
Ane Sillogisme propone, and eik conclude.
Put in exempill, and in similitude,
How mony men in operatioun,
Ar like to beistis in conditioun.

8 Na mervell is, ane man be lyke ane Beist,   50
Quhilk lufis ay carnall and foull delyte;
That schame can not him renye, nor arreist,
Bot takis all the lust and appetyte,
And that throw custum, and daylie ryte,
Syne in thair myndis sa fast is Radicate,
That thay in brutal beistis ar transformate.

32 maner) mater *C*
35 G. G. S. gives, and amends, the non-existent reading, ' decord.'
40 it) ocht þat *MB*   43 his . . . how) þis *M*; ȝow *C*
45 In to . . and argow) And to *MBS;* maid argow *C*
46 Ane Sillogisme) In philosophie *C*
47 Put in) Puttyng *MB*   52 not him renye) nocht derenȝe *MB*
54 custum . . . daylie) þe custome . . . þe dayly *MB*
55 thair myndis) þe mynd *MB*
55-6 Sinne in their mindes is so fast rooted
    That they into brutall beastes are transformed *S*
56 thay . . . ar) he . . . is *MB*

The Taill of the Cok, and the Iasp.

Ane cok sum tyme with feddram fresch and gay,
Richt cant and crous albeit he was bot pure,
Fleu furth vpon ane dunghill soe be day,
To get his dennar set was al his cure.
Scraipand amang the as be auenture,
He fand ane Iolie Iasp, richt precious,
Wes castin furth in sweping of the hous.

Ne Damisellis wantoun, and Insolent,
That fane wald play, and on the streit be sene,
To sweping of the hous thay tak na tent.

Thay

9 This Nobill Clerk, Esope, as I haif tauld,
In gay metir, as poete Lawriate,
Be figure wrait his buke: for he nocht wald
Lak the disdane off hie, nor low estate.   60
And to begin, first of ane Cok he wrate,
Seikand his meit, quhilk fand ane Jolie stone,
Of quhome the Fabill ye sall heir anone.

Finis.

The Taill of the Cok, and the Jasp

10 Ane cok sum tyme with feddram fresch & gay,
Richt cant and crous, albeit he was bot pure,
Flew furth upon ane dunghill sone be day;
To get his dennar set was al his cure.
Scraipand amang the as, be aventure
He fand ane Jolie Jasp, richt precious,
Wes castin furth in sweping of the hous.   70

11 As Damisellis wantoun and Insolent,
That fane wald play, and on the streit be sene,
To swoping of the hous thay tak na tent,
Thay cair na thing, swa that the flure be clene.
Jowellis ar tint, as oftymis hes bene sene,
Upon the flure, and swopit furth anone—
Peradventure, sa wes the samin stone.

12 Sa mervelland Upon the stane (quod he)
'O gentill Jasp! O riche and Nobill thing!
Thocht I the find, thow ganis not for me.   80
Thow art ane Jowell for ane Lord or King.
Pietie it wer, thow suld ly in this mydding,
Be buryit thus amang this muke on mold,
And thow so fair, and worth sa mekill gold.

58 In gay metir, facound and purperat *B*; In gay meteyr & in facund
purpurat *M*; In gray vestiment, and in facound purpurate *C*; With
great invention, as poete Laureate *S*
60 Lak the disdane) tak the disdeyne *M*; wisdome *C*
64 In *C* the first fable follows on the prologue without interval or heading.
70 in sweping) be sweping *H*   74 Thay cair na thing) Quhat be thairin *B*
83 on mold) and mold *MBS*

13 'It is pietie I suld the find, for quhy
     Thy grit vertew, nor yit thy cullour cleir,
     It may me nouther extoll nor magnify :
     And thow to me may mak bot lyttill cheir.
     To grit Lordis thocht thow be leif, and deir,
     I lufe fer better thing of les availl,   90
     As draf, or corne, to fill my tume Intraill.

14 'I had lever ga scrapit heir with my naillis,
     Amangis this mow, and luke my lifys fude,
     As draf, or corne, small wormis, or snaillis,
     Or ony meit wald do my stomok gude,
     Than of Jaspis ane mekill multitude :
     And thow agane, Upon the samin wyis,
     For les availl may me as now dispyis.

15 'Thow hes na corne, and thairof haif I neid,
     Thy cullour dois bot confort to the sicht,   100
     And that is not aneuch my wame to feid.
     For wyfis sayis, lukand werkis ar licht.
     I wald have sum meit, get it geve I micht,
     For houngrie men may not leve on lukis :
     Had I dry breid, I compt not for na cukis.

16 'Quhar suld thow mak thy habitatioun?
     Quhar suld thow dwell, bot in ane Royall Tour?
     Quhar suld thow sit, bot on ane Kingis Croun,
     Exaltit in worschip and in grit honour?
     Rise, gentill Jasp, of all stanis the flour,   110
     Out of this midding, and pas quhar thow suld be ;
     Thow ganis not for me, nor I for the.'

          92 ga scrapit) haif scrapit heir C ; go schraip heir MB
          98 For les availl) for thyne auaill MBC
          99 hes) is C   102 wyfis) Wyse men B
         109 Exaltit) Exault MB
         111 midding) fene M ; ass B
         118 Of this) Of this fabill MB

17 Levand this Jowell law upon the ground,
    To seik his meit this Cok his wayis went.
    Bot quhen, or how, or quhome be it wes found,
    As now I set to hald na Argument.
    Bot of the Inward sentence and Intent
    Of this (as myne Author dois write)
    I sall reheirs in rude and hamelie dite.

18 This Jolie Jasp had properteis sevin :   120
    The first, of cullour it was mervelous,
    Part lyke the fyre, and part lyke to the hevin.
    It makis ane man stark and victorious.
    Preservis als fra cacis perrillous.
    Quha hes this stane, sall have gude hap to speid,
    Or fyre nor water him neidis not to dreid.

                    MORALITAS

19 This gentill Jasp, richt different of hew,
    Betakinnis perfite prudence and cunning,
    Ornate with mony deidis of vertew,
    Mair excellent than ony eirthly thing ;   130
    Quhilk makis men in honour for to Ring,
    Happie, and stark to wyn the victorie
    Of all vicis, and Spirituall enemie.

20 Quha may be hardie, riche, and gratious ?
    Quha can eschew perrell and aventure ?
    Quha can Governe ane Realme, Cietie, or hous,
    Without science ? no man, I yow assure.
    It is riches that ever sall Indure,
    Quhilk Maith, nor moist, nor uther rust can screit ;
    To mannis saull it is eternall meit.   140

120 In *B* this stanza begins the Moralitas.   All other texts put the heading
    before line 127, where the Moralitas proper begins.
125 hap) hoip *CM*
136 Realme, Cietie, or hous) in ane Realme or hous *C*; citie and burchgus *B*
137 no man) nothing *M*; non *B*
139 screit) fret *CS*; ket *B*

21 This Cok, desyrand mair the sempill corne
  Than ony Jasp, may till ane fule be peir,
  Quhilk at science makis bot ane moik and scorne,
  And na gude can : als lytill will he leir.
  His hart wammillis wyse argument to heir,
  As dois ane Sow, to quhome men for the nanis,
  In hir draf troich wald saw precious stanis.

22 Quha is enemie to science and cunning,
  Bot Ignorants, that understandis nocht?
  Quhilk is sa Nobill, sa precious, and sa ding,   150
  That it may not with eirdlie thing be bocht.
  Weill wer that man over all uther, that mocht
  All his lyfe dayis in perfite studie wair
  To get science; for him neidis na mair.

23 Bot now (allace) this Jasp is tynt and hid :
  We seik it nocht, nor preis it for to find.
  Haif we richis, na better lyfe we bid,
  Of science thocht the Saull be bair and blind.
  Of this mater to speik, it wer bot wind.
  Thairfore I ceis, and will na forther say.   160
  Ga seik the Jasp, quha will, for thair it lay.

Finis.

The Taill of the Uponlandis Mous, and the Burges Mous

24 Esope, myne Authour, makis mentioun
  Of twa myis, and thay wer Sisteris deir,
  Of quham the eldest dwelt in ane Borous toun,
  The uther wynnit uponland weill neir ;
  Soliter, quhyle under busk, quhyle under breir,
  Quhilis in the corne, and uther mennis skaith,
  As outlawis dois, and levis on their waith.

142 unto ane fule is peir *HB*   149 Ignorants) Ignorance *C*
155 this Jasp) science *C*
166 Soliter) Richt solitar, quhile wnder buske and brere *AB*
167-8   . . . in other mens food
    As theeues do, that liue by others good *S*

25 This rurall mous in to the wynter tyde,
   Had hunger, cauld, and tholit grit distress;   170
   The uther Mous, that in the Burgh can byde,
   Was Gild brother and made ane fre Burges;
   Toll fre als, but custom mair or les,
   And fredome had to ga quhair ever scho list,
   Amang the cheis in Ark, and meill in kist.

26 Ane tyme when scho was full and unfute sair,
   Scho tuke in mynd hir sister uponland,
   And langit for to heir of hir weilfair,
   To se quhat lyfe scho had under the wand.
   Bairfute, allone, with pykestaf in hir hand,   180
   As pure pylgryme scho passit out off town,
   To seik hir sister baith oure daill and down.

27 Furth mony wilsum wayis can scho walk,
   Throw mosse and mure, throw bankis, busk & breir,
   Scho ran cryand, quhill scho came to a balk:
   'Cum furth to me, my awin Sister deir,
   Cry peip anis!' With that the Mous culd heir,
   And knew hir voce as kinnisman will do,
   Be verray kynd; and furth scho come hir to.

28 The hartlie joy, God! geve ye had sene,   190
   Beis kith quhen that thir Sisteris met;
   And grit kyndnes wes schawin thame betwene,
   For quhylis thay leuch, and quhylis for joy thay gret,
   Quhyle(s) kissit sweit, quhylis in armis plet;
   And thus thay fure quhill soberit wes thair mude,
   Syne ffute ffor ffute unto the chalmer yude.

167 and uther) in uther *AB*   168 waith) wacht *B*
178 for) sar *A*   179 had) led *AB*   184 busk) bush *S*; blak *C*
185 fra fur to fur, cryand fra balk to balk *B*; Cryand on hir fra balk
    to balk *A*; Scho ranne with mony ane hiddeous quaik *C*
187 culd heir) cryit heir *C*; quod heir *B*; couth heir *A*
190 The hartlie joy, God) cheir lord god *AB*
191 thir Sisteris met) twa wer met *AB*
195-6 mude . . . yude) meid . . . ȝeid *B*; mind . . . wend *C*

29 As I hard say, it was ane sober wane,
Off fog & farne ffull febilie wes maid,
Ane sillie scheill under ane steidfast stane,
Off quhilk the entres wes not hie nor braid.   200
And in the samin thay went but mair abaid,
Without fyre or candill birnand bricht,
For comonly sic pykeris luffis not lycht.

30 Quhen thay wer lugit thus, thir sely Myse,
The youngest sister into hir butterie glyde,
And brocht furth nuttis, & candill in steid off spyce;
Giff this wes gude ffair I do it on thame besyde.
The Burges Mous prompit forth in pryde,
And said, 'sister, is this your dayly fude?'
'Quhy not,' quod scho, 'is not this meit rycht gude?'   210

31 'Na, be my saull, I think it bot ane scorne.'
'Madame' (quod scho), 'ye be the mair to blame;
My mother sayd, sister, quhen we wer borne,
That I and ye lay baith within ane wame.
I keip the rate and custome off my dame,
And off my leving into povertie,
For landis have we nane in propertie.'

32 'My fair sister' (quod scho), 'have me excusit.
This rude dyat and I can not accord.
To tender meit my stomok is ay usit,   220
For quhylis I fair alsweill as ony Lord.
Thir wydderit peis, and nuttis, or thay be bord,
Wil brek my teith, and mak my wame fful sklender,
Quhilk wes before usit to meitis tender.'

198 febilie) misterlyk *A* ; maisterlig *B*
199 steidfast) erdfast *AB*
205 glyde) ʒeid *C* ; hyid *AB*
206 candill) corne *S* ; peiss *AB*
215 rate) ryte *AB*
216 leving into povertie) syre liffand in *AB*
221 quhylis) quhy *AB*

33 'Weil, weil, sister' (quod the rurall Mous),
  'Geve it pleis yow, sic thing as ye se heir,
  Baith meit and dreink, harberie and hous,
  Salbe your awin, will ye remane al yeir.
  Ye sall it have wyth blyith and mery cheir,
  And that suld mak the maissis that ar rude,   230
  Amang freindis, richt tender and wonder gude.

34 'Quhat plesure is in the ffeistis delicate,
  The quhilkis ar gevin with ane glowmand brow?
  Ane gentill hart is better recreate
  With blyith curage, than seith to him ane Kow.
  Ane modicum is mair ffor till allow,
  Swa that gude will be kerver at the dais,
  Than thrawin vult and mony spycit mais.'

35 For all hir mery exhortatioun,
  This Burges Mous had littill will to sing.   240
  Bot hevilie scho kest hir browis doun,
  For all the daynteis that scho culd hir bring.
  Yit at the last scho said, halff in hething,
  'Sister, this victuall and your royall feist,
  May weill suffice unto ane rurall beist.

36 'Lat be this hole and cum into my place;
  I sall to you schaw be experience
  My gude friday is better nor your pace;
  My dische likingis is worth your haill expence.
  I have housis anew off grit defence;   250
  Off Cat, nor fall trap, I have na dreid.'
  'I grant,' quod scho; and on togidder thay yeid.

228 will ye remane al yeir) whyles ye remaynen heare *S*
231 and wonder gude) sweit & gud *AB*
235 seith) seik *C*; set *AS*
238 vult) will *C*; vilt *B*
244 royall) rurall *Ht*
245 beist) geast *S*
249 likingis) weschingis *C*
251 nor fall trap) na fall na trap *B*; na trape na fall *A*

37 In stubbill array throw gers and corne,
    And under buskis prevelie couth thay creip,
    The eldest wes the gyde and went beforne,
    The younger to hir wayis tuke gude keip.
    On nicht thay ran, and on the day can sleip,
    Quhill in the morning, or the Laverok sang,
    Thay fand the town, and in blythlie couth gang.

38 Not fer fra thyne unto ane worthie Wane,   260
    This Burges brocht thame sone quhare thay suld be.
    Without God speid thair herberie wes tane,
    In to ane spence with vittell grit plentie;
    Baith Cheis and Butter upon thair skelfis hie,
    And flesche and fische aneuch, baith fresche and salt,
    And sekkis full off meill and eik off malt.

39 Eftir quhen thay disposit wer to dyne,
    Withowtin grace thay wesche and went to meit,
    With all coursis that Cukis culd devyne,
    Muttoun and beif, strikin in tailyeis greit.   270
    Ane Lordis fair thus couth thay counterfeit,
    Except ane thing, thay drank the watter cleir
    In steid off wyne, bot yit thay maid gude cheir.

40 With blyith upcast and merie countenance,
    The eldest Sister sperit at hir gest
    Giff that scho be ressone fand difference
    Betwix that chalmer and hir sarie nest.
    'Ye, dame' (quod scho), 'how lang will this lest?'
    'For evermair, I wait, and langer to.'
    'Giff it be swa, ye ar at eis' (quod scho).   280

253 In stubbill array) in stowthry ay *A*; In skugry ay *B*; rankest gers *B*
254 And under buskis) Wnder cowert full *A*; And wondir sly *B*
263 In to ane spence) in till ane innes *A*
278 'Ye, dame,' quod scho, 'how) '3it deme,' quod scho, 'bot *B*
281 This stanza is lacking in *A*

❧ The Taillis contenit in this present Buke.

The

41 Till eik thair cheir ane subcharge furth scho brocht,
   Ane plait off grottis, and ane dische full off meill;
   Thraf cakkis als I trow scho spairit nocht,
   Aboundantlie about hir for to deill.
   [And mane full fyne] scho brocht in steid off geill,
   And ane quhyte candill out off ane coffer stall,
   In steid off spyce to gust thair mouth withall.

42 This maid thay merie quhill thay micht na mair
   And 'haill yule, haill!' cryit upon hie;
   Yit efter joy oftymes cummis cair,   290
   And troubill efter grit prosperitie.
   Thus as thay sat in all thair jolitie,
   The spenser come with keyis in his hand,
   Oppinnit the dure, and thame at denner fand.

43 Thay taryit not to wesche, as I suppose,
   Bot on to ga quha that micht fformest win.
   The Burges had ane hole, and in scho gois,
   Hir sister had na hole to hyde hir in:
   To se that selie Mous it wes grit sin,
   So desolate and will off ane gude reid,   300
   For verray dreid scho fell in swoun neir deid.

44 Bot as God wald, it fell ane happie cace,
   The Spenser had na laser for to byde,
   Nowther to seik, nor serche, to sker nor chace,
   Bot on he went, and left the dure up wyde.
   The bald Burges his passing weill hes spyde,
   Out off hir hole scho come, and cryit on hie,
   'How fair ye, sister? cry peip, quhair ever ye be.'

---

285 Charteris reading.　And manfully fyne *Bass*; manfulle syne *H*;
   furmage full fyne *B*; And manfully so *S*; main-flour fine *Ht*
287 gust thair mouth) cresch thair teithis *B*
288 quhill) while *Ht*. An early example of this form misunderstood by
   a Scottish scribe or printer.
289 cryit) thay cryit *B*　　300 ane) all *B*　　305 Bot on) Bot in *ÁBSH*

45 This rurall Mous lay flatling on the ground,
  And for the deith scho wes full sair dredand,   310
  For till hir hart straik mony wofull stound,
  As in ane fever scho trimbillit fute and hand.
  And quhan her sister in sic ply hir fand,
  For verray pietie scho began to greit,
  Syne confort hir with wordis hunny sweit.

46 'Quhy ly ye thus? ryse up, my sister deir,
  Cum to your meit, this perrell is overpast.'
  The uther answerit hir with hevie cheir,
  'I may not eit, sa sair I am agast;
  I had lever thir fourty dayis fast,   320
  With watter caill, and to gnaw benis or peis,
  Than all your feist in this dreid and diseis.'

47 With fair tretie yit scho gart hir upryse,
  And to the burde thay went and togidder sat,
  And scantlie had thay drunkin anis or twyse,
  Quhen in come Gib hunter, our Jolie Cat,
  And bad God speid; the Burges up with that,
  And till her hole scho went as fyre on flint;
  Bawdronis the uther be the bak hes hint.

48 Fra fute to fute he kest hir to and ffra,   330
  Quhylis up, quhylis doun, als cant as ony kid;
  Quhylis wald he lat hir rin under the stra,
  Quhylis wald he wink, and play with hir buk heid.
  Thus to the selie Mous grit pane he did,
  Quhill at the last, throw fortune and gude hap,
  Betwix ane burde and the wall scho crap.

---

310 dredand) dredand *S*. Surely an unfamiliar form in the Vale of
    Aylesbury.—(Ed.)
313 ply) plyte *AB*   315 hunny sweit) humbill & sweit *C*
320 fast) haf fast *A*   323 upryse) ryse *HAB*
329 Bawdronis) Gilbert *S* : hes) scho *B*
330-2-3-4, 340 he) scho *AB*   331 cant) tait *AB*
334 pane) harme *B*   335 throw fair fortoun and hap *AB*
336 ane burde) þe dressour *B* ; þe dosour *A*

49 And up in haist behind ane parraling
Scho clam so hie, that Gilbert micht not get hir,
Syne be the cluke thair craftelie can hing,
Till he wes gane, hir cheir wes all the better.   340
Syne doun scho lap quhen thair wes nane to let hir,
And to the Burges Mous loud can scho cry,
'Fairweill, sister, thy feist heir I defy!

50 'Thy mangerie is mingit all with cair,
Thy guse is gude, thy gansell sour as gall.
The subcharge off thy service is bot sair,
Sa sall thow find heir efterwart na ffall.
I thank yone courtyne and yone perpall wall
Of my defence now ffra yone crewall beist.
Almichtie God, keip me fra sic ane ffeist!   350

51 'Wer I into the kith that I come ffra,
For weill nor wo, suld I never cum agane.'
With that scho tuke her leif and furth can ga,
Quhylis throw the corne, and quhylis throw the plane;
Quhen scho wes furth and fre scho wes full fane,
And merilie markit unto the mure.
I can not tell how weill thairefter scho fure.

52 Bot I hard say scho passit to hir den,
Als warme as woll, suppose it wes not greit,
Full beinly stuffit, baith but and ben,   360
Off Beinis, and Nuttis, peis, Ry, and Quheit.
Quhen ever scho list, scho had aneuch to eit,
In quyet and eis withoutin ony dreid;
Bot to hir sisteris feist na mair scho yeid.

337 And) Syne *AB*
339 Syne) And *AB* : cluke) cludges *S*
344 mangerie) managery *A*
346 sair) fair *H*
347 efterwart) heirefterwart *HAB* : na ffall) may fall *AB*
349 yone) ane *C*
357 weill thairefter) eftirwart *AB*
359 woll) weill *C*; wow *B*

MORALITAS

53 Freindis, ye may find, and ye will tak heid,
   In to this fabill ane gude moralitie.
   As fitchis myngit ar with nobill seid,
   Swa interminglit is adversitie
   With eirdlie joy, swa that na estate is frie,
   Without trubill and sum vexatioun :   370
   And namelie thay quhilk clymmis up maist hie,
   That ar not content with small possessioun.

54 Blissed be sempill lyfe withoutin dreid ;
   Blissed be sober feist in quietie ;
   Quha hes aneuch, of na mair hes he neid,
   Thocht it be littill into quantatie.
   Grit aboundance and blind prosperitie
   Oftymes makis ane evill conclusioun :
   The sweitest lyfe thairfoir, in this cuntrie,
   Is sickernes with small possessioun.   380

55 O wanton man ! that usis for to feid
   Thy wambe, and makis it a God to be,
   Lieke to thy self; I warne the weill but dreid,
   The Cat cummis, and to the Mous hes Ee.
   Quhat vaillis than thy feist and royaltie,
   With dreidfull hart, and tribulatioun ?
   Best thing in eird, thairfoir, I say, for me,
   Is blyithnes in hart, with small possessioun.

56 Thy awin fyre, my freind, sa it be bot ane gleid,
   It warmis weill, and is worth Gold to the.   390
   And Solomon sayis, gif that thow will reid,
   'Under the hevin thair can not better be,
   Than ay be blyith and leif in honestie.'
   Quhairfoir I may conclude be this ressoun :
   Of eirthly joy it beiris maist degre,
   Blyithnes in hart, with small possessioun.   *Finis.*

369-372 These lines are badly confused in *C*   381 This stanza is missing in *C*
383 but dreid) on deid *AB*   384 hes Ee) as E *A* ; hies he *S*; hath eye *Ht*
388 blyithnes in hart) sickerness *A* ; mirry hairt *B*
389 my freind) frende *ABHt*
392 thair can not better be) I can nocht better se *AB*   393 honestie) quiete *A*

The Taill of Schir Chantecleir and the Foxe.

57 Thocht brutall beistis be Irrationall,
    That is to say, wantand discretioun,
    Yit ilk ane in thair kynd naturall
    Hes mony divers inclinatioun.   400
    The Bair busteous, the Wolff, the wylde Lyoun,
    The Fox fenyeit, craftie and cawtelous,
    The Dog to bark on nicht and keip the hows.

58 Sa different thay ar in properteis,
    Unknawin to man, and sa infinite,
    In kynd havand sa ffell diuersiteis,
    My cunning is excludit ffor to dyte.
    For thy as now I purpose ffor to wryte
    Ane cais I ffand, quhilk ffell this ather yeir,
    Betwix ane Foxe and ane gentill Chantecleir.   410

59 Ane wedow dwelt, in till ane drop thay dayis,
    Quhilk wan hir ffude off spinning on hir Rok,
    And na mair had fforsuth, as the Fabill sayis,
    Except off hennis scho had ane Lyttill flok ;
    And thame to keip scho had ane Jolie Cok,
    Richt curageous, that to this wedow ay
    Devydit nicht, and crew befoir the day.

60 Ane lyttill ffra this ffoirsaid wedowis hows,
    Ane thornie schaw thair wes off grit defence,
    Quhairin ane Foxe, craftie and cautelous,   420
    Maid his repair, and daylie residence ;
    Quhilk to this wedow did grit violence,
    In pyking off pultrie baith day and nicht,
    And na way be revengit on him scho micht.

402 fenyeit) semis *C*
405 to) unto *B* : sa infinite) infynite *B*
409 ather) hinder *B*
410 ane gentill) gentill *B*

B

61 This wylie Tod, quhen that the Lark couth sing,
 Full sair hungrie unto the Toun him drest,
 Quhair Chantecleir in to the gray dawing,
 Werie for nicht, wes flowen ffra his nest.
 Lowrence this saw, and in his mynd he kest
 The Jeperdie, the wayis, and the wyle,   430
 Be quhat menis he micht this Cok begyle.

62 Dissimuland in to countenance and cheir,
 On kneis fell, and simuland thus he said :
 'Gude morne, my maister, gentill Chantecleir!'
 With that the Cok start bakwart in ane braid.
 'Schir, be my Saull, ye neid not be effraid,
 Nor yit ffor me to start nor fle abak,
 I come bot heir service to yow to mak.

63 'Wald I not serve to yow, it wer bot blame,
 As I have done to your progenitouris ;   440
 Your father full oft fillit hes my wame,
 And send me meit ffra midding to the muris.
 And at his end I did my besie curis,
 To hald his heid, and gif him drinkis warme,
 Syne at the last the Sweit swelt in my arme.'

64 'Knew ye my ffather?' (quod the Cok) and leuch.
 'Yea, my ffair Sone, I held up his heid,
 Quhen that he deit under ane birkin beuch ;
 Syne said the Dirigie quhen that he wes deid.
 Betwix us twa how suld thair be ane feid?   450
 Quhame suld ye traist bot me, your Servitour,
 That to your ffather did sa grit honour?

427 gray) day *Ht*
428 for) of *B*
433 simuland) smyland *BHt* ; flattering *S*
437 start) drede *B*
441 fillit) fulfillit *B*

65 'Quhen I behald your ffedderis ffair and gent,
    Your beik, your breist, your hekill, and your kame,
    Schir, be my Saull, and the blissit Sacrament,
    My hart is warme; me think I am at hame:
    To mak yow blyith, I wald creip on my wame,
    In ffroist and snaw, in wedder wan and weit,
    And lay my lyart loikkis under your feit.'

66 This fenyeit Foxe, ffals and dissimulate,   460
    Maid to this Cok ane cavillatioun:
    'Ye ar, me think, changit and degenerate,
    Fra your ffather off his conditioun;
    Off craftie crawing he micht beir the Croun,
    For he wald on his tais stand and craw.
    This wes na le; I stude beside and saw.'

67 With that the Cok upon his tais hie,
    Kest up his beik, and sang with all his micht.
    (Quod Schir Lowrence) 'weill said, sa mot I the,
    Ye ar your ffatheris Sone and air upricht.   470
    Bot off his cunning yit ye want ane slicht.
    For' (quod the Tod) 'he wald, and haif na dout,
    Baith wink, and craw, and turne him thryis about.'

68 The Cok, infect with wind and fals vanegloir,
    That mony puttis unto confusioun,
    Traisting to win ane grit worschip thairfoir,
    Unwarlie winkand wawland up and doun,
    And syne to chant and craw he maid him boun.
    And suddandlie, be he had crawin ane note,
    The Foxe wes war and hint him be the throte.   480

447 I held) forsuth I held *B*
459 lyart) golden *S*
472 'For,' quod the Tod,) 'Quhat?' quod þe cok *B*
477 wawland) walkit *B*

69 Syne to the woid but tarie with him hyit,
Off that cryme haifand bot lytill dout.
With that Pertok, Sprutok, and Toppok cryit.
The wedow hard, and with ane cry come out.
Seand the cace, scho sichit and gaif ane schout :
'How, murther, hay!' with ane hiddeous beir,
'Allace, now lost is gentill Chantecleir !'

70 As scho wer woid, with mony yell and cry,
Ryvand hir hair, upon hir breist can beit,
Syne, paill off hew, half in ane extasy,   490
Fell doun ffor cair in swoning and in sweit.
With that the selie hennis left thair meit,
And, quhill this wyfe wes lyand thus in swoun,
Fell in that cace in disputatioun.

71 'Allace,' quod Pertok, makand sair murning,
With teiris grit attour hir cheikis fell;
'Yone wes our drowrie, and our dayis darling,
Our nichtingall, and als our Orloge bell,
Our walkryfe watche, us for to warne and tell
Quhen that Aurora with hir curcheis gray,   500
Put up hir heid betwix the nicht and day.

72 'Quha sall our lemman be? quha sall us leid?
Quhen we ar sad, quha sall unto us sing?
With his sweit Bill he wald brek us the breid,
In all this warld wes thair ane kynder thing?
In paramouris he wald do us plesing,
At his power, as nature did him geif.
Now efter him, allace, how sall we leif?'

481 woid) schaw *B*
482 Off that cryme) Off countermaund *B*
483 Toppok) coppok *B*
484 hard) cryit *C*
486 'How, murther, hay !') 'How, murthour, reylock !' *B*
497 drowrie) lemman *S*

73 Quod Sprutok than, 'Ceis sister off your sorrow;
   Ye be to mad ffor him sic murning mais: 510
   We sall ffair weill; I find, Sanct Johne to borrow,
   The prouerb sayis, "als gude lufe cummis as gais."
   I will put on my haly dais clais,
   And mak me fresch agane this Jolie may,
   Syne chant this sang, "wes never wedow sa gay!"

74 'He wes angry and held us ay in aw,
   And woundit with the speir off Jelowsy.
   Off chalmerglew, Pertok, full weill ye knaw,
   Waistit he wes, off Nature cauld and dry;
   Sen he is gone, thairfoir, Sister, say I,   520
   Be blyith in baill, ffor that is best remeid:
   Let quik to quik, and deid ga to the deid.'

75 Than Pertok spak, with feinyeit faith befoir:
   'In lust but lufe he set all his delyte;
   Sister, ye wait, off sic as him ane scoir
   Wald not suffice to slaik our appetyte.
   I hecht be my hand, sen that he is quyte,
   Within ane oulk, ffor schame and I durst speik,
   To get ane berne suld better claw oure breik.'

76 Than Toppok lyke ane Curate spak full crous: 530
   'Yone wes ane verray vengeance from the hevin;
   He wes sa lous, and sa lecherous;
   He had' (quod scho) 'kittokis ma than sevin.
   Bot rychteous God, haldand the balandis evin,
   Smytis rycht sair, thocht he be patient,
   For Adulterie, that will thame not repent.

510 for him sic murning mais) such mourning for to glose *S*
523 Than Pertok spak, with feinyeit faith befoir) Thus sprowtok þat
    feynȝeit fayth befoir *B*
524 he set all his delyte) þat sett all hir delyte *B*
527 hecht) hecht ȝow *B* : he is) ȝe ar *B*
530 Toppok) coppok *B* : Curate) priest *S*
532 lous) lowsie *Ht* ; loweouss *B* ; lowse *S*

77 'Prydefull he wes, and joyit off his sin,
    And comptit not for Goddis favour nor feid,
    Bot traistit ay to rax, and sa to rin,
    Quhill at the last his sinnis can him leid   540
    To schamefull end, and to yone suddand deid.
    Thairfoir it is the verray hand off God
    That causit him be werryit with the Tod.'

78 Quhen this wes said, this wedow ffra hir swoun
    Start up on fute, and on hir kennettis cryde,
    'How! berk, Berrie, Bawsie Broun,
    Rype schaw, Rin weil, Curtes, Nuttieclyde,
    Togidder all but grunching furth ye glyde!
    Reskew my Nobill Cok, or he be slane,
    Or ellis to me se ye cum never agane.'   550

79 With that but baid thay braidet over the bent;
    As fyre off flint thay over the feildis flaw;
    Full wichtlie thay throw wood and wateris went,
    And ceissit not schir Lourence quhill thay saw.
    Bot quhen he saw the Kennettis cum on raw,
    Unto the Cok in mynd he said, 'God sen,
    That I and thow wer fairlie in my den.'

80 Then said the Cok, with sum gude Spirit inspyrit,
    'Do my counsall and I sall warrand the;
    Hungrie thow art, and ffor grit travell tyrit,   560
    Richt faint off force, and may not ferther fle.
    Swyith turne agane, and say that I and ye
    Freindis ar maid, and fellowis ffor ane yeir;
    Than will thay stint, I stand ffor it, and not steir.'

        545 on fute) in haist B
        546 'How! birkye, burrye, bell, balsye broun' B
        547 Nuttieclyde) cutt and clyid B
        555 Kennettis) raches B
        566 frawdis) freindis CHt
        568 falset failyeis ay) wyly beguiles himself S

81 This Tod, thocht he wes fals and frivolus,
    And had frawdis his querrell to defend,,
    Desauit wes be menis richt mervelous;
    For falset failyeis ay at the latter end.
    He start about, and cryit as he wes kend.
    With that the Cok he braid out off the bewch,   570
    Now Juge ye all quhairat Schir Lowrence lewch.

82 Begylit thus, the Tod under the tre
    On kneis fell, and said, 'gude Chantecleir,
    Cum doun agane, and I, but meit or fe,
    Salbe your man and servand ffor ane yeir.'
    'Na, fals theif and revar, stand not me neir.
    My bludy hekill, and my nek sa bla,
    Hes partit freindschip ffor ever betwene us twa.

83 'I wes unwyse that winkit at thy will,
    Quhairthrow almaist I loissit had my heid.'   580
    'I was mair fule,' quod he, 'to be sa still,
    Quhairthrow to put my pray in to pleid.'
    'Fair on, fals theif, God keip me ffra thy feid.'
    With that the Cok over the feildis tuke his flicht,
    And in at the Wedowis Lewer couth he licht.

MORALITAS.

84 Now, worthie folk, suppose this be ane Fabill,
    And overheillit wyth typis figurall,
    Yit may ye find ane sentence richt agreabill,
    Under thir fenyeit termis textuall:
    To our purpose this Cok weill may we call   590
    Nyse proud men, woid and vaneglorious,
    Of kin and blude quhilk ar presumpteous.

        570 out off) unto a B
        576 fals) murther B : not me neir) on reir B
        581 to be sa still) coud nocht be still B
        582 Quhairthrow) But spake B
        592 and blude) or gude B

85 Fy! puft up pryde, thow is full poysonabill;
 Quha favoris the on force man haif ane fall.
 Thy strenth is nocht, thy stule standis unstabill;
 Tak witnes of the Feyndis Infernall,
 Quhilk houndit doun wes fra that hevinlie hall
 To Hellis hole, and to that hiddeous hous,
 Because in pryde thay wer presumpteous.

86 This fenyeit Foxe may weill be figurate,   600
 To flatteraris with plesand wordis quhyte,
 With fals mening and mynd maist toxicate,
 To loif and le that settes thair haill delyte.
 All worthie folk at sic suld haif despyte;
 For quhair is thair mair perrellous pestilence
 Nor gif to learis haistelie credence?

87 The wickit mynd and Adullatioun,
 Of sucker sweit haifand the similitude,
 Bitter as gall, and full of poysoun,
 To taist it is quha cleirlie understude.   610
 For thy, as now schortlie to conclude,
 Thir twa sinnis, flatterie and vaneglore,
 Ar vennomous; gude folk, fle thame thairfoir.

      Finis.

The Taill how this foirsaid Tod maid his Côfessioun to Freir Wolf Waitskaith

88 Leif we this wedow glaid, I yow assure,
 Off Chantecleir mair blyith than I can tell,
 And speik we off the subtell aventure
 And destenie that to this Foxe befell,
 Quhilk durst na mair with waitting Intermell,
 Als lang as Leme or Licht wes off the day,
 Bot, bydand nicht, full styll Lurkand he Lay,   620

   593 This stanza is lacking in *H*
   602 mynd maist toxicate) mouth mellifluate *B*
   603 loif) leif *C*   606 Nor) Than *B*
   613 vennomous) mannis enemeis *C*; perilous *S*
   616 subtell) fatal *B*   618 waitting) miching *B*

89 Quhill that the Goddes off the flude
   Phebus had callit to the harbery,
   And Hesperous put up his cluddie hude,
   Schawand his Lustie Visage in the sky.
   Than Lowrence luikit up, quhair he couth ly,
   And kest his hand upon his Ee on hicht,
   Merie and glade that cummit wes the nicht.

90 Out off the wod unto ane hill he went,
   Quhair he micht se the twinkling sternis cleir,
   And all the planetis off the firmament,   630
   Thair cours, and eik thair moving in the Spheir,
   Sum retrograde, and sum Stationeir,
   And off the Zodiak, in quhat degre
   Thay wer ilk ane, as Lowrence leirnit me.

91 Than Saturne auld wes enterit in Capricorne,
   And Juppiter movit in Sagittarie,
   And Mars up in the Rammis heid wes borne,
   And Phebus in the Lyoun furth can carie;
   Venus the Crab, the Mone wes in Aquarie;
   Mercurius, the God off Eloquence,   640
   Into the Virgyn maid his residence.

92 But Astrolab, Quadrant, or Almanak,
   Teichit off nature be Instructioun,
   The moving off the hevin this Tod can tak,
   Quhat influence and constellatioun
   Wes lyke to fall upon the eirth adoun.
   And to him self he said, withoutin mair,
   'Weill worth my ffather, that send me to the Lair.

93 'My destenie, and eik my weird I ken,
   My aventure is cleirlie to me kend;   650
   With mischeif myngit is my mortall men,
   My misleving the soner bot gif I mend:
   It is reward off sin ane schamefull end.
   Thairfoir I will ga seik sum Confessour,
   And schryiff me clene off my sinnis to this hour.

621 that the) that Thetes the *B*
623 up) of *B* : cluddie hude) heid *C*   649 ken) watt *B*
651 men) Ene *C*; fait *B*   653 It is) Deid is *C*

94 'Allace' (quod he), 'richt waryit ar we thevis,
　Our lyifis set ilk nicht in aventure ;
　Our cursit craft full mony man mischevis ;
　For ever we steill, and ever ar lyke pure :
　In dreid and schame our dayis we Indure ;　　　660
　Syne widdinek, and Crakraip callit als,
　And till our hyre hangit up be the hals.'

95 Accusand thus his cankerit conscience,
　In to ane Craig he kest about his Ee ;
　So saw he cummand ane lyttill than frome hence,
　Ane worthie Doctour in Divinitie,
　Freir Wolff Waitskaith, in science wonder sle,
　To preich and pray wes new cummit ffra the Closter
　With Beidis in hand, sayand his pater noster.

96 Seand this Wolff, this wylie tratour Tod　　　670
　On kneis fell, with hude in to his nek :
　'Welcome, my Gostlie ffather under God'
　(Quod he), with mony binge and mony bek.
　'Ha' (quod the Wolff), 'Schir Tod, for quhat effek
　Mak ye sic feir?　Ryse up, put on your hude.'
　'Father' (quod he), 'I haif grit cause to dude.

97 'Ye ar Mirrour, Lanterne, and sicker way,
　Suld gyde sic sempill folk as me to grace.
　Your bair feit, and your Russet Coull off gray,
　Your lene cheik, your paill pietious face,　　　680
　Schawis to me your perfite halines.
　For weill wer him, that anis in his lyve
　Had hap to yow his sinnis ffor to schryve.'

98 'Na, selie Lowrence' (quod the Wolf), and leuch :
　'It plesis me that ye ar penitent.'
　'Off reif and stouth, Schir, I can tell aneuch,
　That causis me full sair for to repent.
　Bot, ffather, byde still heir upon the bent,
　I you beseik, and heir me to declair
　My conscience, that prikkis me sa sair.　　　690

　　675-6   Make ye such mone, rise up on your foet ?
　　　　　　Father, quoth he, I haue great cause to doet *S*

99 'Weill' (quod the Wolff), 'sit doun upon thy kne.'
    And he doun bairheid sat full humilly,
    And syne began with Benedicitie.
    Quhen I this saw, I drew ane lytill by,
    For it effeiris nouther to heir, nor spy,
    Nor to reveill thing said under that seill:
    Unto the Tod this Gait the Wolf couth kneill.

100 'Art thow contrite, and sorie in thy Spreit
    For thy trespas?' 'Na, Schir, I can not duid:
    Me think that hennis ar sa honie sweit,   700
    And Lambes flesche that new ar lettin bluid;
    For to repent my mynd can not concluid,
    Bot off this thing, that I haif slane sa few.'
    'Weill' (quod the Wolff), 'in faith, thow art ane schrew.'

101 'Sen thow can not forthink thy wickitnes,
    Will thow forbeir in tyme to cum and mend?'
    'And I forbeir, how sall I leif, allace,
    Haifand nane uther craft me to defend?
    Neid causis me to steill quhair evir I wend.
    I eschame to thig, I can not wirk, ye wait,   710
    Yit wald I fane pretend to gentill stait.'

102 'Weill' (quod the Wolff) 'thow wantis pointis twa,
    Belangand to perfyte Confessioun.
    To the thrid part off penitence let us ga:
    Will thou tak pane for thy transgressioun?'
    'Na, Schir, considder my Complexioun,
    Selie and waik, and off my Nature tender;
    Lo, will ye se, I am baith lene and sklender.'

103 'Yit, neuertheles, I wald, swa it wer licht,
    Schort, and not grevand to my tendernes,   720
    Tak part off pane, fulfill it gif I micht,
    To set my selie Saull in way off grace.'
    'Thou sall' (quod he), 'forbeir flesch untill pasche,
    To tame this Corps, that cursit Carioun;
    And heir I reik the full remissioun.'

---

697 couth kneill) couth tell *C*; q^d mele *B*   705 forthink) forbeare *Hl*
714 penitence) pennance *B*   724 this) þi *BHl*

104 'I grant thairto, swa ye will giff me leif
　　To eit puddingis, or laip ane lyttill blude,
　　Or heid, or feit, or paynches let me preif,
　　In cace I fall no flesch unto my fude.'
　　'For grit mister I gif the leif to dude　　　　　730
　　Twyse in the oulk, for neid may haif na Law.'
　　'God yeild yow, Schir, for that Text weill I knaw.'

105 Quhen this wes said, the Wolff his wayis went.
　　The Foxe on fuit he fure unto the fludе—
　　To fang him fisch haillelie wes his intent.
　　Bot quhen he saw the watter, and wallis woude,
　　Astonist all still in to ane stair he stude,
　　And said, 'better that I had biddin at hame,
　　Nor bene ane ffischar in the Devillis Name.

106 'Now may I scraip my meit out off the sand,　　740
　　And I haif nouther boittis nor net bait.'
　　As he wes thus ffor ffalt of meit murnand,
　　Lukand about his leving ffor to lait,
　　Under ane tre he saw ane trip off Gait;
　　Than wes he blyith, and in ane heuch him hid,
　　And ffra the Gait he stall ane lytill Kid.

107 Syne over the heuch unto the see he hyis,
　　And tuke the Kid be the hornis twane,
　　And in the watter outher twyis or thryis
　　He dowkit him, and till him can he sayne:　　750
　　'Ga doun, Schir Kid, cum up Schir Salmond agane!'
　　Quhill he wes deid; syne to the land him drewch,
　　And off that new maid Salmond eit anewch.

729 In cace na flesche vnto my fude I fall *H*; In cace I falt of flesche in
　　to my fude *CB*
730 I gif the leif to gust thy mouth with all *H*
732 I knaw) ye knaw *B*
736 the watter, and wallis woude) thir walterand wawis *B*
737 Astonist all still) All stoneist still *B*
739 Nor bene) Than be *B*

108 Thus fynelie fillit with young tender meit,
    Unto ane derne ffor dreid he him addrest,
    Under ane busk, quhair that the sone can beit,
    To beik his breist and bellie he thocht best.
    And rekleslie he said, quhair he did rest,
    Straikand his wame aganis the sonis heit,
    'Upon this wame set wer ane bolt full meit.'   760

109 Quhen this wes said, the keipar off the Gait,
    Cairfull in hart his Kid wes stollen away,
    On everilk syde full warlie couth he wait,
    Quhill at the last he saw quhair Lowrence lay.
    Ane Bow he bent, ane flane with ffedderis gray
    He haillit to the heid, and, or he steird,
    The Foxe he prikkit fast unto the eird.

110 'Now' (quod the Foxe), 'allace and wellaway!
    Gorrit I am, and may na forther gang.
    Me think na man may speik ane word in play,   770
    Bot now on dayis in ernist it is tane.'
    He harlit him, and out he drew his flane;
    And ffor his Kid, and uther violence,
    He tuke his skyn, and maid ane recompence.

MORALITAS.

111 This suddand deith, and unprovysit end
    Of this fals Tod, without provision,
    Exempill is exhortand folk to amend,
    For dreid of sic ane lyke confusioun;
    For mony now hes gude professioun,
    Yit not repentis, nor for thair sinnis greit,   780
    Because thay think thair lustie lyfe sa sweit.

741 boittis nor net bait) boittis nor ʒit Net *C*; net, bottis, nor bate *B*
748 be) rycht be *B*
769 gang) gane *B*
776 provision) contritioun *B*
778 confusioun) conclusioun *B*
779 now hes gude professioun) gois now to confessioun *B*

112 Sum bene also throw consuetude and ryte,
    Vincust with carnall sensualitie;
    Suppose thay be as for the tym contryte,
    Can not forbeir, nor fra thair sinnis fle;
    Use drawis Nature swa in propertie
    Of beist and man, that neidlingis thay man do,
    As thay of lang tyme hes bene hantit to.

113 Be war, gude folke, and feir this suddane schoit,
    Quhilk smytis sair withoutin resistence.   790
    Attend wyislie, and in your hartis be noit,
    Aganis deith may na man mak defence.
    Ceis of your sin, Remord your conscience,
    Obey unto your God and ye sall wend,
    Efter your deith, to blis withouttin end.

                    Finis.

The Taill of the Sõe & Air of the foirsaid Foxe, callit Father wer : Alswa the Parliamẽt of fourfuttit Beistis, haldin be the Lyoun.

114 This foirsaid ffoxe, that deit ffor his misdeid,
    Had not ane barne wes gottin richteouslie,
    Till airschip be Law that micht succeid,
    Except ane Sone, quhilk in Adulterie
    He gotten had in purches privelie,   800
    And till his Name wes callit Father war,
    That luifit weill with pultrie to tig and tar.

115 It followis weill be ressoun naturall,
    And gre be gre, off richt comparisoun,
    Off euill cummis war, off war cummis werst of all,
    Off wrangus geir cummis fals successioun.
    This ffoxe, Bastard of generatioun,
    Off verray kinde behuifit to be fals;
    Swa wes his Father, and his Grandschir als.

116 As Nature will, seikand his meit be sent,   810
　　Off cace he fand his ffatheris Carioun,
　　Nakit, new slane; and till him hes he went,
　　Tuke up his heid, and on his kne fell doun,
　　Thankand grit God off that conclusioun;
　　And said, 'Now sall I bruke, sen I am air,
　　The boundis quhair thow wes wont ffor to repair.'

117 'Fy! Covetice, unkynd, and venemous:
　　The Sone wes fane he fand his ffather deid,
　　Be suddand schot, ffor deidis odious,
　　That he micht ringe, and raxe in till his steid,   820
　　Dreidand na thing the samin lyfe to leid,
　　In thift, and reif, as did his ffather befoir;
　　Bot to the end attent he tuke no moir.

118 Yit nevertheles, throw Naturall pietie,
　　The Carioun upon his bak he tais.
　　'Now find I weill this prouerb trew' (quod he),
　　'"Ay rinnis the ffoxe, als lang as he fute hais."'
　　Syne with the Corps unto ane peitpoit gais,
　　Off watter ffull, and kest him in the deip,
　　And to the Devill he gaif his banis to keip.   830

119 O fulische man! plungit in warldlynes,
　　To conqueis warldlie gude, and gold, and rent,
　　To put thy Saull in pane, or hevines,
　　To richt thy air, quhilk efter thow art went,
　　Have he thy gude, he takis bot small tent
　　To execute, to do, to satisfie
　　Thy letter will, thy det, and legacie.

794 Obey unto your God) Do wilfull pennance here *B*
799 Adulterie) lemanrie *B*   806 successioun) possessioun *C*
815 bruke) walke *S*
822 thift) stouth *B*
832 and gold, and rent) golde, and rent *C*; gold, or rent *B*
836-7 To sing or say for thy saluatioun:
　　Fra thow be dede, done is thy deuotioun *B*

120 This Tod to rest him, he passit to ane Craig,
     And thair he hard ane busteous Bugill blaw,
     Quhilk, as he thocht, maid all the warld to waig.   840
     Ane Unicorne come lansand over ane Law.
     Than start he up, quhen he this hard and saw;
     With horne in hand, ane bill in breist he bure,
     Ane pursephant semelie, I yow assure.

121 Unto ane bank, quhair he micht se about
     On everilk syde, in haist he culd him hy,
     Schot out his voce, full schyll, and gaif ane schout,
     And on this wyis twyse or thryse did cry.
     With that the beistes in the feild thairby,
     All mervelland, quhat sic ane thing suld mene,   850
     Gritlie agast, thay gaderit on ane grene.

122 Out off ane bus ane bull sone can he braid,
     And red the Text withoutin tarying:
     Commandand silence, sadlie thus he said:
     'The Nobill Lyoun, off all beistis the King,
     Greting to God, helth everlestyng
     To brutall beistis, and Irrationall,
     I send, as to my subjectis grit and small.

123 'My celsitude, and hie magnificence,
     Lattis yow to wait, that evin incontinent,   860
     Thinkis the morne, with Royall deligence,
     Upon this hill to hald ane Parliament.
     Straitlie thairfoir I gif commandement
     For to compeir befoir my Tribunall,
     Under all pane and perrell that may fall.'

124 The morrow come, and Phebus with his bemis
     Consumit had the mistie cluddis gray.
     The ground wes grene, and als as gold it glemis,
     With gers growand gudelie, grit and gay;
     The spyce thay spred to spring on everilk spray;   870
     The Lark, the Maveis, and the Merll, full hie,
     Sweitlie can sing, creippand ffra tre to tre.

851 Gritlie agast) govand agast *B*
852 Out off ane bus) Out of his buist *CHtB*

125 The Leopardis come with Croun off massie gold;
    Beirand thay brocht unto that hillis hicht,
    With Jaspis Jonit, and Royall Rubeis rold,
    And mony diveris Dyamontis dicht,
    With towis proud ane Palyeoun doun thay picht;
    And in that Throne thair sat ane wild Lyoun,
    In Rob Royall, with Sceptour, Swerd, and Croun.

126 Efter the tennour off the cry befoir,   880
    That gais on all fourfuttit beistis in eird,
    As thay commandit wer withoutin moir,
    Befoir thair Lord the Lyoun thay appeird :
    And quhat thay wer, to me as Lowrence leird,
    I sall reheirs ane part of everilk kynd,
    Als fer as now occurris to my mynd.

127 The Minotaur, ane Monster mervelous,
    Bellerophont that beist of Bastardrie,
    The Warwolff, and the Pegase perillous,
    Transformit be assent of sorcerie.   890
    The Linx, the Tiger full off Tiranie :
    The Elephant, and eik the Dromedarie ;
    The Cameill with his Cran nek furth can carie.

128 The Leopard, as I haif tauld beforne,
    The Anteloip, the Sparth furth couth speid,
    The peyntit Pantheir, and the Unicorne ;
    The Rayndeir Ran throw Reveir, Rone, and Reid,
    The Jolie Gillet, and the gentill Steid,
    The Asse, the Mule, the Hors of everilk kynd ;
    The Da, the Ra, the hornit Hart, the Hynd.   900

856 helth everlestyng) ay lestand but ending *B*   868 als as) als like *H*
869 gudelie, grit) gritlie, gude *H*   872 creippand) trippand *CB*
873 The) Thre *B* ; Two *S*
877 towis) powis *C* ; pollis *B* ; silken roapes *S*
880 Slightly varying in *B*
888 Bellerophont) Bellerophant *H* ; Bellorophant *B* ; Bellerophon *S* ;
    Bellepheront *Ht*
893 nek) craig *B*
895 speid) spreid *H* ; hir speid *B*
898 Gillet) Gennet *S* ; Jonet *B*

C

129 The Bull, the Beir, the Bugill, and the Bair,
     The tame Cat, Wildcat, and the Wildwod Swyne,
     The Hardbakkit Hurcheoun, and the Hirpland Hair,
     Baith Otter and Aip, and Pennit Porcupyne;
     The Gukit Gait, the selie Scheip, the Swyne,
     The wyld Once, the Buk, the Welterand Brok,
     The Fowmart, with the Fibert ffurth can flok.

130 The gray Grewhound, with Sleuthound furth can slyde,
     With Doggis all divers and different;
     The Rattoun ran, the Glebard furth can glyde,   910
     The quhrynand Quhitret, with the Quhasill went,
     The Feitho that hes furrit mony fent,
     The Mertrik, with the Cunning and the Con,
     The Bowranbane, and eik the Lerioun.

131 The marmisset the Mowdewart couth leid,
     Because that Nature denyit had hir sicht;
     Thus dressit thay all ffurth, ffor dreid off deid;
     The musk, the lytill Mous with all hir micht
     With haist scho haikit unto that hill of hicht;
     And mony kynd off beistis I couth not knaw,   920
     Befoir thair Lord the Lyoun thay loutit law.

132 Seing thir beistis all at his bidding boun,
     He gaif ane braid, and luikit him about;
     Than flatlingis to his feit thay ffell all doun,
     For dreid off deith thay droupit all in dout.
     He lukit quhen that he saw thame lout,
     And bad thame, with ane countenance full sweit,
     ‘Be not efferit, bot stand up on your feit.

902 tame Cat) wodwyss *B* : Wildwod Swyne) wild wolfyne *B*
906 The bauer bakon and the batterand brok *B*
908 gray) gay *B*
910 Glebard) Glybard *S*; globert *B*
911 quhrynand) quhuiraud *H* ; quherland *B*
914 Bowranbane) Bowrabant *S*; Bourabane *Ht*; lurdane lane *B*
921 the Lyoun) Ilkane *B*
923 luikit him) blenkit all *B*

133 'I lat yow wit my micht is merciabill,
And steiris nane that ar to me prostrait,   930
Angrie, austerne, and als unamyabill
To all that standfray ar to myne estait.
I rug, I reif all beistis that makis debait
Aganis the micht off my Magnyficence :
Se nane pretend to pryde in my presence.

134 'My Celsitude and my hie Maiestie
With micht and mercie myngit sall be ay ;
The lawest heir I can ffull sone up hie,
And mak him maister over yow all I may.
The Dromedarie, giff he will mak deray,   940
The grit Camell, thocht he wer never sa crous,
I can him law als lytill as ane Mous.

135 'Se neir be twentie mylis quhair I am
The Kid ga saiflie be the gaittis syde,
The Tod Lowrie luke not to the lam,
Na revand beistis nouther Ryn nor ryde.'
Thay couchit all efter that this wes cryde ;
The Justice bad the Court ffor to gar fence,
The sutis callit, and ffoirfalt all absence.

136 The Panther, with his payntit Coit Armour,   950
Fensit the Court, as off the Law effeird.
Than Tod Lowrie luikit quhair he couth lour,
And start on fute, all stonist, and all steird,
Ryifand his hair, he cryit with ane reird,
Quaikand ffor dreid, and sichand couth he say :
'Allace this hour, allace this dulefull day !

926 The lyoun lukit quhen he saw þame lout *B*
932 standfray) standis aganis *BS*
935 pryde) quarrell *S*
938 heir) hart *CHt*
944 gaittis) wolf *B*
948 gar fence) go hence *Ht* ; beginne *S*
949 ffoirfalt all absence) forfaytes bring in *S*

137 'I wait this suddand Semblie that I se,
Haifand the pointis off ane Parliament,
Is maid to mar sic misdoars as me;
Thairfoir, geve I me schaw, I will be schent;   960
I will be socht, and I be red absent;
To byde, or fle, it makis no remeid;
All is alyke, thair ffollowis not bot deid.'

138 Perplexit thus in his hart can he mene
Throw ffalset how he micht himself defend;
His Hude he drew laich attour his Ene,
And, winkand with ane Eye, furth he wend;
Clinschand he come, that he micht not be kend,
And, for dreddour that he suld bene arreist,
He playit bukhude behind, ffra beist to beist.   970

139 O fylit Spreit, and cankerit Conscience!
Befoir ane Roy Renyeit with richteousnes,
Blakinnit cheikis and schamefull countenance!
Fairweill thy fame, now gone is all thy grace,
The Phisnomie, the favour off thy face,
For thy defence is foull and diffigurate,
Brocht to the licht, basit, blunt, and blait.

140 Be thow atteichit with thift, or with tressoun,
For thy misdeid wrangous and wickit fay,
Thy cheir changis, Lowrence; thow man luke doun;   980
Thy worschip of this warld is went away.
Luke to this Tod, how he wes in effray,
And fle the filth of falset, I the reid,
Quhairthrow thair followis syn and schamefull deid.

141 Compeirand thus befoir thair Lord and King,
In ordour set as to thair estait effeird,
Of everilk kynd he gart ane part furth bring,
And awfullie he spak, and at thame speird
Geve there wes ony kynd of beistis in eird
Absent, and thairto gart thame deiplie sweir;   990
And thay said: 'nane, except ane Stude gray Meir.'

968 Clinschand) Halting S   969 bene) thoill B
971 The next two stanzas are lacking in B
974 now gone is all thy grace) defylit for ay is C

142 'Ga, mak ane message sone unto that Stude.'
    The Court than cryit : 'now see, quha sall it be?'
    'Cum furth, Lowrie, lurkand under thy hude.'
    'Na, Schir, mercie ! lo, I have bot ane Ee;
    Hurt in the hoche, and cruikit as ye may se;
    The Volff is better in Ambassatry,
    And mair cunning in Clergie fer than I.'

143 Rampand he said, 'ga furth, brybouris baith!'
    And thay to ga withoutin tarying.   1000
    Over Ron and Rute thay ran togidder raith,
    And fand the Meir at hir meit in the morning.
    'Now,' quod the Tod, 'Madame, cum to the King,
    The Court is callit, and ye ar *Contumax*.'
    'Let be, Lowrence' (quod scho), 'your Courtlie Knax.'

144 'Maistres' (quod he), 'cum to the Court ye mon;
    The Lyoun hes commandit so in deid.'
    'Schir Tod, tak ye the Flyrdome, and the Fon,
    I have respite ane yeir, and ye will reid.'
    'I can not spell' (quod he), 'sa God me speid: 1010
    Heir is the Volff, ane Nobill Clerk at all,
    And of this Message is maid principall.

145 'He is Autentik, and ane man of age,
    And hes grit practik of the Chanceliary;
    Let him ga luke, and reid your Privilage,
    And I sall stand, and beir witnes yow by.'
    'Quhair is thy Respite?' (quod the Wolff), in hy.
    'Schir, it is heir, under my hufe weill hid.'
    'Hald up thy heill' (quod he); and so scho did.

146 Thocht he wes blindit with pryde, yit he presumis 1020
    To luke doun law, quhair that hir letter lay.
    With that the meir gird him upon the gumis,
    And straik the hattell off his heid away.
    Halff out off lyif, thair lenand doun he lay:
    'Allace' (quod Lowrence), '**Lupus**, thow art loist.'
    'His cunning' (quod the Meir) 'wes worth sum coist.

996 hoche) hanche *B* ; heid *C*   999 Rampand) Braiding *B*
1001 Rute) ryce *B*   1005 3our carping & 3our knax *B*
    1023 hattell) hattrell *CB*

147 'Lowrence' (quod scho), 'will thow luke on my letter,
      Sen that the Wolff na thing thairoff can wyn?'
      'Na, be Sanct Bryde' (quod he), 'me think it better
      To sleip in haill nor in ane hurt skyn.   1030
      Ane skrow I ffand, and this wes writtin in,
      —For ffyve schillingis I wald not anis fforfaut him—
      Felix quem faciunt aliena pericula cautū.'

148 With brokin skap, and bludit cheikis reid,
      This wretchit Wolff weipand, thus on he went,
      Off his menye markand to get remeid,
      To tell the King the cace wes his Intent.
      'Schir' (quod the Tod), 'byde still upon this bent,
      And ffra your browis wesche away the blude,
      And tak ane drink, ffor it will do yow gude.'   1040

149 To fetche watter this ffraudfull Fox furth fure,
      Sydelingis abak he socht unto ane syke;
      On cace he meittis, cummand ffra the mure,
      Ane Trip of Lambis dansand on ane dyke.
      This Tratour Tod, this Tirrant, and this Tyke,
      The fattest off this flock he ffellit hais,
      And eit his fill; syne to the Wolff he gais.

150 Thay drank togidder, and syne thair Journey takis;
      Befoir the King syne kneillit on thair kne.
      'Quhair is yone Meir, Schir Tod, wes *Contumax?*'   1050
      Than Lowrence said: 'My Lord, speir not at me!
      Speir at your Doctour off Divinitie,
      With his reid Cap can tell yow weill aneuch.'
      With that the Lyoun, and all the laif thay leuch.

1030 and in ane unhurt skyn *B*
1034 brokin skap) bludie skap *H* : bludit cheikis reid) cheikis bla and
      reid *H*
1035 wiping them as he went *S*   1042 syke) slyke *CHt*

151 'Tell on the cais now, Lowrence, let us heir.'
     'This wittie Wolff' (quod he), 'this Clerk off age,
     On your behalff he bad the Meir compeir,
     And scho allegit to ane privilage—
     "Cum neir and se, and ye sall haiff your wage."
     Because he red his rispite plane and weill,   1060
     Yone reid Bonat scho raucht him with hir heill.'

152 The Lyoun said, 'be yone reid Cap I ken
     This Taill is trew, quha tent unto it takis;
     The greitest Clerkis ar not the wysest men;
     The hurt off ane happie the uther makis.'
     As thay wer carpand in this cais, with knakis,
     And all the Court in merines and in gam,
     Swa come the Yow, the Mother off the Lam.

153 Befoir the Justice on hir kneis fell,
     Put out hir playnt on this wyis wofully: 1070
     'This harlet huresone, and this hound off hell,
     Devorit hes my Lamb full doggitly,
     Within ane myle, in contrair to your cry.
     For Goddis lufe, my Lord, gif me the Law
     Off this lurker:' with that Lowrence let draw.

154 'Byde' (quod the Lyoun), 'Lymmer, let us se
     Giff it be suthe the selie yow hes said.'
     'Aa, Soverane Lord, saif your mercie' (quod he),
     'My purpois wes with him ffor to haif plaid;
     Causles he fled, as he had bene effraid;   1080
     For dreid off deith, he duschit ouer ane dyke,
     And brak his nek.' 'Thow leis' (quod scho), 'fals tyke.'

1066 with knakis) in knakis *B*; and knakis *C*; and cracke *Ht*
1067 merines) garray *B*
1075 lurker) lymmar *B*
1079 ffor) bot *B*

155 'His deith be practik may be previt eith :
Thy gorrie gumis and thy bludie snout,
The woll, the flesche yit stikkis on thy teith,
And that is evidence aneuch, but dout.'
The Justice bad ga cheis ane Assyis about;
And so thay did, and fand that he wes fals,
Off Murther, thift, pyking, and tressoun als.

156 Thay band him fast, the Justice bad belyif   1090
To gif the dome, and tak off all his clais ;
The Wolff, that new maid Doctour, couth him schrif;
Syne furth him led, and to the Gallous gais,
And at the ledder fute his leif he tais ;
The Aip was Bowcher, and bad him sone ascend,
And hangit him ; and thus he maid his end.

MORALITAS

157 Richt as the Mynour in his Minorall
Fair Gold with fyre may fra the Leid weill wyn,
Richt so under ane Fabill figurall
Sad sentence man may seik, and efter syne,   1100
As daylie dois the Doctouris of Devyne,
That to our leving full weill can apply
And paynt thair mater furth be Poetry.

158 The Lyoun is the warld be liknes,
To quhom loutis baith Empriour and King,
And thinkis of this warld to get incres,
Thinkand daylie to get mair leving ;
Sum for to reull : and sum to raxe and Ring ;
Sum gadderis geir : sum Gold : sum uther gude,
To wyn this warld, sum wirkis as thay wer wod.   1110

1089   pyking, and tressoun als) and party tresoun als *B*
1095   Bowcher) basare *B*
1098   Leid weill wyn) Copper well win *Ht*
1100   syne) fyne *CHB*
1102-3   Apertly be oure leving can applye
     And preve thare preching be a poesye *B*
1104   liknes) liklynace *B*

159 The Meir is Men of gude conditioun,
   As Pilgrymes Walkand in this wildernes,
   Approvand that for richt Religioun
   Thair God onlie to pleis in everilk place ;
   Abstractit from this warldis wretchitnes,
   Fechtand with lust, presumptioun, and pryde,
   And fra this warld in mynd ar mortyfyde.

160 This Wolf I likkin to Sensualitie,
   As quhen, lyke brutall beistis, we accord
   Our mynd all to this warldis vanitie,   1120
   Lyking to tak and loif him as our Lord :
   Fle fast thairfra, gif thow will richt remord ;
   Than sall Ressoun ryse, Rax and Ring,
   And for thy Saull thair is na better thing.

161 Hir Hufe I likkin to the thocht of deid.
   Will thow remember, Man, that thow man de?
   Thow may brek Sensualiteis heid,
   And fleschlie lust away fra the sall fle,
   Fra thow begin thy mynd to mortifie ;
   Salomonis saying thow may persaif heirin :   1130
   'Think on thy end, thow sall not glaidlie sin.'

162 This Tod I likkin to Temptationis,
   Beirand to mynd mony thochtis vane,
   Assaultand men with sweit perswasionis,
   Ay reddy for to trap thame in ane trayne ;
   Yit gif thay se Sensualitie neir slane,
   And suddand deith draw neir with panis sore,
   Thay go abak, and temptis thame no moir.

1111 gude conditioun) contemplatioun *B*
1112 As Pilgrymes) Of pennance *B* : Walkand) wandrand *H*
1113 As monkis and othir men of religioun *B*
1114 Thair God onlie to pleis) That presis god to pleiss *B*
1116 In wilfull povertee, fra pomp and all pryde *B*
1129-30 Wiss salomone sais, will thow nocht see,
        For as thow may thy sely saull now wyne *B*
1134-5 That daylie sagis men of religioun,
        Cryand to þame, 'Cum to þe warld agane !' *B*
1137 draw neir with) with ithand *B*

163 O Mediatour! mercifull and meik,
    Thow soveraigne Lord, and King Celestiall,   1140
    Thy celsitude maist humillie we beseik,
    Us to defend fra pane and perrellis all,
    And help us up unto thy hevinlie hall,
    In gloir, quhair we may se the face of God.—
    And thus endis the talking of the Tod.

Finis.

The Taill of the Scheip ãd the Doig

164 Esope ane Taill puttis in memorie,
    How that ane Doig, because that he wes pure,
    Callit ane Scheip to the Consistorie,
    Ane certaine breid ffra him ffor to recure.
    Ane fraudfull Wolff was Juge that tyme, and bure   1150
    Authoritie and Jurisdictioun;
    And on the Scheip send furth ane strait summoun.

165 For by the use, and cours, and common style
    On this maner maid his Citatioun:
    ' I, Maister Wolff, partles off fraud and gyle,
    Under the panis off hie Suspensioun,
    Off grit Cursing, and Interdictioun,
    Schir Scheip, I charge the for to compeir,
    And answer to ane Doig befoir me heir.'

1139-1141   O lord eternall, medeator for us mast meke,
             Sitt doun before thy fader celestiall,
             For us synnaris his celsitude beseke, *B*

Note.—These lines replace the original MS. version, and are in the same hand. The original reads—

          O mary myld, mediatour of mercy meke,
          Sitt doun before thy sone celestiall,

1153 curse of common style *Ht*
1158 for) straitiy *B*   1159 to Perry Dogge *S*

166 Schir Corbie Ravin wes maid Apparitour,   1160
    Quha pykit had ffull mony Scheipis Ee ;
    The charge hes tane, and on the letteris bure ;
    Summonit the Scheip befoir the Wolff, that he,
    Peremptourlie, within twa dayis or thre,
    Compeir under the panis in this bill,
    'To heir quhat Perrie Doig will say the till.'

167 This Summondis maid befoir witnes anew ;
    The Ravin, as to his office weill effeird,
    Indorsat hes the write, and on he flew ;
    The selie Scheip durst lay na mouth on eird,   1170
    Till he befoir the awfull Juge appeird,
    The oure off cause, quhilk that the Juge usit than,
    Quhen Hesperus to schaw his face began.

168 The Foxe wes Clerk and Noter in the Cause ;
    The Gled, the Graip, at the Bar couth stand ;
    As Advocatis expert in to the Lawis,
    The Doggis pley togidder tuke on hand,
    Quhilk wer confidderit straitlie in ane band,
    Aganis the Scheip to procure the sentence ;
    Thocht it wes fals, thay had na conscience.   1180

169 The Clerk callit the Scheip, and he wes thair ;
    The Advocatis on this wyse couth propone.
    'Ane certaine breid, worth fyve schilling or mair,
    Thow aw the Doig, off quhilk the terme is gone.'
    Off his awin heid, but Advocate allone,
    The Scheip avysitlie gave answer in the cace :
    'Heir I declyne the Juge, the tyme, the place.

170 'This is my cause, in motive and effect :
    The Law sayis, it is richt perrillous
    Till enter in pley befoir ane Juge suspect ;   1190
    And ye, Schir Wolff, hes bene richt odious
    To me, for with your Tuskis ravenous
    Hes slane full mony kinnismen off mine ;
    Thairfoir, Juge as suspect, I yow declyne.

1167 Summondis) summond is *H* ; summons *S* ; summonds *Ht*
1175 Gled) Kight : Graip) Crow *S*
1194 Juge as suspect) as juge suspect *BS*

171 'And schortlie, of this Court ye memberis all,
     Baith Assessouris, Clerk, and Advocate,
     To me and myne ar ennemies mortall,
     And ay hes bene, as mony Scheipheird wate;
     The place is fer, the tyme is feriate,
     Quhairfoir na Juge suld sit in Consistory,   1200
     Sa lait at evin, I yow accuse ffor thy.'

172 Quhen that the Juge in this wyse wes accusit,
     He bad the parteis cheis, with ane assent,
     Twa Arbeteris, as in the Law is usit,
     For to declair and gif Arbitriment,
     Quhidder the scheip suld answer in Jugement
     Befoir the Wolff; and so thay did but weir,
     Off quhome the Namis efterwart ye sall heir.

173 The Beir, the Brok, the mater tuke on hand,
     For to discyde gif this exceptioun   1210
     Wes off na strenth, nor lauchfully mycht stand;
     And thairupon, as Jugis, thay sat doun,
     And held ane lang quhyle disputatioun,
     Seikand full mony Decreitis off the Law,
     And Glosis als, the veritie to knaw.

174 Of Civile Law volumis full mony thay revolve,
     The Codies and Digestis new and ald;
     Contrait, Prostrait Argumentis thay resolve,
     Sum objecting, and sum can hald;
     For prayer, or price, trow ye that thay wald fald? 1220
     Bot hald the glose, and Text of the Decreis,
     As trew Jugis; I beschrew thame ay that leis.

1198 As mony Scheipheird wate) thocht I mycht not it lat C
1199 feriate) insperate C; desperat Ht; very late S
1205 declair) dissyd B   1206 answer) byd B
1214 Decreitis) decretalis B
1216 Civile) sewall B: volumis full mony) mony volum B
1218 Contrait, prostrait) prowe and contra, strait B
1219 Sum a doctryne, and sum a nother hald B

175 Schortlie to mak ane end off this debait:
    The Arbiteris than sweirand plane,
    The sentence gave, and proces fulminait:
    The Scheip suld pas befoir the Wolff agane,
    And end his pley.   Than wes he nathing fane,
    For ffra thair sentence couth he not appeill.
    On Clerkis I do it, gif this sentence wes leill.

176 The Scheip agane befoir the Wolff derenyeit,   1230
    But Advocate, abasitlie couth stand.
    Up rais the Doig, and on the Scheip thus plenyeit:
    'Ane soume I payit have befoir the hand
    For certane breid;' thairto ane Borrow he fand,
    That wrangouslie the Scheip did hald the breid;
    Quhilk he denyit; and thair began the pleid.

177 And quhen the Scheip this stryif had contestait,
    The Justice in the cause furth can proceid;
    Lowrence the actis, and the proces wrait,
    And thus the pley unto the end thay speid.   1240
    This Cursit Court, corruptit all ffor meid,
    Aganis gude faith, Law, and eik conscience,
    For this fals Doig pronuncit the sentence.

178 And it till put to executioun
    The Wolff chargit the Scheip, without delay,
    Under the panis off Interdictioun,
    The soume off silver, or the breid, to pay.
    Off this sentence (allace) quhat sall I say,
    Quhilk dampnit hes the selie Innocent,
    And Justifyit the wrangous Jugement?   1250

1221 hald) had *C*; held *HB*
1224 than sweirand plane) did sweir full plane *C*; summar and plane *B*
1227 pley) plied *B*   1229 do it) doid *B*; doe give *Ht*
1234 Borrow) borch *B*   1238 Justice) Jugeis *B*
1240 thus) sone *B*
1242 Law, and eik conscience) gud law and conscience *B*

179 The Scheip, dreidand mair the executioun,
    Obeyand to the sentence, he couth tak
    His way unto ane Merchand off the Toun,
    And sauld the woll that he bure on his bak ;
    Syne bocht the breid, and to the Doig couth mak
    Reddie payment, as it commandit was :
    Naikit and bair syne to the feild couth pas.

MORALITAS

180 This selie Scheip may present the figure
    Of pure commounis, that daylie ar opprest
    Be Tirrane men, quhilkis settis all thair cure   1260
    Be fals meinis to mak ane wrang conquest,
    In hope this present lyfe suld ever lest ;
    Bot all begylit, thay will in schort tyme end,
    And efter deith to lestand panis wend.

181 This Wolf I likkin to ane Schiref stout,
    Quhilk byis ane forfalt at the Kingis hand,
    And hes with him ane cursit Assyis about,
    And dytis all the pure men up on land.
    Fra the Crownar haif laid on him his wand,
    Thocht he wer trew as ever wes sanct Johne,   1270
    Slain sall he be, or with the Juge compone.

182 This Ravin I likkin to ane fals Crownair,
    Quhilk hes ane portioun of the Inditement,
    And passis furth befoir the Justice Air,
    All misdoaris to bring to Jugement ;
    Bot luke, gif he wes of ane trew Intent,
    To scraip out Johne, and wryte in Will, or Wat,
    And tak ane bud at boith the parteis tat.

1251 executioun) persecutioun *B*
1252 Obeyand) Obeyit *B* : he couth) and couth *B*   1254 woll) fleiss *B*
1256 it commandit was) he forejugeit wass *B*
1269 Crownar) Baylife *S* : him) thame *B*   1271 he) thay *B*
1273 portioun) porteouss *B*
1274 Justice Air) Justiciar *S*   1278 bud) skat *B* ; tat *H*

183 Of this fals tod, of quhilk I spak befoir,
     And of this Gled, quhat thay micht signify,   1280
     Of thair nature, as now I speik no moir ;
     Bot of this Scheip, and of his cairfull cry
     I sall reheirs ; for as I passit by
     Quhair that he lay, on cais I lukit doun,
     And hard him mak sair lamentatioun.

184 'Allace' (quod he), 'this cursit Consistorie,
     In middis of the winter now is maid,
     Quhen Boreas with blastis bitterlie
     And hard froistes thir flouris doun can faid ;
     On bankis bair now may I mak na baid.'   1290
     And with that word in to ane coif he crap,
     Fra sair wedder, and froistis him to hap.

185 Quaikand for cauld, sair murnand ay amang,
     Kest up his Ee unto the hevinnis hicht,
     And said, 'Lord God, quhy sleipis thow sa lang?
     Walk, and discerne my cause, groundit on richt ;
     Se how I am, be fraud, maistrie, and slicht,
     Peillit full bair : ' and so is mony one
     Now in this warld, richt wonder, wo begone !

186 Se how this cursit sone of covetice,   1300
     Loist hes baith lawtie and eik Law.
     Now few or nane will execute Justice,
     In falt of quhome the pure man is overthraw.
     The veritie, suppois the Juge it knaw,
     He is so blindit with affectioun,
     But dreid, for micht, he lettis the richt go doun.

1279 of quhilk) becauss *B*   1289 And hard) With frawart *B*
1292 sair) hair *B*   1297 slicht) might *Ht*   1300 sone) syn *B*
1301 Exylit hes bayth lufe, lawty, and law *B* ; Bought hath the Lawier,
     and eke the lawe *S*
1306 micht) meid *B*

187 Seis thow not (Lord) this warld overturnit is,
    As quha wald change gude gold in leid or tyn;
    The pure is peillit, the Lord may do na mis;
    And Simonie is haldin for na syn.   1310
    Now is he blyith with okker maist may wyn;
    Gentrice is slane, and pietie is ago,
    Allace (gude Lord) quhy thoilis thow it so?

188 Thow tholis this evin for our grit offence,
    Thow sendis us troubill, and plaigis soir,
    As hunger, derth, grit weir, or Pestilence;
    Bot few amendis now thair lyfe thairfoir.
    We pure pepill as now may do no moir
    Bot pray to the, sen that we ar opprest
    In to this eirth, grant us in hevin gude rest.   1320

Finis.

The Taill of the Lyõn & the Mous

189 In middis of June, that sweit seasoun,
    Quhen that fair Phebus, with his bemis bricht,
    Had dryit up the dew ffra daill and doun,
    And all the land maid with his bemis licht,
    In ane mornyng betwix mid day and nicht,
    I rais, and put all sleuth and sleip asyde,
    And to ane wod I went allone but gyde.

190 Sweit wes the smell off flouris, quhyte and reid,
    The noyes off birdis richt delitious,
    The bewis braid blomit abone my heid,   1330
    The ground growand with gers gratious;
    Off all plesance that place wes plenteous,
    With sweit odouris, and birdis harmony,
    The Morning Myld: my mirth wes mair for thy.

1320 Explicit: quod m̄r. R. H. *B*   1321 sweit) joly sueit *B*
1324 bemis) lemys *B*

191   The Rosis reid arrayit on Rone and Ryce,
        The Prymeros, and the Purpour violat bla ;
        To heir it wes ane poynt off Paradice,
        Sic Mirth the Mavis and the Merle couth ma.
        The blossummis blythe brak up on bank and bra ;
        The smell off Herbis and off fowlis cry,   1340
        Contending wha suld have the victory.

192   Me to conserve than ffra the sonis heit,
        Under the schaddow off ane Hawthorne grene,
        I lenit doun amang the flouris sweit,
        Syne cled my heid, and closit baith my Ene.
        On sleip I fell amang thir bewis bene,
        And in my dreme me thocht come throw the schaw
        The fairest man that ever befoir I saw.

193   His gowne wes off ane claith als quhyte as milk ;
        His Chemeis wes off Chambelate Purpour Broun ;   1350
        His hude off Scarlet, bordourit weill with silk,
        On hekillit wyis, untill his girdill doun ;
        His Bonat round, and off the auld fassoun ;
        His beird wes quhyte ; his Ene wes grit and gray,
        With lokker hair, quhilk over his schulderis lay.

194   Ane Roll off paper in his hand he bair ;
        Ane swannis pen stikand under his eir ;
        Ane Inkhorne, with ane prettie gilt Pennair,
        Ane bag off silk, all at his belt can beir :
        Thus wes he gudelie grathit in his geir.   1360
        Off stature large, and with ane feirfull face :
        Evin quhair I lay he come ane sturdie pace,

1336 Purpour violat bla) Purpour Viola C
1345 cled my heid) maid a corss B
1350 Chemeis) chymmeris B   1354 grit) grene B
1359 can beir) he weir B   1360 grathit) gathered Ht

195 And said, 'God speid, my sone'; and I wes fane
Off that couth word, and off his cumpany;
With reverence I salusit him agane:
'Welcome, Father'; and he sat doun me by.
'Displeis you not, my gude maister, thocht I
Demand your birth, your facultye, and name,
Quhy ye come heir, or quhair ye dwell at hame?'

196 'My sone' (said he), 'I am off gentill blude;　　1370
My native land is Rome withoutin nay;
And in that Towne first to the Sculis I yude,
In Civile Law studyit full mony ane day;
And now my winning is in Hevin ffor ay:
Esope I hecht; my writing and my werk
Is couth and kend to mony cunning Clerk.'

197 'O Maister Esope, Poet Lawriate,
God wait, ye ar full deir welcum to me;
Ar ye not he that all thir Fabillis wrate,
Quhilk in effect, suppois thay fenyeit be,　　1380
Ar full off prudence and moralitie?'
'Fair sone' (said he), 'I am the samin man.'
God wait, gif that my hert wes merie than.

198 I said, 'Esope, my maister venerabill,
I yow beseik hartlie, ffor cheritie,
Ye wald not disdayne to tell ane prettie Fabill,
Concludand with ane gude Moralitie.'
Schaikand his heid, he said, 'my sone lat be,
For quhat is it worth to tell ane fenyeit taill,
Quhen haly preiching may na thing availl?　　1390

199 'Now in this warld, me think, richt few or nane
To Goddis word that hes devotioun;
The eir is deif, the hart is hard as stane,
Now oppin sin without correctioun,
The hart Inclynand to the eirth ay doun;
Sa roustie is the warld with canker blak,
That now my taillis may lytill succour mak.'

1371 native) natale B　　　　1373 Civile Law) Science B
1375-6 Transposed in C and Ht　1386 wald not disdayne) wald dedene B
1393 hard) cauld Ht　　　　1395 hart) eir C

200 'Yis, gentill Schir' (said I), 'for my requeist,
    Not to displeis your Fatherheid, I pray,
    Under the figure off ane brutall beist,   1400
    Ane morall Fabill ye wald denye to say :
    Quha wait, nor I may leir and beir away
    Sum thing thairby heirefter may availl?'
    'I grant' (quod he), and thus begouth ane taill.

       The end of the Prolog, & begiñis
          the Taill :

201 Ane Lyoun at his Pray war foirrun,
    To recreat his limmis and to rest,
    Beikand his breist and belly at the Sun,
    Under ane tre lay in the fair forest ;
    Swa come ane trip off Myis out off thair nest,
    Richt tait and trig, all dansand in ane gyis,   1410
    And over the Lyoun lansit twyis or thryis.

202 He lay so still, the Myis wes not effeird,
    Bot to and fro out over him tuke thair trace ;
    Sum tirlit at the Campis off his beird,
    Sum spairit not to claw him on the face ;
    Merie and glaid thus dansit thay ane space,
    Till at the last the Nobill Lyoun woke,
    And with his pow the maister Mous he tuke.

203 Scho gave ane cry, and all the laif agast
    Thair dansing left, and hid thame sone alquhair; 1420
    Scho that wes tane cryit and weipit fast,
    And said allace oftymes that scho come thair :
    'Now am I tane ane wofull presonair,
    And ffor my gilt traistis Incontinent
    Off lyfe and deith to thoill the Jugement.

1398 Yis) ʒit *HB*   1401 denye) dedene *B*
1405 war) verray *C* ; war *H* ; wery *B*   1411 lansit) th(a)y dansit *C*
1420 thame sone alquhair) thame heir and thair *C*
1422 oftymes that scho come thair) for now and evir mair *B*

204 Than spak the Lyoun to that cairfull Mous:
     'Thow Cative wretche, and vile unworthie thing,
     Over malapart and eik presumpteous
     Thow wes, to mak out over me thy tripping.
     Knew thow not weill I wes baith Lord and King   1430
     Off beistis all?' 'Yes' (quod the Mous), 'I knaw;
     Bot I misknew, because ye lay so law.

205 'Lord! I beseik thy Kinglie Royaltie,
     Heir quhat I say, and tak in patience;
     Considder first my simple povertie,
     And syne thy mychtie hie Magnyfycence;
     Se als how thingis done off Neglygence,
     Nouther off malice nor of presumptioun,
     The rather suld have grace and Remissioun.

206 'We wer repleit and had grit aboundance   1440
     Off alkin thingis, sic as to us effeird;
     The sweit sesoun provokit us to dance,
     And mak sic mirth as nature to us leird.
     Ye lay so still, and law upon the eird
     That, be my sawll, we weind ye had bene deid,
     Elles wald we not have dancit ouer your heid.'

207 'Thy fals excuse,' the Lyoun said agane,
     'Sall not availl ane myte I underta;
     I put the cace, I had bene deid or slane,
     And syne my skyn bene stoppit full off stra,   1450
     Thocht thow had found my figure lyand swa,
     Because it bare the prent off my persoun,
     Thow suld ffor ffeir on kneis have fallin doun.

208 'For thy trespas thow can mak na defence,
     My Nobill persoun thus to vilipend;
     Off thy feiris, nor thy awin negligence,
     For to excuse thow can na cause pretend;
     Thairfoir thow suffer sall ane schamefull end,
     And deith, sic as to tressoun is decreit,
     Upon the Gallous harlit be the feit.'   1460

1438 presumptioun) promissioun *B*   1441 thingis) fude *B*
1460 harlit) hangit *CB*   1467 Kinglie) cumlie *C*

209 'Na, mercie, Lord, at thy gentrice I ase,
　　As thow art King off beistis Coronate,
　　Sober thy wraith, and let it overpas,
　　And mak thy mynd to mercy Inclynate.
　　I grant offence is done to thyne estate,
　　Quhairfoir I worthie am to suffer deid,
　　Bot gif thy Kinglie mercie reik remeid.

210 'In everie Juge mercy and reuth suld be,
　　As Assessouris, and Collaterall ;
　　Without mercie Justice is crueltie,　　　　　　1470
　　As said is in the Lawis speciall :
　　Quhen Rigour sittis in the Tribunall,
　　The equitie off Law quha may sustene ?
　　Richt few or nane, but mercie gang betwene.

211 'Alswa ye knaw the honour Triumphall
　　Off all victour upon the strenth dependis
　　Off his conqueist, quhilk manlie in battell
　　Throw Jeopardie of weir lang defendis.
　　Quhat pryce or loving, quhen the battell endis,
　　Is said off him that overcummis ane man,　　　　1480
　　Him to defend quhilk nouther may nor can ?

212 'Ane thowsand Myis to kill, and eik devoir,
　　Is lytill manheid to ane strang Lyoun ;
　　Full lytill worschip have ye wyn thairfoir,
　　To quhais strenth is na comparisoun ;
　　It will degraid sum part off your renoun
　　To sla ane mous, quhilk may mak na defence,
　　Bot askand mercie at your excellence.

213 'Also it semis not your Celsitude,
　　Quhilk usis daylie meittis delitious,　　　　　　1490
　　To fyle your teith or lippis with my blude,
　　Quhilk to your stomok is contagious ;
　　Unhailsum meit is of ane sarie Mous,
　　And that namelie untill ane strang Lyoun,
　　Wont till be fed with gentill vennesoun.

1468 reuth) truth *H*　　　　　　1471 speciall) spirituall *B*
1477 conqueist) compair *CB*　　　1478 weir) armes *B*

214 'My lyfe is lytill worth, my deith is les,
 Yit and I leif, I may peradventure
 Supple your hienes beand in distres ;
 For oft is sene ane man off small stature
 Reskewit hes ane Lord off hie honour,   1500
 Keipit that wes in poynt to be overthrawin
 Throw misfortoun : sic cace may be your awin.'

215 Quhen this wes said, the Lyoun his langage
 Paissit, and thocht according to ressoun,
 And gart mercie his cruell Ire asswage,
 And to the Mous grantit Remissioun ;
 Oppinnit his pow, and scho on kneis fell doun,
 And baith hir handis unto the hevin upheild,
 Cryand : 'Almichty God mot yow fforyeild !'

216 Quhen Scho wes gone, the Lyoun held to hunt,   1510
 For he had nocht, bot levit on his Pray,
 And slew baith tayme and wyld, as he wes wont,
 And in the cuntrie maid ane grit deray ;
 Till at the last the pepill fand the way
 This cruell Lyoun how that thay mycht tak :
 Off Hempyn cordis strang Nettis couth thay mak.

217 And in ane Rod, quhair he wes wont to ryn,
 With Raipis rude ffra tre to tre it band ;
 Syne kest ane Range on raw the wod within,
 With hornis blast, and Kennettis fast calland.   1520
 The Lyoun fled, and, throw the Ron rynnand,
 Fell in the Net, and hankit fute and heid ;
 For all his strenth he couth mak na remeid.

218 Welterand about with hiddeous rummissing,
 Quhyle to, quhyle ffra, quhill he mycht succour get ;
 Bot all in vane, it vailyeit him na thing ;
 The mair he flang, the faster wes the Net ;
 The Raipis rude wes sa about him plet,
 On everilk syde, that succour saw he nane ;
 Bot styll lyand and murnand maid his mane.   1530

1498 beand) leand B   1504 Paissit) Praised Ht   1510 held) ʒeid B
1524 Welterand) Volvand B   1525 quhill) gif B
1527 wes the Net) was he knett B   1528 plet) knet C

219 'O lainit Lyoun, liggand heir sa law,
 Quhair is the mycht off thy Magnyfycence,
 Off quhome all brutall beist in eird stude aw,
 And dred to luke upon thy Excellence?
 But hoip or help, but succour or defence,
 In bandis strang heir may I ly (allace!)
 Till I be slane, I se nane uther grace.

220 'Thair is na wy that will my harmis wreik,
 Nor creature do confort to my Croun.
 Quha sall me bute? quha sall my bandis breik? 1540
 Quha sall me put fra pane off this Presoun?'
 Be he had maid this lamentatioun,
 Throw aventure, the lytill Mous come neir,
 And off the Lyoun hard the pietuous beir.

221 And suddanlie it come in till hir mynd
 That it suld be the Lyoun did hir grace,
 And said, 'now wer I fals, and richt unkynd,
 Bot gif I quit sumpart off thy gentrace
 Thow did to me:' and on this way scho gais
 To hir fellowis, and on thame fast can cry, 1550
 'Cum help, cum help!' and thay come all in hy.

222 'Lo,' quod the Mous, 'this is the samin Lyoun
 That grantit grace to me quhen I wes tane;
 And now is fast heir bundin in Presoun,
 Brekand his hart with sair murning and mane;
 Bot we him help, off succour wait he nane;
 Cum help to quyte ane gude turne for ane uther,
 Go, lous him sone:' and thay said, 'ye, gude brother.'

223 Thay tuke na knyfe, thair teith wes sharpe anewch.
 To se that sicht, forsuith it wes grit wounder, 1560
 How that thay ran amang the rapis tewch;
 Befoir, behind, sum yeid about, sum under,
 And schuir the raipis off the net in schunder;
 Syne bad him ryse; and he start up anone,
 And thankit thame; syne on his way is gone.

1538 wy) joy *B*   1548 gentrace) gentrice *C*; gentilnes *B*
1555 Brekand his hart) Wrekand his hurt *B*
1562 about) above *S* 1563 net) mastis *B*; Mast *C*

224 Now is the Lyoun fre off all danger,
Lows and delyverit to his libertie,
Be lytill beistis off ane small power,
As ye have hard, because he had pietie.
(Quod I) 'Maister, is thair ane Moralitie   1570
In this Fabill?' 'Yea, sone' (he said), 'richt gude.'
'I pray yow, Schir' (quod I), 'ye wald conclude.'

MORALITAS

225 As I suppois, this mychtie gay Lyoun
May signifie ane Prince, or Empriour,
Ane Potestate, or yit ane King with Croun,
Quhilk suld be walkrife gyde and Governour
Of his pepill, that takis na labour
To reule and steir the land, and Justice keip,
Bot lyis still in lustis, sleuth, and sleip.

226 The fair Forest with levis lowne and le,   1580
With foulis sang, and flouris ferlie sweit,
Is bot the warld and his prosperitie,
As fals plesance myngit with cair repleit.
Richt as the Rois with froist and wynter weit
Faidis, swa dois the warld, and thame desavis
Quhilk in thair lustis maist confidence havis.

227 Thir lytill Myis ar bot the commountie,
Wantoun, unwyse, without correctioun:
Thair Lordis and Princis quhen that thay se
Of Justice mak nane executioun,   1590
Thay dreid na thing to mak Rebellioun,
And disobey, for quhy thay stand nane aw,
That garris thame thair Soveranis misknaw.

228 Be this Fabill ye Lordis of Prudence
May considder the vertew of Pietie;
And to remit sumtyme ane grit offence,
And mitigate with mercy crueltie:
Oftymis is sene ane man of small degre
Hes quit ane kinbute baith of gude and ill,
As Lord hes done Rigour, or grace him till.   1600

1599 Hes quit ane turne baith for gude and evill *C*; hes quyt a commoun *B*;
quitte a King eyther *S*

229 Quha wait how sone ane Lord of grit Renoun,
   Rolland in warldle lust and vane plesance,
   May be overthrawin, destroyit, and put doun
   Throw fals fortoun? quhilk of all variance
   Is haill maistres, and leidar of the dance
   Till Injust men, and blindis thame so soir,
   That thay na perrell can provyde befoir.

230 Thir rurall men, that stentit hes the Net,
   In quhilk the Lyoun suddandlie wes tane,
   Waittit alway amendis for to get   1610
   (For hurt men wrytis in the Marbill Stane).
   Mair till expound as now I lett allane,
   Bot King and Lord may weill wit quhat I mene:
   Figure heirof oftymis hes bene sene.

231 Quhen this wes said (quod Esope): 'my fair child,
   I the beseik and all men for to pray
   That tressoun of this cuntrie be exyld,
   And Justice Regne, and Lordis keip thair fay
   Unto thair Soverane King, baith nycht and day.'
   And with that word he vanist, and I woke;   1620
   Syne throw the Schaw my Journey hamewart tuke.

                    Finis.

The Preiching of the Swallow

232 The hie prudence, and wirking mervelous,
   The profound wit off God omnipotent,
   Is sa perfyte, and sa Ingenious,
   Excellent ffar all mannis Jugement;
   For quhy to him all thing is ay present,
   Rycht as it is, or ony tyme sall be,
   Befoir the sicht off his Divinitie.

1602 lust) wit *H*   1605 maistres) Master *Ht*
1606 Injust) lusty *B* : blindis) bindis *B*
1608 rurall) crewall *B* ; cruell *C*
1616 perswaid the kirkmen ythandly to pray *B*
1621 Explicit : quod m̄r. R. Henrysone.
1624 Ingenious) ingeing *B*   1625 Jugement) argument *B*

233　Thairfoir our Saull with Sensualitie
　　　So fetterit is in presoun Corporall,　　　　　1630
　　　We may not cleirlie understand nor se
　　　God as he is, nor thingis Celestiall:
　　　Our mirk and deidlie corps Naturall
　　　Blindis the Spirituall operatioun,
　　　Lyke as ane man wer bundin in presoun.

234　In Metaphisik Aristotell sayis
　　　That mannis Saull is lyke ane Bakkis Ee,
　　　Quhilk lurkis still als lang as licht off day is,
　　　And in the gloming cummis furth to fle;
　　　Hir Ene ar waik, the Sone scho may not se:　　　1640
　　　Sa is our Saull with fantasie opprest,
　　　To knaw the thingis in nature manifest.

235　For God is in his power Infinite,
　　　And mannis Saull is febill and over small,
　　　Off understanding waik and unperfite,
　　　To comprehend him that contenis all.
　　　Nane suld presume, be ressoun naturall,
　　　To seirche the secreitis off the Trinitie,
　　　Bot trow fermelie, and lat all ressoun be.

236　Yit nevertheles we may haif knawlegeing　　　1650
　　　Off God almychtie, be his Creatouris,
　　　That he is gude, ffair, wyis and bening;
　　　Exempill tak be thir Jolie flouris,
　　　Rycht sweit off smell, and plesant off colouris.
　　　Sum grene, sum blew, sum purpour, quhyte, and reid,
　　　Thus distribute be gift off his Godheid.

237　The firmament payntit with sternis cleir,
　　　From eist to west rolland in cirkill round,
　　　And everilk Planet in his proper Spheir,
　　　In moving makand Harmonie and sound;　　　1660
　　　The fyre, the Air, the watter, and the ground—
　　　Till understand it is aneuch, I wis,
　　　That God in all his werkis wittie is.

1632 thingis) a thing B　　　　　1633 Naturall) materiale B
1649 all ressoun) dirk ressonnis B　　1660 In moving) In morning S

238 Luke weill the fische that swimmis in the se ;
     Luke weill in eirth all kynd off bestiall ;
     The foulis ffair, sa forcelie thay fle,
     Scheddand the air with pennis grit and small ;
     Syne luke to man, that he maid last off all,
     Lyke to his Image and his similitude :
     Be thir we knaw, that God is ffair and gude.   1670

239 All Creature he maid ffor the behufe
     Off man, and to his supportatioun
     In to this eirth, baith under and abufe,
     In number, wecht, and dew proportioun ;
     The difference off tyme, and ilk seasoun,
     Concorddand till our opurtunitie,
     As daylie by experience we may se.

240 The Somer with his Jolie mantill off grene,
     With flouris fair furrit on everilk fent,
     Quhilk Flora Goddes, off the flouris Quene,   1680
     Hes to that Lord as ffor his seasoun sent,
     And Phebus with his goldin bemis gent
     Hes purfellit and payntit plesandly,
     With heit and moysture stilland ffrom the sky.

241 Syne Harvest hait, quhen Ceres that Goddes
     Hir barnis benit hes with abundance ;
     And Bachus, God off wyne, renewit hes
     The tume Pyipis in Italie and France,
     With wynis wicht, and liquour off plesance ;
     And *Copia temporis* to fill hir horne,   1690
     That never wes full off quheit nor uther corne.

242 Syne wynter wan, quhen Austerne Eolus,
     God off the wynd, with blastis boreall,
     The grene garment off Somer glorious
     Hes all to rent and revin in pecis small ;
     Than flouris fair faidit with froist man fall,
     And birdis blyith changit thair noitis sweit
     In styll murning, neir slane with snaw and sleit.

1664-5 weill) we *B*   1686 benit) bewit *C* ; beined *Ht* ; blessed *S*
          1688 The tume) Hir louid *B* ; the toune *S*

243 Thir dalis deip with dubbis drounit is,
   Baith hill and holt heillit with frostis hair;   1700
   And bewis bene laifit bair off blis,
   Be wickit windis off the winter wair.
   All wyld beistis than ffrom the bentis bair
   Drawis ffor dreid unto thair dennis deip,
   Coucheand ffor cauld in coifis thame to keip.

244 Syne cummis Ver, quhen winter is away,
   The Secretar off Somer with his Sell,
   Quhen Columbie up keikis throw the clay,
   Quhilk fleit wes befoir with froistes fell.
   The Mavis and the Merle beginnis to mell;   1710
   The Lark on loft, with uther birdis haill,
   Than drawis furth ffra derne, over doun and daill.

245 That samin seasoun, in to ane soft morning,
   Rycht blyth that bitter blastis wer ago,
   Unto the wod, to se the flouris spring,
   And heir the Mavis sing and birdis mo,
   I passit ffurth, syne lukit to and ffro,
   To se the Soill that wes richt sessonabill,
   Sappie, and to resave all seidis abill.

246 Moving thusgait, grit myrth I tuke in mynd,   1720
   Off lauboraris to se the besines,
   Sum makand dyke, and sum the pleuch can wynd,
   Sum sawand seidis fast ffrome place to place,
   The Harrowis hoppand in the saweris trace:
   It wes grit Joy to him that luifit corne,
   To se thame laubour, baith at evin and morne.

1700 heillit) heled S
1701 bewis) Larkes S: bene laifit) bene baissit C; ar bethit B
1703 bentis bair) fields frore S   1707 Sell) seill CHB: cell S
1720 Moving) Musing Ht

247 And as I baid under ane bank full bene,
    In hart gritlie rejosit off that sicht,
    Unto ane hedge, under ane Hawthorne grene,
    Off small birdis thair come ane ferlie flicht,   1730
    And doun belyif can on the leifis licht,
    On everilk syde about me quhair I stude,
    Rycht mervellous, ane mekill multitude.

248 Amang the quhilks ane Swallow loud couth cry,
    On that Hawthorne hie in the croip sittand :
    'O ye Birdis on bewis, heir me by,
    Ye sall weill knaw, and wyislie understand,
    Quhair danger is, or perrell appeirand ;
    It is grit wisedome to provyde befoir,
    It to deuoyd, ffor dreid it hurt yow moir.'   1740

249 'Schir Swallow' (quod the Lark agane), and leuch,
    ' Quhat haif ye sene that causis yow to dreid?'
    'Se ye yone Churll' (quod scho) 'beyond yone pleuch,
    Fast sawand hemp, and gude linget seid?
    Yone lint will grow in lytill tyme in deid,
    And thairoff will yone Churll his Nettis mak,
    Under the quhilk he thinkis us to tak.

250 'Thairfoir I reid we pas quhen he is gone,
    At evin, and with our naillis scharp and small
    Out off the eirth scraip we yone seid anone,   1750
    And eit it up ; ffor, giff it growis, we sall
    Have cause to weip heirefter ane and all :
    Se we remeid thairfoir ffurth with Instante,
    Nam leuius lædit quicquid prævidimus ante.

1735 croip) toppe *HtS*   1736 hewis) leiffis *C*
1744 and gude linget seid) lose and linget seid ? *C* ; lo se ! and lynget
    sede ? *B*
1754 *prævidimus*) previvimus *C*

251 'For Clerkis sayis it is nocht sufficient
    To considder that is befoir thyne Ee;
    Bot prudence is ane inwart Argument,
    That garris ane man prouyde and foirse
    Quhat gude, quhat evill is liklie ffor to be,
    Off everilk thing behald the fynall end,   1760
    And swa ffra perrell the better him defend.'

252 The Lark, lauchand, the Swallow thus couth scorne,
    And said, scho fischit lang befoir the Net;
    'The barne is eith to busk that is unborne;
    All growis nocht that in the ground is set;
    The nek to stoup, quhen it the straik sall get,
    Is sone aneuch; deith on the fayest fall.'—
    Thus scornit thay the Swallow ane and all.

253 Despysing thus hir helthsum document,
    The foullis ferlie tuke thair flicht anone;   1770
    Sum with ane bir thay braidit over the bent,
    And sum agane ar to the grene wod gone.
    Upon the land quhair I wes left allone,
    I tuke my club, and hamewart couth I carie,
    Swa ferliand, as I had sene ane farie.

254 Thus passit furth quhill June, that Jolie tyde,
    And seidis that wer sawin off beforne
    Wer growin hie, that Hairis mycht thame hyde,
    And als the Quailye craikand in the corne;
    I movit furth, betwix midday and morne,   1780
    Unto the hedge under the Hawthorne grene,
    Quhair I befoir the said birdis had sene.

1758 and foirse) befoir and see *B*
1760 behald the) evin at the *C*; at the *B*
1767 deith on the fayest fall) death on thee fast fall *S*
1769 helthsum) hailsum *B*   1770 ferlie) ferslye *B*
1782 the said) the foresayd *S*
1788 pyme) pryme *B*; pime *S*
1797 tender and small) tender, young and small *SB*

255 And as I stude, be aventure and cace,
       The samin birdis as I haif said yow air,
       I hoip, because it wes thair hanting place,
       Mair off succour, or yit mair solitair,
       Thay lychtit doun : and, quhen thay lychtit wair,
       The Swallow swyth put furth ane piettous pyme,
       Said, 'wo is him can not bewar in tyme.

256 'O, blind birdis ! and full off negligence,   1790
       Unmyndfull of your awin prosperitie,
       Lift up your sicht, and tak gude advertence ;
       Luke to the Lint that growis on yone le ;
       Yone is the thing I bad forsuith that we,
       Quhill it wes seid, suld rute furth off the eird ;
       Now is it Lint, now is it hie on breird.

257 'Go yit, quhill it is tender and small,
       . And pull it up; let it na mair Incres ;
       My flesche growis, my bodie quaikis all,
       Thinkand on it I may not sleip in peis.'   1800
       Thay cryit all, and bad the Swallow ceis,
       And said, ' yone Lint heirefter will do gude,
       For Linget is to lytill birdis fude.

258 'We think, quhen that yone Lint bollis ar ryip,
       To mak us Feist, and fill us off the seid,
       Magre yone Churll, and on it sing and pyip.'
       'Weill' (quod the Swallow), 'freindes hardilie beid ;
       Do as ye will, bot certane sair I dreid,
       Heirefter ye sall find als sour, as sweit,
       Quhen ye ar speldit on yone Carlis speit.   1810

259 'The awner off yone lint ane fouler is,
       Richt cautelous and full off subteltie ;
       His pray full sendill tymis will he mis,
       Bot giff we birdis all the warrer be ;
       Full mony off our kin he hes gart de,
       And thocht it bot ane sport to spill thair blude :
       God keip me ffra him, and the halie Rude.'

260 Thir small birdis haveand bot lytill thocht
    Off perrell that micht fall be aventure,
    The counsell off the Swallow set at nocht,   1820
    Bot tuke thair flicht, and furth togidder fure;
    Sum to the wode, sum markit to the mure.
    I tuke my staff, quhen this wes said and done,
    And walkit hame, ffor it drew neir the none.

261 The Lint ryipit, the Carll pullit the Lyne,
    Rippillit the bollis, and in beitis set,
    It steipit in the burne, and dryit syne,
    And with ane bittill knokkit it, and bet,
    Syne swingillit it weill, and hekkillit in the flet;
    His wyfe it span, and twynit it in to threid,   1830
    Of quhilk the Fowlar Nettis maid in deid.

262 The wynter come, the wickit wind can blaw,
    The woddis grene were wallowit with the weit,
    Baith firth and fell with froistys were maid faw,
    Slonkis and slaik maid slidderie with the sleit;
    The foulis ffair ffor falt thay ffell off feit;
    On bewis bair it wes na bute to byde,
    Bot hyit unto housis thame to hyde.

263 Sum in the barn, sum in the stak off corne
    Thair lugeing tuke, and maid thair residence;   1840
    The Fowlar saw, and grit aithis hes sworne,
    Thay suld be tane trewlie ffor thair expence.
    His Nettis hes he set with diligence,
    And in the snaw he schulit hes ane plane,
    And heillit it all ouer with calf agane.

264 Thir small birdis seand the calff wes glaid;
    Trowand it had bene corne, thay lychtit doun;
    Bot of the Nettis na presume thay had,
    Nor of the Fowlaris fals Intentioun;
    To scraip, and seik thair meit thay maid thame boun.   1850
    The Swallow on ane lytill branche neir by,
    Dreiddand for gyle, thus loud on thame couth cry:

1824 neir the) neir hand *B*   1829 swingillit) scutchit *B*
1834 wer maid faw) and with snow *S*   1844 schulit) showled *S*

265 'In to that calf scraip quhill your naillis bleid,
    Thair is na corne, ye laubour all in vane;
    Trow ye yone Churll for pietie will yow feid?
    Na, na, he hes it heir layit for ane trane;
    Remove, I reid, or ellis ye will be slane;
    His Nettis he hes set full prively,
    Reddie to draw; in tyme be war ffor thy.'

266 Grit fule is he that puttis in dangeir   1860
    His lyfe, his honour, ffor ane thing off nocht;
    Grit fule is he, that will not glaidlie heir
    Counsall in tyme, quhill it availl him nocht;
    Grit fule is he, that hes na thing in thocht
    Bot thing present, and efter quhat may fall,
    Nor off the end hes na memoriall.

267 Thir small birdis ffor hunger famischit neir,
    Full besie scraipand ffor to seik thair fude,
    The counsall off the Swallow wald not heir,
    Suppois thair laubour did thame lytill gude.   1870
    Quhen scho thair fulische hartis understude,
    Sa Indurate, up in ane tre scho flew;
    With that [this] Churll over thame his Nettis drew.

268 Allace! it wes grit hart sair for to se
    That bludie Bowcheour beit thay birdis doun,
    And ffor till heir, quhen thay wist weill to de,
    Thair cairfull sang and lamentatioun:
    Sum with ane staf he straik to eirth on swoun:
    Off sum the heid he straik, off sum he brak the crag,
    Sum half on lyfe he stoppit in his bag.   1880

269 And quhen the Swallow saw that thay wer deid,
    'Lo' (quod scho), 'thus it happinnis mony syis
    On thame that will not tak counsall nor reid
    Off Prudent men, or Clerkis that ar wyis;
    This grit perrell I tauld thame mair than thryis;
    Now ar thay deid, and wo is me thairfoir!'
    Scho tuke hir flicht, bot I hir saw no moir.

    1863 quhill it availl him nocht) mocht *CBHt*
    1873 [this]) thus *Bass*

                                                          E

MORALITAS

270 Lo, worthie folk, Esope, that Nobill clerk,
Ane Poet worthie to be Lawreate,
Quhen that he waikit from mair autentik werk,   1890
With uther ma, this foirsaid Fabill wrate,
Quhilk at this tyme may weill be applicate
To guid morall edificatioun,
Haifand ane sentence, according to ressoun.

271 This Carll and bond of gentrice spoliate,
Sawand this calf, thir small birdis to sla,
It is the Feind, quhilk fra the Angelike state
Exylit is, as fals Apostata :
Quhilk day and nycht weryis not for to ga
Sawand poysoun in mony wickit thocht   1900
In mannis Saull, quhilk Christ full deir hes bocht.

272 And quhen the saull, as seid in to the eird,
Gevis consent unto delectioun,
The wickit thocht beginnis for to breird
In deidlie sin, quhilk is dampnatioun ;
Ressoun is blindit with affectioun,
And carnall lust grouis full grene and gay,
Throw consuetude hantit from day to day.

273 Proceding furth be use and consuetude,
The sin ryipis, and schame is set on syde ;   1910
The Feynd plettis his Nettis scharp and rude,
And under plesance previlie dois hyde ;
Syne on the feild he sawis calf full wyde,
Quhilk is bot tume and verray vanitie
Of fleschlie lust, and vaine prosperitie.

1903 delectioun) in delectatioun *BS*
1911 scharp) stark *B*

274 Thir hungrie birdis wretchis we may call,
    As scraipand in this warldis vane plesance,
    Greddie to gadder gudis temporall,
    Quhilk as the calf ar tume without substance,
    Lytill of availl, and full of variance,   1920
    Lyke to the mow befoir the face of wind
    Quhiskis away and makis wretchis blind.

275 This Swallow, quhilk eschaipit is the snair,
    The halie Preichour weill may signifie,
    Exhortand folk to walk and ay be wair
    Fra Nettis of our wickit enemie,
    Quha sleipis not, bot ever is reddie,
    Quhen wretchis in this warld calf dois scraip,
    To draw his Net, that thay may not eschaip.

276 Allace ! quhat cair, quhat weiping is and wo,   1930
    Quhen Saull and bodie departit ar in twane !
    The bodie to the wormis Keitching go,
    The Saull to Fyre, to everlestand pane.
    Quhat helpis than this calf, thir gudis vane,
    Quhen thow art put in Luceferis bag,
    And brocht to hell, and hangit be the crag ?

277 Thir hid Nettis for to persave and se,
    This sarie calf wyislie to understand,
    Best is bewar in maist prosperite,
    For in this' warld thair is na thing lestand ;   1940
    Is na man wait how lang his stait will stand,
    His lyfe will lest, nor how that he sall end
    Efter his deith, nor quhidder he sall wend.

1917 vane plesance) plesance C   1928 calf dois) wrak do B
1931 departit) pairtit B   1932 wormis Keitching) wormes kitchin S
1934 helpis) help is C   1941 wait) ware Ht

278 Pray we thairfoir, quhill we ar in this lyfe,
  For four thingis: the first, fra sin remufe;
  The secund is fra all weir and stryfe;
  The thrid is perfite cheritie and lufe;
  The feird thing is, and maist for oure behufe,
  That is in blis with Angellis to be fallow.
  And thus endis the preiching of the Swallow.   1950

Finis.

The Taill of the Wolf that gat the Nekherīg throw the wrīkis of the Foxe that begylit the Cadgear.

279 Quhylum thair wynnit in ane wildernes,
  (As myne Authour expreslie can declair),
  Ane revand Wolff, that levit upon purches,
  On bestiall, and maid him weill to ffair;
  Wes nane sa big about him he wald spair,
  And he war hungrie, outher ffor favour or feid,
  Bot in his wraith he weryit thame to deid.

280 Swa happinnit him in watching, as he went,
  To meit ane Foxe in middis off the way;
  He him foirsaw, and fenyeit to be schent,   1960
  And with ane bek he bad the Wolff gude day.
  'Welcum to me' (quod he), 'thow Russell gray;'
  Syne loutit doun, and tuke him be the hand.
  'Ryse up, Lowrence, I leif the for to stand.

281 'Quhair hes thow bene this sesoun ffra my sicht?
  Thow sall beir office, and my Stewart be,
  For thow can knap doun Caponis on the nicht,
  And, lourand law, thow can gar hennis de.'
  'Schir' (said the Foxe), 'that ganis not for me:
  And I am rad, gif thay me se on far,   1970
  That at my figure, beist and bird will skar.'

282 'Na' (quod the Wolff), 'thow can in covert creip
    Upon thy wame, and hint thame be the heid;
    And mak ane suddand schow upon ane scheip,
    Syne with thy wappinnis wirrie him to deid.'
    'Schir' (said the Foxe), 'ye knaw my Roib is reid,
    And thairfoir thair will na beist abyde me,
    Thocht I wald be sa fals as ffor to hyde me.'

283 'Yis' (quod the Wolff), 'throw buskis & throw brais,
    Law can thow lour to cum to thy Intent.'   1980
    'Schir' (said the Foxe), 'ye wait weill how it gais;
    Ane lang space ffra thame thay will feill my sent,
    Then will thay eschaip, suppois I suld be schent;
    And I am schamefull ffor to cum behind thame
    In to the feild thocht I suld sleipand find thame.'

284 'Na' (quod the Wolff), 'thow can cum on the wind,
    For everie wrink, forsuith, thow hes ane wyle.'
    'Schir' (said the Foxe), 'that beist ye mycht call blind,
    That micht not eschaip than ffra me ane myle.
    How micht I ane off thame that wyis begyle?   1990
    My tippit twa eiris, and my twa gray Ene,
    Garris me be kend, quhair I wes never sene.'

285 'Than' (said the Wolff), 'Lowrence, I heir the le,
    And castys ffor perrellis thy ginnes to defend;
    Bot all thy senyes sall not availl the,
    About the busk with wayis thocht thow wend;
    Falset will failye ay at the latter end;
    To bow at bidding, and byde not quhill thow brest,
    Thairfoir I giff the counsall ffor the best.'

1946 fra all) to seiss *B*   1953 purches) cais *C*
1957 wraith) breith *C*   1974 schow) chow *H*
1979 brais) breiris *H*   1983 I suld) thay suld *H*
1995 senyes) son3eis *C*; sayings *S*
1997 Falset will failye ay) Wyly wil beguile himselfe *S*

286 'Schir,' said the Foxe, 'it is Lentring, ye se ;   2000
    I can nocht fische, ffor weiting off my feit,
    To tak ane Banestikill ; thocht we baith suld de,
    I have nane uther craft to win my meit ;
    Bot wer it Pasche, that men suld pultrie eit,
    As Kiddis, Lambis, or Caponis in to ply,
    To beir your office than wald I not set by.'

287 'Than' (said the Wolff), in wraith, 'wenis thow with wylis,
    And with thy mony mowis me to mat ?
    It is ane auld Dog, doutles, that thow begylis :
    Thow wenis to draw the stra befoir the cat !'   2010
    'Schir' (said the Foxe), 'God wait, I mene not that ;
    For and I did, it wer weill worth that ye
    In ane reid Raip had tyit me till ane tre.

288 ' Bot now I se he is ane fule perfay
    That with his maister fallis in ressoning ;
    I did bot till assay quhat ye wald say ;
    God wait, my mynd wes on ane uther thing ;
    I sall fulfill in all thing your bidding,
    Quhat ever ye charge, on nichtis or on dayis.'
    'Weill' (quod the Wolff), 'I heir weill quhat thow sayis.   2020

289 ' Bot yit I will thow mak to me ane aith,
    For to be leill attour all levand leid.'
    'Schir,' said the Foxe, 'that ane word make me wraith,
    For now I se ye haif me at ane dreid ;
    Yit sall I sweir, suppois it be not neid,
    Be Juppiter, and on pane off my heid,
    I sall be trew to you, quhill I be deid.'

2001 I can nouther fische with huke nor Net *C*
2023 that ane word make me wraith) makis *CH* ; let no worde make ye
    wroth *S*

290 With that ane Cadgear, with capill and with creillis,
     Come carpand ffurth ; than Lawrence culd him spy.
     The Foxe the flewer off the fresche hering feillis,   2030
     And to the Wolff he roundis prively :
     'Schir, yone ar hering the Cadgear caryis by ;
     Thairfoir I reid that we se ffor sum wayis
     To get sum fische aganis thir fasting dayis.

291 'Sen I am Stewart, I wald we had sum stuff,
     And ye ar silver seik, I wait richt weill ;
     Thocht we wald thig, yone verray Churlische chuff,
     He will not giff us ane hering off his Creill,
     Befoir yone Churle on kneis thocht we wald kneill ;
     Bot yit I trou alsone that ye sall se,   2040
     Giff I can craft to bleir yone Carllis Ee.

292 'Schir, ane thing is, and we get off yone pelff,
     Ye man tak travell, and mak us sum supple ;
     For he that will not laubour and help him selff,
     In to thir dayis, he is not worth ane fle ;
     I think to work als besie as ane Be.
     And ye sall follow ane lytill efterwart,
     And gadder hering, ffor that sall be your part.'

293 With that he kest ane cumpass ffar about,
     And straucht him doun in middis off the way,   2050
     As he wer deid he fenyeit him, but dout,
     And than upon lenth unliklie lay ;
     The quhyte he turnit up off his Ene tway ;
     His toung out hang ane handbreid off his heid,
     And still he lay, als straucht as he wer deid.

2029 than Lawrence culd him spy) than drew this Boucheour by *C*
2041 craft) traist (?) *C*
2052 And then upon ane lang unliklie bray *C* ; and then all a long
     unlikely he lay *S*

294 The Cadgear fand the Foxe, and he wes fane,
    And till him self thus softlie can he say:
    'At the nixt bait, in Faith, ye sall be flane,
    And off your skyn I sall mak mittennis tway.'
    He lap full lichtlie about him quhair he lay,   2060
    And all the trace he trippit on his tais;
    As he had hard ane pyper play, he gais.

295 'Heir lyis the Devyll' (quod he), 'deid in ane dyke.
    Sic ane selcouth saw I not this sevin yeir;
    I trow ye have bene tussillit with sum tyke,
    That garris you ly sa still withouttin steir:
    Schir Foxe, in Faith, ye ar deir welcum heir;
    It is sum wyfis malisone, I trow,
    For pultrie pyking, that lychtit hes on yow.

296 'Thair sall na Pedder, for purs, nor yit for gluifis,   2070
    Nor yit ffor poyntis pyke your pellet ffra me;
    I sall off it mak mittennis to my lufis,
    Till hald my handis hait quhair ever I be;
    Till Flanderis sall it never saill the se.'
    With that in hy, he hint him be the heillis,
    And with ane swak he swang him on the creillis.

297 Syne be the heid the hors in hy hes hint;
    The fraudfull ffoxe thairto gude tent hes tane,
    And with his teith the stoppell, or he stint,
    Pullit out, and syne the hering ane and ane   2080
    Out of the creillis he swakkit doun gude wane.
    The Wolff wes war, and gadderit spedilie;
    The Cadgear sang, 'huntis up, up, upon hie.'

298 Yit at ane burne the Cadgear luikit about;
    With that the ffoxe lap quyte the creillis ffray;
    The Cadgear wald haif raucht the ffoxe ane rout,
    Bot all ffor nocht, he wan his hoill that day.
    Than with ane schout thus can the Cadgear say:
    'Abyde, and thou ane Nekhering sall haif,
    Is worth my Capill, Creillis, and all the laif.'   2090

2087-8 [transposed in C]   2087 his hoill) his spurs S

299 'Now' (quod the ffoxe), 'I schrew me, and we meit:
    I hard quhat thow hecht to do with my skyn.
    Thy handis sall never in thay mittinnis tak heit,
    And thow wer hangit, Carll, and all thy kyn!
    Do furth thy mercat; at me thou sall nocht wyn;
    And sell thy hering thow hes thair till hie price,
    Ellis thow sall wyn nocht on thy merchandice.'

300 The Cadgear trimillit for teyne quhair that he stude;
    'It is weill worthie' (quod he), 'I want yone tyke,
    That had nocht in my hand sa mekill gude,   2100
    As staff, or sting, yone truker ffor to stryke.'
    With that lychtlie he lap out over ane dyke,
    And hakkit doun ane staff, ffor he wes tene,
    That hevie wes and off the Holyne grene.

301 With that the ffoxe unto the Wolff could wend,
    And fand him be the hering, quhair he lyis;
    'Schir' (said he than), 'maid I not fair defend?
    Ane wicht man wantit never, and he wer wyis;
    Ane hardie hart is hard for to suppryis.'
    (Than said the Wolff): 'thow art ane Berne full bald,   2110
    And wyse at will, in gude tyme be it tald.

302 'Bot quhat wes yone the Carll cryit on hie,
    And schuke his hand,' quod he, 'hes thou no feill?'
    'Schir' (said the Foxe), 'that I can tell trewlie;
    He said the Nekhering wes in till the creill.'
    'Kennis thow that hering?'   'Ye, Schir, I ken it weill,
    And at the creill mouth I had it thryis but doubt;
    The wecht off it neir tit my tuskis out.

303 'Now, suithlie, Schir, micht we that hering fang,
    It wald be fische to us thir fourtie dayis.'   2120
    Than (said the Wolff), 'Now God nor that I hang,
    Bot to be thair, I wald gif all my clays,
    To se gif that my wappinnis mycht it rais.'
    'Schir' (said the ffoxe), 'God wait, I wischit you oft,
    Quhen that my pith micht not beir it on loft.

2113 And schuke his heid quhen that he saw thow fell *C*; . . . didst thou
    not here? *S*   2125 pith) teith *H*

304 'It is ane syde off Salmond, as it wair,
And callour, pypand lyke ane Pertrik Ee;
It is worth all the hering ye have thair,
Ye, and we had it swa, is it worth sic thre.'
'Than' (said the Wolff), 'quhat counsell gevis thou me?' 2130
'Schir' (said the ffoxe), 'wirk efter my devyis,
And ye sall have it, and tak you na suppryis.

305 'First, ye man cast ane cumpas far about,
Syne straucht you doun in middis off the way;
Baith heid, and feit, and taill ye man streik out,
Hing furth your toung, and clois weill your Ene tway;
Syne se your heid on ane hard place ye lay;
And dout not for na perrell may appeir,
Bot hald you clois, quhen that the Carll cummis neir.

306 'And thocht ye se ane staf, have ye na dout,   2140
Bot hald you wonder still in to that steid;
And luke your Ene be clois, as thay wer out,
And se that ye schrink nouther fute nor heid:
Than will the Cadgear Carll trow ye be deid,
And in till haist will hint you be the heillis,
As he did me, and swak you on his creillis.'

307 'Now' (quod the Wolff), 'I sweir the be my thrift,
I trow yone Cadgear Carll he will me beir.'
'Schir' (said the Foxe), 'on loft he will you lift,
Upon his Creillis, and do him lytill deir.   2150
Bot ane thing dar I suithlie to you sweir,
Get ye that hering sicker in sum place,
Ye sall not fair in fisching mair quhill Pasche.

308 'I sall say *In principio* upon yow,
And crose your corps from the top to tay;
Wend quhen ye will, I dar be warrand now
That ye sall de na suddan deith this day.'
With that the Wolff gird up sone, and to gay,
And caist ane cumpas about the Cadgear far;
Syne raucht him in the gait, or he come nar.   2160

2127 And coloured much like the Partrich eye *S*
2148 he will me beir) dow not me beir *CHt*

309 He laid his halfheid sicker hard and sad,
      Syne straucht his four feit ffra him, and his heid,
      And hang his toung furth as the ffoxe him bad;
      Als styll he lay, as he wer verray deid,
      Rakkand na thing off the Carlis ffavour nor feid,
      Bot ever upon the Nekhering he thinkis,
      And quyte forgettis the Foxe and all his wrinkis.

310 With that the Cadgear, wavering as the wind,
      Come rydand on the laid, for it wes licht,
      Thinkand ay on the Foxe that wes behind,   2170
      Upon quhat wyse revengit on him he micht;
      And at the last of the Wolff gat ane sicht,
      Quhair he in lenth lay streikit in the gait;
      Bot giff he lichtit doun, or nocht, God wait!

311 'Softlie,' he said, 'I wes begylit anis;
      Be I begylit twyis, I schrew us baith,
      That evill bot it sall licht upon thy banis,
      He suld have had that hes done me the skaith.'
      On hicht he hovit the staf, ffor he wes wraith,
      And hit him with sic will upon the heid,   2180
      Quhill neir he swonit and swelt in to that steid.

312 Thre battis he bure, or he his feit micht find,
      Bot yit the Wolff wes wicht, and wan away.
      He mycht not se, he wes sa verray blind,
      Nor wit reddilie quhether it wes nicht or day.
      The Foxe beheld that service quhair he lay,
      And leuch on loft, quhen he the Wolff sa seis,
      Baith deif, and dosinnit, fall swonand on his kneis.

313 He that of ressoun can not be content,
      Bot covetis all, is abill all to tyne.   2190
      The Foxe, quhen that he saw the Wolf wes schent,
      Said to him self, 'thir hering sall be myne;'
      I le, or ellis he wes efterwart syne
      That fand sic wayis his Maister for to greif;
      With all the fische thus Lowrence tuke his leif.

2168 wavering as the) als wraith as ony C
2193 syne) fyne CH

314 The Wolff wes neir weill dungin to the deid,
That uneith with his lyfe away he wan,
For with the Bastoun weill brokin wes his heid.
The Foxe in to his den sone drew him than,
That had betraisit his Maister and the man :   2200
The ane wantit the hering off his creillis,
The utheris blude wes rynnand over his heillis.

MORALITAS

315 This Taill is myngit with Moralitie,
As I sall schaw sumquhat, or that I ceis :
The Foxe unto the warld may likkinnit be,
The revand Wolf unto ane man but leis,
The Cadgear Deith, quhome under all man preis :
That ever tuke lyfe throw cours of kynd man dee,
As man, and beist, and fische in to the see.

316 The warld, ye wait, is Stewart to the man,   2210
Quhilk makis man to haif na mynd of Deid,
Bot settis for winning all the craftis thay can ;
The Hering I likkin unto the gold sa reid,
Quhilk gart the Wolf in perrell put his heid :
Richt swa the gold garris Landis and Cieteis
With weir be waistit, daylie as men seis.

317 And as the Foxe with dissimulance and gyle
Gart the Wolff wene to haif worschip for ever,
Richt swa this warld with vane glore for ane quhyle
Flatteris with folk, as thay suld failye never,   2220
Yit suddandlie men seis it oft dissever ;
With thame that trowis oft to fill the sek,
Deith cummis behind and nippis thame be the nek.

2215 Landis and Cieteis) land, certeis *C*
2229 mychtie) ritche *S*
2238 how, haik, upon hicht) hop, hone, on height *S*
2241 thay couth the fur fforfair) they layde the forrow for fayre *S*

318 The micht of gold makis mony men sa blind,
 That settis on Avarice thair felicitie,
 That thay forget the cadgear cummis behind
 To stryke thame, of quhat stait sa ever thay be.
 Quhat is mair dirk than blind prosperitie?
 Quhairfoir I counsell mychtie men to haif mynd
 Of the Nekhering, Interpreit in this kynd.   2230

Finis.

The Taill of the Foxe, that begylit the Wolf, in the schadow of the Mone

319 In elderis dayis, as Esope can declair,
 Thair wes ane Husband, quhilk had ane pleuch to steir.
 His use wes ay in morning to ryse air;
 Sa happinnit him in streiking tyme off yeir
 Airlie in the morning to follow ffurth his feir,
 Unto the pleuch, bot his gadman and he;
 His stottis he straucht with 'Benedicite.'

320 The Caller cryit: 'how, haik, upon hicht;
 Hald draucht, my dowis;' syne broddit thame ffull sair.
 The Oxin wes unusit, young and licht,   2240
 And ffor fersnes thay couth the fur fforfair.
 The Husband than woxe angrie as ane hair,
 Syne cryit, and caist his Patill and grit stanis:
 'The Wolff' (quod he) 'mot have yow all at anis.'

321 Bot yit the Wolff wes neirar nor he wend,
 For in ane busk he lay, and Lowrence baith,
 In ane Rouch Rone, wes at the furris end,
 And hard the hecht; than Lowrence leuch full raith:
 'To tak yone bud' (quod he) 'it wer na skaith.'
 'Weill' (quod the Wolff), 'I hecht the be my hand;   2250
 Yone Carllis word, as he wer King, sall stand.'

322 The Oxin waxit mair reullie at the last;
Syne efter thay lousit, ffra that it worthit weill lait;
The Husband hamewart with his cattell past.
Than sone the Wolff come hirpilland in his gait,
Befoir the Oxin, and schupe to mak debait.
The Husband saw him, and worthit sumdeill agast,
And bakwart with his beistis wald haif past.

323 The Wolff said, 'quhether dryvis thou this Pray?
I chalenge it, ffor nane off thame ar thyne.'   2260
The man thairoff wes in ane felloun fray,
And soberlie to the Wolff answerit syne:
'Schir, be my Saull, thir oxin ar all myne;
Thairfoir I studdie quhy ye suld stop me,
Sen that I faltit never to you, trewlie.'

324 The Wolff said, 'Carle, gaif thou not me this drift
Airlie, quhen thou wes eirrand on yone bank?
And is thair oucht (sayis thou) frear than gift?
This tarying wyll tyne the all thy thank;
Far better is frelie ffor to giff ane plank   2270
Nor be compellit on force to giff ane mart.
Fy on the fredome that cummis not with hart!'

325 'Schir' (quod the husband), 'ane man may say in greif,
And syne ganesay, fra he avise and se:
I hecht to steill, am I thairfoir ane theif?'
'God forbid, Schir, all hechtis suld haldin be!'
'Gaif I my hand or oblissing' (quod he),
'Or have ye witnes, or writ ffor to schaw?
Schir, reif me not, but go and seik the Law!'

326 'Carll' (quod the Wolff), 'ane Lord, and he be leill,   2280
That schrinkis for schame, or doutis to be repruvit,
His saw is ay als sickker as his Seill.
Fy on the Leid that is not leill and lufit!
Thy argument is fals, and eik contrufit,
For it is said in Proverb: "But lawte
All uther vertewis ar nocht worth ane fle."'

2252 waxit) eirit *C*   2271 mart) mark *C*

327 'Schir,' said the husband, 'remember of this thing:
　　Ane leill man is not tane at halff ane taill.
　　I may say, and ganesay, I am na King:
　　Quhair is your witnes that hard I hecht thame haill?'　2290
　　Than said the Wolff, 'thairfoir it sall nocht faill;
　　Lowrence' (quod he), 'cum hidder of that Schaw,
　　And say na thing bot as thow hard and saw.'

328 Lowrence come lourand, for he lufit never licht,
　　And sone appeirit befoir thame in that place:
　　The man leuch na thing, quhen he saw that sicht.
　　'Lowrence' (quod the Wolff), 'thow man declair this cace,
　　Quhairof we sall schaw the suith in schort space;
　　I callit on the leill witnes for to beir:
　　Quhat hard thow that this man hecht me lang eir?'　2300

329 'Schir' (said the Tod), 'I can not hastelie
　　Swa sone as now gif sentence finall;
　　Bot wald ye baith submit yow heir to me,
　　To stand at my decreit perpetuall,
　　To pleis baith I suld preif, gif it may fall.'
　　'Weill' (quod the Wolff), 'I am content for me:'
　　The man said, 'swa am I, how ever it be.'

330 Than schew thay furth thair allegeance but fabill,
　　And baith proponit thair pley to him compleit.
　　(Quod Lowrence): 'now I am ane Juge amycabill:　2310
　　Ye sall be sworne to stand at my decreit,
　　Quhether heirefter ye think it soure or sweit.'
　　The Wolff braid furth his fute, the man his hand,
　　And on the Toddis Taill sworne thay ar to stand.

331 Than tuke the Tod the man furth till ane syde,
　　And said him, 'friend, thow art in blunder brocht;
　　The Wolff will not forgif the ane Oxe hyde,
　　Yit wald my self fane help the, and I mocht;
　　Bot I am laith to hurt my conscience ocht.
　　Tyne nocht thy querrell in thy awin defence;　2320
　　This will not throw but grit coist and expence.

332 'Seis thow not Buddis beiris Bernis throw,
   And giftis garris crukit materis hald ffull evin?
   Sumtymis ane hen haldis ane man in ane Kow.
   All ar not halie that heifis thair handis to hevin.'
   'Schir' (said the man), 'ye sall have sex or sevin,
   Richt off the fattest hennis off all the floik:
   I compt not all the laif, leif me the Coik.'

333 'I am ane Juge' (quod Lowrence than), and leuch;
   'Thair is na Buddis suld beir me by the rycht;   2330
   I may tak hennis and Caponis weill aneuch,
   For God is gane to sleip; as ffor this nycht,
   Sic small thingis ar not sene in to his sicht;
   Thir hennis' (quod he) 'sall mak thy querrell sure,
   With emptie hand na man suld Halkis lure.'

334 Concordit thus, than Lowrence tuke his leiff,
   And to the Wolff he went in to ane ling;
   Syne prevelie he plukkit him be the sleiff:
   'Is this in ernist' (quod he) 'ye ask sic thing?
   Na, be my Saull, I trow it be in heithing.'   2340
   Than saith the Wolff, 'Lowrence, quhy sayis thow sa?
   Thow hard the hecht thy selff that he couth ma.'

335 'The hecht' (quod he) 'yone man maid at the pleuch,
   Is that the cause quhy ye the cattell craif?'
   Halff in to heithing (said Lowrence than), and leuch;
   'Schir, be the Rude, unroikit now ye raif;
   The Devill ane stirk taill thairfoir sall ye haif;
   Wald I tak it upon my conscience
   To do sa pure ane man as yone offence?

336 'Yit haif I communit with the Carll' (quod he);   2350
   'We ar concordit upon this cunnand:
   Quyte off all clamis, swa ye will mak him fre,
   Ye sall ane Cabok have in to your hand,
   That sic ane sall not be in all this land;
   For it is Somer Cheis, baith fresche and ffair;
   He sayis it weyis ane stane, and sumdeill mair.'

  2322 Seest thou not brybes beares all the sway now? *S*
  2324 hen) nedill *C* 2336 Concordit thus) Concordant thus *Ht;* Concord in *C*

337 'Is that thy counsell' (quod the Wolff), 'I do,
    That yone Carll ffor ane Cabok suld be fre?'
    'Ye, be my Saull, and I wer sworne yow to,
    Ye suld nane uther counsell have for me;   2360
    For gang ye to the maist extremitie,
    It will not wyn yow worth ane widderit neip;
    Schir, trow ye not, I have ane Saull to keip?'

338 'Weill' (quod the Wolff), 'it is aganis my will
    That yone Carll for ane Cabok suld ga quyte.'
    'Schir' (quod the Tod), 'ye tak it in nane evill,
    For, be my Saull, your self had all the wyte.'
    'Than' (said the Wolf) 'I bid na mair to flyte,
    Bot I wald se yone Cabok off sic pryis.'
    'Schir' (said the Tod), 'he tauld me quhar it lyis.'   2370

339 Than hand in hand thay held unto ane hill;
    The Husband till his hors hes tane the way,
    For he wes fane; he schaipit ffrom thair ill,
    And on his feit woke the dure quhill day.
    Now will we turne vnto the uther tway.
    Throw woddis waist thir Freikis on fute can fair,
    Fra busk to busk, quhill neir midnycht and mair.

340 Lowrence wes ever remembring upon wrinkis
    And subtelteis the Wolff for to begyle;
    That he had hecht ane Caboik, he forthinkis,   2380
    Yit at the last he findis furth ane wyle,
    Than at him selff softlie couth he smyle.
    The Wolff sayis, 'Lowrence, thow playis bellie blind;
    We seik all nycht, bot na thing can we find.'

341 'Schir' (said the Tod), 'we ar at it almaist;
    Soft yow ane lytill, and ye sall se it sone.'
    Than to ane Manure place thay hyit in haist:
    The nicht wes lycht, and pennyfull the Mone.
    Than till ane draw well thir Senyeours past but hone,
    Quhair that twa bukkettis severall suithlie hang;   2390
    As ane come up, ane uther doun wald gang.

2351 cunnand) cunnad *Ht*; covenant *S*
2372 hors) house *SHt*   2387 Manure place) mannour place *S*

342   The schadow of the Mone schone in the well.
      'Schir' (said Lowrence), 'anis ye sall find me leill;
      Now se ye not the Caboik weill your sell,
      Quhyte as ane Neip, and round als as ane seill?
      He hang it yonder, that na man suld it steill:
      Schir, traist ye weill, yone Caboik ye se hing
      Micht be ane present to ony Lord or King.'

343   'Na' (quod the Wolff) 'mycht I yone Caboik haif
      On the dry land, as I it yonder se,   2400
      I wald quitclame the Carll of all the laif;
      His dart Oxin I compt thame not ane fle;
      Yone wer mair meit for sic ane man as me.
      Lowrence' (quod he), 'leip in the bukket sone,
      And I sall hald the ane, quhill thow have done.'

344   Lowrence gird doun baith sone and subtellie;
      The uther baid abufe, and held the flaill.
      'It is sa mekill' (quod Lowrence) 'it maisteris me,
      On all my tais it hes not left ane naill;
      Ye man mak help upwart, and it haill   2410
      Leip in the uther bukket haistelie,
      And cum sone doun, and make me sum supple.'

345   Than lychtlie in the bukket lap the loun;
      His wecht but weir the uther end gart ryis;
      The Tod come hailland up, the Wolf yeid doun;
      Than angerlie the Wolff upon him cryis:
      'I cummand thus dounwart, quhy thow upwart hyis?'
      'Schir' (quod the Foxe), 'thus fairis it off Fortoun:
      As ane cummis up, scho quheillis ane uther doun!'

2395 round als as ane seill) and als round as ane schell *C*
2402 dart Oxin) durty *S*
2405 quhill thow have done) while thou go downe *S*
2418 thus fairis it off Fortoun) this fair is of fortoun *H* ; thus fares it oft
      in Towne *S*

346 Than to the ground sone yeid the Wolff in haist;   2420
    The Tod lap on land, als blyith as ony bell,
    And left the Wolff in watter to the waist.
    Quha haillit him out, I wait not, off the well.
    Heir endis the Text; thair is na mair to tell.
    Yit men may find ane gude moralitie
    In this sentence, thocht it ane Fabill be.

MORALITAS

347 This Wolff I likkin to ane wickit man,
    Quhilk dois the pure oppres in everie place,
    And pykis at thame all querrellis that he can,
    Be Rigour, reif, and uther wickitnes.   2430
    The Foxe the Feind I call in to this cais,
    Actand ilk man to ryn unrychteous rinkis,
    Thinkand thairthrow to lok him in his linkis.

348 The Husband may be callit ane godlie man,
    With quhome the Feynd falt findes (as Clerkis reids),
    Besie to tempt him with all wayis that he can.
    The hennis ar warkis that fra ferme faith proceidis:
    Quhair sic sproutis spreidis, the evill spreit thair not speids,
    Bot wendis vnto the wickit man agane;
    That he hes tint his travell is full unfane.   2440

349 The wodds waist, quhairin wes the Wolff wyld,
    Ar wickit riches, quhilk all men gaipis to get;
    Quha traistis in sic Trusterie ar oft begyld;
    For Mammon may be callit the Devillis Net,
    Quhilk Sathanas for all sinfull hes set.
    With proud plesour quha settis his traist thairin,
    But speciall grace, lychtlie can not outwin.

2432 Actand) Egging *S*: rinkis) raynes *S*
2433 linkis) chaynes *S*
2440 unfane) fayne *S*
2447 can not outwin) can out wine *S*

350 The Cabok may be callit Covetyce,
    Quhilk blomis braid in mony mannis Ee;
    Wa worth the well of that wickit vyce!   2450
    For it is all bot fraud and fantasie,
    Dryvand ilk man to leip in the buttrie
    That dounwart drawis unto the pane of hell.—
    Christ keip all Christianis from * that wickit well!

              * Actually 'ftom.'

            Finis.

The Taill of the Wolf and the Wedder.

351 Qwhylum thair wes (as Esope can Report)
    Ane scheipheird dwelland be ane Forrest neir,
    Quhilk had ane Hound that did him grit comfort;
    Full war he wes to walk his Fauld but weir,
    That nouther Wolff nor Wildcat durst appeir,
    Nor Foxe on feild, nor yit no uther beist,   2460
    Bot he thame slew, or chaissit at the leist.

352 Sa happinnit it (as euerilk beist man de),
    This Hound off suddand seiknes to be deid;
    Bot than (God wait) the keipar off the fe
    For verray wo woxe wanner nor the weid:
    'Allace' (quod he), 'now se I na remeid
    To saif the selie beistis that I keip,
    For wit(h) the Wolff weryit beis all my scheip.'

353 It wald have maid ane mannis hart sair to se
    The selie scheiphirdis lamentatioun: 2470
    'Now is my Darling deid, allace' (quod he);
    'For now to beg my breid I may be boun,
    With pyikstaff and with scrip to fair off toun;
    For all the beistis befoir bandonit bene
    Will schute upon my beistis with Ire and tene.'

2462 de) sleepe *S*   2464 fe) sheepe *S*
2472 be) me *H*   2473 to fair off toun) fro towne to towne *S*
2476 wrechitlie wan) stoutly stood *S*; wightlie wan *Ht*

354 With that ane Wedder wrechitlie wan on fute:
    'Maister' (quod he), 'mak merie and be blyith;
    To brek your hart ffor baill it is na bute;
    For ane deid Dogge ye na cair on yow kyith.
    Ga ffeche him hither, and fla his skyn off swyth;   2480
    Syne sew it on me; and luke that it be meit,
    Baith heid, and crag, bodie, taill, and feit.

355 'Than will the Wolff trow that I am he;
    For I sall follow him fast quhar ever he fair.
    All haill, the cure I tak it upon me,
    Your scheip to keip at midday, lait and air.
    And he persew, be God, I sall not spair
    To follow him as fast as did your Doig,
    Swa that, I warrand, ye sall not want ane hoig.'

356 'Than,' said the scheipheird, 'this come of ane gude wit;   2490
    Thy counsall is baith sicker, leill, and trew;
    Quha sayis ane scheip is daft, thay lieit of it.'
    With that in hy the Doggis skyn off he flew,
    And on the scheip rycht softlie couth it sew.
    Than worth the Wedder wantoun off his weid:
    'Now off the Wolff' (quod he) 'I have na dreid.'

357 In all thingis he counterfait the Dog;
    For all the nycht he stude, and tuke na sleip,
    Swa that weill lang thair wantit not ane Hog.
    Swa war he wes and walkryfe thame to keip,   2500
    That Lowrence durst not luke upon ane scheip;
    For and he did, he followit him sa fast,
    That off his lyfe he maid him all agast.

358 Was nowther Wolff, Wildcat, nor yit Tod
    Durst cum within thay boundis all about,
    Bot he wald chase thame baith throw rouch and snod.
    Thay bailfull beistis had of thair lyvis sic dout,
    For he wes mekill and semit to be stout,
    That everilk beist thay dred him as the deid,
    Within that woid, that nane durst hald thair heid.   2510

359 Yit happinnit thair ane hungrie Wolff to slyde
     Out throw his scheip, quhair thay lay on ane le;
     'I sall have ane' (quod he), 'quhat ever betyde,
     Thocht I be werryit, for hunger or I de;'
     With that ane Lamb in till his cluke hint he.
     The laif start up, ffor thay wer all agast;
     Bot (God wait) gif the Wedder followit fast.

360 Went never Hound mair haistelie fra the hand,
     Quhen he wes rynnand maist raklie at the Ra,
     Nor went this Wedder baith over Mois and strand,   2520
     And stoppit nouther at bank, busk, nor bra;
     Bot followit ay sa ferslie on his fa,
     With sic ane drift, quhill dust and dirt over draif him,
     And maid ane Vow to God that he suld have him.

361 With that the Wolff let out his Taill on lenth,
     For he wes hungrie, and it drew neir the ene,
     And schupe him for to ryn with all his strenth,
     Fra he the Wedder sa neir cummand had sene.
     He dred his lyfe, and he overtane had bene;
     Thairfoir he spairit nowther busk nor boig,   2530
     For weill he kennit the kenenes off the Doig.

362 To mak him lycht, he kest the Lamb him fra,
     Syne lap ouer leis, and draif throw dub and myre.
     'Na' (quod the Wedder), 'in Faith we part not swa:
     It is not the Lamb, bot the, that I desyre;
     I sall cum neir, ffor now I se the tyre.'
     The Wolff ran still quhill ane strand stude behind him,
     Bot ay the neirar the Wedder he couth bind him.

2519 raklie at the Ra) rashly for the roe *S*
2531 kenenes) cumming *C*; (amended to "cunning," *GGS*); kindnesse *S*
2537 still quhill ane strand) till ane rekill *C*; still and durst not looke *S*
2538 he couth bind) to couth wyn *C*

363 Sone efter that he followit him sa neir,
    Quhill that the Wolff ffor fleidnes fylit the feild ;   2540
    Syne left the gait, and ran throw busk and breir,
    And schupe him ffra the schawis ffor to scheild.
    He ran restles, for he wist off na beild ;
    The wedder followit him baith out and in,
    Quhill that ane breir busk raif rudelie off the skyn.

364 The Wolff wes wer, and blenkit him behind,
    And saw the wedder come thrawand throw the breir ;
    * Syne saw the Doggis skyn hingand on his lind.
    'Na' (quod he), 'is this ye that is sa neir?
    Richt now ane Hound, and now quhyte as ane   2550
        Freir :
    I fled over fer, and I had kennit the cais :
    To God I vow that ye sall rew this rais.

365 'Quhat wes the cause ye gaif me sic ane katche ? '
    With that in hy he hint him be the horne.
    ' For all your mowis ye met anis with your matche,
    Suppois ye leuch me all this yeir to scorne.
    For quhat enchessoun this Doggis skyn have ye borne ? '
    ' Maister' (quod he), ' bot to have playit with yow ;
    I yow requyre that ye nane uther trow.'

366 'Is this your bourding in ernist than ? ' (quod he),   2560
    ' For I am verray effeirit, and on flocht ;
    Cum bak agane and I sall let yow se.'
    Than quhar the gait wes grimmit he him brocht.
    ' Quhether call ye this fair play, or nocht?
    To set your Maister in sa fell effray,
    Quhill he ffor feiritnes hes fylit up the way.

2548 * Bass. has 'Tyne.'
2543 beild) weild *C* ; or els he must needes yeeld *S*
2553 katche) chace *C*

367 'Thryis (be my Saull) ye gart me schute behind;
     Upon my hoichis the senyeis may be sene;
     For feiritnes full oft I ffylit the wind.
     Now is this ye? na, bot ane Hound, I wene;   2570
     Me think your teith over schort to be sa kene.
     Blissit be the busk that reft yow your array,
     Ellis, fleand, bursin had I bene this day.'

368 'Schir' (quod the Wedder), 'suppois I ran in hy,
     My mynd wes never to do your persoun ill;
     Ane flear gettis ane follower commounly,
     In play or ernist, preif quha sa ever will.
     Sen I bot playit, be gracious me till,
     And I sall gar my freindis blis your banis,
     Ane full gude servand will crab his Maister anis.' 2580

369 'I have bene oftymis set in grit effray,
     Bot (be the Rude) sa rad yit wes I never,
     As thow hes maid me with thy prettie play.
     I schot behind, quhen thow overtuke me ever,
     Bot sickkerlie now sall we not dissever.'
     Than be crag bane smertlie he him tuke,
     Or ever he ceissit, and it in schunder schuke.

                        MORALITAS

370 Esope, that poete, first Father of this Fabill,
     Wrait this Parabole, quhilk is convenient.
     Because the sentence wes fructuous and agreabill, 2590
     In Moralitie exemplative prudent;
     Quhais problemes bene verray excellent;
     Throw similitude of figuris, to this day,
     Gevis doctrine to the Redaris of it ay.

2567 schute) looke S   2568 senyeis) sinewes S
2580 crab) helpe S   2604 in) in to H

371 Heir may thow se that riches of array
Will cause pure men presumpteous for to be;
Thay think thay hald of nane, be thay als gay,
Bot counterfute ane Lord in all degre.
Out of thair cais in pryde thay clym sa hie,
That thay forbeir thair better in na steid, 2600
Quhill sum man tit thair heillis over thair heid.

372 Richt swa in service uther sum exceidis,
And thay haif withgang, welth, and cherising,
That thay will lychtlie Lordis in thair deidis,
And lukis not to thair blude, nor thair offspring :
Bot yit nane wait how lang that reull will ring;
Bot he was wyse, that bad his Sone considder :
Bewar in welth, for Hall benkis ar rycht slidder.

373 Thairfoir I counsell men of everilk stait
To knaw thame self, and quhome thay suld forbeir, 2610
And fall not with thair better in debait ;
Suppois thay be als galland in thair geir,
It settis na servand for to uphald weir,
Nor clym so hie, quhill he fall of the ledder ;
Bot think upon the Wolf, and on the wedder !

Finis.

The Taill of the Wolf and the Lamb

374 Ane cruell Wolff, richt ravenous and fell,
Upon ane tyme past to ane Reveir,
Descending from ane Rotche unto ane well,
To slaik his thrist, drank of the watter cleir.
Swa upon cace ane selie Lamb come neir, 2620
Bot of his fa, the Wolff, na thing he wist,
And in the streme laipit to cule his thrist.

375 Thus drank thay baith, bot not of ane Intent;
The Wolfis thocht wes all on wickitnes;
The selie Lamb wes meik and Innocent:
Upon the Rever, in ane uther place,
Beneth the Wolff, he drank ane lytill space,
Quhill he thocht gude, belevand thair nane ill;
The Wolff him saw, and Rampand come him till.

376 With girnand teith and awfull angrie luke,   2630
Said to the Lamb: 'thow Cative wretchit thing,
How durst thow be sa bald to fyle and bruke,
Quhar I suld drink, with thy foull slavering?
It wer Almous the ffor to draw and hing,
That suld presume, with thy foull lippis wyle,
To glar my drink, and this fair watter fyle.'

377 The selie Lamb, quaikand for verray dreid,
On kneis fell, and said: 'Schir, with your leif,
Suppois I dar not say thairoff ye leid;
Bot, be my Saull, I wait ye can nocht preif   2640
That I did ony thing that suld yow grief;
Ye wait alswa that your accusatioun
Failyeis ffra treuth, and contrair is to ressoun.

378 'Thocht I can nocht, Nature will me defend,
And off the deid perfyte experience;
All hevie thing man off the selff discend;
Bot giff sum thing on force mak resistence,
Than may the streme on na way mak ascence,
Nor ryn bakwart: I drank beneth yow far;
Ergo, ffor me your Bruke wes never the war.   2650

2630 awfull angrie) angry austre *B*
2632 and bruke) the bruke *HtS*; this bruke *B*
2635 thy foull) stinkand *B*   2636 fyle) spill *B*
2646 off the selff) of the force *H*   2648 ascence) offens *B*

379 'Alswa my lippis, sen that I wes ane Lam,
    Tuitchit na thing that wes contagious;
    Bot sowkit milk ffrom Pappis off my dam,
    Richt Naturall, sweit, and als delitious.'
    'Weill' (quod the Wolff), 'thy language Rigorous
    Cummis the off kynd swa thy Father before;
    Held me at bait, baith with boist and schore.

380 'He wraithit me, and than I culd him warne
    Within ane yeir, and I brukit my heid,
    I suld be wrokkin on him, or on his barne,   2660
    For his exorbetant and frawart pleid;
    Thow sall doutles ffor his deidis be deid.'
    'Schir, it is wrang, that ffor the ffatheris gilt,
    The saikles sone suld punist be or spilt.

381 'Haiff ye not hard quhat halie Scripture sayis,
    Endytit with the mouth of God Almycht?
    Off his awin deidis ilk man sall beir the prais,
    As pane ffor sin, reward ffor werkis rycht;
    For my trespas quhy suld my sone have plycht?
    Quha did the mis lat him sustene the pane.'   2670
    'Yaa' (quod the Wolff), 'yit pleyis thow agane?

382 'I let the wit, quhen that the ffather offendis,
    I will refuse nane off his Successioun;
    And off his barnis I may weill tak amendis,
    Unto the twentie degre descending doun.
    Thy ffather thocht to mak ane strang poysoun,'
    And with his mouth into my watter did spew.'
    'Schir' (quod the Lamb), 'thay twa ar nouther trew.

2655 Rigorous) outragius *B*   2658 wraithit) wexit *B*
2666 mouth) word *H*   2667 prais) prayis *H*; paiss *B*
2668 pane) pyne *B*   2673 refuse) chereis *C*
2675 twentie) nynt *B*   2676 poysoun) presoun *C*

383 'The Law sayis, and ye will vnderstand,
    Thair suld na man, ffor wrang, nor violence   2680
    His adversar punis at his awin hand,
    Without proces off Law and evidence;
    Quhilk suld have leif to mak lawfull defence,
    And thairupon Summond Peremptourly,
    For to propone, contrairie, or reply.

384 'Set me ane lauchfull Court, I sall compeir
    Befoir the Lyoun, Lord and leill Justice,
    And, be my hand, I oblis me rycht heir,
    That I sall byde ane unsuspect Assyis.
    This is the Law, this is the Instant gyis;   2690
    Ye suld pretend thairfoir; ane Summondis mak
    Aganis that day, to gif ressoun and tak.'

385 'Na' (quod the Wolff), 'thow wald Intruse ressoun,
    Quhair wrang and reif suld dwell in propertie.
    That is ane poynt, and part of fals tressoun,
    For to gar reuth remane with crueltie.
    Be his woundis, fals tratour, thow sall de,
    For thy trespas, and for thy Fatheris als.'
    With that anone he hint him be the hals.

386 The selie Lamb culd do na thing bot bleit;   2700
    Sone wes he deid: the Wolff wald do na grace,
    Syne drank his blude, and off his flesche can eit,
    Quhill he wes full, and went his way on pace.
    Of his murther quhat sall we say, allace?
    Wes not this reuth, wes not this grit pietie,
    To gar this selie Lamb but gilt thus de?

        2682 and evidence) in audiens *B*
        2684 Summond) Summond is *C*
        2685 contrairie, or reply) and contra and reply *B*
        2690 Instant gyis) Instant use *C*; justest wyss *B*
        2691 pretend) proceid *B*
        2695 and part of fals) of oppen fals *B*
        2697 Be his woundis) Be goddis wondis *B*
        2701 deid) hedit *B*   2703 on pace) apace *HB*
        2706 To gar) to heir *B*

MORALITAS

387 The pure pepill this Lamb may signifie,
As Maill men, Merchandis, and all lauboureris,
Of quhome the lyfe is half ane Purgatorie,
To wyn with lautie leving as efferis.   2710
The Wolf betakinnis fals extortioneris
And oppressouris of pure men, as we se,
Be violence, or craft in facultie.

388 Thre kynd of Wolfis in this warld now Rings :
The first ar fals perverteris of the Lawis,
Quhilk under Poete termis falset mingis,
Lettand that all wer Gospell that he schawis ;
Bot for ane bud the pure man he overthrawis,
Smoirand the richt, garrand the wrang proceid :
Of sic Wolfis hellis fyre sall be thair meid.   2720

389 O man of Law ! let be thy subteltie,
With nice gimpis, and fraudis Intricait,
And think that God in his Divinitie
The wrang, the richt, of all thy werkis wait :
For prayer, price, for hie nor law estait,
Of fals querrellis se thow mak na defence ;
Hald with the richt, hurt not thy conscience.

390 Ane uther kynd of Wolfis Ravenous,
Ar mychtie men, haifand full grit plentie,
Quhilkis ar sa gredie and sa covetous,   2730
Thay will not thoill the pure in pece to be ;
Suppois he and his houshald baith suld de
For falt of fude, thairof thay gif na rak,
Bot over his heid his mailling will thay tak.

2708 Maill) evill *S*   2713 in facultie) or usurie *S*
2716 Poete) poleit *B* ; suttell *S*   2718 pure man) trew men *B*
2722 gimpis) quips *S*   2734 his mailling) his house *S*

391 O man! but mercie, quhat is in thy thocht,
    War than ane Wolf, and thow culd understand?
    Thow hes aneuch; the pure husband richt nocht
    Bot croip and caff upon ane clout of land.
    For Goddis aw, how durst thow tak on hand,
    And thow in Barn and Byre sa bene, and big,   2740
    To put him fra his tak and gar him thig?

392 The thrid Wolf ar men of heritage,
    As Lordis that hes land be Goddis lane,
    And settis to the Mailleris ane Village,
    And for ane tyme Gressome payit and tane;
    Syne vexis him, or half his terme be gane,
    With pykit querrellis for to mak him fane
    To flit, or pay his Gressome new agane.

393 His Hors, his Meir, he man len to the Laird,
    To drug and draw in Court or in Cariage;   2750
    His servand or his self may not be spaird
    To swing and sweit, withoutin Meit or wage.
    Thus how he standis in labour and bondage,
    That scantlie may he purches by his maill,
    To leve upon dry breid and watter caill.

394 Hes thow not reuth to gar thy tennentis sweit
    In to thy laubour with faynt and hungrie wame,
    And syne hes lytill gude to drink or eit,
    With his menye at evin quhen he cummis hame?
    Thow suld dreid for rychteous Goddis blame;   2760
    For it cryis ane vengeance unto the hevinnis hie,
    To gar ane pure man wirk but Meit or fe.

2738 croip and caff) cote and cruse _B_
2745 For prayer, pryce, and the gersum tane; _B_
2750 Court) Cairt _B_   2760 suld dreid) suld be rad _B_
2764 Be nocht ane Wolf) Thow art ane Wolf _C_

395 O thow grit Lord, that riches hes and rent,
    Be nocht ane Wolf, thus to devoir the pure;
    Think that na thing cruell nor violent
    May in this warld perpetuallie Indure:
    This sall thow trow and sikkerlie assure,
    For till oppres thow sall haif als greit pane
    As thow the pure had with thy awin hand slane.

396 God keip the Lamb, quhilk is the Innocent,   2770
    From Wolfis byit and fell exortioneris;
    God grant that wrangous men of fals Intent
    Be manifestit, and punischit as effeiris.
    And God, as thow all rychteous prayer heiris,
    Mot saif our King, and gif him hart and hand
    All sic Wolfis to banes out of the land.

Finis.

The Taill of the Paddok & the Mous

397 Upon ane tyme (as Esope culd Report)
    Ane lytill Mous come till ane Rever syde;
    Scho micht not waid, hir schankis were sa schort,
    Scho culd not swym, scho had na hors to ryde: 2780
    Of verray force behovit hir to byde,
    And to and ffra besyde that Revir deip
    Scho ran, cryand with mony pietuous peip.

2767 This is a sentens suth I ʒow assure *B*
2769 had with thy awin hand) anis with thy hand had *B*
2771 and fell) and men *C*; I mene *B*
2775 our King) our Queene *S*

398 'Help over, help over,' this silie Mous can cry,
    'For Goddis lufe, sum bodie over the brym.'
    With that ane Paddok, in the watter by,
    Put up hir heid, and on the bank can clym,
    Quhilk be nature culd douk, and gaylie swym;
    With voce full rauk,* scho said on this maneir:
    'Gude morne (schir Mous), quhat is your erand   2790
        heir?'

399 'Seis thow,' quod scho, 'off corne yone Jolie flat,
    Off ryip Aitis, off Barlie, Peis, and Quheit?
    I am hungrie, and fane wald be thair at,
    Bot I am stoppit be this watter greit;
    And on this syde I get na thing till eit
    Bot hard Nuttis, quhilkis with my teith I bore.
    Wer I beyond, my feist wer fer the more.

400 'I have no Boit; heir is no Maryner;
    And thocht thair war, I have no fraucht to pay.'
    Quod scho, 'sister, lat be thy hevie cheir;   2800
    Do my counsall, and I sall find the way
    Without Hors, Brig, Boit, or yit Galay,
    To bring the over saiflie,—be not afeird!—
    And not wetand the campis off thy beird.'

401 'I haif grit wounder,' quod the lytill Mous,
    'How can thow fleit without fedder or fyn.
    This Rever is sa deip and dangerous,
    Me think that thow suld drounit be thairin.
    Tell me, thairfoir, quhat facultie or gin
    Thow hes to bring the over this watter wan?'   2810
    That to declair the Paddok thus began.

* Orig. has turned letter : 'rank.'

2790 schir) deme *B*
2792 off Barlie, Peis, and Quheit?) of beir, of peiss, and quheit? *B*
2794 greit) deip *C*
2798 Maryner) Marineris *C.* (Seven lines are here omitted in *C*, and a
    composite stanza substituted, consisting of the first line as given,
    and lines 2 to 7 of the fifth stanza of *H* or *Bass.*
2804 campis) compasse *S*   2808 drounit be) drowin to wed *B*

402 'With my twa feit' (quod scho), 'lukkin and braid,
In steid off Airis, I row the streme full styll;
And thocht the brym be perrillous to waid,
Baith to and ffra I row at my awin will.
I may not droun, ffor quhy my oppin Gill
Devoidis ay the watter I resaiff:
Thairfoir to droun forsuith na dreid I haif.'

403 The Mous beheld unto hir fronsit face,
Hir runkillit cheikis, and hir lippis syde,   2820
Hir hingand browis, and hir voce sa hace,
Hir loggerand leggis, and hir harsky hyde.
Scho ran abak, and on the Paddok cryde:
'Giff I can ony skill of Phisnomy,
Thow hes sumpart off falset and Invy.

404 'For Clerkis sayis, the Inclinatioun
Of mannis thocht proceidis commounly
Efter the Corporall complexioun
To gude or evill, as Nature will apply:
Ane thrawart will, ane thrawin Phisnomy.   2830
The auld Proverb is witnes off this 𝔏orum—
Distortum vultum sequitur distortio morum.'

405 'Na' (quod the Taid), 'that Proverb is not trew;
For fair thingis oftymis ar fundin faikin.
The Blaberyis, thocht thay be sad off hew,
Ar gadderit up quhen Primeros is forsakin.
The face may faill to be the hartis takin.
Thairfoir I find this Scripture in all place:
Thow suld not Juge ane man efter his face.

2810 wan?) Than C   2811 That) Thus C: thus) sone C; this H
2813 Airis) Air C   2815 row) swyme C   2820 cheikis) beik B
2825 off falset and Invy) of frawd and als invy B; of false villany S
2827 proceidis) persavis B   2830 thrawart) thrawin H; frawart B
2834 fundin faikin) fowll fakin B; found infakin S
2835 sad) blak B
2838 this Scripture in all place) in scriptour in a place B; this written
in eche place S

G

406 'Thocht I unhailsum be to luke upon,   2840
      I have na cause quhy I suld lakkit be;
      Wer I als fair as Jolie Absolon,
      I am no causer off that grit beutie.
      This difference in forme and qualitie
      Almychtie God hes causit dame Nature
      To prent and set in everilk creature.

407 'Off sum the face may be full flurischand,
      Off silkin toung and cheir rycht amorous,
      With mynd Inconstant, fals, and wariand,
      Full off desait and menis Cautelous.'   2850
      'Let be thy preiching' (quod the hungrie Mous),
      'And be quhat craft thow gar me understand
      That thow wald gyde me to yone yonder land?'

408 'Thow wait' (quod scho), 'ane bodie that hes neid
      To help thame self suld mony wayis cast;
      Thairfoir ga tak ane doubill twynit threid,
      And bind thy leg to myne with knottis fast.
      I sall the leir to swym—be not agast !—
      Als weill as I.' 'As thow?' (than quod the Mous),
      'To preif that play it war richt perrillous.   2860

409 'Suld I be bund and fast quhar I am fre,
      In hoip off help, na than I schrew us baith,
      For I mycht lois baith lyfe and libertie.
      Gif it wer swa, quha suld amend the skaith?
      Bot gif thow sweir to me the murthour aith,
      But fraud, or gyle, to bring me over this flude,
      But hurt or harme.' 'In faith' (quod scho), 'I dude.'

2840 unhailsum) unlusty *B*; irksom *S*
2841 na cause) no wyt *B*
2859 Is that thi counsale, quod the silly mouss *B*
2862 than I schrew) nay than eschrew us *B*
2865 the murthour aith) the mother aith *Ht*
2867 I dude) good *S*
2873 carpand) trappold *CHt*; crabit *B*: Pad) Taid *CB*

410   Scho goikit up, and to the hevin can cry:
      'O Juppiter, off Nature God and King,
      I mak ane aith trewlie to the, that I   2870
      This lytill Mous sall over this watter bring.'
      This aith wes maid.   The Mous, but persaving
      The fals Ingyne of this foull carpand Pad,
      Tuke threid and band hir leg, as scho hir bad.

411   Then fute for fute thay lap baith in the brym;
      Bot in thair myndis thay wer rycht different:
      The Mous thocht off na thing bot ffor to swym,
      The Paddok ffor to droun set hir Intent.
      Quhen thay in midwart off the streme wer went,
      With all hir force the Paddok preissit doun,   2880
      And thocht the Mous without mercie to droun.

412   Persavand this, the Mous on hir can cry:
      'Tratour to God, and manesworne unto me,
      Thow swore the murthour aith richt now, that I
      But hurt or harme suld ferryit be and fre;'
      And quhen scho saw thair wes bot do or de,
      With all hir mycht scho forsit hir to swym,
      And preissit upon the Taiddis bak to clym.

413   The dreid of deith hir strenthis gart Incres,
      And forcit hir defend with mycht and mane.   2890
      The Mous upwart, the Paddok doun can pres;
      Quhyle to, quhyle ffra, quhyle doukit up agane.
      The selie Mous, plungit in to grit pane,
      Gan fecht als lang als breith wes in hir breist,
      Till at the last scho cryit ffor ane Preist.

2877 off na thing bot ffor to swym) na thing bot to fleit and swyme *B*
2878 to droun) to slay *B*
2880 preissit) dowkit *B*
2884 richt now that I) saifly that I *B*
2887 With all hir mycht scho) Scho bowtit up and *B*
2890 forcit) fandit *B* : with mycht and mane) with mony mane *B*
2892 quhyle doukit up agane) quhile dowk, quhile up agane *B*
2894 Gan fecht) can fecht *B*

414 Fechtand thusgait, the Gled sat on ane twist,
    And to this wretchit battell tuke gude heid;
    And with ane wisk, or ony off thame wist,
    He claucht his cluke betuix thame in the threid;
    Syne to the land he flew with thame gude speid,   2900
    Fane off that fang, pyipand with mony pew;
    Syne lowsit thame, and baith but pietie slew.

415 Syne bowellit thame, that Boucheour with his bill,
    And belliflaucht full fettillie thame flaid;
    Bot all thair flesche wald scant be half ane fill,
    And guttis als, unto that gredie gled.
    Off thair debait, thus quhen I hard outred,
    He tuke his flicht, and over the feildis flaw:
    Giff this be trew, speir ye at thame that saw.

MORALITAS

416 My Brother, gif thow will tak advertence   2910
    Be this Fabill, thow may persave and se,
    It passis far all kynd of Pestilence,
    Ane wickit mynd with wordis fair and sle.
    Be war thairfore, with quhome thow fallowis the;
    To the wer better beir the stane barrow,
    For all thy dayis to delf quhill thow may dre,
    Than to be machit with ane wickit marrow.

417 Ane fals Intent under ane fair pretence
    Hes causit mony Innocent for to de.
    Grit folie is to gif over sone credence   2920
    To all that speikis fairlie unto the.
    Ane silkin toung, ane hart of crueltie,
    Smytis more sore than ony schot of arrow.
    Brother, gif thow be wyse, I reid the fle,
    To matche the with ane thrawart, fenyeit marrow.

2896 Fechtand) Sichand *B* : the) a *B*
2898 ony) owthir *B*   2904 fettillie) ferellie *Ht*
2905 all) baith *B*   2909 trew) not true *S*
2914 fallowis the) fellowes bee *Ht*; followis the *B*
2918 pretence) presence *C*

418 I warne the als, it is grit nekligence
 To bind the fast quhair thow wes frank and fre ;
 Fra thow be bund, thow may mak na defence
 To saif thy lyfe, nor yit thy libertie.
 This simpill counsall, brother, tak of me,   2930
 And it to cun perqueir se thow not tarrow,
 Better but stryfe to leif allane in le
 Than to be matchit with ane wickit marrow.

419 This hald in mynde : rycht more I sall the tell
 Quhair by thir beistis may be figurate.
 The Paddok, usand in the flude to duell,
 Is mannis bodie, swymand air and lait
 In to this warld, with cairis Implicate,
 Now hie, now law, quhylis plungit up, quhylis doun,
 Ay in perrell, and reddie for to droun.   2940

420 Now dolorus, now blyth as bird on breir ;
 Now in fredome, now wrappit in distres ;
 Now haill and sound, now deid and brocht on beir ;
 Now pure as Job, now rowand in riches ;
 Now gouins gay, now brats laid in pres ;
 Now full as fitche, now hungrie as ane Hound ;
 Now on the quheill, now wrappit to the ground.

421 This lytill Mous, heir knit thus be the schyn,
 The Saull of man betakin may in deid ;
 Bundin, and fra the bodie may not wyn,   2950
 Quhill cruell deith cum brek of lyfe the threid ;
 The quhilk to droun suld ever stand in dreid,
 Of carnall lust be the Suggestioun
 Quhilk drawis ay the Saull, and druggis doun.

2935 Quhair by) Quhat by *B*
2941-2947 and 2955-2961 are omitted in *C*
2942 wrappit) wappit *H* ; wrapped *Hl* ; wardit *B*
2945 laid in pres) to imbrass *B* 2946 fitche) fysche *B* ; pease *S*
2947 wrappit) wappit *B* ; wrapped *Hl*
2950 wyn) twin *B*   2954 druggis) haldis *B*

422 The watter is the warld, ay welterand,
     With mony wall of tribulatioun :
     In quhilk the saull and body wer steirrand,
     Standand rycht different in thair opinioun :
     The Saull upwart, the body precis doun :
     The Saull rycht fane wald be brocht over I wis,   2960
     Out of this warld, into the hevinnis blis.

423 The Gled is Deith, that cummis suddandlie,
     As dois ane theif, and cuttis sone the battall.
     Be vigilant, thairfoir, and ay reddie,
     For mannis lyfe is brukill, and ay mortall :
     My freind, thairfoir, mak the ane strang Castell
     Of Faith in Christ ; for deith will the assay,
     Thow wait not quhen—evin, morrow or midday.

424 Adew, my freind ; and gif that ony speiris
     Of this Fabill, sa schortlie I conclude,   2970
     Say thow, I left the laif unto the Freiris,
     To mak exempill and ane similitude.
     Now Christ for us that deit on the Rude,
     Of saull and lyfe as thow art Salviour,
     Grant us till pas in till ane blissit hour.

                    Finis.

        2956 wall) wayiss *B* ; waves *S*
        2957 wer steirrand) ay waverand *B*
        2958 rycht different) distinyt and *B*
        2959 Saull) spreit *B*
        2960-2961 The natur of the saule wald our be borne
                   Out of this warld unto the hevinly trone *B*
        2963 and cuttis sone) and endis *B*
        2966 Castell) wall *S*
        2967 Of Faith in Christ) of gud deidis *B*
        2969 speiris) aske *S*
        2971 the Freiris) the learneds taske *S*

The Testament of Cresseid

HENRIE CHARTERIS, EDINBURGH

1593

The Testament of Cresseid

1 ANE doolie sessoun to ane cairfull dyte
  Suld correspond, and be equivalent.
  Richt sa it wes quhen I began to wryte
  This tragedie, the wedder richt fervent,
  Quhen Aries, in middis of the Lent,
  Schouris of haill can fra the north discend,
  That scantlie fra the cauld I micht defend.

2 Yit nevertheles within myne oratur
  I stude, quhen Titan had his bemis bricht
  Withdrawin doun, and sylit under cure   10
  And fair Venus, the bewtie of the nicht,
  Uprais, and set unto the west full richt
  Hir goldin face in oppositioun
  Of God Phebus direct discending doun.

3 Throw out the glas hir bemis brast sa fair
  That I micht se on everie syde me by
  The Northin wind had purifyit the Air
  And sched the mistie cloudis fra the sky,
  The froist freisit, the blastis bitterly
  Fra Pole Artick come quhisling loud and schill,   20
  And causit me remufe aganis my will.

4 For I traistit that Venus, luifis Quene,
  To quhome sum tyme I hecht obedience,
  My faidit hart of lufe scho wald mak grene,
  And therupon with humbill reverence,
  I thocht to pray hir hie Magnificence;
  Bot for greit cald as than I lattit was,
  And in my Chalmer to the fyre can pas.

      7 micht defend) my3t me defende *TSJK*
    15 fair) sore *A*
    20 quhisling) whiskyng *TSJK*

5 Thocht lufe be hait, yit in ane man of age
   It kendillis nocht sa sone as in youtheid,   30
   Of quhome the blude is flowing in ane rage,
   And in the auld the curage doif and deid,
   Of quhilk the fyre outward is best remeid ;
   To help be Phisike quhair that nature faillit
   I am expert, for baith I have assailit.

6 I mend the fyre and beikit me about,
   Than tuik ane drink my spreitis to comfort,
   And armit me weill fra the cauld thairout :
   To cut the winter nicht and mak it schort,
   I tuik ane Quair, and left all uther sport,   40
   Writtin be worthie Chaucer glorious,
   Of fair Creisseid, and worthie Troylus.

7 And thair I fand, efter that Diomeid
   Ressavit had that Lady bricht of hew,
   How Troilus neir out of wit abraid,
   And weipit soir with visage paill of hew ;
   For quhilk wanhope his teiris can renew
   Quhill Esperus rejoisit him agane,
   Thus quhyle in Joy he levit, quhyle in pane.

8 Of hir behest he had greit comforting,   50
   Traisting to Troy that scho suld mak retour,
   Quhilk he desyrit maist of eirdly thing
   Forquhy scho was his only Paramour ;
   Bot quhen he saw passit baith day and hour
   Of hir ganecome, than sorrow can oppres
   His wofull hart in cair and hevines.

---

32 doif) dul *TS/K*   34 be Phisike) the Physick *A*
36 mend) made *TS/K*   38 armit) warmed *SJ*
48 Esperus) esperance *A* (*see* note, p. 252)
51 Traisting to Troy) To Troy trusting *SJ*
55 than) in *TSJ*   63 fair) false *A*

9 Of his distres me neidis nocht reheirs,
  For worthie Chauceir in the samin buik
  In gudelie termis and in Joly veirs
  Compylit hes his cairis, quha will luik.   60
  To brek my sleip ane uther quair I tuik,
  In quhilk I fand the fatall destenie
  Of fair Cresseid, that endit wretchitlie.

10 Quha wait gif all that Chauceir wrait was trew?
   Nor I wait nocht gif this narratioun
   Be authoreist, or fenyeit of the new
   Be sum Poeit, throw his Inventioun,
   Maid to report the Lamentatioun
   And wofull end of this lustie Creisseid,
   And quhat distres scho thoillit, and quhat deid.   70

11 Quhen Diomeid had all his appetyte,
   And mair, fulfillit of this fair Ladie,
   Upon ane uther he set his haill delyte
   And send to hir ane Lybell of repudie,
   And hir excludit fra his companie.
   Than desolait scho walkit up and doun,
   And sum men sayis into the Court commoun.

12 O fair Creisseid, the flour and A per se
   Of Troy and Grece, how was thou fortunait!
   To change in filth all thy Feminitie,   80
   And be with fleschlie lust sa maculait,
   And go amang the Greikis air and lait
   Sa giglotlike, takand thy foull plesance!
   I have pietie thou suld fall sic mischance.

66 fenyeit) forged *TS/K*
70 And what distresse she was in or she deyde *TS/K*
74 Lybell of repudie) lybel repudy *TS/K*
77 into the Court commoun) in the Court as commune *TS/K*
86 brukkilnes) brutelnesse *TS/K*

13 Yit nevertheless quhat ever men deme or say
    In scornefull langage of thy brukkilnes,
    I sall excuse, als far furth as I may,
    Thy womanheid, thy wisdome and fairnes :
    The quhilk Fortoun hes put to sic distres
    As hir pleisit, and nathing throw the gilt   90
    Of the, throw wickit langage to be spilt.

14 This fair Lady, in this wyse destitute
    Of all comfort and consolatioun,
    Richt privelie, but fellowschip, on fute
    Disagysit passit far out of the toun
    Ane myle or twa, unto ane Mansioun
    Beildit full gay, quhair hir father Calchas
    Quhilk than amang the Greikis dwelland was.

15 Quhen he hir saw, the caus he can Inquyre
    Of hir cumming; scho said, siching full soir :   100
    'Fra Diomeid had gottin his desyre
    He wox werie, and wald of me no moir.'
    Quod Calchas, 'douchter, weip thou not thairfoir ;
    Peraventure all cummis for the best ;
    Welcum to me, thou art full deir ane Gest.'

16 This auld Calchas, efter the Law was tho,
    Wes keiper of the Tempill as ane Preist,
    In quhilk Venus and hir Sone Cupido
    War honourit, and his Chalmer was thame neist,
    To quhilk Cresseid with baill aneuch in breist   110
    Usit to pas, hir prayeris for to say.
    Quhill at the last, upon ane Solempne day,

94 Right prively, without felowship, or refute, *TSJK*
95 Disagysit) Disshevelde *TSJK*   97 Beildit) Bylded *TASJK*
109 was thame neist) was neist *A TSJK*
110 aneuch) enewed *TSJ*; renewed *K*

17 As custome was, the pepill far and neir
    Befoir the none, unto the Tempill went,
    With Sacrifice, devoit in thair maneir :
    Bot still Cresseid, hevie in hir Intent,
    Into the Kirk wald not hir self present,
    For giving of the pepill ony deming
    Of hir expuls fra Diomeid the King :

18 Bot past into ane secreit Orature   120
    Quhair scho micht weip hir wofull desteny,
    Behind hir bak scho cloisit fast the dure
    And on hir kneis bair fell doun in hy.
    Upon Venus and Cupide angerly
    Scho cryit out, and said on this same wyse,
    'Allace that ever I maid you Sacrifice.

19 'Ye gave me anis ane devine responsaill
    That I suld be the flour of luif in Troy,
    Now am I maid ane unworthie outwaill,
    And all in cair translatit is my Joy,   130
    Quha sall me gyde? quha sall me now convoy
    Sen I fra Diomeid and Nobill Troylus
    Am clene excludit, as abject odious?

20 'O fals Cupide, is nane to wyte bot thow,
    And thy Mother, of lufe the blind Goddes !
    Ye causit me alwayis understand and trow
    The seid of lufe was sawin in my face,
    And ay grew grene throw your supplie and grace.
    Bot now allace that seid with froist is slane,
    And I fra luifferis left and all forlane.'   140

130 all in cair) in all care *A*
134 is nane) none is *TSJK*
138 grew) grow *A*
139-140 slane, forlane) shorn, forlorn *A*

21 Quhen this was said, doun in ane extasie,
Ravischit in spreit, intill ane dreame scho fell,
And be apperance hard, quhair scho did ly,
Cupide the King ringand ane silver bell,
Quhilk men micht heir fra hevin unto hell;
At quhais sound befoir Cupide appeiris
The seven Planetis discending fra thair Spheiris,

22 Quhilk hes power of all thing generabill
To reull and steir be thair greit Influence,
Wedder and wind, and coursis variabill: 150
And first of all Saturne gave his sentence,
Quhilk gave to Cupide litill reverence,
Bot, as ane busteous Churle on his maneir,
Come crabitlie with auster luik and cheir.

23 His face [fronsit], his lyre was lyke the Leid,
His teith chatterit, and cheverit with the Chin,
His Ene drowpit, how sonkin in his heid,
Out of his Nois the Meldrop fast can rin,
With lippis bla and cheikis leine and thin;
The Iceschoklis that fra his hair doun hang   160
Was wonder greit, and as ane speir als lang.

24 Atouir his belt his lyart lokkis lay
Felterit unfair, ouirfret with Froistis hoir,
His garmound and his gyis full gay of gray,
His widderit weid fra him the wind out woir;
Ane busteous bow within his hand he boir,
Under his girdill ane flasche of felloun flanis,
Fedderit with Ice, and heidit with hailstanis.

144 ringand) tynkyng *T*; tinging *SJK*
149 steir) stir *A*   153 busteous) boistous *K*
155 fronsit) frounsed *TSJ*; frownced *K*: orig. reads 'frosnit.'
156 cheverit) shevered *T*; checkered *A*
164 gyis) gate *TSJ*; guise *A*; gite *K*

25 Than Juppiter, richt fair and amiabill,
   God of the Starnis in the Firmament,   170
   And Nureis to all thing generabill,
   Fra his Father Saturne far different,
   With burelie face, and browis bricht and brent,
   Upon his heid ane Garland, wonder gay,
   Of flouris fair, as it had bene in May.

26 His voice was cleir, as Cristall wer his Ene,
   As goldin wyre sa glitterand was his hair;
   His garmound and his gyis full [gay] of grene,
   With golden listis gilt on everie gair;
   Ane burelie brand about his midill bair;   180
   In his richt hand he had ane groundin speir,
   Of his Father the wraith fra us to weir.

27 Nixt efter him come Mars, the God of Ire,
   Of strife, debait, and all dissensioun,
   To chide and fecht, als feirs as ony fyre;
   In hard Harnes, hewmound and Habirgeoun,
   And on his hanche ane roustie fell Fachioun;
   And in his hand he had ane roustie sword;
   Wrything his face with mony angrie word,

28 Schaikand his sword, befoir Cupide he come   190
   With reid visage, and grislie glowrand Ene;
   And at his mouth ane bullar stude of fome
   Lyke to ane Bair quhetting his Tuskis kene,
   Richt Tui[t]lyeour lyke, but temperance in tene;
   Ane horne he blew, with mony bosteous brag,
   Quhilk all this warld with weir hes maid to wag.

167 flasche) fasshe *TSJ*; flush *A*   173 burelie) burly *TSJK*
178 gyis) gyte *TSJK*; guise *A* : [gay] supplied from *TK*
182 weir) bere *TSJK*   190 sword) brande *TSJK*
192 bullar) blubber *TSJK*
194 Tui[t]lyeour) tulsure *TSJ*; Souldiour- *A*; tulliure *K* (*see* note, p. 255)

29 Than fair Phebus, Lanterne & Lamp of licht
Of man and beist, baith frute and flourisching,
Tender Nureis, and banischer of nicht,
And of the warld causing, be his moving   200
And Influence, lyfe in all eirdlie thing,
Without comfort of quhome, of force to nocht
Must all ga die that in this warld is wrocht.

30 As King Royall he raid upon his Chair
The quhilk Phaeton gydit sum tyme upricht;
The brichtnes of his face quhen it was bair
Nane micht behald for peirsing of his sicht.
This goldin Cart with fyrie bemis bricht
Four yokkit steidis full different of hew,
But bait or tyring, throw the Spheiris drew.   210

31 The first was soyr, with Mane als reid as Rois,
Callit Eoye into the Orient;
The secund steid to Name hecht Ethios,
Quhitlie and paill, and sum deill ascendent;
The thrid Peros, richt hait and richt fervent;
The feird was blak, callit Philologie
Quhilk rollis Phebus doun into the sey.

32 Venus was thair present that goddes [gay],
Hir Sonnis querrell for to defend and mak
Hir awin complaint, cled in ane nyce array,   220
The ane half grene, the uther half Sabill black;
Quhyte hair as gold kemmit and sched abak;
Bot in hir face semit greit variance,
Quhyles perfyte treuth, and quhyles Inconstance

202 to) is *A*   203 But all must die *A*
205 upricht) unright *TSJK*
216 Philologie) (Phlegonie) Philogie *A* ; Phlegone *SJK*
218 [gay] supplied from *TK*   220 Hir) His *T*

33 Under smyling scho was dissimulait,
  Provocative, with blenkis Amorous,
  And suddanely changit and alterait,
  Angrie as ony Serpent vennemous
  Richt pungitive, with wordis odious.
  Thus variant scho was, quha list tak keip,   230
  With ane Eye lauch, and with the uther weip.

34 In taikning that all fleschelie Paramour
  Quhilk Venus hes in reull and governance,
  Is sum tyme sweit, sum tyme bitter and sour
  Richt unstabill, and full of variance,
  Mingit with cairfull Joy and fals plesance,
  Now hait, now cauld, now blyith, now full of wo,
  Now grene as leif, now widderit and ago.

35 With buik in hand than come Mercurius,
  Richt Eloquent, and full of Rethorie,   240
  With polite termis and delicious,
  With pen and Ink to report al reddie,
  Setting sangis and singand merilie:
  His Hude was reid, heklit atouir his Croun,
  Lyke to ane Poeit of the auld fassoun.

36 Boxis he bair with fine Electuairis,
  And sugerit Syropis for digestioun,
  Spycis belangand to the Pothecairis,
  With mony hailsum sweit Confectioun,
  Doctour in Phisick cled in ane Skarlot goun,   250
  And furrit weill, as sic ane aucht to be,
  Honest and gude, and not ane word culd le.

222 Quhyte hair as gold) With hair as gold *A* ; Bright heer *K*
230 variant) vertant *A*   236 fals) fair *A*
257 Haw) Hew *A*

II

37 Nixt efter him come Lady Cynthia,
   The last of all, and swiftest in hir Spheir,
   Of colour blak, buskit with hornis twa,
   And in the nicht scho listis best appeir.
   Haw as the Leid, of colour nathing cleir ;
   For all hir licht scho borrowis at hir brother
   Titan, for of hir self scho hes nane uther.

38 Hir gyse was gray, and ful of spottis blak,   260
   And on hir breist ane Churle paintit full evin,
   Beirand ane bunche of Thornis on his bak,
   Quhilk for his thift micht clim na nar the hevin.
   Thus quhen thay gadderit war, thir Goddes sevin,
   Mercurius thay cheisit with ane assent
   To be foirspeikar in the Parliament.

39 Quha had bene thair, and liken for to heir
   His facound toung, and termis exquisite,
   Of Rethorick the prettick he micht leir,
   In breif Sermone ane pregnant sentence wryte :   270
   Befoir Cupide veiling his Cap alyte,
   Speiris the caus of that vocatioun,
   And he anone schew his Intentioun.

40 'Lo !' (quod Cupide), 'quha will blaspheme the name
   Of his awin God, outher in word or deid,
   To all Goddis he dois baith lak and schame,
   And suld have bitter panis to his meid.
   I say this by yone wretchit Cresseid,
   The quilk throw me was sum tyme flour of lufe,
   Me and my Mother starklie can reprufe.   280

260 gyse) gyte *TSJK*   262 bunche) busshe *TSJK*
270 sentence) Sermon *A*
271 veiling his Cap alyte) wailling his capalite *A*
275 or). Original has 'in'   276 lak) losse *TSJK*
280 starklie) she stately *TSJK*

41 'Saying of hir greit Infelicitie
   I was the caus, and my Mother Venus,
   Ane blind Goddes, hir cald, that micht not se,
   With sclander and defame Injurious;
   Thus hir leving unclene and Lecherous
   Scho wald returne on me and my Mother,
   To quhome I schew my grace abone all uther.

42 'And sen ye ar all sevin deificait,
   Participant of devyne sapience,
   This greit Injurie done to our hie estait   290
   Me think with pane we suld mak recompence;
   Was never to Goddes done sic violence.
   Asweill for yow, as for myself I say,
   Thairfoir ga help to revenge I yow pray.'

43 Mercurius to Cupide gave answeir
   And said : 'Schir King my counsall is that ye
   Refer yow to the hiest planeit heir,
   And tak to him the lawest of degre,
   The pane of Cresseid for to modifie;
   As god Saturne, with him tak Cynthia.'   300
   'I am content' (quod he), 'to tak thay twa.'

44 Than thus proceidit Saturne and the Mone,
   Quhen thay the mater rypelie had degest,
   For the dispyte to Cupide scho had done,
   And to Venus oppin and manifest,
   In all hir lyfe with pane to be opprest,
   And torment sair, with seiknes Incurabill,
   And to all lovers be abhominabill.

283 Shee called a blind goddess, and might not see *SJTK*
286 returne) retorte *TSJK*
297 Refer yow) Utter you *A*

45 This duleful sentence Saturne tuik on hand,
   And passit doun quhair cairfull Cresseid lay,   310
   And on hir heid he laid ane frostie wand;
   Than lawfullie on this wyse can he say:
   'Thy greit fairnes and all thy bewtie gay,
   Thy wantoun blude, and eik thy goldin Hair,
   Heir I exclude fra the for evermair.

46 'I change thy mirth into Melancholy,
   Quhilk is the Mother of all pensivenes;
   Thy Moisture and thy heit in cald and dry;
   Thyne Insolence, thy play and wantones
   To greit diseis; thy Pomp and thy riches   320
   In mortall neid; and greit penuritie
   Thou suffer sall, and as ane beggar die.'

47 O cruell Saturne! fraward and angrie,
   Hard is thy dome, and to malitious;
   On fair Cresseid quhy hes thou na mercie,
   Quhilk was sa sweit, gentill and amorous?
   Withdraw thy sentence and be gracious
   As thou was never; so schawis thow thy deid,
   Ane wraikfull sentence gevin on fair Cresseid.

48 Than Cynthia, quhen Saturne past away,   330
   Out of hir sait discendit doun belyve,
   And red ane bill on Cresseid quhair scho lay,
   Contening this sentence diffinityve:
   'Fra heit of bodie I the now depryve,
   And to thy seiknes sal be na recure,
   Bot in dolour thy dayis to Indure.

312 lawfullie) awfully *K*
328 so schawis thow) so sheweth through *TSJK*
329 wraikfull) wrackful *A*
301-329 are misplaced in *A*, occurring after Charteris, line 357
325 quhy hes thou na) wha shewst noe *SJ*

49 'Thy Cristall Ene minglit with blude I mak,
Thy voice sa cleir, unplesand hoir and hace,
Thy lustie lyre ouirspred with spottis blak,
And lumpis haw appeirand in thy face.　　　　340
Quhair thou cũmis, Ilk man sal fle the place.
This sall thou go begging fra hous to hous
With Cop and Clapper lyke ane Lazarous.'

50 This doolie dreame, this uglye visioun
Brocht to ane end, Cresseid fra it awoik,
And all that Court and convocatioun
Vanischit away, than rais scho up and tuik
Ane poleist glas, and hir schaddow culd luik:
And quhen scho saw hir face sa deformait
Gif scho in hart was wa aneuch God wait.　　　　350

51 Weiping full sair, 'Lo quhat it is' (quod sche),
'With fraward langage for to mufe and steir
Our craibit Goddis, and sa is sene on me!
My blaspheming now have I bocht full deir.
All eirdlie Joy and mirth I set areir.
Allace this day, allace this wofull tyde,
Quhen I began with my Goddis for to Chyde.'

52 Be this was said ane Chyld come fra the Hall
To warne Cresseid the Supper was reddy,
First knokkit at the dure, and syne culd call:　　　　360
'Madame your Father biddis yow cum in hy.
He hes mervell sa lang on grouf ye ly,
And sayis your prayers bene to lang sum deill:
The goddis wait all your Intent full weill.'

338 hoir) heer *TSJ*; hoarse *K*
342 This) Thus *A TSJK*
350 wa aneuch) wo I ne wyte *TK*: ne wat nat I, shee wate *SJ*
357 my Goddis) my goddes *A TK*
364 wait) do know *A*

53 Quod scho : 'Fair Chyld ga to my Father deir,
And pray him cum to speik with me anone.'
And sa he did, and said : 'douchter quhat cheir ?'
'Allace' (quod scho), 'Father my mirth is gone.'
'How sa' (quod he) ; and scho can all expone
As I have tauld, the vengeance and the wraik   370
For hir trespas, Cupide on hir culd tak.

54 He luikit on hir uglye Lipper face,
The quhilk befor was quhyte as Lillie flour,
Wringand his handis oftymes he said allace
That he had levit to se that wofull hour,
For he knew weill that thair was na succour
To hir seiknes, and that dowblit his pane.
Thus was thair cair aneuch betuix thame twane.

55 Quhen thay togidder murnit had full lang,
Quod Cresseid : 'Father, I wald not be kend.   380
Thairfoir in secreit wyse ye let me gang
Into yone Hospitall at the tounis end.
And thidder sum meit for Cheritie me send
To leif upon, for all mirth in this eird
Is fra me gane, sic is my wickit weird.'

56 Than in ane Mantill and ane bawer Hat,
With Cop and Clapper wonder prively,
He opnit ane secreit yet, and out thair at
Convoyit hir, that na man suld espy,
Into ane Village half ane myle thairby,   390
Delyverit hir in at the Spittaill hous,
And daylie sent hir part of his Almous.

386 Than) Whan *TSJK*
399 thairfoir) there *TSJK* : better) bitter *K*
401 ouirquhelmit) ouerheled *T* : ouerwheled *K*
402 God) Now *SJ*   410 blaiknit bair) blake & bare *TSJK*
411 the of thy) or sound thy *A* ; helpe thy sair *TSJK*
413 on breird) unberd *TSJ* ; unberth *K*
414 God gif) God if *ATSJ*

57 Sum knew her weill, & sum had na knawledge
   Of hir becaus scho was sa deformait,
   With bylis blak ouirspred in hir visage,
   And hir fair colour faidit and alterait.
   Yit thay presumit for her hie regrait
   And still murning, scho was of Nobill kin :
   With better will thairfoir they tuik hir in.

58 The day passit, and Phebus went to rest,   400
   The Cloudis blak ouirquhelmit all the sky.
   God wait gif Cresseid was ane sorrowfull Gest,
   Seing that uncouth fair and Harbery :
   But meit or drink scho dressit hir to ly
   In ane dark Corner of the Hous allone.
   And on this wyse weiping, scho maid her mone :

The Complaint of Cresseid

59 'O sop of sorrow, sonkin into cair :
   O Cative Creisseid, for now and ever mair,
   Gane is thy Joy and all thy mirth in Eird,
   Of all blyithnes now art thou blaiknit bair.   410
   Thair is na Salve may saif the of thy sair,
   Fell is thy Fortoun, wickit is thy weird :
   Thy blys is baneist, and thy baill on breird,
   Under the Eirth, God gif I gravin wer :
   Quhair nane of Grece nor yit of Troy micht heird.

60 'Quhair is thy Chalmer wantounlie besene?
   With burely bed and bankouris browderit bene,
   Spycis and Wyne to thy Collatioun,
   The Cowpis all of gold and silver schene :
   The sweit Meitis, servit in plaittis clene,   420
   With Saipheron sals of ane gud sessoun :
   Thy gay garmentis with mony gudely Goun,
   Thy plesand Lawn pinnit with goldin prene :
   All is areir, thy greit Royall Renoun.

417 bankouris) bankers *TK*; boukers *A* ; brankers *SJ*
421 Saipheron) savery *TSJK*: sessoun) facioun *TSJK*

61 'Quhair is thy garding with thir greissis gay?
And fresche flowris, quhilk the Quene Floray:
Had paintit plesandly in everie pane,
Quhair thou was wont full merilye in May,
To walk and tak the dew be it was day
And heir the Merle and Mawis mony ane,   430
With Ladyis fair in Carrolling to gane,
And se the Royall Rinkis in thair array,
In garmentis gay garnischit on everie grane.

62 'Thy greit triumphand fame and hie honour,
Quhair thou was callit of Eirdlye wichtis Flour,
All is decayit, thy weird is welterit so.
Thy hie estait is turnit in darknes dour.
This Lipper Ludge tak for thy burelie Bour.
And for thy Bed tak now ane bunche of stro,
For waillit Wyne, and Meitis thou had tho,   440
Tak mowlit Breid, Peirrie and Ceder sour:
Bot Cop and Clapper, now is all ago.

63 'My cleir voice, and courtlie carrolling,
Quhair I was wont with Ladyis for to sing,
Is rawk as Ruik, full hiddeous hoir and hace,
My plesand port all utheris precelling:
Of lustines I was hald maist conding.
Now is deformit the Figour of my face,
To luik on it, na Leid now lyking hes:
Sowpit in syte, I say with sair siching,   450
Ludgeit amang the Lipper Leid allace.

427 pane) way *SJ*
432-437 and 444 and 446-7 are omitted in *TSJ* and *K* and two irregular
    stanzas are made up of the remaining lines, in rather haphazard order.
438 burelie) goodly *TSJK*   441 Peirrie) pirate *TSJK*
445 rawk as Ruik) rank and rouk *A*
449 na Leid now lyking hes) no pleople (*sic*) hath lykyng *TSJ*
450 Sowpit in syte) Solped in syght *T*; Soe sped in sight *SJ*
451 Ludgeit) Lyeing *T*
454 and 455 are interchanged in *TSJ* and *K*; 453 is omitted in *TSJ* and *K*

64 'O Ladyis fair of Troy and Grece, attend
My miserie, quhilk nane may comprehend.
My frivoll Fortoun, my Infelicitie :
My greit mischeif quhilk na man can amend.
Be war in tyme, approchis neir the end,
And in your mynd ane mirrour mak of me :
As I am now, peradventure that ye
For all your micht may cum to that same end,
Or ellis war, gif ony war may be.   460

65 'Nocht is your fairnes bot ane faiding flour,
Nocht is your famous laud and hie honour
Bot wind Inflat in uther mennis eiris.
Your roising reid to rotting sall retour :
Exempill mak of me in your Memour,
Quhilk of sic thingis wofull witnes beiris,
All Welth in Eird, away as Wind it weiris.
Be war thairfoir, approchis neir the hour :
Fortoun is fikkill, quhen scho beginnis & steiris.'

66 Thus chydand with hir drerie destenye,   470
Weiping, scho woik the nicht fra end to end.
Bot all in vane ; hir dule, hir cairfull cry
Micht not remeid, nor yit hir murning mend.
Ane Lipper Lady rais and till hir wend,
And said : 'quhy spurnis thow aganis the Wall,
To sla thy self, and mend nathing at all?

67 'Sen thy weiping dowbillis bot thy wo,
I counsall the mak vertew of ane neid.
To leir to clap thy Clapper to and fro,
And leir efter the Law of Lipper Leid.'   480
Thair was na buit, bot furth with thame scho yeid,
Fra place to place, quhill cauld and hounger sair
Compellit hir to be ane rank beggair.

454 frivoll) freyle *TSJ*   455 amend) commend *A*
456 The rest of the stanza in *T* and *SJ* is not sufficiently coherent for analysis.
468-9 omitted in *K*   469 not in *T* or *SJ*
473 mend) end *SJ*   479 To) Go *A TSJK*

68 That samin tyme of Troy the Garnisoun,
Quhilk had to chiftane worthie Troylus,
Throw Jeopardie of Weir had strikken doun
Knichtis of Grece in number mervellous,
With greit tryumphe and Laude victorious
Agane to Troy [richt] Royallie they raid
The way quhair Cresseid with the Lipper baid.   490

69 Seing that companie thai come all with ane stevin
Thay gaif ane cry and schuik coppis gude speid.
Said 'worthie Lordis for goddis lufe of Hevin,
To us Lipper part of your Almous deid.'
Than to thair cry Nobill Troylus tuik heid,
Having pietie, neir by the place can pas :
Quhair Cresseid sat, not witting quhat scho was.

70 Than upon him scho kest up baith hir Ene,
And with ane blenk it come into his thocht,
That he sumtime hir face befoir had sene.   500
Bot scho was in sic plye he knew hir nocht,
Yit than hir luik into his mynd it brocht
The sweit visage and amorous blenking
Of fair Cresseid sumtyme his awin darling.

71 Na wonder was, suppois in mynd that he
Tuik hir figure sa sone, and lo now quhy ?
The Idole of ane thing, in cace may be
Sa deip Imprentit in the fantasy
That it deludis the wittis outwardly,
And sa appeiris in forme and lyke estait,   510
Within the mynd as it was figurait.

489-490 raid . . . baid) rode . . . stode *TSJK*
491 that companie) the troup *A*
495 thair) her *TSJ*
507 cace) face *A*

72 Ane spark of lufe than till his hart culd spring
And kendlit all his bodie in ane fyre.
With hait Fewir ane sweit and trimbling
Him tuik, quhill he was reddie to expyre.
To beir his Scheild, his Breist began to tyre
Within ane quhyle he changit mony hew,
And nevertheless not ane ane uther knew.

73 For Knichtlie pietie and memoriall
Of fair Cresseid, ane Gyrdill can he tak,   520
Ane Purs of gold, and mony gay Jowall,
And in the Skirt of Cresseid doun can swak;
Than raid away, and not ane word [he] spak,
Pensive in hart, quhill he come to the Toun,
And for greit care oft syis almaist fell doun.

74 The lipper folk to Cresseid than can draw,
To se the equall distributioun
Of the Almous, bot quhen the gold thay saw,
Ilk ane to uther prevelie can roun,
And said: 'Yone Lord hes mair affectioun,   530
How ever it be, unto yone Lazarous
Than to us all, we knaw be his Almous.'

75 'Quhat Lord is yone' (quod scho), 'have ye na feill,
Hes done to us so greit humanitie?'
'Yes' (quod a Lipper man), 'I knaw him weill,
Schir Troylus it is, gentill and fre:'
Quhen Cresseid understude that it was he,
Stiffer than steill, thair stert ane bitter stound
Throwout hir hart, and fell doun to the ground.

---

521 This line is repeated in the original.
522 swak) shake *K*
525 oft syis) some say *A*
539 *K* omits 5 stanzas of *T*

76 Quhen scho ouircome, with siching sair & sad,   540
   With mony cairfull cry and cald ochane:
   'Now is my breist with stormie stoundis stad,
   Wrappit in wo, ane wretch full will of wane.'
   Than swounit scho oft or scho culd refrane,
   And ever in hir swouning cryit scho thus:
   'O fals Cresseid and trew Knicht Troylus.

77 'Thy lufe, thy lawtie, and thy gentilnes,
   I countit small in my prosperitie,
   Sa elevait I was in wantones,
   And clam upon the fickill quheill sa hie: 550
   All Faith and Lufe I promissit to the,
   Was in the self fickill and frivolous:
   O fals Cresseid, and trew Knicht Troilus.

78 'For lufe, of me thou keipt gude continence,
   Honest and chaist in conversatioun.
   Of all wemen protectour and defence
   Thou was, and helpit thair opinioun.
   My mynd in fleschelie foull affectioun
   Was Inclynit to Lustis Lecherous:
   Fy fals Cresseid, O trew Knicht Troylus.   560

79 'Lovers be war and tak gude heid about
   Quhome that ye lufe, for quhome ye suffer paine.
   I lat yow wit, thair is richt few thairout
   Quhome ye may traist to have trew lufe agane.
   Preif quhen ye will, your labour is in vaine.
   Thairfoir, I reid, ye tak thame as ye find,
   For thay ar sad as Widdercock in Wind,

---

540 Quhen scho ouircome) Whan she, ouercome *T*; When she overcame *A*
   (*see* note, p. 258).   541 cald ochane) colde atone *TSJ*
543 full will of wane) fulwyl of one *TSJ*
544 Then fell in swoun, full oft ere she would fane *A*; Than fel in
   swoun ful ofte or she wolde fone *TSJ*

80 'Becaus I knaw the greit unstabilnes
　　Brukkill as glas, into my self I say,
　　Traisting in uther als greit unfaithfulnes :　　570
　　Als unconstant, and als untrew of fay.
　　Thocht sum be trew, I wait richt few ar thay,
　　Quha findis treuth lat him his Lady ruse :
　　Nane but my self as now I will accuse.'

81 Quhen this was said, with Paper scho sat doun,
　　And on this maneir maid hir Testament.
　　'Heir I beteiche my Corps and Carioun
　　With Wormis and with Taidis to be rent.
　　My Cop and Clapper and myne Ornament,
　　And all my gold the Lipper folk sall have :　　580
　　Quhen I am deid, to burie me in grave.

82 'This Royal Ring, set with this Rubie reid,
　　Quhilk Troylus in drowrie to me send,
　　To him agane I leif it quhen I am deid,
　　To mak my cairfull deid unto him kend :
　　Thus I conclude schortlie and mak ane end,
　　My Spreit I leif to Diane quhair scho dwellis,
　　To walk with hir in waist Woddis and Wellis.

83 'O Diomeid, thou hes baith Broche and Belt,
　　Quhilk Troylus gave me in takning　　590
　　Of his trew lufe,' and with that word scho swelt.
　　And sone ane Lipper man tuik of the Ring,
　　Syne buryit hir withouttin tarying :
　　To Troylus furthwith the Ring he bair,
　　And of Cresseid the deith he can declair.

547 lawtie) laude *TSJ*　　　　549 elevait) efflated *A* ; effated *TSJ*
551-2 Omitted in *SJ*　　　　554 continence) countenance *ASJT*
556-7 Omitted in *SJ*　　　　562 quhome) whan *T*
565 Omitted in *SJ*　　　　570 unfaithfulnes) brutelnesse *TSJ*
577 beteiche) bequeath *A TSJ*　583 drowrie) Dowry *A TSJK*

84 Quhen he had hard hir greit infirmitie,
   Hir Legacie and Lamentatioun,
   And how scho endit in sic povertie,
   He swelt for wo, and fell doun in ane swoun,
   For greit sorrow his hart to brist was boun :   600
   Siching full sadlie, said : ' I can no moir,
   Scho was untrew, and wo is me thairfoir.'

85 Sum said he maid ane Tomb of Merbell gray,
   And wrait hir name and superscriptioun,
   And laid it on hir grave quhair that scho lay,
   In goldin Letteris, conteining this ressoun :
   ' Lo, fair Ladyis, Crisseid, of Troyis toun,
   Sumtyme countit the flour of Womanheid,
   Under this stane lait Lipper lyis deid.'

86 Now, worthie Wemen, in this Ballet schort,   610
   Made for your worschip and Instructioun,
   Of Cheritie, I monische and exhort,
   Ming not your lufe with fals deceptioun.
   Beir in your mynd this schort conclusioun
   Of fair Cresseid, as I have said befoir.
   Sen scho is deid, I speik of hir no moir.

                    Finis.

---

607 fair Ladyis) clear Ladies *A*   609 lait Lipper) laith Lipper *A*
613 Ming) Wing *A*   614 schort) sore *TSJ*

Orpheus and Eurydice

BANNATYNE MS.

Orpheus and Eurydice

1 THE nobilnes and grit magnificens
  of prince and lord, quhai list to magnifie,
  his ancestre and lineall discens
  Suld first extoll, and his genolegie,
  So that his harte he mycht inclyne thairby
  The moir to vertew and to worthiness,
  herand reherss his elderis gentilness.

2 It is contrair the Lawis of nature
  A gentill man to be degenerat,
  Nocht following of his progenitour   10
  The worthe rewll, and the lordly estait ;
  A ryall rynk for to be rusticat
  Is bot a monsture in comparesoun,
  had in dispyt and full derisioun.

3 I say this be the grit lordis of grew,
  Quhich set thair hairt, and all thair haill curage,
  Thair faderis steppis Justly to persew,
  Eiking the wirschep of thair he lenage ;
  The anseane and sadwyse men of age
  Wer tendouris to yung and Insolent,   20
  To mak thame in all vertewis excellent.

4 Lyk as a strand, or watter of a spring,
  haldis the sapour of the fontell well,
  So did in grece ilk Lord and worthy king,
  of forbearis thay tuk knawlege and smell,
  Among the quhilk of ane I think to tell ;
  Bot first his gentill generatioun
  I sall reherss, with your correctioun.

3 ancestre) ancestry *A* ; ancester *C*   12 rynk) renk *C* ; reulre *A*
19 sadwyse) sad wyse *C*   25 knawlege) tarage *C*; carage *A*
129   I

5 Upone the mont of elecone,*
The most famouss of all arrabea,   30
A goddes dwelt, excellent in bewte,
gentill of blude, callit memoria ;
Quhilk Jupiter that goddess to wyfe can ta,
And carnaly hir knew, and eftir syne,
apone a day bare him fair dochteris nyne.

6 The first in grew wes callit euterpe,
In our language gud delectatioun ;
The secound maid clippit melpomyne,
As hony sueit in modelatioun ;
Thersycore is gud instructioun   40
of every thing—the thrid sister, I wiss,
Thus out of grew in latyne translait Is.

7 Caliope, that madin mervalouss,
The ferd sistir, of all musik maistress,
and mother to the king schir orpheouss,
quhilk throw his wyfe wes efter king of traiss ;
Clio, the fyift, that now is a goddess,
In Latyne callit meditatioun,
of everything that hes creatioun.

8 The sext sister is callit herato,   50
quhilk drawis lyk to lyk in every thing ;
The sevint lady was fair polimio,
quhilk cowth a thowsand sangis sueitly sing ;
Talia syne, quhilk can our saulis bring
In profound wit and grit agilite,
Till undirstand and haif capacitie.

* MS. 'electon.'

29 elecone) Elicone *C* ; Elicounee *A*
33 goddess) god *A C*
38 clippit) namyt *A C*
40 Thersycore) Tersitor *C A*
50 sister is) lady was *C A*

9   Urania, the nynt and last of all,
    In greik langage, quha cowth it rycht expound,
    Is callit armony celestiall,
    Reiosing men with melody and sound.   60
    Amang thir nyne calliope wes cround,
    And maid a quene be michty god phebuss,
    off quhome he gat this prince schir orpheouss.

10 No wondir wes thocht he wes fair and wyse,
    gentill and gud, full of liberalitie,
    his fader god, and his progenetryse
    a goddess, finder of all armony :
    quhen he wes borne scho set him on hir kne,
    and gart him souk of hir twa paupis quhyte
    The sueit lecour of all musik perfyte.   70

11 Incressand sone to manheid up he drew,
    off statur large, and frely fair of face ;
    [H]Is noble fame so far it sprang and grew,
    Till at the last t[h]e michty quene of trace,
    excelland fair, haboundand in richess,
    a message send unto that prince so ying,
    Requyrand him to wed hir and be king.

12 Euridices this lady had to name ;
    and quhene scho saw this prince so glorius,
    hir erand to propone scho thocht no schame,   80
    with wordis sueit, and blenkis amorouss,
    Said, 'welcum, Lord and lufe, schir orpheuss,
    In this provynce ye salbe king and lord !'
    Thay kissit syne, and thus thay can accord.

58 greik) our *AC.*   [*C* breaks off here, and does not resume
   till line 175 of *AB.*]
64 wes) Is *A*   65 and gud, full) and full *A*
71 Quhen he was auld, sone to manhed he drewe *A*
84 thay can accord) war at accord *A*

13 Betuix orpheuss and fair erudices,
    fra thai wer weddit, on fra day to day
    The low of lufe cowth kyndill and incress,
    with mirth, and blythness, solace, and with play
    off wardly Joy; allace, quhat sall I say?
    Lyk till a flour that plesandly will spring,   90
    quhilk fadis sone, and endis with murnyng.

14 I say this be erudices the quene,
    quhilk walkit furth in to a may mornyng,
    Bot with a madyn, untill a medow grene,
    To tak the air, and se the flouris spring;
    quhair in a schaw, neir by this lady ying,
    a busteouss hird callit arresteuss,
    kepand his beistis, Lay undir a buss.

15 And quhen he saw this Lady solitar,
    bairfut, with schankis quhyter than the snaw,   100
    preckit with lust, he thocht withoutin mair
    hir till oppress, and to his cave hir draw:
    Dreidand for evill scho fled, quhen scho him saw;
    and as scho ran, all bairfute on a buss
    Scho strampit on a serpent vennemuss.

16 This crewall venome wes so penetrife,
    As natur is of [all] mortall pusoun,
    I[n] peisis small this quenis harte can rife,
    and scho annone fell on a deidly swoun:
    Seand this caiss, proserpyne maid hir * boun,   110
    quhilk clepit is the goddes infernall,
    ontill hir court this gentill quene can call.

* MS. 'him': 'hir' has been written in the margin in a later hand.

95 the air) the dewe *A*
97 arresteuss) arystyus *A*
102 to his cave hir draw) till hir can he draw *A*
105 strampit) trampit *A*
112 ontill) And till *A*

17 And quhen scho vaneist was and unwisible,
   hir madyn wepit with a wofull cheir,
   cryand with mony schowt and voce terrible,
   quhill at the last king orpheus can heir,
   and of hir cry the causs sone cowth he speir.
   Scho said, 'allace ! euridicess, your quene,
   Is with the phary tane befoir my Ene.'

18 This noble king inflammit all in yre,   120
   and rampand as a Lyoun rewanuss,
   With awfull Luke, and Ene glowand as fyre,
   sperid the maner, and the maid said thuss :
   'Scho strampit on a serpent venemuss,
   and fell on swoun ; with that the quene of fary
   clawcht hir upsone, and furth with hir cowth cary.'

19 Quhen scho had said, the king sichit full soir,
   his hairt neir brist for verry dule and wo ;
   half out of mynd, he maid no tary moir,
   bot tuk his harp, and on to wod cowth go,   130
   wrinkand his handis, walkand to and fro,
   quhill he mycht stand, syne sat doun on a stone,
   and till his harp thussgait [he] maid his mone.

[*The Complaint of Orpheus*]

20 'O dulful herp, with mony dully string,
   turne all thy mirth and musik in murning,
   and seiss of all thy sutell songis sueit ;
   now weip with me, thy lord and cairfull King,
   quhilk lossit hes in erd all his lyking ;
   and all thy game thow change in gole, and greit,
   Thy goldin pynnis with mony teiris weit ;   140
   and all my pane for * till report thow preiss,
   cryand with me, in every steid and streit,
   "quhair art thow gone, my luve ewridicess ? "
           * MS. 'foll.'

    134 dully) dolly *A*   140 mony) thi *A*

21 Him to reioss yit playit he a spring,
    quhill that the fowlis of the wid can sing,
    and treis dansit with thair levis grene,
    him to devod from his grit womenting;
    Bot all in vane, that wailyeit no thing,
    his hairt wes so upoun his lusty quene;
    The bludy teiris sprang out of his ene,   150
    Thair wes no solace mycht his sobbing sess,
    bot cryit ay, with cairis cauld and kene,
    'quhair art thow gone, my lufe euridicess?'

22 'Fair weill my place, fair weill plesandis and play,
    and wylcum woddis wyld and wilsum way,
    my wicket werd in wildirness to ware;
    my rob ryell, and all my riche array,
    changit salbe in rude russet and gray,
    my dyademe in till a hate of hair;
    my bed salbe with bever, brok, and bair,   160
    in buskis bene with mony busteouss bess,
    withowttin song, sayand with siching sair,
    "quhair art thow gone, my luve euridicess?"

23 'I the beseik, my fair fadir phebuss,
    Haif pety of thy awin sone orpheuss;
    wait thow nocht weill I am thy sone and chyld?
    now heir my plaint, peinfull * and peteuss;
    Direk me fro this deid so doloruss,
    Quhilk gois thus withouttin gilt begyld;
    Lat nocht thy face with cluddis to be oursyld;   170
    Len me thy lycht, and lat me nocht go leiss,
    To find that fair in fame that was nevir fyld,
    My lady quene and lufe, euridices.

* MS. apparently 'pelfull.'

148 that wailyeit) thai comfort *A*
154 place). *A* suggests ' place ' as an alternative reading.
158 and gray) of gray *A*
170 face) late *A* : to be oursyld) be ourfyld *A*

24 'O Jupiter, thow god celestiall,
and grantschir to my self, on the I call
To mend my murning and my drery mone;
Thow gif me forss, that [I] nocht fant nor fall,
Till I hir fynd; forsuth seik hir I sall,
and nowthir stint nor stand for stok nor stone.
Throw thy godheid grant me quhair scho is gone,   180
gar hir appeir, and put my hairt in pess.'
King orpheuss thus, with his harp allone,
Soir weipand for his wyfe euridices.

25 Quhen endit wer thir songis lamentable,
he tuk his harp and on his breist can hing,
Syne passit to the hevin, as sayis the fable,
To seik his wyfe, bot that welyeid no thing:
By wedlingis streit he went but tareing,
Syne come doun throw the speir of saturne ald,
Quhilk fadir is to all the stormis cald.   190

26 Quhen scho wes socht outhrow that cauld regioun,
Till Jupiter his grandschir can he wend,
quhilk rewit soir his Lamentatioun,
and gart his spheir be socht fro end to end;
Scho was nocht thair; and doun he can descend
Till mars, the god of battell and of stryfe,
and socht his spheir, yit gat he nocht his wyfe.

27 Than went he doun till his fadir phebus,
god of the sone, with bemis brycht and cleir;
bot quhen he saw his awin sone orpheuss   200
In sic a plicht, that changit all his cheir,
and gart annone ga seik throw all his spheir;
bot all in vane, his lady come nocht thair:
he tuk his leif and to venus can fair.

176 *C* resumes here   180 grant) gyde *AC*
187 welyeid) availit *C*; avalit *A*   190 stormis) sternis *AC*
191 outhrow) out throu *AC*   194 spheir) spere, speir *AC*

28 Quhen he hir saw, he knelit and said thuss :
'wait ye nocht weill I am your awin trew knycht?
In luve none leler than schir orpheuss ;
And ye of luve goddass, and most of micht,
of my lady help me to get a sicht.'
'fforsur,' quod scho, 'ye mone seik nedirmair.'   210
Than fra venus he tuk his leif but mair.

29 Till mercury but tary is he gone,
quhilk callit is the god of eloquens,
bot of his wyfe thair gat he knawlege none.
with wofull hairt he passit doun frome thens ;
on to the mone he maid no residens :
Thus from the hevin he went onto the erd,
Yit be the way sum melody he lerd.

30 In his passage amang the planeitis all,
he hard a hevinly melody and sound,   220
passing all instrumentis musicall,
causit be rollyn of the speiris round ;
Quhilk armony of all this mappamound,
Quhilk moving seiss unyt perpetuall,
Quhilk of this warld pluto the saule can call.

31 Thair leirit he tonis proportionat,
as duplare, triplare, and emetricus,
enolius, and eik the quadruplait,
Epoddeus rycht hard and curius ;
off all thir sex, sueit and delicius,   230
rycht consonant fyfe hevinly symphonyss
componyt ar, as clerkis can devyse.

32 ffirst diatesserone, full sueit, I wiss
And dyapasone, semple and dowplait,
And dyapenty, componyt with the dyss ;
Thir makis fyve of thre multiplicat :
This mirry musik and mellefluat,
Compleit and full of nummeris od and evin,
Is causit be the moving of the hevin.

234 dowplait) duplycate C   236 makis) mak C

33 Off sic musik to wryt I do bot doit,   240
    Thairfoir of this mater a stray I lay,
    For in my lyfe I cowth nevir sing a noit;
    bot I will tell how orpheus tuk the way,
    To seik his wyfe attour the gravis gray,
    hungry and cauld, with mony wilsum wone,
    Withouttin gyd, he and his harp allone.

34 he passit furth the space of twenty dayis,
    fer and full fer, and ferrer than I can tell,
    and ay he fand streitis and reddy wayis;
    Till at the last unto the yet of hell   250
    he come, and thair he fand a porter fell,
    with thre heidis, wes callit serberus,
    a hound of hell, a monstour mervellus.

35 Than orpheus began to be agast,
    Quhen he beheld that ugly hellis hound;
    he tuk his harp and on it playit fast,
    Till at the last, throw sueitnes of the sound,
    This dog slepit and fell doun on the ground;
    Than orpheus attour his wame install,
    and neddirmair he went, as ye heir sall.   260

36 He passit furth ontill a ryvir deip,
    our it a brig, and on it sisteris thre,
    quhilk had the entre of the brig to keip,
    Electo, mygra, and thesaphone,
    Turnit a quheill wes ugly for to se,
    and on it spred a man hecht exione,
    Rolland about rycht windir wo begone.

37 Than orpheus playd a Joly spring,
    The thre susteris full fast thay fell on sleip,
    The ugly quheill seisit of hir quhirling;   270
    Thus left wes none the entre for to keip.
    Thane exione out of the quheill gan creip,
    And stall away; and orpheus annone,
    Without stopping, atour the brig is gone.

248 Fer and full ferther than I can tell *CA*
261 Than come he till ane rywir wonder depe *CA*

38　Nocht far frome thyne he come unto a flude,
　　Drubly and deip, and rythly doun can rin,
　　Quhair tantelus nakit full thristy stude,
　　And yit the wattir yeid aboif his chin;
　　quhen he gaipit thair wald no drop cum In;
　　quhen he dowkit the watter wald discend;　　　280
　　Thus gat he nocht his thrist [to slake] no[r] mend.

39　Befoir his face ane naple hang also,
　　fast at his mowth upoun a twynid [threid],
　　quhen he gaipit, It rollit to and fro,
　　and fled, as it refusit him to feid.
　　Quhen orpheus thus saw him suffir neid,
　　he tuk his harp and fast on it can clink:
　　The wattir stud, and tantalus gat a drink.

40　Syne our a mure, with thornis thik and scherp,
　　Wepand allone, a wilsum way he went,　　　290
　　And had nocht bene throw suffrage of his harp,
　　With fell pikis he had bene schorne and schent;
　　As he blenkit, besyd him on the bent
　　he saw lyand speldit a wofull wycht,
　　nalit full fast, and titius he hecht.

41　And on his breist thair sat a grisly grip,
　　quhilk with his bill his belly throw can boir,
　　both maw, myddret, hart, lever, and trip,
　　he ruggit out—his panis was the moir.
　　Quhen orpheus thus saw him suffir soir,　　　300
　　he tuke his herp and maid sueit melody—
　　The grip is fled, and titius left his cry.

275 Syne come he till a wonder grisely flud *CA*
283 twynid) tolter *CA*
284 rollit) rokkit *CA*
286 Than Orpheus had reuth of his grete nede *CA*
293 blenkit) blent *CA*
294 lyand speldit) speldit *CA* : wofull) wonder wofull *CA*
295 titius) Theseus *CA*
302 and titius) Theseus *CA*
318 with) of *CA* : full birnand) full hate birnand *CA*
324 And) Thare fand he *CA* : his foull crewaltie) his crueltee *CA*

42 Beyond this mure he fand a feir full streit,
  myrk as the nycht, To pass rycht dengerus,
  ffor sliddreness skant mycht he hald his feit,
  In quhilk thair wes a stynk rycht odiuss,
  That gydit him to hiddouss hellis houss,
  Quhair rodomantus and proserpina
  Wer king and quene ; and orpheus in can ga.

43 O dully place, [and] grundles deip dungeoun,   310
  furness of fyre, and stink intollerable,
  pit of dispair, without remissioun,
  Thy meit wennome, Thy drink is pusonable,
  Thy grit panis and to compte unnumerable ;
  Quhat creature cumis to dwell in the
  Is ay deand, and nevirmoir sall de.

44 Thair fand he mony cairfull king and quene,
  With croun on heid, with brass full birnand,
  quhilk in thair lyfe full maisterfull had bene,
  and conquerouris of gold, richess, and land.   320
  hectore of troy, and priame, thair he fand ;
  and alexander for his wrang conqueist ;
  antiochus als for his foull incest.

45 And Julius cesar for his foull crewaltie ;
  and herod with his brudiris wyfe he saw ;
  and nero for his grit Iniquitie ;
  And pilot for his breking of the law ;
  Syne undir that he lukit, and cowth knaw
  Cresus, that king none mychtiar on mold
  ffor cuvatyse, yet full of birnand gold.   330

46 Thair saw he pharo, for the oppressioun
  of godis folk on quhilk the plaigis fell ;
  and sawll, for the grit abusioun
  Was Justice to the folk of Israell ;
  Thair saw he acob and quene Jesabell,
  Quhilk silly nabot, that wes a propheit trew,
  For his wyne yaird withouttin mercy slew.

47 Thair saw he mony paip and cardynall,
In haly kirk quhilk did abusioun,
and bischopis in thair pontificall, 340
Be symonie and wrang Intrusioun;
abbottis and all men of religioun,
ffor evill disponyng of thair place and rent,
In flame of fyre wer bittirly torment.

48 Syne neddirmair he went quhair pluto was,
and proserpyne, and hiddirwart he drew,
Ay playand on his harp quhair he cowth pass;
Till at the last erudices he knew,
Lene and deidlyk, and peteouss paill of hew,
Rycht warsche and wane, and walluid as the weid, 350
hir Lilly lyre wes lyk unto the leid.

49 Quod he, 'my lady leill, and my delyt,
ffull wo is me to se yow changit thus;
quhair is your rude as ross with cheikis quhyte,
your cristell ene with blenkis amorus,
your Lippis reid to kiss delicius?'
quod scho, 'as now I der nocht tell, perfay;
Bot ye sall wit the causs ane uthir day.'

50 Quod pluto, 'schir, thocht scho be lyk ane elf,
Scho hes no causs to plenye, and for quhy? 360
Scho fairis alsweill daylie as dois my self,
or king herod for all his chevelry:
It is langour that putis hir in sic ply;
War scho at hame in hir cuntre of trace,
Scho wald rewert full sone in [fax *] and face.'

* There is a blank space here in the MS.

341 and wrang Intrusioun) for wrang ministration *CA*
342 all men of) men of all *CA*
343 place and rent) placis rent *CA*
360 Scho hes) Thare is *CA*
361 fairis . . . dois) fare . . . did *C*; fare . . . dois *A*
365 rewert) refete *CA*; fax *CA*

51 Than orpheus befoir pluto sat doun,
  And in his handis quhit his herp can ta,
  And playit mony sueit proportioun,
  With baiss tonis in Ipotdorica,
  With gemilling in yporlerica;   370
  quhill at the last for rewth and grit petie,
  Thay weipit soir, that cowth him heir or se.

52 Than proserpene and pluto bad him ass
  his waresoun—And he wald haif rycht nocht
  Bot Licience with his wyfe away to pass
  To his cuntre, that he so far had socht.
  Quod proserpyne, 'sen I hir hiddir brocht,
  We sall nocht pairte without conditioun.'
  Quod he, 'thairto I mak promissioun.'

53 'Euridices than be the hand thow tak,   380
  and pass thi way, bot undirneth this pane:
  Gife thow turnis or blenkis behind thy bak,
  We sall hir haif to hell for evir agane.'
  Thocht this was hard, yit orpheus was fane,
  and on thay went, talkand of play and sport,
  Till thay almost come to the outwart port.

54 Thus orpheus, with inwart lufe repleit,
  So blindit was with grit effectioun,
  pensyfe in hart apone his lady sueit,
  Remembrit nocht his hard conditioun.   390
  Quhat will ye moir? in schort conclusioun,
  he blent bakwart, And pluto come annone,
  And on to hell with hir agane is gone.

55 Allace! it wes grit pety for to heir
  of orpheus the weping and the wo,
  how his lady, that he had bocht so deir,
  Bot for a luk so sone wes tane him fro.
  flatlingis he fell, and micht no fordir go,
  And Lay a quhyle in swoun and extasy;
  Quhen he ourcome, this out of lufe gan cry: 400

56 'Quhat art thow, luve, how sall I the defyne?
   Bittir and sueit, crewall and merciable,
   plesand to sum, to uthir plent and pyne,
   Till sum constant, to uthir wariable;
   hard is thy law, thy bandis unbrekable;
   Quho sservis the, thocht thay be nevir so trew,
   Perchance sum tyme thay sall haif causs to rew.

57 'Now find I weill this proverb trew,' quod he,
   '"hart on the hurd, and handis on the soir;
   Quhair Luve gois, on forss mone turne the E."   410
   I am expart, and wo is * me thairfoir,
   Bot for a Luke my lady is forloir.'
   Thus chydand on with luve, our burne and bent,
   A wofull wedo hamewart is he went.

MORALITAS

Now, wirthy folk, boece, that senatour,
To wryt this fenyeit fable tuk in cure,
In his gay buke of consolatioun,
ffor our doctrene and gud instructioun;
quhilk in the self suppoiss it fenyeid be,
and hid under the cloik of poetre,   420
Yit maister trivat doctour nicholass,
quhilk in his tyme a noble theologe wass,
Applyis it to gud moralitie,
rycht full of fructe and seriositie.
ffair phebus is the god of sapience;
Caliope, his wyfe, is eloquence;
Thir twa mareit gat orpheus belyfe,
Quhilk callit is the pairte intelletyfe
Off manis saule, and undirstanding fre,
And seperat fra sensualitie.   430
Euridices is our effectioun,
Be fantesy oft movit up and doun;

MS. 'wois.'

410 mone turne the E) turnis the ee *CA*   415 Now) Lo *CA*
421 trivat) trowit *C*; trewit *A*   429 and) in *CA*

Quhile to ressone it castis the delyte,
Quhyle to the flesche it settis the appetyte.
Arestius, this [hird] that cowth persew
Euridices, is nocht bot gud vertew,
That bissy is to keip our myndis clene;
Bot quhen we fle outthrow the medow grene
Fra vertew, till this warldis vane plesans,
myngit with cair and full of variance,   440
The serpentis stang, that is the deidly syn,
That posownis the saule without and in;
And than is deid, and eik oppressit doun
Till wardly lust, and all our affectioun.
Thane perfyte wisdome weipis wondir soir,
Seand thus gait our appetyte misfair;
And to the hevin he passit up belyfe,
Schawand to us the Lyfe contemplatyfe,
The perfyte wit, and eik the fervent luve
We suld haif allway to the hevin abuve;   450
Bot seildin thair our appetyte is fundin,
It is so fast within the body bundin;
Thairfoir dounwart we cast our myndis E,
Blindit with lust, and may nocht upwartis fle;
Sould our desyre be socht up in the spheiris,
Quhen it is tedderit in thir warldly breiris,
Quhyle on the flesch, quhyle on this warldis wrak:
And to the hevin full small intent we tak.
Schir orpheus, thow seikis all in vane
Thy wyfe so he; Thairfoir cum doun agane,   460
And [pas] unto the monster mervellus,
With thre heidis, that we call cerberus,
Quhilk fenyeid is to haif so mony heidis,
For to be takin thre maner of deidis.

438 outthrow) out throu *CA*
441 The serpent stangis that is dedely syn *CA*
447 And passis up to the hevyn belyve *CA*
449 wit) will *A C*
451 fundin) found *A C*: bundin) bound *A C*
456 thir warldly breiris) this warldis breris *A C*
458 full small) small *A C*

The first is in the tendir yong bernage,
The secound deid is in the middill age,
The thrid is in greit eild quhen men ar tane.
Thus cerberus to swelly sparis nane,
Bot quhen our mynd is myngit with sapience,
and plais upoun the herp of eloquence;   470
That is to say, makis persuasioun
To draw our will and our affectioun,
In every eild, fra syn and fowll delyte,
The dog our sawll na power hes to byte.

The secound monstour[is] ar the sistiris thre,
Electo, migera, and thesaphany,
Ar nocht ellis, in bukis as we reid,
Bot wickit thocht, ill word, and thrawart deid.
Electo is the bolling of the harte,
Mygera the wickit word inwart,   480
Thesaphony is operatioun,
That makis fynall executioun
In deidly syn; and thir thre turnis ay
The ugly quheill, is nocht ellis to say,
Bot warldly men sumtyme ar cassin he
upone the quheill, in gret prosperitie,
and with a quhirle, onwarly, or thai wait,
ar thrawin doun to pure and law estait.
Off exione that on the quheill wes spreid,
I sall yow tell of sum pairte, as I haif red: 490
he was of lyfe brukle and lecherouss,
and in that craft hardy and curaguss,
That he wald luve in to no lawar place
Bot Juno, quene of nature and goddace.
And on a day he went up on the sky,
and socht Juno, thinkand with hir to ly:
Scho saw him cum and knew his foull intent.
a rany clud one fra the firmament
Scho gart discend, and kest betuix thame two;
and in that clud his nature yeid him fro,   500

469-70 Bot quhen that resoun and intelligence, Plais . . . etc. *AC*
480 inwart) outwert *AC*   485 Bot) That *AC*

off quhilk was generat the sentowriss,
half man, half horss, upoun a ferly wiss.
Thane for the inwart craving and offens
That Juno tuke for his grit violens,
Scho send him doun unto the sistiris thre,
Upone a quheill ay turnyt for to be.
Bot quhen ressoun and perfyte sapience
playis upone the herp of eloquens,
and persuadis our fleschly appetyte
To leif the thocht of this warldly delyte, 510
Than seissis of our hert the wicket will,
Fra frawart language than the tong is still,
Our synfull deidis fallis doun on sleip,
Thane exione out of the quheill gan creip;
That is to say, the grit solicitud,
Quhyle up, quhyle doun, to win this warldis gud,
seissis furthwith, and our affectioun
waxis quiet in contemplatioun.

THIS tantalus, of quhome I spak of aire,
quhill he levit he was a gay ostlaire, 520
and on a nycht come travilland thairby
The god of richess, and tuk harbery
with tantalus; and he till his supper
Slew his awin sone that was [him] leif and deir,
Syne in a sew, with spycis soddin weill,
he gart the god eit up his flesche ilk deill.
For this dispyt, quhen he wes deid annone,
Was dampnit in the flud of acherone,
Till suffer hungir, thrist, nakit and cawld,
Rycht wo begone, as I befoir haif tould. 530
This hungry man and thirsty, tantalus,
Betaknis men gredy and covetouss,
The god of riches that ar ay reddy
For to ressaif, and tak in harbery;

487 wait) witte *C*   491 of lyfe) on lyve *AC*   497 foull) full *AC*
507-8   Bot quhen that reson and intelligence,
        Playis apon the harp of conscience   *AC*
509 to 514 are missing in *AC*   517 affectioun) complexion *AC*
534 tak) call *AC*

K

And till him sieth his sone in pecis small,
That is the flesch and blud, with grit travell,
To full the bag, and nevir fund in thair hairt
Upoun thame self to spend, nor tak thair pairte.
Allace, in erd quhair is thair mair foly,
Than for to want, and haif haboundantly,   540
Till haif distress on bed, on bak and burd,
And spair till wyn [of] men of gold a hurd?
And in the nycht sleip soundly thay may nocht,
To gaddir geir so gredy is thair thocht.
Bot quhen [that] ressoun and intelligence
Smytis upoun the herp of conscience,
Schawand to ws quhat perrell on ilk syd
That thai incur quhay will trest or confyd
Into this warldis vane prosperitie,
quhilk hes thir sory properteis thre,   550
That is to say, gottin with grit Labour,
Keipit with dreid, and tynt with grit dolour.
This grit avariss, be grace quha undirstud,
I trow suld leif thair grit solicitude
off ythand thochtis and he besines
To gaddir gold, [and] syne leif in distres;
Bot he suld eit and drink quhen evir he list
off cuvatyse, to slaik the birnand thrist.
This titius lay nalit on the bent,
And [with] the grip his bowellis revin and rent,   560
Quhill he levit, he set al his * intentioun
To find the craft of divinatioun,
and lyrit it unto the spamen † all,
To tell befoir sic thingis as wald befall,
quhat lyfe, quhat deth, quhat destany and werd,
provydit ware unto every man on erd.

* MS. 'alhis.'   † MS. 'spyne.' See p. 266.

542 wyn [of]) othir *A C*.   546-550. These lines are omitted in *A C*.
546 Smytis) Playis *A C*: conscience) eloquence *A C*
555 And Ithand thouchtis, and thair besynes *A C*
557 eit and drink) drink ineuch *A C*

Appollo than for this abusioun,
Quhilk is the god of divinatioun,
for he usurpit of his facultie,
put him to hell, and thair remanis he.   570
Ilk man that heiris this conclusioun
Suld dreid to serss be constillatioun
Thingis to fall undir the firmament,
Till ye or na quhilk ar indefferent,
Without profixit causs and certane,
quhilk nane in erd may knaw bot god allane,
Quhen orpheus upoun his harp can play,
That is our undirstanding for to say,
Cryis, 'o man, recleme thi folich harte,
Will thow be god and tak on the his parte?   580
To tell thingis to cum that nevir wilbe,
Quhilk god hes kepit in his prevetie?
Thow ma no mair offend to god of micht,
Na with thi spaying reif fra him his richt;'
This perfyte wisdome with his melody
fleyis the spreit of fenyeid profecy,
and drawis upwart our affectioun.*
Fra wichcraft, spaying, and sorsery,
and superstitioun of astrology,
Saif allanerly sic maner of thingis   590
quhilk upoun trew and certane caussis hingis,
The quhilk mone cum to thair caus indure,
On verry forss, and nocht throw avanture,
As is the clippis and the conjunctioun
of sone and mone be calculatioun,
The quhilk ar fundin in trew astronomy,
Be moving of the speiris in the sky;
All thir to speik it may be tollerable,
And none udir quhilk no caussis stable.
This ugly way, this myrk and dully streit,   600
Is nocht ellis bot blinding of the spreit,

* A line appears to be omitted.

559 This titius) Thir Theseus *C*; This theseus *A*
564 tell) fele *A*   567 this) his *A C*   569 of) in *A C*
570 The following forty-five lines are omitted in *A C*

With myrk cluddis and myst of Ignorance,
affetterrit in this warldis vane plesance,
And bissines of temporalite ;
To kene the self a styme it may nocht se,
For stammeris * on eftir effectioun,
Fra Ill to war ale thus to hale gois doun,
That is wan howp throw lang hanting of syn,
and fowll dispair that mony fallis In.
Than orpheus our ressoun is full wo,   610
and twichis on his harp and biddis ho,
Till our desyre and fulich appetyte
Bidis leif this warldis full delyte.
Than pluto, god and quene of hellis fyre,
Mone grant to ressoun on forss the desyre.
Than orpheus hes wone euridices,
Quhen our desyre with ressoun makis pess,
And seikis up to contemplatioun,
of syn de[te]stand the abutioun.
Bot ilk man suld be wyse, and warly se   620
That he bakwart cast nocht his myndis E,
Gifand consent, and delectatioun,
off fleschly lust and for the affectioun ;
for thane gois bakwart to the sone agane
our appetyte, as it befoir was slane,
In warldly lust and vane prosperite,
and makis ressoun wedow for to be.

Now pray we god sen our affectioun
Is allway promp and reddy to fall doun,
That he wald undirput his haly hand   630
of mantenans, and gife us forss to stand
In perfyte luve, as he is glorius.
And thus endis the taill of orpheus.

                        Finis : quod $\overline{mr}$. R. H.

* MS. 'scammeris.'

616 Than) Bot *A C*   620 be wyse, and warly se) bewar, & wisely see *A C*
624 sone) syn *A C*   626 vane prosperite) sensualitee *A C*
630 undirput his) help us wyth *A C*   631 forss) grace *A C*

Robene and Makyne

BANNATYNE MS.

[Robene and Makyne]

1 ROBENE sat on gud grene hill,
   Kepand a flok of fe :
   mirry makyne said him till,
   'Robene, thow rew on me ;
   I haif the luvit lowd and still,
   Thir yeiris two or thre ;
   my dule in dern bot gif thow dill,
   Dowtless but dreid I de.'

2 Robene ansert, 'be the rude,
   nathing of lufe I knaw,   10
   Bot keipis my scheip undir yone wid,
   Lo quhair thay raik on raw :
   quhat hes marrit the in thy mude,
   makyne, to me thow schaw ;
   Or quhat is lufe, or to be lude ?
   Fane wald I leir that law.'

3 'At luvis lair gife thow will leir,
   Tak thair ane a b c :
   be heynd, courtass, and fair of feir,
   Wyse, hardy, and fre ;   20
   So that no denger do the deir,
   quhat dule in dern thow dre ;
   preiss the with pane at all poweir,
   be patient and previe.'

4 Robene anserit hir agane,
   'I wait not quhat is luve ;
   Bot I haif mervell incertane
   Quhat makis the this wanrufe :
   The weddir is fair, & I am fane,
   my scheip gois haill aboif ;   30
   And we wald play us in this plane,
   They wald us bayth reproif.'

151

5 'Robene, tak tent unto my taill,
  And wirk all as I reid,
And thow sall haif my hairt all haill,
  Eik and my madinheid.
Sen god sendis bute for baill,
  And for murning remeid,
I dern with the, bot gif I daill,
  Dowtles I am bot deid.'   40

6 'Makyne, to morne this ilk a tyde,
  And ye will meit me heir,
Peraventure my scheip ma gang besyd,
  quhill we haif liggit full neir;
Bot mawgre haif I and I byd,
  Fra thay begin to steir;
quhat lyis on hairt I will not hyd;
  Makyn, than mak gud cheir.'

7 'Robene, thow reivis me roif and rest;
  I luve bot the allone.'   50
'Makyne, adew, the sone gois west,
  The day is neir hand gone.'
'Robene, in dule I am so drest,
  That lufe wilbe my bone.'
'Ga lufe, makyne, quhair evir thow list,
  ffor lemman I [bid] * none.'

8 'Robene, I stand in sic a styll;
  I sicht, and that full sair.'
'Makyne, I haif bene heir this quhyle;
  at hame god gif I wair.'   60
'my huny, robene, talk ane quhill,
  gif thow will do na mair.'
'Makyne, sum uthir man begyle,
  ffor hamewart I will fair.'

* The MS. is corrupt here, the reading being 'lid ' or 'lue.'
(*See* note, p. 267.)

9 Robene on his wayis went,
als licht as leif of tre ;
mawkin murnit in hir intent,
and trowd him nevir to se.
Robene brayd attour the bent ;
Than mawkyne cryit on hie,   70
'Now ma thow sing, for I am schent !
quhat alis lufe at me ? '

10 Mawkyne went hame withowttin faill,
Full wery eftir cowth weip :
Than robene in a fulfair daill
Assemblit all his scheip.
Be that sum pairte of mawkynis aill
Outthrow his hairt cowd creip ;
he fallowit hir fast thair till assaill,
and till hir tuke gude keip.   80

11 'Abyd, abyd, thow fair makyne,
a word for ony thing ;
For all my luve it salbe thyne,
Withowttin depairting.
all haill, thy harte for till haif myne
Is all my cuvating ;
my scheip to morne quhill houris nyne
Will neid of no keping.'

12 'Robene, thow hes hard soung & say,
In gestis and storeis auld,   90
The man that will nocht quhen he may
sall haif nocht quhen he wald.
I pray to Jesu every day
mot eik thair Cairis cauld,
that first preiss with the to play,
be firth, forrest, or fawld.'

13 'Makyne, the nicht is soft and dry,
   The wedder is warme & fair,
   And the grene woid rycht neir us by
   To walk attour all quhair;   100
   Thair ma na Janglour us espy,
   That is to lufe contrair;
   Thairin, makyne, bath ye & I
   Unsene we ma repair.'

14 'Robene, that warld is all away
   and quyt brocht till ane end,
   and nevir agane thairto perfay
   Sall it be as thow wend;
   For of my pane thow maid it play,
   and all in vane I spend;   110
   as thow hes done, sa sall I say,
   murne on, I think to mend.'

15 'Mawkyne, the howp of all my heill,
   my hairt on the is sett,
   and evirmair to the be leill,
   quhill I may leif but lett;
   nevir to faill, as utheris feill,
   quhat grace that evir I gett.'
   'Robene, with the I will nocht deill;
   Adew, for thus we mett.'   120

16 Malkyne went hame blyth annewche,
   Attour the holttis hair;
   Robene murnit, and Malkyne lewche;
   Scho sang, He sichit sair;
   and so left him, bayth wo & wrewche,
   In dolour & in cair,
   Kepand his hird under a huche,
   amangis the holtis hair.

                    quod : $\overline{mr}$. robert Henrysone.

Sum Practysis of Medecyne

BANNATYNE MS.

Sum Practysis of Medecyne

1 GUK, guk, gud day, ser, gaip quhill ye get it,
Sic greting may gane weill gud laik in your hude
ye wald deir me, I trow, becauss I am dottit,
To ruffill me with a ryme; na, ser, be the rude,
your saying I haif sene, and on syd set it,
as geir of all gaddering, glaikit, nocht gude;
als your medicyne by mesour I haif meit met It,
The quhilk, I stand ford, ye nocht understude,
Bot wrett on as ye culd To gar folk wene;
For feir my lougis wes flaft, ⎫   10
or I wes dottit or daft,   ⎬   heir be it sene.
Gife I can ocht of the craft, ⎭

2 Becaus I ken your cunnyng in to cure
Is clowtit and clampit and nocht weill cleird,
My prettik in pottingary ye trow be als pure,
And lyk to your lawitnes, I schrew thame that leid;
Is nowdir fevir, nor fell, that our the feild fure,*
Seiknes nor sairnes, in tyme gif I seid,
Bot I can lib thame & leiche thame fra lame & lesure,   20
With salvis thame sound mak: on your saule beid,
That ye be sicker of this sedull I send yow,
With the suthfast seggis, ⎫
that glean all egeis,   ⎬   of malis to mend yow.
With dia and dreggis,   ⎭

---

* In the second half of this line, the MS. has, ' in tyme gif I seid' (deleted).

DIA CULCAKIT.

3 Cape cukmaid and crop the colleraige,
    ane medecyne for the maw, and ye cowth mak it,
    with sueit satlingis and sowrokis, The sop of the sege,
    The crud of my culome, with your teith crakit ;   30
    Lawrean and linget seid, and the luffage,
    The hair of the hurcheoun nocht half deill hakkit,
    With the snowt of ane selch, ane swelling to swage ;
    This cure is callit in our craft Diaculcakkit.
    Put all thir in ane pan, with pepper and pik,
    Syne sottin to thiss,   ⎫
    The count of ane sow kiss,   ⎬ For the collik.
    Is nocht bettir, I wiss,   ⎭

DIA LONGUM.

4 Recipe, thre ruggis of the reid ruke,   40
    The gant of ane gray meir, The claik of ane guss,
    The dram of ane drekterss, the douk of ane duke,
    The gaw of ane grene dow, The leg of ane lowss,
    fyve unce of ane fle wing, the fyn of ane fluke,
    With ane sleiffull of slak, that growis in the sluss ;
    myng all thir in ane mass with the mone cruke.
    This untment is rycht ganand for your awin uss,
    With reid nettill seid in strang wesche to steip,
    For to bath your ba cod,   ⎫
    quhen ye wald nop and nod ; ⎬ To latt yow to sleip. 50
    Is nocht bettir, be god,   ⎭

DIA GLACONICON.

5 This dia is rycht deir and denteit in daill,
  Causs it is trest & trew, thairfoir that ye tak
  sevin sobbis of ane selche, the quhidder of ane quhaill,
  The lug of ane lempet is nocht to forsaik,
  The harnis of ane haddok, hakkit or haill,
  With ane bustfull of blude of the scho bak,
  With ane brewing caldrun full of hait caill,
  For it wilbe the softar and sweittar of the smak;   60
  Thair is nocht sic ane lechecraft fra lawdian to lundin:
  It is clippit in our cannon, ⎫
  Dia glecolicon,   ⎬ quhair fulis ar fundin.
  For till fle awaye son,   ⎭

DIA CUSTRUM.

6 The ferd feisik is fyne, and of ane felloun pryce,
  Gud for haising, and hosting, or heit at the hairt;
  Recipe, thre sponfull of the blak spyce,
  With ane grit gowpene of the gowk fart;
  The lug of ane lyoun, the guse of ane gryce;   70
  ane unce of ane oster poik at the nether parte,
  annoyntit with nurice doung, for it is rycht nyce,
  Myngit with mysdirt and with mustart;
  Ye may clamp to this cure, & ye will mak cost,
  bayth the bellox of ane brok, ⎫
  With thre crawis of the cok ⎬ Is gud for the host.
  The schadow of ane yule stok, ⎭

7 Gud nycht, guk, guk, for sa I began,
  I haif no come at this tyme langer to tary,   80
  bot luk on this letter, and leird, gif ye can,
  The prectik and poyntis of this pottingary;
  Ser, minister this medecyne at evin to sum man,
  and or pryme be past, my powder I pary,
  Thay sall bliss yow, or ellis bittirly yow ban;
  For it sall fle thame, in faith, out of the fary:
  Bot luk quhen ye gadder thir gressis & gerss,
  outhir sawrand or sour,   ⎫
  That it be in ane gude oure: ⎬   Ane uthir manis erss.
  It is ane mirk mirrour,   ⎭   90

quod mr. ro^t henrysone.

Ane Prayer for the Pest

BANNATYNE MS.

Ane Prayer for the Pest

1 O ETERNE god, of power infinyt,
 To quhois hie knawledge na thing is of obscure
 That is, or was, or evir salbe, perfyt,
 in to thy sicht, quhill that this warld indure;
 Haif mercy of us, Indigent and peure;
 Thow dois na wrang to puneiss our offens:
 O Lord, that is to mankynd haill succure,
 Preserve us fra this perrelus pestilens.

2 We the beseik, o Lord of lordis all,
 thy eiris inclyne and heir our grit regrait;   10
 We ask remeid of the in generall,
 That is of help and comfort desolait;
 bot thow with rewth our hairtis recreat,
 We ar bot deid but only thy clemens:
 We the exhort, on kneis law prostrait,
 Preserf us fra this perrellus pestilens.

3 We ar richt glaid thow puneiss our trespass
 be ony kind of uthir tribulatioun,
 Wer it thy will, o lord of hevin, allaiss,
 that we sowld thus be haistely put doun,   20
 and dye as beistis without confessioun,
 That nane dar mak with uthir residence.
 O blissit Jesu, that woir the thorny croun,
 Preserve us frome this perrelus pestilens.

4 Use derth, o lord, or seiknes, and hungir soir,
 and slaik thy plaig that is so penetryve.
 Thy pepill ar perreist: quha ma remeid thairfoir,
 bot thow, o lord, That for thame Lost thy lyve?
 Suppoiss our syn be to the pungityve,
 Oure deid ma nathing our synnys recompens.   30
 Haif mercy, lord, we ma not with the stryve:
 preserve us etc.

2 *Bd* omits "hie": thing) think *Bd*   3 perfyt) is perfyt *Bd*
10 regrait) degrait *Bd*   27 perreist) preist *Bd*
163

5 Haif mercy, lord, haif mercy, hevynis king!
Haif mercy of thy pepill penetent;
Haif mercy of our petouss punissing;
retreit the sentence of thy Just Jugement
Aganis us synnaris, that servis to be schent:
Without mercy, we ma mak no defens.
Thow that, but rewth, upoun the rude was rent,
preserve us frome this perrellus pestilens.   40

6 Remmember, Lord, how deir thow hes us bocht,
That for us synnaris sched thy pretius blude,
Now to redeme that thow hes maid of nocht,
That is of vertew barrane and denude;
Haif rewth, Lord, of thyne awin symilitude;
Puneiss with pety and nocht with violens.
We knaw it is for our Ingratitude
That we ar puneist with this pestilens.

7 Thow grant us grace for till amend our miss,
And till evaid this crewall suddane deid;   50
We knaw our syn is all the cause of thiss,
for oppin syn thair is set no remeid.
The Justice of god mon puneiss than bot dreid,
for by the law he will with non dispens:
quhair Justice laikis thair is Eternall feid,
of god that sowld preserf fra pestilens.

8 Bot wald the heiddismen that sowld keip the law
Pueneiss the peple for thair transgressioun,
Thair wald na deid the peple than owrthraw:
bot thay ar gevin so planely till oppressioun,   60
That god will not heir thair intercessioun;
bot all ar puneist for thair Innobediens
be sword or deid withowttin remissioun,
And hes Just cause to send us pestilens.

53 bot dreid) be deid *Bd*
64 *Bd* has Finis here, after which the Supplication follows as in *B*
71 send grace) but grace *Bd*: and us Imbrace) for to arrace *Bd*

9 Superne/ Lucerne/ guberne/ this pestilens,
preserve/ and serve/ that we not sterve thairin.
Declyne/ that pyne/ be thy Devyne prudens.
O trewth/ haif rewth/ lat not our slewth us twin.
Our syt/ full tyt/ wer we contryt/ wald blin.
Dissiver/ did never/ quha evir the besocht.   70
Send grace/ with space/ and us Imbrace/ fra syn.
Latt nocht be tynt that thow so deir hes bocht.

10 O prince preclair/ this cair/ cotidiane,
We the exhort/ distort/ it in exyle.
Bot thow remeid/ this deid/ is bot ane trane,
for to dissaif/ the laif/ and thame begyle.
Bot thow sa wyiss/ devyiss to mend this byle
Of this mischief/ quha ma releif/ us ocht
for wrangus win/ bot thow our syn ourfyll?
Latt not be tynt etc.   80

11 Sen for our Vyce/ that Justyce/ mon correct,
O king most hie/ now pacifie/ thy feid :
Our syn is huge/ Refuge/ we not suspect ;
As thow art Juge/ deluge us of this dreid.
In tyme assent/ or We be schent with deid ;
We us repent/ and tyme mispent forthocht :
Thairfoir/ Evirmoir/ be gloir/ to thy godheid
Lat nocht be tynt that thow sa deir hes bocht.

ffinis. 'q. henrysone.' *

* Added in a later hand.

76 and thame begyle) falsly and begyle *Bd*   79 ourfyll) oursyle *Bd*
84 deluge) dislug *Bd* : dreid) steid *Bd*
86 and) all *Bd* : forthocht) for thocht *Bd*
    No ascription in *Bd*

The Garmont of Gud Ladeis

Bannatyne MS.

[The Garmont of Gud Ladeis]*

1　WALD my gud lady lufe me best,
　and wirk eftir my will,
　I suld ane garmond gudliest
　Gar mak hir body till.

2　Off he honour suld be hir hud,
　upoun hir heid to weir,
　garneist with governance so gud,
　na demyng suld hir deir.

3　Hir sark suld be hir body nixt,
　Of chestetie so quhyt,　　　　　　　　　　　10
　With schame and Dreid togidder mixt,
　The same suld be perfyt.

4　Hir kirtill suld be of clene constance,
　Lasit with lesum Lufe,
　The mailyeis of continwance
　for nevir to remufe.

5　Hir gown suld be of gudliness,
　Weill ribband with renowne,
　Purfillit with plesour in ilk place,
　furrit with fyne fassoun.　　　　　　　　　　20

6　Hir belt suld be of benignitie,
　Abowt hir middill meit ;
　Hir mantill of humilitie,
　To tholl bayth wind & weit.

7　Hir hat suld be of fair having,
　And hir tepat of trewth ;
　Hir patelet of gud pansing ;
　Hir hals ribbane of rewth.

8 Hir slevis suld be of esperance,
   To keip hir fra dispair ;   30
   hir gluvis of gud govirnance,
   to gyd hir fyngearis fair.

9 Hir schone suld be of sickernes,
   In syne that scho nocht slyd ;
   Hir hoiss of honestie, I ges,
   I suld for hir provyd.

10 Wald scho put on this garmond gay,
    I durst sweir by my seill,
    That scho woir nevir grene nor gray
    That set hir half so weill.   40

        ffinis of the garmont of
        gud ladeis.   [quod $\overline{mr}$ ro^t Henrysoun.*]

             * Added in another hand.

The Bludy Serk.

BANNATYNE MS.

The Bludy Serk *

1 THIS hindir † yeir I hard be tald
 Thair was a worthy king;
 Dukis, erlis, and barronis bald
 He had at his bidding.
 The lord was anceane and ald,
 And sexty yeiris cowth ring;
 he had a dochter fair to fald,
 a Lusty Lady ying.

2 Off all fairheid scho bur the flour,
 And eik hir faderis air,   10
 Off lusty laitis and he honour,
 Meik bot and debonair.
 Scho wynnit in a bigly bour;
 On fold wes none so fair;
 princis luvit hir paramour,
 In cuntreis our all quhair.

3 Thair dwelt alyt besyde the king
 A fowll gyane of ane;
 stollin he hes the lady ying,
 away with hir is gane,   20
 and kest hir in his dungering,
 Quhair licht scho micht se nane;
 hungir and cauld and grit thristing
 Scho fand in to hir wame. ‡

---

 * Title in the margin in a later hand, and above, in the same hand,
'Fable VII.'
 † G. G. S. reads 'hundir.' ‡ G. G. S. reads 'wane' (*see* note, p. 271).

4 He wes the laithliest on to luk
   that on the ground mycht gang;
   His nailis wes lyk ane hellis cruk,
   Thairwith fyve quarteris lang.
   Thair wes nane that he ourtuk,
   In rycht or yit in wrang,   30
   Bot all in schondir he thame schuke—
   The gyane wes so strang.

5 He held the lady day and nycht
   Within his deip dungeoun;
   he wald nocht gif of hir a sicht,
   for gold nor yit ransoun,
   Bot gife the king mycht get a knycht,
   To fecht with his persoun—
   To fecht with him both day and nycht,
   Quhill ane wer dungin doun.   40

6 The king gart seik baith fer and neir,
   beth be se and land,
   off ony knycht gife he micht heir
   wald fecht with that gyand.
   a worthy prince that had no peir
   hes tane the deid on hand,
   For the luve of the Lady cleir,
   and held full trew cunnand.

7 That prince come prowdly to the toun
   of that gyane to heir,   50
   and fawcht with him his awin persoun,
   and tuke him presoneir;
   And kest him In his awin dungeoun,
   allane withouttin feir,
   With hungir, cauld, and confusioun,
   As full weill worthy weir.

8 Syne brak the bour, had hame the bricht,
  Unto hir fadir deir;
  Sa evill wondit was the knycht
  That he behuvit to de.   60
  Unlusum was his likame dicht,
  His sark was all bludy;
  In all the warld was thair a wicht
  So peteouss for to sy?

9 The lady murnyt and maid grit mone,
  With all hir mekle micht:
  'I luvit nevir lufe bot one,
  that dulfully now is dicht.
  God sen my lyfe were fra me tone,
  or I had sene yone sicht,   70
  or ellis in begging evir to gone
  furth with yone curtass knycht.'

10 he said, 'fair lady, now mone I
  De, trestly ye me trow;
  Tak ye my sark that is bludy,
  and hing It forrow yow;
  first think on it, and syne on me,
  quhen men cumis yow to wow.'
  The lady said, 'be mary fre,
  Thairto I mak a wow.'   80

11 Quhen that scho lukit to the serk,
  Scho thocht on the persoun,
  and prayit for him with all hir harte,
  That Lowsd hir of bandoun,
  quhair scho was wont to sit full merk
  In that deip dungeoun;
  and evir quhill scho wes in quert,
  That wass hir a lessoun.

12 Sa weill the lady luvit the knycht,
  that no man wald scho tak.
  Sa suld we do our god of micht,   90
  That did all for us mak ;
  quhilk fullely to deid wes dicht
  for sinfull manis saik ;
  Sa suld we do both day and nycht,
  With prayaris to him mak.

MORALITAS

13 This king is lyk the trinitie,
  Baith in hevin and heir ;
  The manis saule to the Lady ;
  The gyane to Lucefeir ;   100
  The knycht to chryst, that deit on tre,
  And coft our synnis deir ;
  The * pit to hell, with panis fell ;
  The syn to the woweir.

14 The lady was wowd, bot scho said nay,
  With men that wald hir wed ;
  Sa suld we wryth all syn away,
  That in our breistis bred.
  I pray to Jesu chryst verrey,
  For us his blud that bled,   110
  To be our help on domysday,
  quhair lawis are straitly led.

15 The saule is godis dochtir deir,
  And eik his handewerk,
  That was betrasit with lucifeir,
  quha sittis in hell full merk.
  Borrowit with chrystis angell cleir,
  hend men, will ye nocht herk ?
  ffor his lufe that bocht us deir,   120
  Think on the bludy serk.

    ffinis quod m̄r
    R. Henrici.

   * 'gyane' deleted.

The Ressoning betuix Aige and Yowth

BANNATYNE MS.

The Ressoning betuix Aige and Yowth

Yowth.

1 Quhen fair flora, the godes of the flowris,
  Baith firth and feildis freschely had ourfret,
  And perly droppis of the balmy schowris
  Thir widdis grene had with thair water wet,
  Movand allone In mornyng myld I met
  A mirry man, that all of mirth cowth mene,
  Singand the sang that richt sweitly was sett :
  'O yowth, be glaid in to thy flowris grene.'

Aige.

2 I lukit furth a litill me befoir,
  And saw a cative on ane club cumand,   10
  With cheikis clene and lyart lokis hoir ;
  His ene was how, his voce was hess hostand,
  Wallowit richt wan, and waik as ony wand ,
  Ane bill he beure upoun his breist abone,
  In Letteris Leill but lyis, with this legand,
  'O yowth, thy flowris fedis fellone sone.'

Yowth.

3 This yungman lap upoun the land full licht,
  And mervellit mekle of his makdome maid ;
  'Waddin I am,' quod he, 'and woundir wicht,
  with bran as bair, and breist burly and braid ;   20
  na growme on ground my gairdone may degraid,
  nor of my pith may pair of wirth a prene ;
  My face is fair, my fegour will not faid :
  O yowith, be glaid in to thy flowris grene.'

5 Movand) musand *M*   7 richt sweitly) suttellie *MF*
11 clene) leyn *MF M Bd*   13 richt) and *MF M Bd* : ony) ane *M*
16 fellone) ferly *M MF*   18 makdome) misdum *M*
22 a prene) half a prene *M MF*
179

AIGE.

4 This senyeour sang bot with a sobir stevin;
  schakand his berd, he said, 'my bairne, lat be;
  I was within thir sextie yeiris and sevin
  Ane freik on fold, als forss and als fre,
  als glaid, als gay, als ying, als yaip as yie;
  Bot now tha dayis ourdrevin ar & done;   30
  Luke thow my laikly luking gif I lie:
  O yowth, thy flowris fadis fellone sone.'

YOWTH.

5 Ane uthir verss yit this yungman cowth sing:
  'At luvis law a quhyle I think to leit,
  In court to cramp clenely in my clething,
  And luke amangis thir lusty ladeis sweit;
  of mariage to mell with mowthis meit,
  In secreit place, quhair we ma not be sene,
  And so with birdis blythly my bailis beit:
  O yowth,' &c.   40

AIGE.

6 This awstrene greif anssuerit angirly:
  'for thy cramping thow salt baith cruke & cowre;
  Thy fleschely lust thow salt also defy,
  and pane the sall put fra paramour;
  Than will no bird be blyth of the in bouir;
  quhen thy manheid sall wendin as the mone,
  Thow sall assay gif that my song be sour:
  O yowth, thy flowris fedis fellone sone.'

28-29 Ane freik on fold, bayth frak, forty, and fre,
        Als glaid, als gay, als ȝoung, als ȝaip as ȝe ; *MF*
31 laikly luking) laythly *M MF*; lycome *M*; lykyme *Bd*
32 fellone) ferly *M MF*
37 mowthis meit) mowis met *M*
38 secreit place) sacreit wyse *MF*; secreitnes *Bd*
41 This ancient man gaif ansuer angrielie *MF*
44 Quhen pane sall the depryve for paramour *MF*
46 wendin) mynnis *MF*; move *Bd*

YOWITH.

7 This mirry man of mirth yit movit moir :
  'My corps is clene withowt corruptioun,   50
  My self is sound, but seiknes or but soir,
  My wittis fyve in dew proportioun,
  My Curage is of clene complexioun,
  My hairt is haill, my levar, & my splene ;
  Thairfoir to reid this roll I haif no ressoun :
  O yowth,' &c.

AIGE.

8 The bevar hoir said to this berly berne :
  'This breif thow sall obey, sone be thow bald ;
  Thy stait, thy strenth, Thocht it be stark and sterne,
  The feveris fell & eild sall gar the fald ;   60
  Thy corps sall clyng, thy curage sall wax cald,
  Thy helth sall hynk, and tak a hurt but hone,
  Thy wittis fyve sall vaneis, Thocht thow not wald :
  O yowth, thy flowris,' &c.

9 This go[w]*and grathit with [sic] † grit greif,
  he on his wayis wrethly went but wene ;
  This lene awld man luche Not, bot tuk his leif,
  And I abaid undir the levis grene :
  Of the sedullis the suthe quhen I had sene,
  Of trewth, me thocht, thay triumphit in thair tone : 70
  'O yowth, be glaid in to thy flowris grene !
  O yowth thy flowris faidis fellone sone !'

ffinis : quod m̄r Robert hendersone.

* 'w' deleted in the MS.   † inserted above the line.

51 My self is sauf fra seiknes and fra sair *MF*
52 in dew) ar dowbill in *MF*   53 is omitted in *MF*   58 obey) abyd *MF*
59 it) Johne *MF*   60 &) for *MF*   63 vaneis) wane *MF*
65 gowand) galʒart *MF* : with sic grit greif) and began to greif *MF*
66 And on full sone he went his wayis but wein *MF*
69 That takkin suthlie, fra that I had sein *MF*
70 triumphit) tremefit *Bd* ; trevist *MF*

The Prais of Aige

CHEPMAN & MYLLAR
EDINBURGH, 1508

[The Prais of Aige] *

1 WYTHIN a garth, under a rede rosere,
　　Ane ald man, and decrepit, herd I syng;
　　Gay was the note, suete was the voce et clere:
　　It was grete joy to here of sik a thing.
　　'And to my dome,' he said, in his dytyng,
　　'For to be † yong I wald not, for my wis
　　Off all this warld to mak me lord et king:
　　The more of age the nerar hevynnis blis.

2 'False is this warld, and full of variance,
　　Besoucht with syn and other sytis mo;　　　　　　10
　　Treuth is all tynt, gyle has the gouvernance,
　　Wrechitnes has wroht all welthis wele to wo;
　　Fredome is tynt, and flemyt the lordis fro,
　　And covatise is all the cause of this;
　　I am content that youthede is ago:
　　The more of age the nerar hevynnis blisse.

3 'The state of youth I repute for na gude,
　　For in that state sik perilis now I see;
　　Bot full smal grace, the regeing of his blude
　　Can none gaynstand quhill that he agit be;　　　20
　　Syne of the thing that tofore joyit he
　　Nothing remaynis ‡ for to be § callit his;
　　For quhy it were bot veray vanitee:
　　The more of age the nerar hevynnis blisse.

---

* The poem is untitled in C. & M. and bears no ascription.
† *Orig.* has 'tobe.'　　‡ *Orig.* reads 'remayms.'　　§ *Orig.* 'tobe'

---

1 Wythin) In tyl *M*　　　10 Oursel with syt and other synnyss mo *M*
11 is all tynt) is tynt *M*
12 and wrachitness his turnyt all fra weil to vo ; *M*
　　Wrechitnes hes wrocht all weill to wo *B*
13 flemyt) fremmit *Bd*　　18 sik) grit *M*　　19 full smal) speciall *Bd*
19-20 can nane gane stand the ragyne of his blud,
　　　　na ʒit be stabil one til he agit be ; *M*　　23 were) wes, *all other texts*
185

4 'Suld no man traist this wrechit warld, for quhy
Of erdly joy ay sorow is the end ;
The state of it can noman certify,
This day a king, to morne na gude to spend.
Quhat have we here bot grace us to defend?
The quhilk god grant us for to mend oure mys,   30
That to his glore he may oure saulis send ;
The more of age the nerar hevynnis blisse.'

[ffinis : quod hendersone] *

* from *B*.

27 state) gloyr *M*   31 glore) joy *M*

The Want of Wyse Men

CHEPMAN & MYLLAR, AND
BANNATYNE MS.

The Want of Wyse Men

1 Me ferlyis of this grete confusioun;
I wald sum clerk of connyng walde declerde,
Quhat gerris this warld be turnyt up so doun.
Thare is na faithfull fastnes founde in erd;
Now ar noucht thre may traistly trow the ferde;
Welth is away, and wit is worthin wrynkis;
Now sele is sorow this is a wofull werde,
Sen want of wyse men makis fulis to sit on binkis.

2 That tyme quhen levit the * king Saturnus,
For gudely gouvernance this warld was goldin cald;   10
For untreuth we wate noucht quhare to it turnis;
The tyme that Octauiane, the monarch, coud hald,
Our all was pes, wele set as hertis wald:
Than regnyt reule, & resone held his rynkis;
Now lakkis prudence, nobilitee is thralde,
Sen want of wyse men makis fulis to sitt on bynkis.

3 Arestotill for his moralitee,
Austyn,† or ambrose, for dyvine scripture,
Quha can placebo, & noucht half dirige,
That practik for to pike & pill the pure,   20
He sall cum in, and thay stand at the dure;
For warldly wyn sik walkis, quhen wysar wynkis;
Wit takis na worschip, sik is the aventure,
Sen want of wysemen makis fulis to sit on binkis.

* *Orig.* 'quhen the lovit.'   † *Orig.* Anstyn.

1 ferlyis) mervellis *B*   2 sum clerk of connyng) sum cunnand clerk of clergy *B*
3 up so doun) upsyd doun *B*
6 wit is worthin wrynkis) wit is now wrochtin to wrinkis *B*
7 Now sele is sorow) No seill is sover now *B*   8 makis) garris *B*
9 That tyme) As bukis beiris witnes *B*
11 Nou ellis we wat, forsuth, quhithir it turnis *B*
12 The tyme that) The quhilk *B*; the monarch) the man riche *B*
13 hertis) menis hairtis *B*   14 reule) gud rewll *B*
15 prudence, nobilitee is) nobilite, prudens now is *B*
17 for his) for all his grit *B*   18 for dyvine) for all thair devyne *B*
19 noucht half dirige) nocht to haif derige *B*   20 pill) peill full bair *B*
21 in, and thay) in sone, quhen that thay *B*
22 wyn) wonyng *B*   23 sik is) sa is now *B*
189

4 Now, but defense, rycht lyis all desolate,
   Rycht, na resone under na rufe has rest;
   youth his but raddour, & age is obystynate,
   Mycht but mercy, the pore ar all opprest.
   Lerit folk suld tech the peple of the best,
   Thouch lare be lytil, fer lesse in tham sinkis: 30
   It may noucht be this warld ay thus suld lest,
   That want of wyse men makis fulis sitt on binkis.

5 For now is exilde all ald noble corage,
   Lautee, lufe, and liberalitee;
   Now is stabilitee fundyn in na stage,
   Nor degest connsele wyth sad maturitee;
   Peas is away, all in perplexitee;
   Prudence and policy ar banyst our al brinkis:
   This warld is ver, sa may it callit be,
   That want of wisemen makis fulis sitt on bynkis.   40

6 Quhare is the balance of just & equitee?
   Nothir meryt is preisit, na punyst is trespas;
   All ledis lyvis lawles at libertee,
   Noucht reulit be reson, mare than ox or asse;
   Gude faith is flemyt, worthin fraellar than glas;
   Trew lufe is lorne, & lautee haldis no lynkis;
   Sik gouvernance I call noucht worth a fasse,
   Sen want of wise men makis fulis sitt on binkis.

25 This stanza and the following are interchanged in *B*
   Now) Weir *B*
26 na) and *B*   28 pore) pure folkis *B*   30 fer lesse) 3it ferles *B*
33 For now is exilde all ald) Lord, quhiddir ar exylit all *B*
34 and) with kyndnes and *B*
35 No thing is fundin now stable in no stagis *B*
36 wyth sad maturitee) availis with moralite *B*
37 all in perplexitee) flemit is all proplexite *B*
38 and policy) and wisdome *B*
39 The worldis war may seyme weill callit to be *B*
41 balance of just & equitee?) balme of Justice, evin equite *B*
42 preisit) present *B*   43 ledis) leidis now *B*

7 now wrang hes warrane, and law is bot wilfulness;
  quha hes the war Is worthin on him all the wyte,   50
  For trewth is tressoun, and faith is fals fekilness;
  Gylle is now gyd, and vane lust is also delyte;
  Kirk is contempnit, thay compt nocht cursing a myte;
  Grit god is grevit, That me rycht soir forthinkis:
  The causs of this ony man may sone wit,
  That want of wysmen garis fulis sit on binkis.

8 Lue hes tane leif, and wirschip hes no vdir wane;
  with passing poverty pryd is Importable;
  Vyce is bot vertew, wit is with will soir ourgane;
  as lairdis so laddis, daly chengeable;   60
  but ryme or ressone all Is bot heble hable;
  Sic sturtfull stering in to godis neiss it stinkis;
  Bot he haif rew, all is unremedable,
  For want of, &c.

9 O lord of lordis, god & gouvernour,
  Makar & movar, bath of mare & lesse,
  Quhais power, wisedome, & honoure,
  Is infynite, salbe, & ewir wes,*
  As in the principall mencioun of the messe,
  All thir sayd thingis reforme as thou best thinkis;   70
  Quhilk ar degradit, for pure pitee redresse,
  Sen want of wise [men] makis [fulis] sit in binkis.

Finis.

   * *Orig.* 'ewir was wes.'

44 ox or asse) one ass *B*   45 fraellar) frewollar *B*
47 our governante nocht keipis gud rewll nor compass *B*
49 These two stanzas following appear only in *B*
67 & honoure) gudnes, and he honour *B*
69 as thy evangell planely dois express *B*
70 thingis) faltis *B*
71 Quhilk ar degradit) as it is deformit *B*
72 That without fulis may wysemen sit on binkis *B*

The Abbay Walk

BANNATYNE MS.

The Abbay Walk

1 ALLONE as I went up and doun
  in ane abbay was fair to se,
  Thinkand quhat consolatioun
  Was best in to adversitie,
  On caiss I kest on syd myne E,
  And saw this writtin upoun a wall:
  'off quhat estait, man, that thow be,
  Obey and thank thy god of all.

2 'Thy kindome and thy grit empyre,
  Thy ryaltie, nor riche array,   10
  Sall nocht endeur at thy desyre,
  Bot as the wind will wend away ;
  Thy gold and all thy gudis gay,
  quhen fortoun list will fra the fall ;
  Sen thow sic sampillis seis ilk day,
  Obey and thank thy god of all.

3 'Job wes maist riche in writ we find,
  Thobe maist full of cheritie :
  Job woux pure, and thobe blynd,
  Bath tempit with adversitie.   20
  Sen blindness wes infirmitie,
  and poverty wes naturall,
  Thairfoir rycht patiently bath he and he
  Obeyid and thankit god of all.

4 'Thocht thow be blind, or haif ane halt,
  Or in thy face deformit ill,
  Sa it cum nocht throw thy defalt,
  Na man suld the repreif by skill.
  Blame nocht thy Lord, sa is his will ;
  Spurn nocht thy fute aganis the wall ;   30
  Bot with meik hairt and prayer still
  obey, &c.

6 saw) fand *MF*   10 Thy) In *Bd*
15 Sen þir but dout þou man assay *MF*   17 In writ) I wait *MF*
25 For thocht þow be hurt or halt *MF*   29 thy Lord) þi god *MF*

5 'God of his justice mon correct,
　　and of his mercy petie haif;
　　he is ane Juge to nane suspect,
　　To puneiss synfull man and saif.
　　Thocht thow be lord attour the laif,
　　and eftirwart maid bound and thrall,
　　ane pure begger, with skrip and staif,
　　obey, &c.　　　　　　　　　　　　　　40

6 'This changeing and grit variance
　　off erdly staitis up and doun
　　Is nocht bot causualitie and chance,
　　as sum men sayis, without ressoun,
　　Bot be the grit provisioun
　　of god aboif that rewll the sall;
　　Thairfoir evir thow mak the boun
　　To obey, &c.

7 'In welth be meik, heich nocht thy self;
　　be glaid in wilfull povertie;　　　　　50
　　Thy power and thy warldis pelf
　　Is nocht bot verry vanitie.
　　Remember him that deit on tre,
　　For thy saik taistit the bittir gall;
　　quha heis law hairtis and lawis he;
　　obey and thank thy god of all.'

Finis: quod mr ro^t henrysone.

---

39 ane) Or *MF*　　43 Cowmis nowdir throw fortoun nor chance *MF*
46 rewll) gyd *MF*　　47 Thairfoir quhone evir 3e till him bown *MF*
50 wilfull) wofull *MF*　　　　　54 taistit the) gustit *MF*
55 Quhilk rasis þe law and humilis þe hie *MF*

The Annunciation

GRAY MS.

The Annunciation

1 FORCY as deith Is likand lufe,
   Throuch quhome al bittir suet is,*
   No thing Is hard, as writ can pruf,
   Till him in lufe that letis ;
   Luf us fra barret betis ;
   Quhen fra the hevinly sete abufe,
   In message gabriell couth muf,
   And with myld mary metis,
   And said, 'god wele the gretis ;
   In the he will tak Rest and Rufe,   10
   but hurt of syne, or yit Reprufe :
   In him sett thi decretis.'

2 This message mervale gert that myld,
   And silence held but soundis,
   As weill aferit, a maid Infild :
   the Angell It expoundis,
   how that hir Wame but woundis
   Consave It suld, fra syne exild.
   And quhen this carpin wes compilit
   Brichtnes fra bufe aboundis :   20
   thane fell that gay to groundis,
   of goddis grace na thing begild,
   wox in hir chaumer chaist with child,
   with crist our kyng that cround is.†

---

  * MS. 'suetis.'   † MS. 'croundis.'

3 Thir tithingis tauld, the messinger
Till hevin agane he glidis :
That princes pure, withoutyn peir,
Full plesandly applidis,
And blith with barne abidis.
O worthy wirschip singuler,   30
To be moder and madyn meir,
As cristin faith confidis ;
that borne was of hir sidis,
our maker goddis sone so deir,
quhilk erd, wattir, & hevinnis cler,
throw grace and virtu gidis.

4 The miraclis ar mekle & meit,
fra luffis Ryver Rynnis ;
The low of luf haldand the hete
unbrynt full blithlie birnis ;   40
quhen gabriell beginnis
With mouth that gudely may to grete,
The wand of aarone, dry but wete,
To burioun nocht blynnis ;
The flesch all donk within Is,
upone the erd na drop couth fleit ;
Sa was that may maid moder suete,
And sakeless of all synnis.

5 Hir mervalus haill madinhede
god in hir bosum bracis,   50
And hir divinite fra dreid *
Hir kepit in all casis.
The hie god of his gracis
Him self dispisit us to speid,
and dowtit nocht to dee one deid :
He panit for our peacis,
And with his blude us bacis ;
Bot quhen he Ras up, as we Rede,
the cherite of his godhede
Was plane in every placis.   60

* G. G. S. reads 'deid.'

6 O lady lele and lusumest,
  Thy face moist fair & schene Is !
  O blosum blithe and bowsumest,
  Fra carnale cryme that clene Is !
  This prayer fra my splene Is,
  That all my werkis wikkitest
  Thow put away, and mak me chaist
  Fra termigant that teyn Is,
  And fra his cluke that kene Is ;
  And syne till hevin my saule thou haist,   70
  Quhar thi makar of michtis mast
  Is kyng, and thow thair quene Is.

                          quod R. Henrisoun.

The Thre Deid Pollis

BANNATYNE MS.

The Thre Deid Pollis

1 O sinfull man, in to this mortall se
   quhilk is the vaill of murnyng and of Cair,
   With gaistly sicht, Behold oure heidis thre,
   Oure holkit ene, oure peilit pollis bair:
   As ye ar now, Into this warld we wair,
   Als fresche, als fair, als lusty, to behald;
   Quhan thow lukis on this suth examplair
   Off thy self, man, thow may be richt unbald.

2 For suth it is, that every man mortall
   Mon suffer deid, and de, that lyfe hes tane;   10
   Na erdly stait aganis deid ma prevaill;
   The hour of deth and place Is uncertane,
   Quhilk Is referrit to the hie god allane;
   Heirfoir haif mynd of deth, that thow mon dy; *
   This fair exampill to se quotidiane,
   Sowld causs all men fra wicket vycis fle.

3 O wantone yowth, als fresche as lusty may,
   farest of flowris, renewit quhyt & reid,
   Behald our heidis : O lusty gallandis gay,
   full laichly thus sall ly thy lusty heid,   20
   holkit and how, and wallowit as the weid,
   Thy crampand hair, & elk thy cristall ene;
   full cairfully conclud sall dulefull deid;
   Thy example heir be us it may be sene.

* This line is repeated in the MS.

2 the vaill of) þe well and of *MF*   9 For suth) Off treuthe *MF*
10 suffer deid) thole þe dethe *MF*   15 fair) sair *MF*
20 laichly) laithly *MF*   22 cristall) lustie *MF*

4 O ladeis quhyt, in claithis corruscant,
   poleist with perle, and mony pretius stane ;
   With palpis quhyt, and hals [so] elegant,
   Sirculit with gold, & sapheris mony ane ;
   Your finyearis small, quhyt as quhailis bane,
   arrayit with ringis, and mony rubeis reid :   30
   as we ly thus, so sall ye ly ilk ane,
   with peilit pollis, and holkit thus your heid.

5 O wofull pryd, the rute of all distres,
   With humill hairt upoun our pollis penss :
   man, for thy miss, ask mercy with meikness ;
   Aganis deid na man may mak defenss.
   the empriour, for all his excellenss,
   King & quene, & eik all erdly stait,
   peure & riche, sal be but differenss,
   Turnit in ass, and thus in erd translait.   40

6 This questioun, quha can obsolve, lat see,
   quhat phisnamour, or pcrfyt palmester—
   quha was farest, or fowlest, of us thre ?
   or quhilk of us of kin was gentillar ?
   or maist excellent in science, or in lare,
   in art, musik, or in astronomye ?
   heir sowld be your study and repair,
   and think, as thus, all your heidis mon be.

7 O febill aige, [ay] drawand neir the dait
   of dully deid, and hes thy dayis compleit,   50
   Behald our heidis with murning & regrait ;
   fall on thy kneis ; ask grace at god greit,
   with oritionis, and haly salmes sweit,
   Beseikand him on the to haif mercy,
   Now of our sawlis bydand the decreit
   of his godheid, quhen he sall call & cry.

---

33 wofull) wilfull *MF*   38 erdly) uþer *MF*
45 excellent) expert *MF*   47 sowld be) still sould be *MF*
48 And think rycht sure, as þus all heidis man ly *MF*
51 with) for *MF*   52 god greit) god, and greit *MF*
56 quhen he sall call & cry) to rew and glorifie *MF*

8 Als we exhort, that every man mortall,
　for his saik that maid of nocht all thing,
　for our sawlis to pray in general
　To Iesus chryst, of hevin and erd the king;　　60
　that throwch his blude we may ay leif & ring
　With the hie fader, be eternitie,
　The sone alswa, The haly gaist conding,
　Thre knit in ane be perfyt unitie.

Finis: quod patrik Johnistoun.

59 for our sawlis to) For mercy cry, and *MF*
61 Throw ȝour prayar that we and ȝe may Regnne *MF*
64 In *B* follows, 'ffinis: quod patrik Johnistoun.' In *MF*, the ascription reads, 'Quod Mr Robert Henrysoun.'

The Ressoning betuix Deth and Man

BANNATYNE MS.

O

The Ressoning betuix Deth and Man

DETH.

1 'O mortall man, behold, tak tent to me,
  Quhilk sowld thy mirrour be baith day & nicht;
  all erdly thing that evir tuik lyfe mon die:
  Paip, empriour, king, barroun, & knycht,
  Thocht thay be in thair roall stait and hicht,
  may not ganestand, quhen I pleiss schute the derte;
  waltownis, Castellis, and towris nevir so wicht,
  may nocht risist quhill it be at his herte.'

THE MAN.

2 'Now quhat art thow That biddis me thus tak tent,
  And mak ane mirrour day & nicht of the?   10
  Or with thy Dert I sowld richt soir repent?
  I trest trewly off that thow sall sone lie.
  Quhat freik on fold sa bald dar maniss me,
  Or with me fecht, owthir on fute or horss?
  Is non so wicht, or stark in this cuntre,
  Bot I sall gar him bow to me on forss.'

DETH.

3 'My name, forswth, sen that thou speiris,
  Thay call me deid, Suthly I the declair,
  Calland all man and woman to thair beiris,
  Quhen evir I pleiss, quhat tyme,* quhat place, or   20
    quhair:
  Is nane sa stowt, Sa fresche, Nor yit sa fair,
  Sa yung, Sa ald, Sa riche, nor yit sa peur,
  Quhair evir I pass, Owthir lait or air,
  mon put thame haill on forss undir my cure.'

  * Written on the margin of the MS.

12 sone lie) le *Bd*

MAN.

4 'Sen it is so, That nature can so wirk,
  That yung and awld, with riche & peure, mon die,
  In my yowtheid, allace, I wes full Irk,
  Cowld not tak tent To gyd and governe me,
  Ay gude to do, ffra evill deidis to fle,
  Trestand ay yowtheid wold with me abyde,   30
  fulfilland evir my sensualitie
  In deidly syn, and specialy in pryd.'

DETH.

5 'Thairfoir repent and remord thy conscience;
  Think on thir wordis I now upoun the cry:
  O wrechit man, O full of Ignorance,
  All thy plesance thow sall richt deir aby;
  Dispone thy self and cum with me in hy,
  Edderis, askis, and wormis meit for to be;
  Cum quhen I call, thow ma me not denny,
  Thocht thow war paip, Empriour, and king all thre.'   40

MAN.

6 'Sen it is swa ffra the I may not chaip,
  This wrechit warld for me heir I defy,
  And to the deid, To lurk under thy Caip,
  I offer me with hairt richt humly;
  Beseiking god, The divill, myne Ennemy,
  No power haif my sawill till assay.
  Jesus, on the, with peteous voce, I cry,
  Mercy on me to haif on domisday.'

                              ffinis : quod hendersone.

35 O full of) o wofull of *Bd*
37 Dispone for þe and cum with me and try *Bd*
38 for to be) to be *Bd*

Aganis Haisty Credence of Titlaris

Bannatyne MS.

Aganis Haisty Credence of Titlaris

1 FFALS titlaris now growis up full rank,
  nocht ympit in the stok of cheretie,
  howping at thair lord to gett grit thank;
  Than haif no dreid on thair nybouris to lie
  Than sowld ane lord awyse him weill, I se,
  Quhen ony taill Is brocht to his presence,
  Gif it be groundit in to Veretie,
  or he thairto gif haistely creddence.

2 Ane worthy lord sowld wey ane taill wyslie,
  the tailltellar, and quhome of it is tald;   10
  gif it be said for luve, or for Invy,
  and gif the tailisman abyd at It he wald;
  Than eftirwart the pairteis sowld be cald
  for thair excuse To mak lawfull defence:
  Than sowld ane Lord the ballance evinly hald,
  and gif not at the first haistie creddence.

3 It is no wirschep for ane nobill Lord,
  for the fals tailis To put ane trew man doun,
  And gevand creddence to the first recoird,
  he will not heir his excusatioun;   20
  The tittillaris so in his heir can roun,
  The Innocent may get no awdience;
  Ryme as it may, thair is na ressoun
  To gif till taillis hestely creddence.

4 Thir teltellaris oft tymes dois grit skaith,
    and raissis mortall feid and discrepance,
    and makis Lordis with thair serwandis wreith,
    and baneist be withowt[in] cryme perchance.
    It is the grund of stryf and all distance,
    moir perrellus than ony pestillence,   30
    Ane lord in flatterreris to haif plesance,
    Or to gif lyaris hestely creddence.

5 O thow wyse Lord, quhen cumis a flatterrer
    The for to pleiss, and hurt the Innocent,
    will tell ane taill of thy familiar,
    Thow sowld the pairteis call Incontinent,
    And sitt doun sadly in to Jugement,
    and serche the causs weill, or thow gif sentence,
    or ellis heireftir, in cais thow may repent,
    That thow to tailis gaif so grit creddence.   40

6 O wicket tung, sawand dissentioun,
    of fals taillis to tell That will not tyre,
    Moir perrellus Than ony fell pusoun,
    The pane of hell thow sall haif to thi hyre.
    Richt swa thay sall that hes Joy or desyre
    To gife his Eir To heird with patience ;
    for of discord It kendillis mony fyre,
    Throwcht geving talis hestely creddence,

7 Bakbyttaris to heir it is no bowrd,
    For thay ar excommunicat in all place ;   50
    Thre personis severall he slayis with ane wowrd—
    him self, The heirar, and the man saiklace.
    Within ane hude he hes ane dowbill face,
    Ane bludy tung, undir a fair pretence.
    I say no moir ; bot god grant Lordis grace,
    To gife to taillis nocht hestely creddence.

ffinis : quod m̄r Robert Hendersone.

27 with thair serwandis wreith) with freyndes and nychtbours wraithe *MF*
28 baneist) troublit *MF*   45 that hes Joy or desyre) with mynd þat dois *MF*
49 To heir bakbyttaris, traist weill, it is na bourd *MF*
50 excommunicat) planlie curst *MF*   54 pretence) presance *MF*

APPENDIX

The Morall Fabillis: Thomas Bassandyne, Edinburgh, 1571. Small 8vo.

Collation: A-G⁸ H⁴ ; 60 leaves.

Contents: A1a title ; A1b *The Taillis contenit in this present Buke;* A2a-H3b (pp. 3-118) text ; H4 blank.

This little book is a curiosity in more senses than one. Another example of the art of Thomas Bassandyne would have been interesting in any case, but this edition has the distinction of being almost entirely printed in the cursive 'lettres de civilité.' Some time after my discovery of the edition, I saw a letter written by the late E. Gordon Duff to Mr George P. Johnston, Secretary of the Edinburgh Bibliographical Society. The letter was attached to the descriptive slips of the Bibliographical Society, which, since 1932, have been kept in the National Library of Scotland, and read :

GORDON ARMS, YARROW,
SELKIRK,
July 7, 1914.

DEAR MR JOHNSTON,

I meant to have written you before to tell you of a most interesting book I saw lately at York Minster, a copy of the " Morall Fabillis of Esope the Phrygian, Compylit in Eloquent and ornate Scottis Meter be M. Robert Henryson, Edinburgh "—Imprinted att Edinburgh be me Thomas Bassandyne, dwelland at the nether Bow, Anno 1571.

It is a curious little book, half of it printed in the curious cursive "lettres de civilité." They have at York several other early Scottish books of which D. and E. could quote no copies.* I am re-reading the printed catalogue carefully and marking all the Scottish books to 1700.

Yrs sincerely,
E. GORDON DUFF.

---

* The editor has visited the library of York Minster in an attempt to trace these Scottish rarities, and has communicated the result of his search to the Keeper of Printed Books in the National Library of Scotland. The Minster Library certainly is rich in early Scottish books, some of which are unique or rare, but none of which rates in importance with the Henryson.

And an investigation of the slips of the Bibliographical Society revealed two entries relating to the book: the first by Mr G. P. Johnston, recording the details of Duff's communication, the second by Mr H. G. Aldis, with a pencil note: '. . . requires to be checked and divisions of lines marked.' That the existence of the edition should have been known to such excellent bibliographers as Gordon Duff and Aldis in 1914, the year of the completion of Gregory Smith's S.T.S. edition of Henryson, is a piece of improbability only surpassed by the fact that, as far as the present editor is aware, these three separate pieces of evidence—Mr Kellas Johnstone's note, Mr Gordon Duff's letter, and the Edinburgh Bibliographical Society slips—have lain useless from that time to this.

Every title-page on which the words 'Newlie imprinted' appear (the Charteris print of the *Fables* for example) does not necessarily imply the existence of an earlier edition. The meaning and use of the word 'Newlie' in this connection are too ambiguous for that. But in the case of the Bassandyne edition, the matter is left in no doubt. The description reads 'Newlie corectit, and Vendicat, fra mony Errouris, quhilkis war ouersene in the last prenting, quhair baith Lynes, and haill Versis war left owt.' This was a not infrequent claim. At the end of John Scot's edition of Lyndsay's *Dreme*, in the printer's epistle to the reader, the formula appears in similar terms:

> Gentyll redaris, I wyll adverteis ȝow that
> thare is of thir Bukis, Imprentit in France,
> The quhilkis ar verray fals. And
> wantis the tane half, and all
> wrang spelit, and left out
> heir ane lyne, and thar
> twa wordis.

And in the Henrie Charteris (1568) edition of the *Warkis*, the same claim is made, at considerable length, in the address to the reader, and, on the title-page, in terms almost identical with that of the Bassandyne Henryson. '. . . Newly correctit, and vindicate from the former errouris quhairwith thay war befoir corruptit: and augmentit with sindrie warkis quhilk was not befoir Imprentit.' The 'last prenting,' in the case of the

Henryson, was probably the Charteris print of the previous year—
at least, it is unlikely that another unknown edition appeared in
the interval and has since been utterly lost—unlikely, but (in the
light of recent events) not impossible. Let us assume, for the
moment, that the Charteris print is the 'last prenting' referred
to, and compare the two texts to see how far Thomas Bassandyne's
claim to have 'corectit and Vendicat' the *Fables* is justified.

Certainly the Bassandyne copy does contain lines that are not
in the Charteris print, and at least one 'haill Verse.' The stanza
beginning, 'O wantoun man!' (l. 381) for example, which is
lacking in Charteris, is present both in Harleian and Bassandyne.
And the stanza, 'Fy! puft up pryde, . . . (l. 593), which is not
in Harleian, is in both Charteris and Bassandyne: so that, on
the score of completeness at least, Bassandyne's claim is justified.
His is the most complete single text of the *Fables*.

Concerning the *nature* of the text presented by Bassandyne,
one can justly say that it is better in every way than either Charteris
or Harleian. It is not only more complete than either, but it
shows no trace of Anglicisation in spelling or in word-forms.
The terminations are more definitely and consistently Scots, and
there are fewer traces of misreading and misunderstanding in the
text. On these grounds, the editor has chosen the Bassandyne
print as the basis of his text of the *Fables*, and has reproduced it
(apart from slight normalisation, indicated in the text) literally,
believing that it may be interesting to students of early Scottish
printing and poetry to have an accurate text of this hitherto
unknown edition.

There is another aspect of this text which is not uninteresting,
and that is the type in which it is printed. It was obviously this
feature of the book which interested Mr Gordon Duff, and, when
the facts are known, it is not surprising. There is certainly no
earlier known instance of the use of civilité type in Scotland;
it is doubtful even if there is an earlier use in any English
printed book. The type was first used by Robert Granjon of
Lyons, in his *Dialogue de la Vie et de la Mort*, etc. (Lyons,
1557), in the Dedication of which the printer gives an account
of the reasons which led him to engrave the new 'lettre
Françoyse d'art de main.' The invention earned him a ten
years' Royal Patent, which, however, failed to protect his rights

in the matter. In 1559 the type was used in Antwerp for a book called *La Civilité puérile distribuée par petits chapitres*, a translation from Erasmus by Jehan Louveau, printed by Jehan Bellère, and from this publication the type took the name by which it was commonly known. Civilité was rapidly popularised and freely used in the S. Netherlands, while Plantin purchased some from Granjon and commissioned the latter to engrave him some new characters. In Antwerp and Ghent the type was promptly and freely imitated. The best accounts of the type are to be had in *Les Caractères de Civilité de J. Enschedé en Zonen* (Haarlem, MDCCCCXXVI) and Sabbe et Audin, *Les Caractères de Civilité de Robert Granjon et les Imprimeurs flamands* (Anvers-Lyon, 1921). The type was used in the printing of the colophon to *The Grammer-Warre. . . . Imprinted at London by Henry Binneman, dwelling in Knight Rider streate, at the signe of the Mermayde. Anno* 1576; and was used in the printing of wine-licenses granted by Raleigh, in accordance with the monopoly granted him in 1583 (see article in the *Trans. of the Bibliographical Society*, xiii. p. 291, and facsimiles: *English Current Writing and Early Printing*, by Hilary Jenkinson); but there seems to be no known occasion of its use for the text of any English book earlier than that date. It is little short of amazing that this uncommon type should make its first appearance in an Edinburgh printing-house; yet the natural suspicion that the Henryson may have been printed in France or the Netherlands is not supported by the evidence of the text. The body of the *Fables* is entirely in civilité, while Roman has been used for all the Moralitas sections. (*See* facsimile, *frontispiece*). There are two cuts in the book: the first, on the title-page, a portrait of Esop surrounded by creatures and objects from the Fables; the second (leaf A3b) an illustrative cut of the *Cock and the Jasp*. These engravings are both of interest. In the first place, they supply the lost originals for the coloured drawings in the Harleian MS. of the *Fables*. Previous editors have agreed that the Harleian MS. was obviously derived from a printed original, but no such original could be found. Whether the Bassandyne text should be regarded as the parent of the Harleian will be discussed below; but there is no denying the family resemblance between the *Cock and the Jasp* in the two texts (readers may conveniently compare the facsimiles in this edition with those of the Harleian in the S.T.S. edition) or between the drawing to the *Preiching of the Swallow* and some of the details on the Bassandyne title-page. It is possible, too, that the book noted in Foulis of Colinton's note-book, '1673, January 6. For Æsop's Fables in Scots to Archie, with the cuts £1, 7. o,' may be Bassandyne's text, or a lost reprint of it.

But the cut on the title-page of Bassandyne's edition is to be found again and again, with only the slightest variation, in dozens of fifteenth century editions of Æsop, printed in Germany and elsewhere. Examples are to be found in several volumes of Albert Schramm, *Bilderschmuck der Frühdrucke* (v., viii., xii. etc.), in sufficient number to show that Bassandyne's title-page is perhaps one of the latest examples of a long tradition. This matter will be discussed at greater length in the editor's bibliography of Henryson, which is in course of preparation, and will be published separately.

If Thomas Bassandyne had this type in Edinburgh in 1571, it is at least surprising that no other example of its use has come down to us.* The natural suspicion that the book might have been printed abroad, in France or the Netherlands, where the type was common, is dispelled by the nature of the text. The book has none of the blemishes common in Scots books printed 'furth of the realm.' There are no signs of imperfect understanding of the text, no un-Scots usages or spellings, no instances even of the use of 'et' as in the Chepman & Myllar pamphlets. Further, a comparison of the book with other productions of Bassandyne's press (and the Harleian MS.) is productive of new evidence, which, for the sake of clearness, is set out below.

1. The capital A on page 6 of the Henryson is identical with that on page 341 of Bassandyne's Lyndesay (1574) and is similar to one in the Harleian MS.

2. The capital T on p. 3 of the Henryson is identical with that on p. 95, etc., of the Lyndesay.

3. The Roman type used in the Henryson has no lower-case or capital '3'. Neither has the Roman in the Lyndesay. Both use lower-case and capital 'z' instead.

4. The cut of the *Cock and the Jasp* on p. 6 of the Henryson is almost identical with one in the Harleian MS., and

* See notes p. xlii

some of the details from the title-page of the Henryson reappear in the Harleian drawing to the *Preiching of the Swallow.*

5. But the Bassandyne Henryson supplies lines that are not in Harleian.

In view of this evidence, and in default of any good evidence to the contrary, it would seem (*a*) that the Henryson is a genuine product of Bassandyne's press, and (*b*) that the printed text and the Harleian MS. have no direct relationship, but derive from a common original.

The Fabulous tales of / Esope the Phrygian, Compiled / 𝔪𝔬𝔰𝔱𝔢 𝔢𝔩𝔬𝔮𝔲𝔢𝔫𝔱𝔩𝔶 𝔦𝔫 𝔖𝔠𝔬𝔱𝔱𝔦𝔰𝔠𝔥𝔢 / Metre by Master Robert / Henrison, & 𝔫𝔬𝔴 𝔩𝔞𝔱𝔢𝔩𝔶 / 𝔈𝔫𝔤𝔩𝔦𝔰𝔥𝔢𝔡.

𝔈𝔳𝔢𝔯𝔶 tale 𝔐𝔬𝔯𝔞𝔩𝔦𝔷𝔢𝔡 most 𝔞𝔭𝔱𝔩𝔶 to / 𝔱𝔥𝔦𝔰 𝔭𝔯𝔢𝔰𝔢𝔫𝔱 𝔱𝔦𝔪𝔢, 𝔴𝔬𝔯𝔱𝔥𝔶 / 𝔱𝔬 𝔟𝔢 𝔯𝔢𝔞𝔡. / [Ornament: (Mackerrow 186,) with Motto: *Occulta Veritas Tempora patet.*]/ Imprinted at London by / Richard Smith./ Anno. 1577.

Collation : ¶⁴ ***¹ A-G⁸ H² ; 63 leaves.

Contents : ¶1a title ; ¶1b *The bookes paſport;* ¶2a *To his worſhipfull and eſpecial good friend Maſter Richard Stoneley;* ¶3a-¶4a *The argument betweene Eſope and the Tranſlatour;* ¶4b *His verdict on his labour;* *** *The Contentes of the Booke;* A1a-H2a (pp. 1-115) text ; H2a *The Epilogue;* H2b blank.

The volume was carefully described in David Laing's edition (1865) and his description was fully reprinted in the S.T.S. edition, where any interested will find it. The printer (who was also the printer of George Gascogne's *Steel Glas*) seems also to be the translator, and according to him, the work was 'Finished in the Vale of Aylesburie the thirtenth of August Anno Domini 1574.' It is obviously not a text that could possibly add much to the sum of our knowledge of Henryson's *Fables.* Apart altogether from the entire Anglicisation of the text, it is apparent that the translator has failed to understand, not only the difficulties and obscurities of his original, but many of the most elementary points of language and syntax. A few of his most desperate remedies are recorded in the footnotes. The question

of the possible relation between this text and the Harleian MS.
is to some extent bound up with the relation between Harleian
and Bassandyne. Smith, in his Dedication of the translation,
writes: 'There came into my hande a Scottishe pamphlet of
the Fabulous Tales of Esope, a worke, Sir, as I thinke, in that
language wherein it was written, verie eloquent and full of great
invention.' So far as we know, there were only two possible
printed texts for Smith to read, the Charteris and the Bassandyne, and of the two, Smith's version much more closely
resembles the latter. But the relation between Smith and the
Harleian MS. is closer than either of these resemblances; and,
as we are bound to accept his statement that he worked from a
printed text, we are again driven to assume the existence of
another early text of the *Fables*, possibly that which served as
common original to Bassandyne and Harleian. A fuller account
of the evidence for these conclusions will be given in the editor's
forthcoming bibliography.

COMMENTARY

The marginal numbers refer to lines

THE MORALL FABILLIS

Prolog

3. *polite:* not 'polite' in the modern sense, but 'poleit,' or 'polished'—a stereotyped use of the epithet as applied to the 'termis' of the Scots *rhétoriquers.*

5. *caus:* seems to be dissyllabic in value here, and in all other texts.

8. *bustious:* an epithet of very wide application; in the text of Henryson alone, it is used to denote: healthy, strong, sturdy, rough, fresh, brave, fierce, overbearing, etc. [Derivation uncertain.]

10. *abreird:* = *on breird,* from *breird,* the first shoots. Cp. A.-S. *brord,* frumenti spicæ, and Lancashire dialect, *bruart,* for new-sprung blades of corn. The word still survives in lowland Scots: only last summer I was counselled by an old lady of my acquaintance to 'hain at the breird.'

12. *sentence:* (accented on the second syllable), *sententia* or 'moral.'

13. *dyte:* the written word. Cp. Mod. English 'indictment, ditty, dictate.'

22. *B* gives the best reading for this line.

28. This quotation has been used as a clue in the attempt to discover Henryson's original for the fables, and seems to point to Gualterus Anglicus' version of Romulus, which begins—

> *' Ut juvet, ut prosit, conatur pagina præsens :*
> *Dulcius arrident seria picta jocis.'*

The quotation appears on the title-page of the Charteris text (1570).

31. *In Mother toung of Latyng:* 'into the vernacular, from Latin . . .' the necessary medieval convention of apology for use of the 'Mother toung.' Cp. line 36.

34. Henryson's 'Lord,' if he ever existed, has not been identified.

35. Gregory Smith gave the reading 'decord,' as from the Charteris print, and emended it to 'record,' but, on examining photographs of the Charteris print, I found no trace of the reading 'decord.' It reads 'record,' as in *//* and *Bass.*

44. *brutal:* cp. this purely generic use of the epithet with that in l. 1400, when the sense is 'irrational.'

58*n. facound purpurat C:* 'facound' is here a substantive = 'eloquence.'

60. *Lak the disdane:* 'make light of . . .'

The Taill of the Cok, and the Jasp

69. *Jasp:* (A.F. *jaspe,* L. *iaspis*) used here in the general sense of 'jewel.'

83. The reading 'on mold' suggests the familiar verse-tag, meaning 'on the earth.' The alternative reading '*and* mold' is apparently an attempt to provide 'muke' with a synonym.

102. *lukand werkis:* Cp.

'ʒit have I hard oft said be men na clerkis,
Till idill folk full lycht beyn lukand warkis.'

(Douglas.)

126. *Moralitas:* Gregory Smith follows *B* in beginning the Moralitas at l. 120. All the other texts agree in beginning it at l. 127, and there, properly speaking, the Moralitas does begin.

139. *screit:* this form is unknown, and I have seen no satisfactory explanation of it. The reading 'ket,' in *B,* is little better: 'fret' in *HCS* makes excellent sense, and is probably the original reading.

149. *Ignorants,* the reading of all the texts except *C,* is certainly the better reading.

The Taill of the Uponlandis Mous, and the Burges Mous

164. *Borous toun:* a town with borough rights. This word is still preserved in the full form of the place-name Bo'ness, on the Firth of Forth—Borrowstounness.

165. *uponland:* compare *Fables,* l. 1268, p. 46. See Glossary.

168. *waith:* (O.N. *veiðr*) hunting; 'wacht' in *B* is probably an arbitrary rhyme-form of the same word.

173. *but custom mair or les:* free of custom, both the great (*magna custuma,* levied on exports and imports) and the little (*parva custuma,* levied on market goods).

176. *unfute sair:* Gregory Smith quotes several lines from the *Thrie Priestes of Peblis* to explain this phrase:

. . . Thrie Priests went unto collatioun,
Into ane privie place of the said toun,
Quhair that they sat, *richt soft and unfute sair;* . . .

. . . Quhair that they sat, *full easily and soft.*

And Diebler quotes a thirteenth century version of the fable (*Reliquiæ Antiquæ*, I, 320), in which the mouse is described: '. . . Movit igitur iter facili pede.'

179. *under the wand:* not 'in a state of subjection,' as is suggested by Laing, but 'in the open.' See Glossary.

183. *wilsum wayis:* one of the most common M. Sc. verse-tags. Cp. *Orpheus and Eurydice* (p. 138, l. 290).

187. *Cry peip anis.* Cp. *Kingis Quair*, st. 57 :

'Now suete bird, say ones to me pepe.'

198. misterlyk, *A;* maisterlig, *B.* G. G. S., probably on the strength of the *B* form, translates 'masterfully.' The word actually is 'skilfully' (Scots, *Mister*, *myster*, craft, art). But probably the reading of *C*, *H* and *Bass* should be preferred. (Cp. Burns, *To a Mouse*, l. 20, 'Its silly wa's . . .')

203. *For comonly sic pykeris luffis not lycht:* Fergusson (*Scottish Proverbs*, S.T.S. 1924), A. 310. Cp. *Owl and the Nightingale*, 229-30 :

'Vor eurich þing þat schuniet riȝt
hit luueþ þuster & hatiet liȝt.'

and John, iii. 20.

207. *I do it on thame besyde:* 'I leave it to them.' A common rhetorical turn.

248. *My gude friday is better nor your pace:* 'My Good Friday (which is a most rigid fast) is more plentiful than your Easter (which is a time of feast).

253. *In stubbill array:* B gives the best reading here—'In skugry ay' (always stealthily). The reading 'stowthry,' in *A*, is connected with the sense of stolen or smuggled goods (*stoutherie*, *stouthrief*, etc.). Cp. l. 686.

263. *ane innes* (*A*) used in plural in sing. sense. G. G. S. quotes the *Wallace*, iv. 381 (S.T.S. p. 60) :

'For him he gert ane innys graithit be.'

281. *ane subcharge:* an additional course.

283. *Thraf cakkis:* (O.E. þearf, unleavened) cakes of unleavened bread. See *N.E.D.*, *s.v.* 'Tharf.'

285. *And mane full fyne.* This reading is supplied from *C—Bass*, *H*, *S*, and *Ht* being defective. *B's* reading, 'furmage,' cheese (A.F. *fourmage*), is good enough sense but makes the line hypermetrical. 'Mane' is fine bread, and the word is usually used with 'bread' in a descriptive sense.

288. *This*, for 'thus.' A common M. Sc. usage.

300. *will off ane gude reid:* at a loss for good counsel. 'Will of rede' and 'will of wane' are quite common. Cp. *Testament of Cresseid,* l. 543, and the word 'wilsum,' l. 183 *supra.*

326. *Gib hunter:* Gib, or Gilbert, one of the 'character' names of the cat. His Reynardian name is Tybert.

329. *Bawdronis:* another familiar name for the cat, which persisted late in Scots usage. Cp. R. Fergusson, *The King's Birth-Day in Edinburgh,* l. 81 :

> 'If *baudrins* slip but to the door.'

336. *ane burde:* B reads 'þe dressour' (the dresser), and *Ā* 'þe dosour' (a hanging). The latter reading is supported by l. 348, 'I thank yone courtyne . . .', and perhaps refers to the protection curtain drawn over the upper shelves of the larder.

345. *Thy guse is gude :* For this proverbial expression, see Fergusson, A. 145.

  gansell: (O.F. *ganse aillie*) garlic sauce, served with goose. L. F. Salzmann, in *More Medieval Byways,* p. 136, cites (from the Wardrobe Account, 1306/7) the name *Gaunsaillie,* as that of a minstrel who received payment at the court of Edward I. in that year, but is unaware of the significance of the word.

347. *perpall wall :* partition wall, a wall built with parpens—single bricks or stones, faced on both sides. See *N.E.D., s.v.* 'Parpen.' Cp. l. 337, 'parraling.'

360. *but and ben :* (O.E. *beūtan, beinnan,* without, within) the outer and inner room of the Scots single-doored, two-roomed dwelling-house. Direct entry is possible only to the kitchen, or 'but,' and the parlour, or 'ben,' is entered from the kitchen.

391. *And Solomon sayis :* The passage does not occur, with the authority of Solomon, in the Scriptures. I quote from G. G. S.'s note : 'It suggests a memory-blend of *Ecc.* iii. 22 ("Et deprehendi nihil esse melius quam lætari hominem in opere in suo, et hance esse partem illius") and *Prov.* xvi. 8 ("Melius est parum cum iustitia quam multi fructus cum iniquitate") ; but it is most probably, in the light of Henryson's use of Lydgate, a rendering of *Prov.* xvii. 1.'

  Lydgate's version runs :

> 'Salamon writeth, how it is better behalf
> A smal morsel of brede with joy and rejoysyng,
> Than at festis to have a rosted calf
> With hevy chiere and froward grucchyng.'

The reference to Solomon seems, then, to be misplaced in
Henryson's fable, and should, properly speaking, accompany
ll. 234-238. Fergusson, A. 164, quotes:

> 'Beter is lyte to have in ese
> Than much to have(n) in malese.'

See, too, *King Alexander*, l. 7365.

The Taill of Schir Chantecleir and the Foxe

That the central theme of this fable had passed into proverbial
use is indicated by the phrase in the *Kingis Quair*, l. 1088:

> 'The wyly fox, the wedowis inemye.'

400. *inclinatioun :* sing. in form, but plural sense.

402. *fenyeit :* a better reading than the 'semis' of *C*.

411. *drop :* metathetical form of 'dorp' ('thorp') = village. Probably
from the O.E. metathesised form 'þrop,' as in Thrupp (Berks),
Throope (Wilts), Souldrop (Beds.); but, although the change
of initial þr to *dr* is common enough in W.-Mid and S.W.
of England, the editor knows of no Scots instance.

416. *curageous :* sprightly.

428. *Werie for nicht :* weary of the night.

429. *Lowrence :* Scots familiar name for the fox, the equivalent of
the English 'Reynard.' The origins of the name would seem
to be doubtful. Jamieson suggests Corn. *luern*, Arm. *luarn*,
'vulpes,' but inclines to the belief that the name 'lowrie'
derives from some root expressive of deception. Cp. Du.
loeren, late M.H.G. and M.L.G. *lûren*, to lie in wait. Sibbald
substantiates this with a specimen derivation: 'Teut. *lorer*,
fraudator; *lorerye*, fraus, *lore*, illecebra.' If this is so,
Lowrence is an attributive title, like Noble the Lion, etc.,
and the form 'Lawrence' in Henryson is a misleading variant.
In support of this suggestion, see *Fables*, l. 2294:

> 'Lowrence come lourand, for he lufit never licht.'

449. *Dirigie.* The first word of the Antiphon at Matins in the Office
for the Dead, and used as a name for that service. (Ps. v. 8,
Dirige, Domine, Deus meus, in conspectu tuo viam meam.)
Cp. the *Want of Wyse Men*, p. 189, l. 19.

459. *lyart loikkis :* grey, or hoary, locks. Cp. *Testament of Cresseid*,
p. 110, l. 162, and Burns, 'Cottar's Saturday Night,' l. 105:

> 'His lyart haffets wearing thin an' bare.'

477. *wawland :* 'rolling his eyes.' A better reading than that
provided by *B*, 'walkit.'

483. *Pertok, Sprutok, and Toppok.* Familiar hen-names. 'Pertok' ('partlot' in *B*) is, of course, Chaucer's Pertelote. 'Sprutok,' which occurs also in *The Tale of Colkelbie's Sow,* l. 117, may, as Gregory Smith suggests, be connected with *Sprotinus,* the cock in the Latin Reynard, or with 'sprutlit,' speckled, as in Douglas, *Virgil,* 46, 4 : 'And twys faldit thare sprutillit skynnis but dout.' 'Coppok,' the reading of *B,* is probably to be preferred to the other texts on this point. It has the support of alliteration, and is closer to the Reynardian form, Coppe (*Caxton,* Coppen). Cp., too, Gower, *Vox Clamantis,* i. 545 (ed. Macaulay), and the editor's note on the passage. If 'Toppok' is preferred, it should probably be taken to convey the sense of top or crest, as in 'tappit hen.' The '-ok' endings are probably onomatopœic coinages.

486. *'How, murther, hay !'* The reading 'reylock' in *B* has been dismissed by previous editors as probably corrupt. It was, however, pointed out by Professor Bruce Dickins, in the *T.L.S.,* 21st February 1924, that the word was a technical term in Scots law. 'It is suggested that *reylock* is a corrupt form of the O.E. law term *rēaflāc,* "robbery," "rapine," which, like *hāmsōcn* (hamesucken), survived in Scots legal terminology. It is found as *reyflake, revelayk* (=roboria) in the fifteenth-century vernacular translation of the Assize Willelmi (Sc. Acts Parl. [1844], i. 381). "Hi, murder, robbery !" gives excellent sense.

The Charteris and Harleian reading *hay* would suggest that the term was no longer familiar in the sixteenth century, but that need not exclude the possibility of its use by Henryson, who, to judge from his fable of *The Sheep and the Dog,* was well acquainted with the terminology and procedure, at any rate, of the canon law.'

497. *drowrie :* An uncommon use of the word. It is commonly used to signify love in the abstract sense, illicit or otherwise, a love token or gift, or the marriage-gift. In the sense of love, it is used in the *Bruce,* viii. 497-8 :

> 'Than mycht he weil ask a lady
> Hyr amowris, and hyr drowery.'

In the sense of a love-token, it is used in the *Test. of Cresseid,* l. 583, and, as the marriage or Morwyn gift it is quoted by Jamieson from the Acts Ja. IV., 1503, Ed. 1814, p. 240 : '. . . the donation & gift of our souerane lady the qwenis drowry & morwyn-gift eftir the form of the charteris.' As it is used here, as a personal noun, it is by no means common.

500. *curcheis :* (O.F. *couvrechés*, pl. of *couvrechef*) kerchief, commonly used as a cap or mutch. A false singular, 'curch,' was formed, and the true singular, 'curches,' became a fallacious plural. This is an example of the correct singular use.

511. *Sanct Johne to borrow.* Cp. Lyndsay, *The Complaynt of the Commoun Weill of Scotland* (Laing, i. p. 38, l. 996) :

> 'Fair weill, quod I, and with sanct Jhone to borrow.'

Compare, too, the *Wallace*, iii. 336 ; *Colkelbie's Sow* (Laing, p. 258, l. 153), and uses in Chaucer, Lydgate, James I., etc. St John as a witness or guarantor. Cp. *The Sheep and the Dog*, l. 1234 :

> '. . . thairto ane Borrow (*B* borch) he fand.'

515. '*wes never wedow sa gay !*' The song has not been identified.

517. *chalmerglew :* cp. Lyndsay (ed. Laing, ii. p. 110, l. 2163).

523-4. The reading in *B* for these lines makes better sense.

533. *kittokis :* 'Kittok,' a familiar name for a woman, frequently disrespectful and used in the sense of 'paramour' or 'wanton.' Dunbar's *Kynd Kyttok* and Lyndsay's *Kittie's Confessioun* illustrate the use of the name.

545. *kennettis :* see Glossary. Described by Reginald Scot as 'a hound of scent.'

546 *et seq.* Compare the names of the widow's dogs with those in Chaucer's version of the tale. *Berk* (birkye, *B*) is probably a form of the word 'birkie,' still in use, for 'a game fellow'— a trusty, stout-hearted dog. *Berrie* is the same name as Perrie, in the *Sheep and the Dog*, p. 43, l. 1166. See *N.E.D.*, *s.v.* 'Pirrie.' *Bell* (*B*) is a common name for a collie-bitch to this day. *Bell* and *Bawsie Broun* appear together in Dunbar's *Dance of the Seven Deadly Synnis*, l. 30 :

> 'Blak Belly and Bawsy Broun.'

Perhaps both dogs owe their names to their colour ; cp. Burns, *The Twa Dogs*, l. 31, 'His honest, sonsie, baws'nt face.' See *N.E.D.*, *s.v.* 'Bausond.' *Rype schaw* (search covert) and *Rin weil* are obviously attributive names. *Curtes* (Cortois), the Reynardian name for the dog ; and *Nuttieclyde*, 'brown Clyde,' a name, according to Gregory Smith, still in use.

568. *falset failyeis ay at the latter end.* Note Richard Smith's anglicisation of this typical senténce.

575. *ffor ane yeir :* the term of hire.

582. *in to pleid :* in jeopardy.

603. *loif and le :* to flatter and lie. A better reading than that in *C*, 'leif.'

The Taill how this foirsaid Tod maid his Cōfessioun to Freir Wolf Waitskaith.

618. *waitting:* hunting. Cp. *waith*, l. 168 *supra.*

621. This line is defective in all texts but *B*, which supplies the missing two syllables, '*Thetes.*'

623. Compare the 'cloudy hood' of Hesperus, the evening star, with the kerchief of Aurora, in l. 500 *supra.*

629. *sternis* (O.N. *stjarna*). This form of the plural survives at least as late as Fergusson, *Hallow-Fair*, ll. 1-2 :

> 'At *Hallowmas*, whan nights grow lang,
> And *starnies* shine fu' clear.'

642-3. *But Astrolab :* Without astrolabe, etc. The fox knew the moving of the heavenly bodies by 'kind' as the Cock in Chaucer also did.

649-52. There is obviously something wrong with these four lines. *B* offers the best reading. Sir W. A. Craigie suggests that 'ken' and 'men' are dittographies of 'kend' and 'mend,' and that 'Ene' in *C* is an attempt at improvement.

661. *widdinek, and Crakraip :* withy-neck, a criminal hanged with a rope of willow twigs ; *Crakraip*, crack-rope, a self-explanatory name for a gallows-bird.

666. *Doctour in Divinitie.* The Wolf appears again in this role, in the fable of the *Trial of the Fox*, p. 38, l. 1052, where his red cap suggests the title.

667. *Waitskaith :* one who lies in wait to do hurt, or 'skaith.' The name occurs in Caxton's *Reynard :* 'Ther is prentout, wayte scathe, and other of my frendis and alyes.'

675. *feir* may here mean either 'fear' or 'demeanour.'

684. *and leuch :* not so much 'laughed' as 'giggled.' Cp. l. 446 *supra.*

693. *Benedicitie :* the invocation of blessing before confession.

698. *Art thow contrite.* This is the first part of the Catholic sacrament of penance, *Contritio*. The second part, *Confessio*, is not reported here for the reason advanced in ll. 694-7. In the 'thrid part off penitence,' or *Satisfactio*, the Fox is no more satisfactory.

730. *For grit mister :* in the case of extreme need. The word is used to denote need, either as a verb or substantive, and sometimes, particularly, need of food :

> 'And now her heart is like to melt away
> Wi' heat and *mister*.'
> (Ross's *Helenore*.)

Jamieson suggests a derivation from S.G. *mist-a*, Dan. *mist-er*, to lose, to sustain the want or loss of a thing.

731. *for neid may haif na law :* Fergusson, A. 649 ; *Piers Plowman,* xx. l. 10 ; Heywood, p. 43.

736. *wallis woude :* the stormy waves ; 'walterand,' in *B*, developes the sense.

751. *Schir Salmond :* cp. the earlier episode in the *Brus* xix. 649 *et seq.*, and the French *Ysopet :* 'Quant Ysangrin vit le mouton si le salua . . . Et li dit : "Sawmon, Dieu te gart !" '

763. *couth he wait :* stalk. Cp. ll. 618, 168, *supra* (notes).

776 *et seq.* (*B*) *contritioun, confessioun, wilfull pennance, etc.* The readings in Bannatyne, here as elsewhere, show fewer traces of Protestant revision, than those of the other texts.

The Taill of the Sõe & Air of the foirsaid Foxe, callit Father wer : Alswa the Parliamẽt of four-futtit Beistes, haldin be the Lyoun.

800. *in purches :* in bastardy [cp. O.F. *porchais*, an intrigue]. Douglas, *Virgil*, 303, 4, has :

> ' Son to the bustuous nobyl Sarpedon,
> In *purches* get ane Thebane wensche apoun.'

Elsewhere in Henryson it has the sense of hunting for food, and of fraud.

801. *Father war : i.e.* worse than his father, on the analogy of ' Father-better.' Fergusson (MS. 1035), ' Mony ar father war, few father better.' See the following stanza.

808. *Off verray kinde :* by birth and nature. Note how cunningly the accent falls in this line.

827. 'Ay rinnis the ffoxe, als lang as he fute hais.' Cp. Dunbar, *Epetaphe for Donald Owre* (ed. Mackay Mackenzie), p. 66 :

> ' Ay rinnis the fox
> Quhill he fute hais,'

and Knox, *Hist.*, ed. Laing, i. 116—'So that the Scotesh proverbe was trew in him : "So long rynnis the fox, as he fute hes." ' Fergusson, A. 8.

836. *To execute, to do, to satisfie :* 'execute' in the legal sense—cp. mod. 'executors,' to do, to act for, on behalf of : cp. 'agent.' This couplet as it stands in *C, H,* and *Bass*, is probably a Protestant revision of the original couplet, represented by *B*.

840. *maid all the warld to waig.* Cp. *Testament of Cresseid*, p. 110, ll. 195-6.

843. *breist :* the reading 'buste' in *B* is probably the more correct : ' in a box or case.'

852. *Out of ane bus :* the reading here should probably be 'buist' as in *CHB.* See note on l. 843 *supra.*

854. *sadlie :* solemnly, impressively.

855. *Nobill Lyoun :* the conventional Reynardian epithet for the lion, in Willem, Leeu, and Caxton.

864. *compeir :* (Lat. *compar -ere* ; Fr. *compar -oir*) to present oneself at court, civil or ecclesiastical, in obedience to a summons. Cp. the *Priests of Peblis :*

> 'And sent to him his officer, but weir
> Thus but delay befoir him to *compeir.*'

873. There appears to be an attempt at a heraldic jest here, as Professor Bruce Dickins has pointed out (*Times Literary Supplement,* 21st February 1924). The 'Three Leopards' (*B*) are the leopards of the English arms, and the lion is, of course, the Scots lion, enthroned, with sceptre, sword, and crown, as on the Scots arms, who is thus being royally served. Compare the lines in Dunbar's *Thrissil and the Rois,* 96-99, for a similar heraldic picture of the King of the Beasts. See notes, p. 238.

883. Gatherings of beasts, similar to this, and founded on the medieval *Bestiary,* are common in Middle English and Middle Scots literature. Chaucer, in the *Parliament of Foules,* the author of the *Kingis Quair,* and Montgomerie, in the *Cherrie and the Slae,* give similar lists. Montgomerie's list may, as Gregory Smith suggests, owe something to Henryson's.

888. *Bellerophont.* For the nature of this 'beist of Bastardrie,' about which previous editors have been silent, the reader is referred to the Workes of Armo | *rie deuided into three Bookes, enti* | tuled, the Concordes of Armorie, Ar | morie of Honor, and of Cotes and | Creastes, Collected and gathered | by *Iohn Bossewell* Gentleman. | London : Henrie Ballard, 1597 (p. 66) :

'Chymere. The field is partie per bend sinister, Gules and Sable, a Chymere, siluer. This Chymere is a Beast or monster hauing three heads, one like a Lyon, an other like a Goate, the third like a Dragon, fingũt & Chymeram triformem bestiam : ore Leo, postremis partibus Draco, media Caprea. Quam quidam Philosophi non animal, sed Cilitiæ montẽ esse aiunt, quibusdam locis Leones & Capreas nutrientem, quibusdã ardentem, quibusdã plenam serpentibus. Hunc Bellerophons, habitabilẽ fecit, vnde Chymerã dicitur occidisse.

This Bellerophons, or Bellerophon, the sonne of Glaucus, king of Ephyra, a man of much beautie and prowesse, was ardently

beloued of Stenobia, the wife of Pretus king of Ephyra, next
after Glaucus, when she desired him to cōmit adoultrie with
her, he fearing the vengance of Iupiter, God of hospitalitie,
and remembring the friendship her husband had shewed
him, refused, and put her away from him : Which she dis-
deyning, and being in a wood rage, accused him to her husband,
that he rauished her, but he like a sober man, would not slea
him in his owne house, deliuering him letters to his wiues
father, sent him into Lycia, who perceiuing the mind of
Pretus, encouraged, & sent Bellerophon to destroy the two
Monsters, Solymos, and Chimæra, that he might be slaine
under the colour of a valiant enterprise.   But he atchyuing
it nobly, retourned with honor.   This historie foloweth more
at large set forth in yᵉ Latin toongue by Stockmahere, in his
Commentaries upon the Emblemes of Alciate.—Emb. iii. in
these words. . . .'

891. *The Tiger full off Tiranie :* cp. the *Kingis Quair,* l. 1086 :

> ' The fery tigere, full of felonye.'

895. *the Sparth :* probably a heraldic beast, but so far unidentified.
As an animal the Sparth is unidentified.   As a battleaxe he
is common enough, and if the passage is corrupt, which there
is reason to believe it may be, the word may have been so
intended.   I am indebted here, as on many other occasions,
to Professor Bruce Dickins for suggestions that throw light
on the obscurity of the text.   He writes, ' Could the original
reading have been

> " Thre leopardis as I haif tauld beforne,
>   The Anteloip, the Swan furth couth hir speid "

—a reference to the arms of Henry IV. with their supporters.
(Henry IV. had, as supporters to the royal arms of England,
a black antelope and a white swan, Henry V. and Henry VI.
a lion and an antelope [W. A. Copinger, *Heraldry Simplified,*
p. 236, *Manchester,* 1910]).'
  If the word ' sparth ' is to be retained, then we must seek for
some reading that will use it in its normal signification.
Professor Dickins suggests

> ' The anteloip with a sparth furth couth speid '

—a reference to the heraldic antelope, armed, like the
Norwegian lion, with a battleaxe.

896. *The peyntet Pantheir :* ' peyntet ' probably means ' spotted,' as
in Spenser, *Amoretti,* 53.   (But cp. *Kingis Quair,* l. 1080 :
' The pantere, like unto the *smaragdyne* ' [*i.e.* ' the emerald '].

In a Latin Bestiary printed by A. W. Rendell, *Physiologus* (London, 1928), p. 96, the panther is thus described: 'Qui niger ex albo conspergitur orbiculato.' 'Conspergitur' is glossed 'depingitur.' See J. Hall, *Selections from Early Middle English* (Oxford, 1920), p. 194, and Notes.

898. *The Jolie Gillet:* mare. *B* Jonet, *S* Gennet, a small Spanish horse. For 'gillet,' see Dunbar's *Tua Mariit Wemen* (ed. Mackay Mackenzie), l. 114:

'He fepillis like a farcy aver that flyrit one a gillot.'

902. (*B*) *wodwyss:* satyrs, or 'wild-men': glossed in *Prompt. Parv.* as *silvanus, satirus*. Gregory Smith quotes from the Revels Account, 1513, when they appear as 'woodwossys or wyld men.' They commonly figure in heraldry as supporters.

903. *Hurcheoun:* (O.F. *erichon*), urchin, hedgehog.
Hirpland: limping—the characteristic uneven gait of the hare. Cp. Burns, *Holy Fair*, l. 7:

'The hares were hirplin' down the furrs,'

and Keats, *Eve of St Agnes*, l. 3:

'The hare limped trembling through the frozen grass.'

906. *The wyld Once:* probably a heraldic beast of the leopard kind. In a *History of Mediaeval Ireland from* 1100-1513, by Edmund Curtis (p. 36, note), we read: 'The best Irish accounts of the battle are in Loch Cé, and in *Ann. Clon*. Gilla-na-naer O Dovailin is called in *Loch Cé* "the bearer of the leopard standard" (*fear iomchar na h-onchon*); however, "*onchu*" was a heraldic beast of uncertain species and the O'Briens also had an "onchu."' In the *English-Irish Dictionary*, T. O'Neill Lane (Nutt, 1904), is the entry 'Leopard, *oncú*.'

907. *Fibert:* beaver (Lat. *fiber*). The appearance of the beaver in this line makes it more difficult to explain the 'baver bakon' (*B*) in the preceding line; although the polecat appears twice, once in this line ('fowmart') and in l. 912 ('Feitho').

910. *Rattoun*: (F. *raton*) little rat. Quite a common form of the word. I have found it in Topsell, *Fourefooted Beastes*, for rats of various kinds. Cp. Burns, *Halloween*, l. 194:

'A ratton rattl'd up the wa'.'

See Lyndsay (ed. Laing), iii. 2495, 3982.

Glebard: (*B* globert; *S* glybard). I have been unable to identify this animal, which is (from the context) most probably one of the rodent kind and is most certainly not the glowworm, as is tentatively suggested by G. G. S. See note on l. 913.

911. *quhrynand:* whining, not 'striking,' as in G. G. S. Cp. A.S. *hrinan,* and Lyndsay, *Answer to the Kingis Flyting,* l. 60 (ed. Laing, p. 107): '. . . quhimperand with mony quhryne.'

913. *Mertrik:* marten. Topsell (*Fourefooted Beastes,* 1607, pp. 495-6) writes, 'princes and great Nobles are clothed therewith, every skinne being woorthe a Frenche crowne or foure shillings at the least.' In the Welsh laws of Howel dda (10th cent.) 'Tri wrllys a ddyly y frenines: croen beleu; a llostlydan a charlwng.' (Three furs which the queen is entitled to: the skin of a marten; of a beaver; or an ermine.) And in the *Leges Wallicæ,* lib. ii., cap. viii., § viii.: 'Tres sunt lymbi regis que ad regem de iure pertinent: scilicet, *llostledan* [fiber]; beleu [martes]; et *carrlung* [mustela candida]: pellis llostledan [fibri] dimidium libre valet: carrlung [mustela candida], lxᵃ denarios; beleu [martis] xxᵗⁱ iiiiᵒʳ denarios valet; et si in predatione inventi fuerint, regis erunt.'

Cyvreithian Cymru: 'There are three kinds of vermin in law: a marten; a beaver; and an ermine; [they are recognisable] in law for their skins [with which the] queen's robes [are adorned] wherever [they may be killed].'

It is at least possible that the third of these, the ermine, is the unidentified 'glebard'; in so complete a list of vermin it is strange to find the ermine absent. It occurs in a similar context in the *Kingis Quair,* l. 1095.

the Cunning and the Con: the rabbit (cony) and the squirrel.

914. *Bowranbane:* (Bourabant *S:* Bourabane *Ht:* lurdane lane *B*) the Werewolf(?) *Bass, S* and *H* offer almost identical readings, and that of *B* is probably an attempt to improve a corrupt text—as far as we are concerned, however, confusion is worse confounded. In default of any better suggestion, the editor offers the following:—*Bourré: subst. masc.* Espèce d'animal fantastique ainsi nommé à Paris, et qui étoit appelé à Orléans le *mulet odet,* à Blois et à Angers le *lou garou,* et à Tours le *roy huguet,* d'où le nom *huguenot. Variantes:* Bourré, Bourry, Bourru (*Dictionnaire Historique de l'Ancien Langage François,* par La Curne de Sainte-Palaye (1877), t. iii.). Sir W. A. Craigie writes (of *Bowranbane* and *Glebard*): 'If they are Henryson's (and not due to later corruptions), he probably found them in some list similar to his own, and may not have known what they meant.' *

Lerioun: perhaps a young rabbit. Jamieson gives 'Lepron, Leproun: a young rabbit or hare': and quotes from Burgh Records, Edinburgh, ii. 231 '. . . conyngis and leprones.'

---

* See notes p. xli

[O.F. *leporin*, a hare.] Other suggestions are (F. *liron*) the grey dormouse, and (F. *levron*) a small greyhound.

918. *Musk:* G. G. S. suggests the civet-cat, and quotes Florio, *s.v.* 'Lattitio : a kind of Muske or Zivet-cat.'

930. *And steiris nane that ar to me prostrait.* Cp. Dunbar's *Thrissil and the Rois*, l. 119 :

> ' Quhois noble yre is *parcere prostratis* '

(ed. Mackay Mackenzie, p. 110). The editor's note on the line reads : 'The MS. reads *proceir*, but the reference is clearly to the motto cited, in connection with the armorial bearings of the kings of Scotland, in *Le Simbol Armorial*, etc., Paris, 1455 : *Parcere prostratis scit nobilis ira leonis*, which is almost the line in the text (see Note in S.T.S. edition). The scribe has probably expanded wrongly a sign of abbreviation.'

948. *gar fence :* a term used in Scots law, at the opening of a Court or Parliament for the formula in which the lieges are ordered to abstain from all unnecessary disorder or interruption.

949. *absence :* absentees, defaulters. Cp. 'Ignorance' (*C*) l. 149, for 'Ignorantis.'

950. *his payntit Coit Armour :* cp. l. 896, 'The peyntet Pantheir,' and note.

970. *bukhude :* hide-and-seek. Cp. l. 333 *supra*.

999. *Rampand :* rearing, in anger: the term is probably used descriptively here, but it cannot, of course, be divorced entirely from its heraldic significance. The heraldic jape in stanza 125 has already been noted ; and it may as well be said here that the student of medieval poetry, art, and architectural ornament will lose the significance of much of his study unless he is conversant at least with the terms and forms of heraldry. The unnatural natural history of Middle Scots and Middle English poetry is as dependent on heraldic form and jargon, as are the decorative arts as found, for example, in Roslin Chapel or Melrose Abbey. Cp. note on l. 873.

1004. *Contumax :* a Sc. legal term, borrowed from O.F. law. Guilty of contempt of Court.

1005. *Courtlie Knax :* that is, your lawyer's quibbles, not courtier's blandishments.

1014. *Chanceliary :* the chancery hand, ultimately derived from the old Roman cursive, in which charters and other legal and business documents were written. Cp. the corresponding passage in Caxton's *Reynard* (chap. 27) where the wolf says :

'I can wel frenshe latyn englissh and duche. I have goon to
scole at oxenford I haue also wyth olde and auncyent doctours
ben in the audyence and herde plees | and also haue gyuen
sentence | I am lycensyd in bothe lawes | what maner wrytyng
that ony man can deuyse | I can rede it as perfyghtly as my
name.'

1030. *To sleip in haill.* Cp. Fergusson, MS. 823.

1033. *Felix quem:* quoted by Erasmus in his *Adagia*, and translated by Richard Taverner, 1539, 'He is happy, whom other
mens perills maketh ware.' The proverb appears in many
Scots collections: 'Better learn frae your neebor's skaith
than your ain.' Fergusson's *Scottish Proverbs* (S.T.S. 1924),
B. 152, has the proverb. Cp. Chaucer, *Troilus and Criseyde*,
iii. 329 :

'For wise ben by foles harm chastised.'

1044. *Ane Trip of Lambis:* the collective noun 'trip' is the correct
technical use for sheep, goats and swine. Cp. l. 744 *supra*,
'ane trip off Gait': that it is correctly used of mice, in
l. 1409 *infra*, I am not so sure.

1052. *your Doctour off Divinitie:* cp. l. 666 *supra*, and note.

1064. *The greitest Clerkis.* Fergusson, A. 857, Heywood, p. 115, and
Chaucer, *Canterbury Tales*, A. 4054. Diebler (*Henrisone's
Fabeldichtungen*, 1885, p. 51) points out the parallel between
this line and the concluding words of Caxton's *Reynard*,
chap. 27, sect. i.: 'Now I here wel | it is true that I long
syth haue redde and herde | that the beste clerkes ben not
the wysest men|'

1083. *be practik:* by experience. In this case, the modern sense is
'by circumstantial evidence.'

1089. *party tresoun* (*B*). Surely the sense of 'party' here is not
'partly' or 'pretty,' as G. G. S. suggests, but 'petty-treason'—
treason against a subject, as opposed to betrayal of the
sovereign. In this case the fox owed no allegiance to the
ewe, but the act of violence committed on the lamb, in open
violation of the lion's proclamation of peace, is construed as
treason in the second degree.

1095. *Bowcher:* Executioner: for 'basare' (*B*), cp. Barbour, *Legends*,
Cristofore, 597 : and *N.E.D.*, *s.v.* 'Baser.'

1111 *et seq.* Here, as elsewhere, *B* gives readings that show less
trace of Protestant revision.

1126. *Will thow remember, Man.* The reminder, and the tone, are
among the commonplaces of medieval literature ; surviving
in song and ballad to a later day. In 'Ane compendious
booke of Godly and Spirituall Songs . . . with sundrie . . .

ballates changed out of prophaine Sanges,' &c. (Andro Hart, *Edinb.*, 1621) appears the ballad, 'Remember, O thou man':

'Remember, O thou man, O thou man, O thou man,
Remember, O thou man, thy time is spent.
Remember, O thou man,
How thou art dead and gone,
And I did what I can,
Therefore, repent.'

1134. (*B*) *sagis*: assays, assails, or lays siege to.

The Taill of the Scheip ãd the Doig

1148. *Consistorie*: the Consistory Court, or ecclesiastical court. Lord Hailes (*Ancient Scottish Poems*, 1770) and others have remarked on the fulness and precision with which the form of process in this court are here described.

1156-7. *hie Suspensioun, grit Cursing, and Interdictioun.* For a full account of these ecclesiastical penalties, see Gregory Smith's edition (iii., p. 20, l. 1148, 9, note), when reference is also made to a full text of a vernacular 'terrible cursing,' by Gawin, Archbishop of Glasgow, dated 28th October 1525.

1159. (*S*) *Perry Dogge*: cp. l. 546 *supra*, for 'Berrie'; and see l. 1166 *infra*.

1160. *Schir Corbie Ravin*: (F. *corbeau*), Sir Corbie, the Raven. Frequently 'Corbun' or 'Corboun.' 'An of messagers corbun' (*Cursor Mundi*, v. 1892). Cp. Lindsay, 1592, p. 41,

'He send furth Corbie Messenger,'

and Fergusson, MS. 596, when the sense is 'a messenger whose tidings come not at all or too late.'
Apparitour: the officer of the consistorial court.

1173. *Quhen Hesperus to schaw his face began.* Lord Hailes writes: 'The Wolf held his court while the sun was down. "On every Wednesday morning next after Michaelmas Day, *at cocks crowing*, there is by ancient custom a court held by the Lord of the honour of Raleigh, which is vulgarly called the *lawless court*—because held at an unlawful or lawless hour"—Blount, *Customs of Manours*, p. 147.' Cp. note on *Testament of Cresscid*, l. 48.

1198. (*C*) *thocht I mycht not it lat*: though I could not prevent it. The sense of 'lat' here is the common one; 'let,' to hinder or obstruct, and not 'to say' (O.N. *láta*) as G. G. S. suggests.

1217. *Codies and Digestis new and ald:* a reference, as Lord Hailes points out, 'to the ridiculous division of the Pandects, into *digestum vetus, infortiatum, et novum,* made by Bulgarus in the twelfth century' (*Ancient Scottish Poems,* 1770).

1218. *B* is the only text to give a correct reading here. The readings of *C, H,* and *Bass* are probably a scribal misreading of 'Contra et pro, strait . . . &c.'

1219. *B* gives the best version of this line.

1228. *couth he not appeill:* 'No appeal lay from the judgement of the arbiters. They were judges chosen by the parties themselves, and parties cannot appeal from their own deed' (Hailes, *u.s.,* p. 329).

1234. *ane Borrow:* (Borch *B*), see note on l. 511 *supra.*

1241. *meid:* cp. Chaucer, *Canterbury Tales,* A. 3380-1 :

> 'And, for she was of toune, he profreth meede ;
> For som folk wol ben wonnen for richesse,'

and Langland, *Piers Plowman,* B., Prol. 215, and iii. 12, etc.

1265. Hailes (*u.s.,* p. 329) writes : 'It is remarkable that the whole satire of the fable is aimed at the ecclesiastical judge, whereas the application is to the civil. Henrysoun probably stood more in awe of the court spiritual than of the temporal.'

1273. *portioun:* a misreading for 'porteouss' (*B*), which was originally the portable breviary, then any book or manual (cp. the *Portuus of Nobilnes,* Chepman & Myllar, 1508, cited in the Introduction), and in this case was 'a roll of the names of offenders, which, by the old practice of the Justiciary Court, was prepared by the Justice-Clerk from the informations of crimes furnished by the local authorities' (Bell, *Dict. of the Law of Scotland*). The form 'portouns' in Lyndsay's *Satyre of the Thrie Estaits* (1602), l. 769, is probably due to a misprint (turned letter).

1278. *tat:* (skat *B*) exact. Cp. *scat,* tribute (O.N. *skattr*).

1286. *Consistorie:* the word requires here to be shortened to some such form as 'Constorie.' Cp. 'Constry' (Lyndsay, ed. Laing, iii. p. 149, l. 5757).

1292. *sair:* the reading 'hair' (*B*) has alliterative justification.

1296. *discerne:* adjudge. 'The saidis lordis and estatis of parliament findis, *decernis,* and declaris, that the said Frances, sumtyme erll Bothuile, hes committit and done oppen and manifest tressoun aganis our said souerane lord,' &c. (Acts Ja. VI., 1593, Edin. 1814, p. 11).

1306. *micht:* meid (*B*) makes a better reading here.

Q

The Taill of the Lyon & the Mous.

1328. *quhyte and reid*: the traditional colours of flowers in the courtly allegory.

> 'Of blomyt branchis and flowris quhite and rede'
>> (Douglas, *Virgil*, xii., Prol.)

The actual flowers are usually lilies and roses, and have several contrasted significations—the lily-white symbolising chastity, loyalty, modesty, etc. ; the rose-red symbolising courage, pride, lust, youth, etc.

1345. Here as elsewhere the Catholic tendencies of *B* have been submitted to a Protestant recension.

1348. These first three stanzas of this fable come nearer to the conventional opening of the Chaucerian dream-allegory than Henryson approaches elsewhere.

1350. *Chemeis:* loose gown or robe. *B's* reading *chymmeris* is the plural of 'chymmer' or 'chimer,' a loose gown (O.F. *chamarre*, m.L. *chimera*). *Chambelate:* a wool-and-silk woven cloth. In medieval tradition the wool was always camel's-wool, Cp. the *Kingis Quair*, st. 157 :

> 'For chamelot, the camel full of hare.'

See *N.E.D.*, *s.v.* 'camelet.'

1352 *et seq.* Compare the closely parallel lines in the *Testament of Cresseid*, ll. 244-5.

1358. *prettie gilt:* perhaps 'party-gilt'; partly made of, or covered with, beaten gold.

1386. Cp. l. 1401, and note.

1401. *denye*. The reading 'dedene' in *B* is *not* an error, as G. G. S. states. There are other uses of 'dedene' in the sense of 'deign':

> '—I *dedeinye* not to ressaue
> Sic honour certis quhilk feris me not to haue.'
>> (Douglas, *Virgil*, 23, 30.)
> '—My Lordis to heir that will *deden* . . .'
>> (*Colkelbie Sow*, Prohem.)

Also, *Lancelot of the Laik*, ll. 948, 240.

1407-8. Cp. ll. 756-7 *supra*.

1442. *The sweit sesoun :* early summer ; a common medieval phrase for the opening of the year.

1455. *vilipend :* to abuse or treat slightingly (O.F. *vilipender*, or ad. Lat. *vilipendere*). The whole negotiations are conducted in full legal style.

1460. *harlit:* not 'hanged' but 'dragged.' Cp. l. 772 *supra.*

1469. *Assessouris:* court officials who act as assistant or adviser to a judge or magistrate.

1517. *Rod:* path ; not the same word as 'road.' See *N.E.D.*, *s.v.* 'Rod.'

1520. *Kennettis:* see l. 555 *supra.*

1562. *about:* 'above' in *S.* One of the few instances in which the English text gives a more satisfactory reading than any of the Scots versions.

1580. *lowne and le:* unruffled and sheltered from the wind. G. G. S. quotes Holland, *Buke of the Howlat,* l. 18 :

      ' The Land lowne was and le, with lyking and luf.'

1599. *kinbute:* literally, the wergeld paid by a murderer to the relations of his victim, and so, by extension, a debt or obligation.

1614. Attempts to identify these lines with any particular historical events have been, and are bound to be, futile.

The Preiching of the Swallow.

1633. *deidlie :* mortall, sinful, in the theological sense.

1636. Aristotle, *Metaph. I. M.,* i. 3.

1657. *sternis:* cp. l. 629 *supra,* and note.

1661. *The fyre, the Air, the Watter, and the ground:* the four elements, which play so large a part in medieval physiology, medicine, etc. These lines seem to have been closely imitated by an anonymous poet, quoted by G. G. S. (*Henryson,* iii. p. 26).

1679. *furrit on everilk fent:* cp. l. 912 *supra.*

1685. *Harvest.* Henryson gives the seasons their old names : Somer, Harvest, Wynter, and Ver.

1686. *Hir barnis benit: benit* is a past part. from *bene* pleasant, comfortable ; used here in the sense of 'filled.'

1730. *ferlie :* the usual sense of this word is 'strange' or 'wonderful,' but it is probably better rendered here, and under, at l. 1770, as G. G. S. suggests, by 'sudden.'

1735. *croip :* the top, or crest, of a tree.

1754. *Nam levius . . .* No immediate source for this line has been discovered. It looks like a variant of *Nam provisa minus tela nocere solent,* at v. 10 of Gualterus Anglicus, *De Hirundine et Avibus* (L. Hervieux, *Les Fabulistes latins,* ii. 394).

1763. *scho fischet lang befoir the Net:* Fergusson, A. 379, MS. 419.
Cp. *Towneley Plays*, p. 104, l. 139 ; Heywood's *Proverbs*,
p. 67, etc.

1766. *The nek to stoup :* Fergusson, A. 486.

1775. Cp. *Piers Plowman*, l. 6 :

> 'Me byfel a ferly—of fairy, me thou3te.'

1788. *pyme :* cry. No other example of the word has been recorded.

1807. *friendes hardilie beid :* 'so be it, friends, by all means.'

1817. The sense is, of course, 'God and the holy Rood keep me from
him' ; not the sense suggested by the order of the sentence
as printed.

1822. *markit to the mure :* cp. l. 356 *supra.*

1825 *et seq.* All editors have commented on the accuracy of this
account of flax preparation. Dunfermline, which is still the
chief centre of the linen industry in Scotland, was associated
with the manufacture at least as early as 1491, when six
'wabsters' were charged with 'strubblance' or breach of the
peace. This passage, therefore, may record an instance of
local observation and description, though the methods and
terms are, of course, quite general. It is, at any rate, the
earliest known verse-account of the flax industry.

1863. The two readings, *mocht (CBHt)* and *nocht (Bass H)*, require
different senses of 'quhill.' In the first case it would be
'while'—'While it might avail . . . ,' and in the second,
'till'—'Till it avails him not (is too late to be of any use.)'

1890. *autentik :* serious, important. Cp. the use in *The Trial of the
Fox*, l. 1013 *supra :*

> 'He is Autentik, and ane man of age.'

1950. It has been suggested that Montgomerie, in the *Cherrie and
the Slae* (st. 13), is alluding to Henryson and this fable :

> 'To lait I knaw, quha hewes to hie,
> the speill sall fall into his eye :
> to lait I went to schooles :
> to lait I hard the swallow preich,
> to lait experience dois teich—
> the School-maister of fooles.'

The conjunction of the 'School-maister' allusion with the
undoubted reference to this fable makes the surmise a
tempting one.

The Taill of the Wolf that gat the Nekherīg throw the wrikis of the Foxe that begylit the Cadgear

1952. *As myne Authour:* the source of this fable, one of Henryson's best, is yet unknown, but Professor Bruce Dickins suggests that it may be an elaboration of the Bestiary story of the Fox feigning death in order to catch carrion-crows or ravens.*

1962. *Russell:* (O.F. *russel*, reddish) one of the traditional names of the fox in the Reynard cycle. Cp. Chaucer, *Nun's Priest's Tale*, B. 4525.

1995. *senyes:* the reading of *C*, 'sonȝeis,' is certainly the better reading here.

1997. *Falset will failye ay.* Cp. l. 568 *supra*, and note.

1998. Cp. Fergusson, A. 184.

2001. *I can nocht fische:* a reference to the adage in Heywood's *Proverbs*, p. 60. Cp. the lines in *Macbeth*, I. vii. 44:

> 'Letting "I dare not" wait upon "I would,"
> Like the poor cat i' the adage?'

and see, too, Fergusson, A. 904, MS. 1542; Chaucer, *Hous of Fame*, 1783-5; and Trinity Coll. Camb. MS. (*c.* 1250):

> 'Cat lufat visch ac he nele his feth wete.'

2010. *to draw the stra befoir the cat:* Fergusson, A. 519; Heywood, p. 150.

2013. *reid Raip:* a 'bowcher's' or hangman's rope.

2036. *silver seik:* usually greedy or miserly; here, 'short of cash.' '*Argentangia*, the syluer sickness,' also called the 'silver-quinsy.' (Elyot, *Lat. Dict.*, 1548.)

2041. *traist* (?): (*C*) probably a misprint, caused by a misreading of 'craft,' 'c' and 't,' and 's' and 'f' being easily confused.

2063. *the Devyll . . . deid in ane dyke.* Fergusson, A. 744:

> 'Seldome lyes the divel dead by ane dycksyd.'

Cp. *Towneley Plays*, p. 123, l. 229.

2068-9. *sum wyfis malisone . . . For pultrie pyking.* Cp. Sᵣ Johne Rowlis' Cursing upoun the steilaris of his fowlis (Bann. MS., S.T.S., ii. 277), l. 10: 'Godis braid malesone mot thay haif.'

2074. *Till Flanderis:* to the skin-merchants of the Low Countries.

2083. *huntis up.* Cp. *Romeo and Juliet*, III. v. 34. An ancient song, written, according to Puttenham (*Arte of English Poesie*, 1589), by 'one Gray,' in the time of Henry VIII.

---

* See notes p. xl

and the Protector Somerset. References to the air are to be found in Alex. Scott's *Of May*, *c.* 1560 (S.T.S., p. 23, l. 13), and in the *Complaynt of Scotlande*, 1549 (E.E.T.S., p. 66, and Introd., pp. lxxxvii., lxxxviii.). See, for a full account of the tune, Chappell's *Popular Music of the Olden Time*, i. 60.

2089. *Nekhering:* a blow on the neck, or cuff on the ear. G. G. S. quotes a gloss: 'A Nekherynge, *colaphus*,' from *Cath. Angl.*, 1483, p. 251 (ed. Herrtage, E.E.T.S.).

2102. *lychtlie he lap.* Cp. *The Ressoning betuix Aige and Yowth*, l. 17, p. 179.

2108. *Ane wicht man:* cp. Fergusson, A. 10.

2120. *thir fourtie dayis:* Lent.

2148. The reading of *CHt*, 'dow not me beir' is better here, and accords better with ll. 2149-50.

2154. *In principio.* The first words of *Genesis* and the *Gospel of St John*; commonly used as a piece of ecclesiastical jargon.

2175. '*Softlie*': either as printed, part of the Cadger's speech, or a descriptive adverb, meaning 'under his breath.' There is no indication in the MSS. or printed texts which reading should be adopted.

2198. *Bastoun:* this form preserves the 's' as in O.F. *baston.*

2213. *gold sa reid:* red is the conventional colour of gold in medieval and Renaissance literature, surviving, indeed, to our own day. [Cædmon's *Genesis*, 2404: 'Hi . . . ȝesawon ofer since salo hlifian, reced ofer *readum golde*': Stewart, *Cron. Scot.*, ii. 98 (1535): 'Sex thousand ȝeirlie. . . . Into tribute of fynest *gold so reid.*' And Scott, *Bride of Lammermoor*, ii.: 'From the red gold keep thy finger.']

The Taill of the Foxe, that begylit the Wolf, in the schadow of the Mone

The somewhat primitive methods of agriculture described in this fable are curiously and exactly paralleled by those apparently employed in the Island of Lewis in the early nineteenth century. In a letter to Sir Walter Scott in 1803, James Hogg commented on the Lewis method of ploughing in the following terms:

'I could venture a wager that Cain himself had a more favourable method of tilling the ground. The man was walking by the side of the plough, and guiding it with his right hand. With the left he carried a plough-pattle over his shoulder, which he frequently heaved in a threatening manner at such of the horses as lagged behind; but as it had the same effect on them all, and rather caused the most fiery ones to rush on, he was obliged sometimes to throw it at the lazy ones. The coulter is very slender, points straight down, and is so placed that if it at all rip the ground it hath no effect in keeping the plough steady. The horses, impatient in their nature, go very fast, and the plough being so ticklish, the man is in a perpetual struggle, using every exertion to keep the plough in the ground, and after all, the furrow is in many places a mere scrape. The four ponies go all abreast, and such a long way before the plough, that at a little distance I could not imagine they had any connection with the man or it. They were all four tied to one pole, and a man, to whom the *puller* is a much more applicable name than the *driver*, keeps hold of it with both hands, and walking backward as fast as he can, pulls them on. Those of them that walk too fast he claps the pole to their nose, which checks them. He finds means also to carry a small goad, with which he strikes the lazy ones on the face, asserting that that makes them spring forward. I had once an old brown mare—if he had struck her on the face he would have got her no farther in that direction. A man can scarcely conceive a more disagreeable employment than that of this "driver" as he is called. The ploughman's post being such a very troublesome one he is mostly in a bad humour, and if the line of horses angle, the plough in spite of his teeth is pulled out of the land to the side on which the line is advanced. This puts him into a rage, and he immediately throws the pattle, or a stone, at the hindmost. Now, although the man may be a tolerable good archer, yet passion may make him miss, and the driver run a risk of meeting with the fate of Goliath of Gath. But granting this should never happen, and the ploughman's aim should always hold good, yet " I own 'tis past my comprehension " how a man can walk so fast the whole day in a retrograde direction without falling, when he must that moment be trodden under foot by the horses. In fact I have seen many people who would be often missing their feet on such land although walking with their face foremost ; and it is a fact that many of these drivers are hurt by accidents of the above nature.'

(*The Ettrick Shepherd*, E. C. Batho. Cambridge, 1927.)

2234. *in streiking tyme :* to 'streik' the plough is to draw the first furrow ; in the first of spring, or ploughing-time.

2236 and 2238. *Gadman* and *Caller :* goadsman, or the hand who leads the ploughing-team out to the fields. The *Caller* is the driver. In this case the caller and gadman seem to be one and the same.

2240. *licht :* not in weight but in temper. The opposite sense would be 'sad ' [L. *satis*], serious.

2241. And in their high spirits they spoiled the furrow.

2243. *Patill :* familiar to most readers by its use in Burns' *To a Mouse*, i. 5-6 :

' I wad be laith to rin an' chase thee,
Wi' murdering pattle.'

The tool used by the ploughman for scraping clay from his plough.

2249. *bud:* usually used in the sense of 'bribe'; here rather as 'gift' or 'offer.' Cp. l. 1278 *supra.*

2259. *this, Pray:* the sense 'this (or 'thus'), pray?' adopted by G. G. S. and other editors may be correct, but there is equal justification for the interpretation 'this prey?' with 'prey' in the sense of something seized or taken by force. See *N.E.D., s.v.* 'prey' (4).

2270. *plank.* Previous editors have treated this as an arbitrary rhyme-form of 'plack,' but this is not the case. The form 'plank' connects with the Gaelic word *plang,* 'plack'; for similar nasal infix, compare such forms as 'ballant' beside 'ballat.' The plack was a small copper coin, worth ⅓d. (or four pennies Scots), and was used commonly to express the idea of something trifling and valueless. The printer's Advertisement at the end of Lyndsay's *Works* (St Andrews, 1554) concludes: 'thay ar nocht worthe ane plake.'

2285-6. *For it is said in Proverb, 'But lawte . . .'* I have been unable to identify this proverb with any in Scripture. Cp. Barbour's *Brus,* i. 365-374.

2314. *on the Toddis Taill.* It is unlikely that any pun is intended here.

2322. *Buddis:* cp. l. 1278 and l. 2249 *supra,* and notes.

2332. *God is gane to sleip.* The Sleep of God was a common expression for times of hardship and oppression. Cp. the well-known passage in the Peterborough Chronicle:

> '. . . þe land was al fordon mid suilce dædes, and hi sæden openlice ðat Crist slep and his halechen.'

2335. Fergusson, A. 877, and Heywood, p. 111 *n.* Cp. the line in the *Canterbury Tales,* A. 4134, for an almost identical version of the proverb:

> 'With empty hand men may none haukes tulle.'

2353. *Cabok,* cheese; Mod. Scots, 'kebbock.'

2355. *Somer Cheis:* cheese made in summer, when the milk is at its best. The phrase survives yet in Scots use.

2372. *hors: C H Bass, etc.* Probably a scribal error for 'hous' (house) as in *S Ht.* The latter reading is supported by l. 2374, 'woke the dure' (watched or guarded the door).

2383. *bellie blind:* 'Blind-man's buff' or 'Blind-Harry.' The phrase is a common one in M. Sc. poetry. For a note on the identity of Blind Harry and the web of confusion which has been spun round the name, see *Dunbar,* ed. Mackenzie, Appendix D, p. 242.

2401. *quitclame :* (A.F. *quiteclamer*) legal term for a formal discharge or release.

2402. *dart :* draught, a perfectly easily-understood form. dart = dra^t, with the usual scribal abbreviation and Scots metathesis of 'r.'

2418. *thus fairis it off Fortoun :* perhaps the commonest of medieval poetic commonplaces—the wheel of Fortune. *S* is more laughably at fault here than over any other reading.

2424. *thair is na mair to tell :* a more honest statement of the case than is usual in Chaucer, who used the phrase as a detaining hand upon the arm of his reader while he gathered breath for another thousand lines.

2441. *wyld :* beguiled, through the wiles or 'wrinkis' of the Foxe.

The Taill of the Wolf and the Wedder

2531. *kenenes.* This reading agrees in sense with the emendation 'cunning' supplied by G. G. S. for the orig. 'cumming' of *C*. But the sense of the passage is better met by the original reading. The Wolf knew nothing of the Dog's 'cunning,' but of his 'cumming' he had good reason to know.

2553. *katche :* not 'catch' but 'chase,' as in *C*.

2557. *enchessoun :* (O.F. *encheson*, F. *encheoir*, lit. to fall in, hence to be in fault). Here, 'reason, occasion.'

2608. *Hall benkis.* Cp. *The Priests of Peblis,* 614 :

'For wit thou weil, Hal binks ar ay slidder'

and Fergusson, A. 335.

The Taill of the Wolf and the Lamb

2632. *and bruke.* There is little to choose between this reading and 'the bruke' *Ht S*, 'this bruke' *B* ; but the latter reading seems to be supported by l. 2650 *infra*.

2648. *ascence :* certainly a better reading than 'offens' (*B*).

2673. *refuse :* spare, or let go ; 'chereis' (*C*) would have some such sense as 'favour.'

2679 *et seq.* A brief account of the state of the law as it concerned the ordinary man. This passage should be compared with the longer account in the *Scheip and the Doig*, pp. 42 *et seq.*

2690. *Instant gyis :* the present or recognised custom.

2697. *Be his woundis :* a full form of the oath later abbreviated to ''Swounds !'

2708. *Maill men:* tenants. Cp. '*mailling*,' l. 2734 = small farm for which rent is paid ; and ' Mailleris,' l. 2744 = cottars or small farmers.

> ' Ye saw yoursel how weel his *mailin'* thrave.'
>
> *(Fergusson,* 1785, p. 77.)

2716. *Poete:* (*C H Bass*) a scribal error for 'poleit,' as in *B. S* has the right sense, with 'suttell.'

2738. *croip and caff:* crops and cattle ; the small-holder's sole sources of income.

2743. *Goddis lane:* by God's gift or loan. G. G. S. quotes Chaucer, *C. T.,* D. 1861 :

> ' . . . God be thanked of his loone ! '

2744. *Village:* permission to pasture cattle.

2745. *Gressome:* in Scots law, the fine paid by a tenant to his superior on taking up, or renewing, a holding. '*Gressumas* diċimus summas pecuniae, quae in principio assedationes aut solvuntur aut promittuntur, supra annuam mercedem ' (Craig, *Jus Feudale,* 1732, *Gloss.* p. 49. [G. G. S.])

2750. *Court:* the reading in *B,* ' Cairt,' is almost certainly right.

2752. *withoutin Meit or wage.* These were not the usual conditions. It was customary to provide meals on these occasions.

2755. *watter caill:* soup made without meat. Cp. l. 321 *supra.*

The Taill of the Paddok & the Mous

2790. *schir Mous:* deme (*B*) accords better with the rest of the text, in which the mouse is referred to as ' scho'—cp. l. 2779 *et seq.*

2809. *facultie or gin:* skill or contrivance.

2819. *fronsit:* frounced, wrinkled. Cp. *Testament of Cresseid,* l. 155 :

> ' His face frosnit, his lyre was lyke the Leid,'

where ' frosnit ' is a misprint for ' fronsit.' The error occurs again in *The Flyting of Montgomerie and Polwart,* l. 575 :

> ' With scoiris and crakis athort his *froisnit* front.'

2827. *proceidis:* G. G. S. assumes that this reading and ' persavis' (*B*) are scribal misreadings of ' persewis ' (written ' persevis '), but there is no reason to reject the *C H Bass* reading.

2830. This line should almost certainly read : 'Ane thrawin will, ane thrawin Phisnomy.' See the reading of *C.*

2831. *Lorum:* a popular abbreviated form of 'culorum,' the end of 'in secula seculorum,' signifying conclusion. For similar corruptions the reader is referred to *Merry Wives of Windsor*, I. i. 5, 6 :

> '. . . justice of peace, and Coram.
> *Shal.* Ay, cousin Slender, and Cust-alorum.'

2834. *For fair thingis:* Fergusson, A. 801.

2838. *in all place:* the reading (*B*) 'in a place' is probably to be preferred.

2842. *Jolie Absolon:* traditional medieval type of perfect beauty. Cp. Chaucer's *Ballade* from the *Legend of Good Women*, Prol. B, ll. 249-69 :

> ' Hyd, Absolon, thy gilte tresses clere ;'

2854-5. Cp. ll. 2044-5 *supra.*

2873. *carpand:* deceiving or lying. If the reading 'trappald' (*CHt*) be taken, some emendation is necessary. G. G. S. suggests crappald (scribal confusion of 'c' and 't') and quotes 'crapault' (=toad) from Caxton. (Fr. *crapand.*)

2883. *manesworne:* (now obsolete except in Scots and northern dialects) perjured, forsworn.

2897. *battell:* in the old sense of 'duel,' as in the phrase 'ordeal of battle.'

2904. *belliflaucht:* a particular method of skinning, in which the skin is pulled whole over the head.

2910. The Moralitas is in 8-line Ballade form.

2927. *frank and fre :* technical phrase, derived from feudal law.

2945. Now gay gowns, now poor clothes, tended as carefully as though they *were* fine.

The reading of *B* is more obvious and satisfactory.

2946. *fitche :* fitchew, or fish (as in *B*)?

2972. *exempill and ane similitude.* Cp. l. 47 *supra.*

The Testament of Cresseid

4. *tragedie :* in the medieval sense—a fall from felicity to misery, implying no sense of dramatic construction.

fervent : intense or bitter ; used of cold until 1634. *N.E.D.* quotes from Stewart, *Croniklis of Scotland*, ii. 337, 'The fervent frost so bitter wes' (1535).

5. *Aries :* the Ram, the sign of the Zodiac which the sun entered on 13th March and left on 11th April.

in middis of the Lent : about the beginning of April. This exact dating of a poem by the signs of the Zodiac, or the Christian calendar (or even more explicit statement) is in the true medieval tradition. Cp. Chaucer, *Legend of Good Women*, Prol. B, 108, or *Hous of Fame*, 63 and 111.

15. *the glas:* Kinaston's note on this passage runs : *Per vitra, etc.:* Id est, per fenestram vitreis quadris compactam quarum rarior erat vsus, nisi in templis aut ecclesijs, ob magnos nempe sumptus in compagibus plumbeis componendis, cum artifices nondum excogitassent machinam instar molendini ad plumbeos bacillos ducendos & in canali formandos iam accommodatum, sed magno labore solebant crebris morsubus dolabræ excauare virgulas plumbeas vt quadræ vitreæ illis inhærerent immotæ.'

Pedro de Ayala, the Spanish ambassador, in a letter dated 25th July 1498, wrote : 'The towns and villages are populous. The houses are good, all built of hewn stone, and provided with excellent doors, glass windows, and a great number of chimneys.'

(*The Days of James IV:* ed. G. Gregory Smith, 1900.)

23. *To quhome sum tyme I hecht obedience:* Henryson represents himself here, and here only, as a worshipper in the temple of Love.

27. *lattit:* prevented. Cp. 'thocht I mycht not it lat' (*Fables* (*C*) l. 1198).

36. *I mend the fyre:* for a comparable picture of a winter interior, see Douglas's *Æneid*, Prol., Bk. vii.

43. *thair I fand:* Chaucer, *Troilus and Criseyde*, v. 1030 *et seq.*

48. *Esperus:* this reading in *C* and *T* has been taken to be a confusion of original 'esperance' with 'Hesperus,' the (morning and) evening star. *SJ* and *A* have the 'correct' reading, and *K* has made the necessary emendation in his translation, with a marginal note, 'esperance, that is hope.' Cp. the *Garmont of Gud Ladeis*, p. 170 :

'Hir slevis suld be of esperance.'

'Esperance' is presumably intended to balance 'wanhope,' or despair in the previous line. But Professor Bruce Dickins, of Leeds University, writing on this subject to the *Times Literary Supplement*, 11th December 1924, shed a new light on the matter. He wrote :

' . . . But is this conclusive? Kinaston had consulted more than one of the printed versions of the poem, and when baffled by their readings had sought the advice of Scottish friends ; but to my mind the form "tulliure," which he substitutes at v. 194 for the meaningless "tulsure" of Thynne and the rest,

negatives in advance the suggestion that he had access to
a purer text than that presented by the Charteris print.

I suggest that the reading "Esperus" should be retained, but in an
unusual sense—a sense hitherto unrecognised by the *N.E.D.*,
though there is unquestionably an example at vv. 197-8 of *The
Second Anniversary*, where Donne is describing the flight of
Mistress Elizabeth Drury's soul 'twixt earth and heaven :

> " Venus retards her not, to enquire if shee
> Can (being one starre) Hesper, and Vesper bee."

Venus is, of course, both Evening and Morning Star—Hesper
when she follows, Phosphor when she goes before, the sun
(Cicero, *De Natura Deorum*, 2, 2, 53). In this passage of
Donne, however, the juxtaposition of "Hesper" and "Vesper"
makes it clear that, by a strange transference of meaning,
"Hesper" is used of the Morning Star.

"Esperus" is almost certainly to be found in the same sense
in the second stanza of the Scots song, "Lusty May with
Flora quene," which is as early as the first half of the sixteenth
century. In the Bannatyne manuscript of 1568 it begins :

> "Than esperus that is so bricht,
> Till wofull hairtis castis his lycht,"

which is modernized and anglicized to

> "Then Aurora that is so bright,
> To wofull hearts he casts great licht,"

in the 1682 edition of Forbes's Aberdeen "Cantus."

It will be seen that the two lines quoted present a pretty close
parallel to the passage from Henryson.

In view of the references I have given I cannot see that there is
any need to abandon the Charteris reading ; Donne shows
that "Esperus" can be used in the sense of the Morning
Star, which brings light to woeful hearts, as the song from
the Bannatyne manuscript suggests. And it is particularly
appropriate that "Esperus," who is also Venus, should comfort
the faithful lover.'

(See also the reply by Mr W. M. L. Hutchinson, *T.L.S.*, 25th
December 1924.)

50. *Of hir behest: Troilus and Criseyde*, v. 1423 *et seq.*
61. *ane uther quair :* this 'other quair,' if it ever existed, is not known
to exist now.*
74. *Lybell of repudie :* 'a bill of divorcement' : the *libellum repudii*
of the Vulgate. Wycliffe translates it : 'a libel, that is, a litil

* See notes p. xxxix

boke of forsakyng.' For 'libell' in the sense of a book of any
kind, cp. Lyndsay, *Testament and Complaynt of our Soverane
Lordis Papyngo*, ll. 19-21 (S.T.S. *ed. Hamer*, i. 56-57) :

> ' Quintyng, Mersar, Rowle, Henderson, hay & holland,
> Thocht thay be ded, thar libells bene levand,
> Quhilkis to reheirs makeith redaris to reiose.'

77. *into the Court commoun :* that is, became a prostitute. Cp. the
word 'courtesan.'

78. *A per se :* paragon. The phrase derives from the vocabulary of
printing, and means, literally : '*A* by itself' = the word, 'A' ;
just as the character '&' is still called the 'ampersand,' *i.e.*
'& by itself' = the word 'and.' 'A' being the first letter of
the alphabet, the phrase came to be applied to whatever was
first and highest in esteem. Cp. *Crying of Play*, 133 : 'In
Edinburgh, Quhilk is the lampe & A per se of this regioun
. . .' and examples from Dunbar, Douglas, Stewart, Lyndsay,
etc., in Craigie's *Dictionary of the Older Scottish Tongue*.

79. *how was thou fortunait :* how evil was thy fortune.

84. *fall :* in the sense of 'obtain' or 'come in for.' See *N.E.D. s.v.*
'Fall,' *v.* 54.

87. *excuse :* vindicate. Cresseid's womanhood, wisdom, and fairness
are not qualities that require extenuation.

91. *wickit langage :* slanderous tongues—*Rumor.*

97. *Beildit :* (*North.* beldau) decorated. The 'Bylded' of *TA* is a
corruption, due probably to inability to understand the original.

106. *efter the Law was tho :* according to the law at that time.

107-8. Calchas was not a priest of Venus and Cupid in Chaucer, but
a priest of Apollo (*Troilus and Criseyde*, i. 69-72). Henryson
probably altered his service deliberately for the sake of
dramatic effect.

129. *outwaill :* outcast. (For 'wale' = choose, see l. 440 *infra.*
The word is still common in Scots use.) Literally, 'chosen
for rejection.'

133. *abject odious :* 'abject' is here a substantive, = 'outcast.'

140. *forlane :* perhaps 'deflowered' : cp. *N.E.D. s.v.* 'forlane,' where
it is explained as the past participle of 'forlie,' to prostitute, or
violate. But the sense is more probably 'forsaken.' G. G. S.
quotes Rolland's *Court of Venus* (S.T.S., 127, l. 496) for a
very similar use of the word :

> ' Be quite for3et, ouirsene, and all forlane.'

147 *et seq.* With this description of the Planets compare Dunbar's
Goldyn Targe (ed. Mackenzie, p. 115), ll. 109-117.

149. *Influence:* in the astrological sense. 'The supposed flowing from the stars of an ethereal fluid acting upon the character and destiny of men, and affecting sublunary things generally.'

155. *frosnit:* a corruption of 'fronsit' or 'frounced' as it is given, correctly, in *T.* The correct form occurs in the *Fables,* l. 2819, 'hir fronsit face.' Kinaston again has the right sense — 'frownced that is wrinkeled.'

his lyre was lyke the Leid: 'his lere that is his cullor' (*K*). Lead, according to medieval alchemy, was the metal of Saturn. Cp. Chaucer, *Hous of Fame,* iii. ll. 358-59 :

'And the leed, withouten faile,
Is lo, the metal of Saturne.'

164. *gyis:* dress or robe. The correct reading is certainly 'gyte' (O.F. *guite,* a gown or dress). Here it may be taken either as 'robe' or 'hat' (Godefroy, *Dictionnaire Historique de l'Ancien Langage Français*). The usual English sense is 'garment'— so used till 1614. 'And she cam after in a gyte of reed' (Chaucer, *Canterbury Tales,* A. 3954).

167. *flasche:* Thynne and Speght both read 'fasshe' (O.F. *fais* or *faisse,* bundle or sheaf), but 'flash' is common in this sense in 16th and 17th century writers. The *N.E.D. s.v.* Flash, *sb.*[3], is disposed to attribute these usages to the example of Henryson, and quotes Fairfax, *Tasso* (1600), XI. xxviii. 201 :

'Her ratling quiver at her shoulders hong,
Therein a flash of arrowes feathered weele.'

178. *gyis:* gyte *TK.* See note on l. 164 *supra.*
[gay] supplied from *T* and *K.* See, too, l. 218 *infra.*

187-8. *roustie:* not 'rusty' in the common sense, but 'bronze'—as red as rust. Bronze, however, is not the metal of Mars :

'For yren Martes metal is,
Which that god is of bataile ;'
(Chaucer, *Hous of Fame,* iii. 356-7.)

194. *Tuilyeour lyke: C* reads *Tuitl3eour; T, tulsure,* as also do Stow (1561) and Speght (1598) ; and *A, Souldiour.* Kinaston's note reads : 'Propter ignorantiam veræ significationis Scotici vocabuli *Tullieur* erratum est fere in omnibus impressionibus in quibus perpaeram describitur *Tulsur.* vox hæc apud Scotos hominem trucem & efferum significat qualem nos Angli vocamus *a Swaggerer,* & Itali *uno Brauo.*

196. Cp. *Fables,* l. 840 :

'Quhilk, as he thocht, maid all the warld to waig.'

205. *upricht:* (unricht, *TAK*). The latter reading is probably the more correct, corresponding, as it does, with Chaucer's 'amis' in *Troilus and Criseyde*, v. 664-5 :

> 'The sonnes sone, Pheton, be on-lyve
> And that his fadres cart amis he dryve.'

But compare *Fables*, l. 470 (p. 19) :

> 'Ye ar your ffatheris sone and air upricht.'

211. The names of the four steeds derive from Ovid's *Metamorphoses*, ii. 153-5 :

> 'Aeöus, Aethon, Phlegon, and the firie Pyrois
> The restlesse horses of the Sunne began to ney so hie.'
>
> (Golding's translation, 1567.)

In both *Charteris* and *Thynne*, *Phlegon* appears as *Philologee*. *K* and *SJ* give the correct reading.

231. *lauch . . . weip :* G. G. S. explains these forms as infinitives with the value of the subjunctive. But the more natural explanation is that 'lauch' is an eccentric form of 'leuch,' the preterite ; 'weip' is the normal form—cp. A.S. 'weop.'

244-5. *heklit:* with these two lines compare the description of Æsop, *Fables*, ll. 1352-3, p. 49. The meaning is fringed, like the hackle of a cock, or folded. Kinaston glosses it in a marginal note : 'hecled that is wrapped or folded.' As a poetic headdress this 'turban' survived well into the eighteenth century, as in the portrait of the poet James Thomson, for example.

246-52. Cp. Chaucer's Doctour of Physic in *Prol.* 410 *et seq.*

260. *gyse :* gyte *T.* See note on ll. 164, 178 *supra.*

261. *ane Churle :* an allusion to the fate of the Man in the Moon. Cp. Chaucer, *Troilus and Criseyde*, Bk. i., ll. 1013-4 :

> 'Quod Pandarus, thou hast a ful gret care
> Lest that the cherl may falle out of the mone.'

Cp., too, Shakespeare, *Midsummer Night's Dream*, v. i. 251 ; and *Tempest*, II. ii. 131.

272. *vocatioun :* calling together, convocation. Cp. line 346 *infra.*

275. See note on ll. 107-8 *supra.*

290. *Injurie :* the form 'injure,' found in *T*, is better Scots and, metrically, makes a better line.

299. *modifie :* to judge or assess ; Scots legal usage, still in use. Cp. the form 'moderator' in the Scots Church Assembly.

308. *abhominabill :* a common, but fallacious form of the word, due to the popular and incorrect derivation, 'ab homine' : used from the time of Wyclif, and very common in Shakespeare.

318. In the medieval physiology, moisture and heat were component qualities of the 'sanguine' humour—cold and dryness of the melancholic.

332. *bill:* (Anglo-L. *billa*, altered from Med. L. *bulla*, a seal) any sealed or formal document ; used until 1788 in the sense of 'indictment.'

337. The late Sir J. Y. Simpson demonstrated by these lines that leprosy in this country was, as on the Continent, truly the Greek Elephantiasis (*Edin. Med. and Surg. Journal,* 1841).

343. The leper's cup, or begging-bowl, and clap-dish, to give warning of his approach. Scott discusses this passage in the notes to *Sir Tristrem* (*Poetical Works,* v., pp. 452-54).

358. *the Hall:* the great hall of the medieval house where all the members of the household ate together.

362. *on grouf:* (O.N. *ágrúfu*), cp. modern 'grovelling.' The form still exists in Scots use. A friend of mine lately heard a young mother with a crying infant being advised to 'turn the bairn agrufe.'

382, 391. *Hospitall, Spittaill hous:* Laing (*Henryson,* p. 261) writes : 'There is reason to believe that a spittall house existed in Dunfermline ; and the name Spittal Street, at the east end of the town, is still retained. This may have afforded Henryson an opportunity of personally witnessing the victims of this frightful malady.' The opportunity, in Henryson's day, was not so hard to come by ; there were leper communities all over the country. Cp. the names Spittal (near Berwick), Spittal Street, Edinburgh, and Liberton (supposed to be a corruption of Lipper-toun).

407. *The Complaint of Cresseid* follows the model of Chaucer's *Compleynt of Faire Anelyda upon Fals Arcyte.*

413. *on breird.* See notes to *Fables,* l. 10.

416. With this account of Cresseid's forfeited delights, G. G. S. compares *Philotus* (ed. Bannatyne Club), §§ 10 *et seq.* ; and Lyndsay's *Squyer Meldrum* (ed. Laing, i., p. 189, ll. 927 *et seq.*).

440. *waillit:* choice. See note on l. 129 *supra.*

480. *leir:* Skeat and Sir W. A. Craigie advocate the rejection of this reading in favour of 'leve.'

483. In the old Burrow Lawis of Scotland, cap. 64, it is enjoined, that 'Leper folke sall nocht gang fra dure to dure, but sall sit at the posts of the Burgh, and seik almes (with cop and clapper) fra thame that passes in and forth.' (Laing : *Henryson,* p. 262.)

490, 494. *the Lipper . . . us Lipper:* leper folk, as in lines 526, 580.

507. *Idole:* (late L. *idolum,* a. G. εἴδωλον, fr. εἴδος, form or shape), insubstantial mental image. *N.E.D.* quotes, 'Vain idols and phantoms of blessedness' (1899).

R

540. *ouircome :* Professor Bruce Dickins, of Leeds University, has pointed out (*Test. of Cresseid*, Edinburgh, 1925, p. 38) that the usual punctuation, a comma between 'scho' and 'ouircome,' destroys the sense. 'Ouircome' here, as in *Orpheus and Eurydice*, l. 400 (p. 141), means 'revived.'

541. *cald ochane !* The Gaelic 'ochane' or 'O hone' (exclamation of sorrow) has puzzled *T*, who read 'atone.' It is possible to read 'cald' either as 'called' or 'cold'; I have chosen the latter. It is necessary to supply some such phrase as 'She cried' before the next line.

550. *the fickill quheill :* the wheel of Fortune. Cp. *Fables*, ll. 2418-9 (p. 82).

567 *sad :* reliable (literally, 'heavy'). Used ironically here for 'unsad,' as in Chaucer, *Clerkes Tale* (E. 995-6):

> ' O stormy peple ! unsad, and ever untrewe !
> Ay undiscreet, and chaungynge as a vane.'

583. *drowrie :* (*AT* dowry). See note on *Fables*, l. 497. Cp. *Gawain*, 1057.

588. *Wellis :* the fountains associated with the chaste Diana.

589. *Broche and Belt.* There is no mention in Chaucer of the belt, which is probably Henryson's addition. It may be intended to signify the cincture of chastity, as the brooch represented the badge of true love, worn over the heart. For the brooch, see *Troilus and Criseyde*, v. 1661-1666, 1669, 1688-1694.

610. *Ballet :* the term probably applies to the whole poem, which is written in Ballade-royal verse.

Orpheus and Eurydice

2. *rynk :* (renk, *C*; reulre *A*). Probably the reading in *A* is a misreading of *C*.

25. *knawlege :* (tarage *C ;* carage *A*). Probably the best reading is 'tarage' (*C*), meaning 'flavour': 'carage' is a likely misreading of 'tarage,' and 'knawlege' is an obvious case of substitution for an unfamiliar reading.

52. *polimio :* Polyhynmia, from the secondary form 'Polymnia.'

92. Cp. *Testament of Cresseid*, ll. 429 *et seq.*, and Lyndsay's *Squyer Meldrum* (ed. Laing, i., p. 189, ll. 927 *et seq.*).

121. *rampand as a Lyoun.* Cp. notes to *Fables*, l. 999, p. 238.

134 *et seq.* This 'Complaint of Orpheus' is similar in construction to that of Cresseid in the *Testament*. Cresseid's is a nine-line decasyllabic stanza, rhyming *aabaabbab ;* that of Orpheus is a ten-line decasyllabic stanza, rhyming *aabaabbcbc.*

138. *lyking:* for a similar use of the word, see the lyric printed by Sir E. K. Chambers from the *Sloane* MS. 2593 (*Early English Lyrics*, 1926):

> 'Lullay, mine liking, my dere sone, mine sweting.'

139. *gole, and greit:* bitter crying and lamentation. (Cp. Lyndsay, *Monarchie*, 6003):

> 'Thare salbe gowlyng and gretyng.'

140. *pynnis:* pins or pegs of a harp.

159. *hate of hair:* cp. the *Testament of Cresseid*, l. 386 (p. 118):

> 'Than in ane Mantill and ane bawer Hat'

—apparently one of the insignia of poverty and misery.

188. *wedlingis streit:* Watling Street; here, the Milky Way, or Galaxy. Cp. Chaucer, *Hous of Fame*, Bk. ii., ll. 427 *et seq.*:

> 'Now' quod he tho, 'cast up thyn ÿe;
> See yonder, lo, the Galaxÿe,
> The which men clepe the Milky Wey,
> For hit is white : and somme, parfey,
> Callen hit Watlynge strete,'

and Douglas, *Virgil*, III. viii. (ed. Small, ii., p. 151, ll. 11 *et seq.*):

> 'Of euery sterne the twinkilling notis he,
> That in the stil heuin move cours we se,
> Arthuris huyfe, and Hyades betaiknand rane,
> Syne Watling streit, the Horne, and the Charle wane.'

G. G. S. writes : 'The ascription of the name of a great road to the Via lactea ("Hac iter est Superis ad magni tecta tonantis," Ovid, *Metam.*, i. 170) was common in Europe. The English also spoke of "Walsingham Way" (see Blomfield's *Norfolk*), the Italians of *Strada di Roma*, and the Spaniards of the *Santiago road* (see Skeat, Chaucer, iii. 263, and Langland, ii. p. 8).' (*Henryson*, iii. p. 54.)

190. *Quhilk fadir is to all the stormis cald:* cp. the *Testament of Cresseid*, ll. 155-169 (pp. 110-111 *supra*).

206-7. '*wait ye nocht weill I am your awin trew knycht?*' Orpheus appears here in thoroughly medieval guise, vowing service to the queen of love, like Palamon in the *Knight's Tale:*

> 'Emforth my myght, thy trewe servant be,
> And holden werre alwey with chastitee ;
> That make I myn avow, so ye me helpe.'
> (*Canterbury Tales*, A. 2235-7.)

212-13. *Till mercury . . . quhilk callit is :* cp. *Testament of Cresseid,* ll. 239-245, and ll. 267-270 (pp. 113, 114 *supra*).

219. With Henryson's account of the music of the spheres, and music in general, and with his ingenuous disclaiming of all knowledge of the science (1. 240 *infra*), cp. G. Douglas, *Palice of Honour*, ed. Small, i. p. 20, ll. 12 *et seq.*, and ll. 21 *et seq.*

223. *mappamound :* (A.F. *mappemonde*, ad. Med. L. *mappa mundi*), the map of the world : in early use (as here), the world itself.

> ' With that he racht me a roll : to rede I begane,
> The royetest ane ragment with mony ratt rime,
> Of all the mowis in this mold, sen God merkit man,
> The mouing of the mapamound, and how the mone schane.'
> (Douglas, *Virgil*, 239, a. 55.)

And Lyndsay, *The Dreme* (ed. Laing, p. 32, l. 833) :

> ' Quhilkis als is nocht in al the Mapamound.'

224. *Quhilk moving seiss unyt perpetuall.* This line has been rejected as corrupt, and, as it stands, is certainly difficult. G. G. S. suspects (and not unreasonably) the repetition of ' quhilk' at the head of three successive lines. But the original reading of the Chepman & Myllar text is not ' Quhilk' but ' Quhill.' Accepting this reading, the sense may be taken to be—

> '. . . Which harmony of all this universe
> (In perpetual unison, until moving cease),
> Pluto called the soul of this world.'

The ' Quhilk' at the head of the last line is unnecessary but resumes the sense after the interpolation. And the point of the phrase, ' Quhill moving seiss,' is admirably illustrated in Lyndsay's *Dialog betuix Experience and ane Courteour*, ll. 6038-9, in which, describing the end of creation, he says :

> ' And everilk Planeit in his speir
> Sall rest, withouttin more moveyng.'

See too, ll. 6241-6247, and Laing's note. Orpheus's journey through the heavens may be compared with the flight in Lyndsay's *Dreme*, i., pp. 15-20, especially ll. 505-511.

Henryson's knowledge of the terms of music may have been derived from Boethius' *De Musica*. Cp. Chaucer, *Nun's Priest's Tale* (B. 4483-4) :

> ' Therwith ye han in musyk moore feelynge
> Than hadde Boece, or any that kan synge.'

The following well-known passage from Higden's *Polychronicon*,
1495, fol. 101 (printed by Wynkyn de Worde), illustrates the
reputed origin, and sense, of some of these terms :

'Here wyse men I tell, that Pictagoras passed som tyme by a
smythes hous, and herde a swete sowne, and accordynge in
the smytynge of four hamers vpon an anuelt, and therefore
he lette weye the hamers, & found that one of the hamers
weyed twyes so moche as another. Another weyed other halfe
so moche as another ; and another weyed so moche as another,
and the thyrde dele of another. As though the fyrste hamer
were of syx pounde, the second of twelue, the thyrde of eyght,
the fourth of ix.—When these accordes were founden,
Pictagoras gaue them names, and so that he called in nombre,
double, he called in sownes DYAPASON, and that he called in
nombre *other halfe*, he called in sowne DYAPENTE, & that that
in nombre is called *alle and the thyrde dele*, hete in sownes
DYATESSERON, and that that in nombres is called *alle & the
eyghteth dele*, hete in tewns, DOUBLE DYAPASON. As in melody
of one strenge, yf the strenge be streyned enlonge vpon the
holownesse of a tree, and departe euen atwo by a brydge sette
there vnder in eyther part of the strenge, the sowne shall be
Dyapason, if the strenge be streyned and touched. And yf
the strenge be departed euen in thre, and the brydge sette
vnder, soo that it depart bytwene the twey deles and the
thyrde, then the lenger dele of the strenges, yf it be touched,
shal gyue a sowne called Dyatesseron. And yf it be departed
in nyne, and the brydge sette vnder bytwene the laste parte
and the other dele, and the lenger dele of the strenge, yf it
be touched, shall gyue a sowne that hete Tonus.'

227. *duplare, triplare :* double and triple time.

    Emetricus : (? Gr. ἐμμετρία, ἡ ; fit measure, proportion, μετρικός, of
or relating to measure or measuring). This, even more than
Epoddeus, is 'rycht hard and curius.' The editor has discovered no use of the term denoting (as it should here do)
a particular musical ratio. It is at least possible that the
original form was *epitritus* (Gr. ἐπίτριτος) or sesquitertius = one
and a third, or the ratio of four to three. Admitting the
common confusion of manuscript 't' and 'c,' we have *epitricus*,
which a puzzled and well-intentioned copyist might normalise
to *emetricus*. But, like my author, I submit the theory only
until some better-informed student explains the reading as
it stands :

      'Off sik musik to wryt I do bot doit.'

228. *Enolius:* Boethius, *De Musica* (*Opera Omnia* . . . Basle, 1546), p. 1171, 'Divisio chromatis hemiolij'; Ducange (*Glossarium*, &c.) gives 'hemiolus = Numerus sesquialter'; and Groves (*Dict. of Music*, ii. 608) gives: Hemiolia (Gr. ἡμιόλιος; Lat. *sesquialtera;* Fr. *hémiole;* Ital. *emiolia*). 'Literally, the whole and a half; technically, the proportion of two to three. In this latter sense the word is used, in the musical terminology of the Middle Ages, to denote the perfect fifth, the sound of which is produced on the monochord by two-thirds of the open string.'

229. *Epoddeus* (Epogdŏŏs, -ŏus, ἐπόγδοος): a whole and an eighth—the proportion of nine to eight (or *sesquioctavus*); Boethius, p. 1062 (Diagram), gives 'Epogdous.'

235. *componyt with the dyss:* or 'componyt with the "bis"'—'bisdiapente,' the interval of a double fifth.

264. *Electo, mygra, and thesaphone:* the Eumenides, or Furies: Alecto, Megaera, and Tisiphone.

266. *exione:* Ixion, king of the Lapithæ, who, for his ingratitude in attempting the love of Hera, was made father of a Centaur, and chained for ever to a rolling wheel. (Ovid, *Metamorphoses*, Bk. iv.)

282. *ane naple:* probably 'an apple'; though Jamieson records the form 'napple'—'a sweet wild root' . . . apparently *Orobus tuberosus*, or Heath-pea (. . . diligently digged for and greedily chewed by boys). But the form is more probably a product of the opposite process to that by which 'una naránja' becomes 'an orange.'

295. *titius:* (Theseus *C*, l. 178). Tityus, son of Gæa, who for his attempted violence to Artemis, was destroyed by Zeus with a flash of lightning; after which he was cast into Tartarus, where vultures and snakes devoured his liver as he lay outstretched on the ground. Cp. Chaucer's *Boece*, iii., Metrum 12: 'The foul that highte voltor, that etith the stomak or the gyser of Tycius, is so fulfild of his song that it nil eten ne tiren no more.' The order of incidents in Orpheus' search follows closely the account of Boethius, but Henryson most probably knew the story in the *Georgics*, the *Aeneid*, Bk. vi., and in Ovid (*Metamorphoses*, Bk. iv.). Cp., too, Chaucer's *Troilus and Criseyde*, i. 786-7:

> 'As sharp as doth he, Ticius, in helle,
> Whos stomak foules tiren evere mo.'

317 ff. With this passage compare the lines in Lyndsay's *Dialog betuix Experience and ane Courteour*, 5729-50 (ed. Laing, iii. pp. 148-9).

338 *et seq.* *Thair saw he mony paip and cardynall:* cp. Dante, *Inferno*, Canto xix.

369. *Ipotdorica:* Hypodorian or Locrian, a plagal mode in medieval music, a fourth below the authentic Dorian mode.

370. *gemilling:* (gemynyng *C*) perhaps 'second part.' The form suggests some connection with *gemel*, 'twin, or double.' The form is used in a technical musical sense by Douglas, *Palice of Honour* (ed. Small, i. 20, ll. 19-21):

> 'In modulation hard I play and sing.
> Faburdoun, pricksang, discant, countering,
> Cant organe, figuration, and gemmell.'

N.E.D., s.v. 'Gimmal,' quotes Palsgrave, 'Gymell song, *jumeau.*

yporlerica: *Hypolocrian*, a rejected plagal mode, a fourth below the authentic Locrian. See above, note to l. 369.

400. *ourcome:* recovered. Cp. the use in *Testament of Cresseid*, l. 540 (p. 124 *supra*), and note.

401. *Quhat art thow, luve, how sall I the defyne ? :* an attempt at the extravagant rhetorical 'character of love,' full of apparent paradox and contradiction. Cp. the song of Troilus in *Troilus and Criseyde*, Bk. i., ll. 400 *et seq.:*

> 'If no love is, O God, what fele I so?'

for a similar attempt. Chaucer writes:

> 'O quike deth ! O swete harm so queynte !'
> 'For hete of cold, for cold of hete, I dye !'

etc. This rather frigid and elaborate rhetoric was most highly cultivated in the Petrarcan sonnet-form.

409. For the second part of this proverb, Sir W. A. Craigie has provided an Icelandic parallel: 'Tungan leikr við tanna sár,' —'the tongue plays with the sore tooth.'

411. *expart:* (L. *expertus*) experienced (in the matter). Cp. *Testament of Cresseid*, l. 35 (p. 106 *supra*).

414. *wedo:* the obsolete masculine use, from O.E. *widewa*, corresponding to feminine *widewe*.

415. *boece:* Boethius, *De Consolatione*, iii., Metrum 12.

421. *maister trivat:* (trowit *C*: trewit *A*) Nicholas Trivet (? 1258-1328) Dominican friar, author of a *Chronicle* (Annales sex Regum Angliæ . . . . [1136-1307]) from which Chaucer took the story of Constance (Man of Lawe's Tale) ; and several theological works, including In [librum] *Boetii de consolatione philosophiæ.* The commentary was as widely known and read as the original, and Laing (*Henryson*, p. 256) quotes from the inventory of the

library of the Cathedral Church of Glasgow, drawn up in the
year 1442, . . . 'Item, liber Boetii cum glossa Trevet.' How
closely Henryson follows Trivet in the Moralitas may be seen
by comparison with the following extracts [1] :

'*Per* orpheum inte*lligitur* pars intellectiua instructa sap*ient*ia et
eloq*uen*cia. vn*de* dicitur filius phebi et calliope. . . . et eius
filius d*icitu*r quilib*et* eloq*uen*cia instructus et quia phebus est
de*u*s sapient*i*e . . . Cui*u*s ux*or* est eur[i]dice s*cilicet* pa*rs*
homin*is* aff*ect*iua q*uam* s*ibi* copulare cupit. ariste*u*s qui inter-
pr*e*tatur uirt*us*. s*e*t illa dum fugit p*er* pr*a*ta i*d* e*st* amena
pr*e*sentis uite calcat s*er*pentem no*n* ip*s*um *conter*endo s*et* seip*s*am
que s*up*erior est inf*er*iori s*cilicet* s*en*suali*t*ati appli*cando* a qua
mordetur dum p*er* s*en*suali*t*atem ei occa*s*ione mortis datur (?)
sicq*u*e ad inferos descendit i*d* e*st* t*er*renor*um* curis se s*u*biciendo
orpheus aut*em* i*d* e*st* inte*llectus* uolens ea*m* a talibus abstrah*ere*
modula*c*ionibus placat super*os*. i*d* e*st* p*er* suaue*m* eloq*uen*ciam
coniuncta*m* sap*ienc*ie ra*ti*onatu*r* commenda*ndo* celestia. ut
ab istis t*er*renis ip*s*am abstrahat s*et* quia ascensus ad celestia
difficultatem ha*b*et prop*ter* s*u*btracci*on*em multar*um* delect-
a*c*ionu*m* qu*e* impediunt uirtute*m* p*er* qua*m* sit ascensus. . . .
Deind*e* cum dicit. s*t*up*et* o*st*endi*t* quo*modo* orpheus placu*er*it
monstra inf*er*nalia p*r*imo incipiens a cane qui fingitur Janitor
inferni et h*a*b*ere* tria capita. per istum cane*m* intel*ligitu*r t*er*ra.
. . . S*ecundum* ysidor*um* libro xj. ethi*mologiarum* c. de port-
entis. p*er* hu*n*c canem trium capitum signa*n*tur tres p*ar*tes
etatis p*er* quas mors homi*n*em deuorat. i*d* e*st* p*er* infanciam
iuue*n*tute*m* et senectute*m* quar*um* quel*ib*et admiratu*r* sapienciam. Deind*e* describit aliud mo*n*stru*m* v*b*i notand*um* q*uod*
om*n*e scelus uel est in cogita*c*ione uel in s*er*mone u*el* in opere
pr*opter* q*uod* ponu*n*tur tres dee sceler*i*s que p*ropter* co*n*nexione*m*
istorum adinuice*m* d*ic*untu*r* sorores. quar*um* prima uocatur
allecto. secunda thesiphone. t*er*cia meg*er*a. . . . Tertium
mo*n*str*um* quod describit est pena yrionis [yxionis] de quo
fingitu*r* q*uod* uoluit *con*cumb*er*e cum Junone. vn*de* accepit
cognom*en* audacis q*uia* uoluit i*t*a alte amore*m* querere. cui
Juno apposuit nubem in q*ua* recepto semi*n*e nati sunt centauri.
ipse a*ut*em adiudicat*u*s inf*er*no *con*tinu*e* uoluitu*r* in rota. . . .
s*et* Juno interponit nubem quia p*er* hanc uitam incurrit ho*m*o
obscuritate*m* rac*i*onis vn*de* nascuntur centauri qui in p*ar*te sunt
homines et in p*ar*te equi. quia in p*ar*te sunt rac*i*onales et in
p*ar*te irrac*i*onales qui apud inferos in rota uoluitur quia deditus
curis te*m*poralib*us* *con*tinu*e* eleuatur pr*o*speritate et deprim-

<hr>

[1] Text taken from the transcript of MS. Mm. 2. 18 in the Cambridge
University Library, printed in the S.T.S. edition, pp. liii.-lv.

itur aduersitate que quidem rotacio desistit quando homo sapiencia instructus talia contempnit. . . . Quartum monstrum quod tangit est pena tantali qui fingitur lacerasse filium suum et dedisse eum diis ad comedendum pro quo dampnatus in inferno. dicitur habere aquam usque ad mentum et poma ante os suum pendencia et cum fame et siti deficere. quia tamen pomum uel aquam carpere subterfugiunt tantalus auarum signat qui filium suum lacerat dando eum diis ad comedendum quia quicquid natura causarum habet lacerat et exponit vnde diuicias acquirat quibus tamen cum habundauerit in egestate est. quia non sustinet in necessitatibus suis ea expendere quia delectatus vsu pecunie non ult' aceruum diminuere vnde dicit et tantalus perditus longa siti. scilicet auaricie. spernit flumina et diuicias que more fluminis labuntur. Quintum monstrum est pena ticii qui fingitur uoluisse concumbere cum latona matre apollinis qui est deus diuinacionis. latona dicitur quasi latitonai id est certitudo futuri temporis que in dubio iacet. Quequidem incertitudo quia est causa memorandi artem diuinacionis dicitur mater apollinis. set sagittis apollinis occiditur quia diuersis speciebus intentus nimio studio quasi mortuus absorbetur. . . . Deinde cum dicit tandem ostendit quomodo uxor orpheo reddita fuerit et circa hoc duo facit primo ostendit quomodo reddita. secundo quomodo fuerit perdita. . . . Deinde cum dicit. vos hec fabula. applicando fabulam hortatur uitare illud quod contemplacionem summi boni impedit. vnde communiter homines alloquendo dicit, hec ea fabula respicit nos. quia scilicet ad uestram informacionem est inducta quicunque queritis. id est uultis ducere mentem. id est contemplacionem mentis in supernum diem. id est bona superna. Nam qui uictus. scilicet cupiditate terrenorum. flexerit lumina scilicet rationem et intellectum a celesti bono in specus tartareum id est ad terrena fauendo cupiditati ut supra expositum est quicquid precipuum trahit. id est quicquid boni laborando aquisiuit per sapienciam et eloquenciam perdit dum uidit inferos id est dum est intentus istis terrenis et temporalibus que sunt infima. et hic terminatur liber tercius continens prosas 12 et metra 12.'

428. *the pairte intelletyfe* : medieval philosophy, following Aristotle, divided the soul into several parts or kinds, the nutritive, sensitive, intellectual, etc.

520. *ostlaire* : innkeeper. [*Hospiciarius*, Prompt. Parv.]

       ' So wunnit thair ane wundir gay ostleir
       Without the toun, until ane fair maneir.'
            (Dunbar, (?) *The Freiris of Berwik*, 51.)

563. [*Spamen*] supplied from *C*, l. 436 ; the *B* reading is 'spyne.'

571 *et seq.* The sense of this rather difficult passage is :

'Each man that hears this conclusion should fear to attempt to find out, by study of the constellations, what things are likely to happen under heaven ; which (things) are indifferent to 'yea' or 'nay,' being without certain and predetermined cause, and which none on earth but God alone may know.'

584. *spaying :* cp. l. 563 *supra* [spamen], and note thereon.

592. This line appears to be corrupt. Sir W. A. Craigie suggests the emendation :

'The quhilk mone cum *and* to þair *end* indure.'

634. The ascription to ' m̄r. R. H.,' which occurs only in *B*, is supported by the gloss in Gavin Douglas's hand to the word ' Muse' in the Cambridge MS. (Gale 03.12) of his *Æneid.* See Introduction, p. xiii.

Robene and Makyne

This pastoral ballad of Henryson's is considerably indebted, in form and spirit, to the old French and Provençal *pastourelles ;* but no really convincing resemblance has yet been detected. In *Modern Language Notes*, Nov. 1931 (vol. 46), p. 457, Mr W. Powell Jones, of Western Reserve University, attempts to demonstrate that Henryson's original is to be found in a *pastourelle* by one Baudes de la Kakerie (contained in a manuscript of the thirteenth century), and quotes extracts from the poem. It is certainly more like *Robene* in type than is the usual *pastourelle*, but the resemblance is still not convincing. In the old French poem 'the poet . . . sees a shepherdess approach a swain and beg him vociferously to love her. Robin resists her until he is attracted by another girl to whom he flees. This girl will have nothing to do with him, so he goes back to the one who had offered him her love, but now she mocks him.' It will be seen that, although there is a broad similarity between the action of the two poems, they are quite unlike in detail ; and this dissimilarity is accentuated by the quotations which Mr Powell Jones gives. Corresponding to the passage in Henryson,

'mirry makyne said him till,' etc.

is this in the French poem :

'"mignot Robin,
tes ex mar esgardai,
se cist maus ne m'assoage, je morrai."
cele a dit "o ! que ferai ?
d'amer morrai,
ja nen vivrai
se toi nen ai que j'aim si bien."'

5. *lowd and still :* openly and in secret ; *i.e.* continually.

12. *raik on raw :* a common alliterative tag in M. Scots verse. The late Professor Gregory Smith gives a number of examples in his note on the passage. (*Henryson*, iii. 59-60.)

17-24. This advice, given to Robin by Makyne, is an excellent summary of the rules laid down for lovers in the 'Statutes of Love.' For a full analysis of this subject, see W. A. Neilson's *Origins and Sources of the Court of Love*, 1899.

19. *heynd :* not 'kind,' as some editors have wished to read it, but 'courteous' or 'gentle.'

20. *Wyse, hardy, and fre :* wise, courageous, and generous.

21. *denger :* no previous editor has noted the meaning of 'denger' in this line. G. G. S. glosses it as 'danger, or harm.' The original sense was 'dominion or power' [L. Lat. *dominiarium*], as in Chaucer, *Cant. Tales, Prol.*, A. 663 :

> ' In daunger hadde he at his owene gise
> The yonge girles of the diocise,'

and later, 'difficulty,' 'chariness,' 'coyness,' or 'disdain. For the latter uses, cp. the *Romaunt of the Rose*, l. 3371 :

> ' My silf I knowe full well Daungere,
> And how he is feers of his cheere
> At prime temps love to manace,'

and ll. 1491-2 :

> ' The proude-hertid Narcisus,
> That wes in love so daungerous.'

See, too, the works of Gower (ed. Macaulay), ii. 476.

24. *be patient and previe :* the most binding injunction of all. Cp. the poem ascribed to Dunbar (S.T.S. ii. 312-3), 'Gif ye wald lufe and luvit be,' in which each stanza ends with the refrain :

> ' Be secreit, trew, and pacient.'

39. *I dern :* in derne, or in secret.

56. [*bid*]. The MS. reading is doubtful here, but seems to be either 'lue' or 'lid.' Sir W. A. Craigie suggests that '*lid* must be a slip on the part of Bannatyne, for which either *luve* or *list* would be a natural emendation, but still better is *bid* = ask for, as in the *Fables*, 157, 'na better lyfe we bid.'

58. *sicht :* see *N.E.D. s.v.* 'sight, *v.*²'

96. *firth, forrest, or fawld :* a common alliterative sequence, like 'roif and rest' in l. 49, and 'holttis hair' in l. 122, etc. 'Firth' is a coppice or wooded ground.

116. *but lett :* without hindrance. The same use as in *Fables*, l. 1198 (C) '. . . Thocht I mycht not it lat.' (See note on this line.)

Sum Practysis of Medecyne

1. *Guk, guk :* the exact use of this expression here is rather doubtful. 'Guk' is presumably 'gowk,' and 'guk-guk,' as G. G. S. notes, is Scots for 'cuckoo'; but the intended application here is not clear. G. G. S. quotes from Montgomerie, *Cherrie and the Slae,* 701 : 'Go, go, we do not heir bot guckis,' that is, *Nugamur duntaxit* (in Dempster's translation).

8. *I stand ford :* cp. *Fables,* ll. 676 and 2867 *supra.*

17. *I schrew thame that leid :* cp. *Fables,* 1222 *supra.*

20. *lib :* either 'cut' in the sense of simple surgery, or in the commoner and more restricted sense of 'castrate.' There may, on the other hand, be a connection with O.E. *lyb,* a medicine, drug or simple, as G. G. S. suggests, but there is no other instance of the verbal use either in Old or Middle English, or in Scots.

22. *sedull :* (Fr. *cedule*) cp. Lyndsay, 'Cedule,' a schedule or writing (ed. Laing, i. 70, 234). Cp. *Aige and Yowth,* l. 69.

24. 'That glean all ages'? Other suggestions for this line are *glean,* from *gleam,* 'to smear,' and *egeis* = 'eggs,' in supposed allusion to the medieval practice of compounding drugs with eggs. But the candid editor is well-advised to admit that there are many words and passages in this poem that defy any exact interpretation.

26. *dia :* 'compounded of': the familiar pharmaceutical prefix, used here, as occasionally elsewhere, as a separate word. Cp. Langland, Passus B, xx. 173 :

> 'And to dryue away Deth · with dyas and drogges.'

Cp., too, the combinations *diatesseron, diapente,* etc. Cp. *Orpheus and Eurydice,* ll. 233 *et seq.*

dreggis : probably 'drugs.' Cp. the Langland quotation above— the form exhibiting the common confusion with *dreg (dredge),* a preparation (F. *dragée*).

27. *Dia :* in the four 'prescriptions' means 'compounded of.' *Dia Culcakit*—prescription for the colic, etc.

Cape : take. Cp. 'Recipe' in l. 40 *infra.*

cukmaid : obscure ; may be 'excrement.'

colleraige : Arsesmart, the water-pepper plant.

31. *luffage :* lovage (*Levisticum officinale*), popular medicinal herb, used mainly as a diuretic.

36. *sottin :* perhaps 'sprinkle' or 'mix in.' G. G. S. suggests a connection with *soudie,* 'hotch-potch.'

40. *reid ruke:* 'red rook.' 'But why,' asks G. G. S., 'red rook, except for alliterative purposes, or in burlesque verse?' The particular form of humour favoured by the author of this grotesque piece is the prescription of impossible and non-existent ingredients. Hence the 'red rook'; hence the 'gaw of ane grene dow' (l. 43)—the dove having no gall in medieval physiology (see *N.E.D. s.v.* 'gall,[2]' esp. examples from Orm and Lydgate); and hence the 'fyve unce of ane fle wing.'

42. *The dram of ane drekterss: drek* is drake; for *terss*, see *N.E.D. s.v.* 'Tarse[1]'; *dram* is used in the sense of a liquid measure.

45. *slak:* Thomas Ruddiman, in his edition of G. Douglas (1710), glosses '*Slike*': '*Scot. Bor.* call *a kind of Sea-weed, very soft and slippery*, SLAKE, which they also eat.'

52. *deir and denteit in daill:* 'deir and denteth (dainty)' is a common alliterative tag. The Dia Glaconicon, like the curate's egg, is good in parts.

58. *scho bak:* the she bat.

61. *fra lawdian to lundin:* from Lothian to Lundin (in Fifeshire)— *i.e.* from south to north. See Introduction, p. xiv.

70. *guse:* Jamieson gives '*guse:* the long gut or *rectum*,' without any illustration or justification.

77. *yule stok:* 'winter cabbage, or kale'; probably so-called because of the use made of them in Yule and Hallowe'en celebrations. Cp. Burns, *Halloween*, ll. 28-36.

84. *I pary:* I wager. (L. *pariare*; Fr. *parier*.)

86. *out of the fary:* out of this world. Cp. Dunbar:

> ' Bot evir be reddy and addrest
> To pass out of this frawdful fary.'

90, 91. *It is ane mirk mirrour.* A coarse application of the proverb, 'A mirk mirroor is a man's mind' (Fergusson: *Proverbs*, A. 70).

Ane Prayer for the Pest

Visitations of the plague were so frequent in the late fourteenth and early fifteenth century that it is fruitless to speculate on the particular outbreak to which the poem refers.

27. *perreist:* the Bann. draft has *preist*, a form which probably represents no difference in the sense.

37. *servis:* common aphetic form of 'deserves.'

53. *bot dreid:* without fail. *Bd* has 'be deid' (by death).

64. The *Finis* which occurs here in the *Bd* text serves only to separate the first part of the poem from the elaborate

Supplication which follows. With the intricate internal rhyme-system of these stanzas compare Dunbar's *Ballat of our Lady*, and the conclusion of some of the sections of the *Flyting of Dunbar and Kennedie* (ed. Mackay Mackenzie, pp. 160 and 12, 20, etc.). This device of ending a poem with a sort of firework-display of metre and rhyme is a common one in Scots poetry. The actual words used in the first stanza of Henryson's *finale* inevitably suggest Dunbar's *Ballat*, and if the Henryson attribution is to be credited, it is at least possible that Dunbar was here indebted to the older poet. But as it was certainly a common tradition, it is more than likely that the *Eterne, Superne* tag was also a poetical commonplace of which only these examples survive.

66. *serve :* used here in the sense of 'grant.'

71. *with space :* with time (or opportunity). G. G. S. quotes Dunbar, *Man, sen thy lyfe is ay in Weir* (Mackay Mackenzie, p. 147):

> 'Thyne awin gud spend quhill thow hes spais.'

74. *distort :* in the literal sense—'turn aside.'

84. *deluge = disluge, i.e.* dislodge, or remove.

86. *mispent forthocht :* the two terms are practically synonymous : 'misspent and wasted.'

The Garmont of Gud Ladeis

Henryson here elaborates an idea often suggested in earlier verse, the robing of his lady in the graces and virtues. He perhaps took the idea from a long, tedious poem by Oliver de la Marche, the *Triumphe des Dames (alias, Le Parement des Dames)*, c. 1500 ; but, as G. G. S. points out, it was an easy and natural extension of the old chivalric 'significations' such as we have in the contemporary Scots MS. of Gilbert of the Haye. It was carried a degree farther by Jean de la Motte, in his *Voie d'Enfer et de Paradis*, who speaks of a 'cotte de vilonie, manteau de maudisson et descri,' &c. If Henryson owes anything to de la Marche it is the idea and only the idea, and his merit is the greater for having recast a prolix 1400-line allegory into this brief and graceful form. The idea was resumed in 1572 by the unknown author of the *Lamentation of Lady Scotland*, etc. Scotland says :

> ' My bodie was weill cled with Policie ;
> My hat was of Justice and Equitie ;
> My coller, of trew Nichtbour lufe it was,
> Weill prenit on with Kyndnes and solas ;
> My Gluifis wer of fre Liberalitie :

> My Sleifis wer of to borrow and len glaidlie ;
> My Lais and Mailȝies of trew permanence ;
> My stomak maid was of clene Conscience ;
> My waist was gyrdit with Sobrietie ;
> My leggs and feit schod with Simplicitie . . . .'

(Cranstoun : *Satirical Poems of the Time of the Reformation*,
S.T.S. 1891, ii. 226-228.)

8. *deir :* not 'harm,' as G. G. S. gives it, but 'frighten,' as in *Robene and Makyne*, p. 151, l. 21.

15. *mailyeis :* eyelet-holes.

27. *patelet :* ruff. Cp. Dunbar : *A General Satyre*, ed. Mackenzie, p. 153, l. 64 :

> ' Sic skaith and scorne, so mony paitlattes worne.'

29. *esperance :* hope. See *Testament of Cresseid*, l. 48, and note.

38. *my seill :* either 'my seal' or 'my happiness' (sele).

The Bludy Serk

1. *hindir :* not 'hundir' as in previous texts. G. G. S. gives the sense as 'a long time ago,' which connects up, in sense, with 'Thair was a worthy king.' The phrase 'This hindir yeir' connects directly with 'I hard be tald.' It is only a variant on one of the commonest of opening phrases in Middle Scots poetry—cp. Dunbar's 'This hinder nycht, halff sleiping as I lay'; 'This hindir nycht in Dunfermeling'; 'In secreit place this hyndir nycht'; 'Musing allone this hinder nicht,' etc. : and in early English lyrics, 'This endris night. . . .' (E. K. Chambers : *Early English Lyrics*, 1926, pp. 119, 121.)

12. *bot and :* 'and also.'

15. *luvit hir paramour :* cp. Barbour, *Brus*, xiii. 485 :

> ' That he his sistir paramouris
> Lufit.'

18. *a fowll gyane of ane :* a particularly foul giant. See Table of Grammatical Characteristics, *Introd.*, p. xxxviii.

24. *wame :* not 'wane' (dwelling) as in G. G. S.

57. *the bricht :* for this substantival use of adjectives in M. Scots, see Table of Grammatical Characteristics, *Introd.*, p. xxxvii.

58. *deir :* the fact that 'deir' is not a perfect rhyme does not justify the substitution of 'fre' or any other word here. 'Merk' and 'quert' in ll. 85 and 87 depend equally on assonance.

96. *mak:* perhaps a false formation (for the sake of rhyme) of the
past participle ('with prayers to him made'). Cp. the dupli-
cation of 'mak' as a rhyme word in this stanza (ll. 92, 96) with
'nycht' (ll. 33, 39) ; but see note on l. 58 *supra.*

118. *hend:* cp. *Robene and Makyne,* l. 19, 'heynd.' Here 'hend men'
is the equivalent of 'gentle readers.'

The Ressoning betuix Aige and Yowth

11. *lyart lokis hoir:* there is little distinction in meaning possible
between 'lyart' and 'hoir' ; 'lyart' is used perfunctorily here,
as often, for the sake of alliteration.

18. *makdome* (misdum *M*): 'makdome' = 'comeliness' is common in
M. Scots writers ; *e.g.* in Dunbar, *Tua Mairit Wemen and the
Wedo,* l. 73 (ed. Mackay Mackenzie, p. 86) :

    'To manifest my makdome to multitude of pepill.'

    It is used, too, in the sense of 'appearance,' as in Pitscottie's
    Chronicles : '. . . one called Alexander M'Cullo, and the other
    THE SQUYER OF CLEISCH, who wer both verrie lyk in makdome
    to the King,' etc. If the reading *misdum* from *M* be accepted,
    it must be read in the sense of 'misdoom' or 'misjudgement.'
    (See *N.E.D., s.v.* 'Misdoom.')

21. *growme on ground:* like 'freik on fold,' l. 28 *infra,* a common
alliterative tag both in M. Scots and M. English verse.

22. *pair:* aphe_tic form of *empair, appair,* impair, detract from.
G. G. S. quotes *Catholic Tractates* (S.T.S.), p. 10, l. 27 : 'nother
eikand nor pearand ane word.'

28. *forss:* for this adjectival use (=*forcy*), see Dunbar, *Doun by ane
Rever* (S.T.S. ii. 306, l. 35) :

    'Sum wyse, sum wicht, sum forss, sum fell.'

    forty in *MF* is almost certainly a scribal error for 'forcy,' 'c' and
    't' being here, as often, confused.

31. *laikly :* probably merely a corruption of *laythly (M MF).*

35. *cramp:* the sense certainly seems to be 'strut,' 'swagger'—but
no very conclusive account of the form has yet been given.
See G. G. S.'s note (S.T.S. iii., p. 66). Note the antithesis
between 'cramping' and 'cruking, cowering' at l. 42.

39. *birdis:* ladies. See *N.E.D. s.vv.* 'Bird,' 'Burd,' 'Bride': and
cp. the ballad-titles, *Burd Ellen and Young Tamlene, Burd
Isabel and Earl Patrick.*

52. *My wittis fyve :* the five senses.

59. *it:* (Johne *MF*). The MF reading probably needs no emendation. 'Johne' is used as it is used in Johne Uponland (*Piers Plowman*), etc., for 'any man.' Sir W. A. Craigie suggests a misreading of 'thow' (þow).

65. *gowand:* (galzart *MF*). The form 'gowand' has baffled all Henryson's editors. See G. G. S.'s jocose note on the subject (S.T.S. iii. 67): 'galzart' is, of course, *galliard*, a gay or spirited fellow.

69. *sedullis:* see *Sum Practysis of Medecyne*, l. 22, and note.

70. *triumphit.* The *MF* reading 'trevist' (traversed, ran contrary) is certainly the most satisfactory here : 'tremefit' (*Bd*) is perhaps a corruption of the same reading.

The Prais of Aige

1. *Wythin a garth:* cp. Dunbar's *Of Deming* (ed. Mackay Mackenzie, p. 23), l. 3 :

'Within ane garth under a tre.'

3. *et.* This abbreviation for 'and' and its possible significance are discussed in Appendix, p. 221.

5. There are obviously two senses to be taken from this line, according to which punctuation is preferred ; but the question does not greatly affect our understanding of the poem.

13. *flemyt:* put to flight ; 'fremmit' (*Bd*) may be a corruption of the same word, or have its usual sense of 'exiled,' 'estranged.'

19-20. Cp. the readings in *Bd* and *M.*

The Want of Wyse Men

The refrain of this poem seems to have been a proverbial expression, and is preserved in the *Wisdom of Solomon* (*E.E.T.S.*, 43, p. 23, 765-6); in Fergusson's *Proverbs* (1641) A. 273 ; Hislop, *Proverbs of Scotland* (1862), p. 63 ; Henderson (1881), p. 22 ; and Cheviot (1896), p. 108. Bannatyne has rehandled the poem, apparently with a view to casting it into six-foot lines.

2. *declerde:* cp. *dude*, ll. 2867, 676, *supra*, etc.

7. *is sover now* (*B*) : 'is secure now.'

17. *moralitee:* moral philosophy.

18. *Austyn:* Augustine.

19. *placebo:* In the Latin rite : Vespers for the Dead, the first antiphon of which is *Placebo Domino*, etc. Psalms, cxiv. 9, Vulgate. Used commonly, and perhaps here, of time-servers and flatterers. Cp. Caxton, *Reynard the Fox* (ed. Arber, 1878, p. 11).

dirige: (dergie, dregy, etc.) modern, dirge. See note on *Fables*, l. 449, p. 18 *supra*.

S

26. *under na rufe has rest:* this collocation of 'rufe' and 'rest' is perhaps, as G. G. S. states, a persistence of the alliterative tag 'roif and rest' (cp. *Robene and Makyne*, l. 49, p. 152) even though the sense is different.

27. *his:* may be 'is' with initial 'h' (cp. the *Cock and the Jewel*, Bann. l. 4, 'heir' for 'eir') or a typographical error for 'hes' = 'has.'

30. *fer lesse:* the *B* reading, 'ferles' = marvels, is the better reading here.

39. *ver:* a typographical error for *wer* = 'waur,' 'worse.'

47. *a fasse:* something of no value. Cp. G. Douglas, *Aeneid*, iv., Prol. (ed. Small, ii. 169, 22):

> 'Sayis nocht ʒour sentence thus, scant worth a fas.'

60. *laddis:* serving-men. With this contrast of 'lairds' and 'lads' compare Lyndsay's *Testament . . . of our Souerane Lordis Papyngo*, 391 (ed. Laing, i. p. 75):

> 'Pandaris, pykthankis, custronis, and clatteraris
> Loupis up, from laddis, syne lychtis among lardis,'

and the proverb: 'Lay up like a laird, and seek like a lad' (Kelly, *Sc. Prov.*, 240).

The Abbay Walk

See the note on this poem, Introduction, p. xxviii.

23. *he and he:* the one and the other. Cp. Douglas, *Æneid* (ed. Small, iii. 160):

> 'And gan begyn desyre, baith he and he,
> In bodeis ʒit for to returne agane.'

28. *by skill:* with reason, on good grounds.

50. *wilfull:* willing. See *MF* reading.

54. *taistit* (gustit *MF*): these two words are the same in sense. Cp. the *Fables*, l. 287, p. 13 *supra*.

The Annunciation

4. *in lufe that letis:* 'letis' is an unusual form. G. G. S. suggests that *let* is connected with O.E. *lætan*, in the sense of 'think,' or 'consider': but even so the reading is not very convincing.

10. *Rest and Rufe:* cp. *Robene and Makyne*, l. 49, and *Prais of Aige*, l. 26, and notes.

12. *decretis:* almost certainly ought to be *decreit is.* Cp. ll. 2 and 24 of the poem when *suet is* and *cround is* appear as *suetis* and *croundis*. If *decretis* be taken as a noun, the sense must be 'resolves.'

13. *mervale* is here a verb.
 that myld: for this substantival use, see note to the *Bludy Serk*,
 l. 57. Cp. l. 21 *infra*, 'that gay.'
15. *Infild:* undefiled.
28. *applidis:* hearkens, or consents. See *N.E.D. s.v.* Apply³.
 The form 'applidis' is unusual, but many words are distorted
 through the exigencies of rhyme in this poem.
33. *sidis:* womb. Cp. Dunbar, *Ros Mary: Ane Ballat of our Lady*,
 l. 41 (ed. Mackay Mackenzie, p. 176):
> 'Thy blessit sydis bure the campioun.'
51. *dreid:* the MS. reads *dreid* = danger or harm, not *deid* = death,
 as in earlier editions.
57. *bacis:* the meaning is doubtful. Perhaps it is used for 'establishes'
 as in the *Mirrour for Magistrates*, xl., 'By bloudshed they
 doe . . . bace . . . their state.'
68. *termigant:* the false god of the Mahometans. (Ital. *Trivigante*,
 O.F. *Tervagan*.) In the English miracle plays he represented
 a blustering bully, which sense is intended by Dunbar in the
 Dance of the Sevin Deidly Synnis (ed. Mackay Mackenzie,
 p. 123), l. 115:
> 'Thae tarmegantis, with tag and tatter.'

 Cp., too, *Hamlet*, III. ii. 16. The word is not found in its
 modern sense of a shrewish woman till about 1660.

The Thre Deid Pollis

10. With the sentiment of this line, compare *Fables*, l. 2208, p. 76 *supra*.
18. *quhyt & reid.* See note on *Fables*, l. 1328, p. 48 *supra;*
 'quhyte quhilk is takin to be þe symboll and tokin gevin
 commounlie in diuise of colouris to signifie sempilnes and
 loyaltie, and reid signifying manli[nes] and heroyicall courage'
 (Buchanan, *The Chamæleon* (S.T.S., pp. 42-43).
22. *crampand:* curly. See note on *Aige and Yowth*, l. 35.
41. This stanza inevitably reminds the reader of a more effective
 handling of the material, in *Hamlet*, v. i.
65. *patrik Johnistoun: MF* gives the poem to 'Mr Robert
 Henrysoun.' Patrick Johnston is named as dead by Dunbar
 in the *Lament for the Makaris*, l. 71 (ed. Mackay Mackenzie,
 p. 22):
> 'He hes Blind Hary and Sandy Traill
> Slaine with his schour of mortall haill,
> Quhilk Patrik Johnestoun myght nocht fle ;
> *Timor mortis conturbat me.*'

 See Dr Mackenzie's note, *u.s.*, p. 202.

The Ressoning betuix Deth and Man

13. *freik on fold:* common alliterative tag. Cp. *growme on ground*,
'Aige and Yowth,' l. 21, p. 179 *supra*, and note.

43. *under thy Caip:* either to be covered by Death's mantle, or to
be lapped in lead. *Caip of leid* is a Scots phrase for a coffin
(Bellenden, *Cron.* B. xvi. c. 19: 'Kyng Hary . . . miserabilly
deceassit, and wes brocht in ane caip of leid in Ingland,' and
Knox, *Hist.* [1846], i. 179, etc.).

It may interest the reader to see a seventeenth century specimen
of this kind of graveyard dialogue. It is taken from a poetical MS.
('Blooms & Blossoms,' 1623) in the University Library of Edinburgh:

THE DIALOGUE BETWIXT DEATH & A YONGUE MAN SICKE

> *death:* Sʳ I arrest yᵒ in the high kings name
> *man:* arrest me Rascall knowest thou who I am
> *death:* o passing well Sʳ Anthropos of claye
>   Nay swagger not yᵒ must yᵒ shall obeye
> *man:* I must I shall (proud sergeant) at whose suite
> *d:* at natures Sʳ.   *m:* what action?   *d:* tes for fruite
> *m:* fetcht by whom? or for me?
> *d:* by Adam sir, long since at Edens tree
> *m:* what have I with Adams debts to doe?
> *d:* Sʳ as yᵒ are heire you're liable there to.
> *m:* hes heire of what?   *d:* of that he left his kin
> *m:* what heretage?   *d:* the inheritance of sin.

Aganis Haisty Credence of Titlaris

The poem was first titled by Lord Hailes, and late editors have
adopted the title.

23. *Ryme . . . ressoun:* see *N.E.D. s.v.* 'Rime' and Cranstoun's
edition of *Montgomerie* (S.T.S., p. 352). This is one of the
earliest examples of the phrase.

46. *heird:* 'hear it.' Cp. notes on ll. 676, 2867, etc.

GLOSSARY

ABBREVIATIONS : *T. C.*, The Testament of Cresseid. *O. E.*, Orpheus and Eurydice. *Pract. of Med.*, Sum Practysis of Medecyne. *R. M.*, Robene and Makyne.

adj., adjective ; *adj. phr.*, adjectival phrase ; *adv.*, adverb ; *conj.*, conjunction ; *n.*, noun ; *n. pl.*, noun, plural ; *prep.*, preposition ; *pron.*, pronoun ; *v.*, verb ; *v. p.*, verb, participle ; *v. pp.*, verb, past participle.

A

Abaid, *n.*, delay
  v. past, abode
Abak, *adv.*, away, backwards
Abasitlie, *adv.*, humbly
Abbay, *n.*, abbey
Abbottis, *n. pl.*, abbots
A b c, *n.*, alphabet
Abhominabill, *adj.*, abominable, hateful. *See* Note, *T. C.*, 308
Abide, abyd(e), *v.*, remain ; abide ; obey ; abide by ; continue ; wait for ; stay
Abill, *adj.*, ready (of ground for seed)
Abject, *n.*, outcast, cast-off
Aboif, *adv.*, above
Abone, *adv.* and *prep.*, above
Aboundance, *n.*, plenty, abundance
About, *adv.*, thoroughly, all round
Abraid, *v. past*, started, jumped
Abreird. *See* Breird
Absence, *n.* (= *absentis*), absentees (from court)
Absolve, *v.*, answer, resolve
Abstractit, *v. past*, withdrawn, removed
Abusioun, *n.*, abuse, misdirection
Aby, *v.*, pay for
Accuse, *v.*, blame, accuse, protest against (legal)
Actand, *v. p.*, actuating, 'moving'
Actis, *n. pl.*, acts (of a Court)

Adoun, *adv.*, downwards
Adversar, *n.*, adversary
Advertence, advertens, *n.*, heed, warning
Affectioun, *n.*, inclination, affection
Afferit. *See* Effrayit
Affetterrit, *v. pp.*, fettered
Agane, aganis, *prep.*, against
  adv., again
Agilite(e), *n.*, acuteness
Ago, *v. pp.*, gone, past
Agreabill, *adj.*, agreeable, suitable
Aige, age, ege, *n.*, age
Aigit, *v. pp.*, aged
Aill, *n.*, ailment, trouble, distress
Aip, *n.*, ape
Air, *n.*, air, heir, oar
  n., eyre, circuit (*Justice—A.*)
  adv., before, early
Airschip, *n.*, heirship
Aith, ath, *n.*, oath
Aitis, *n.*, oats
Albeit, *conj.*, albeit, although
Ale, *pron.*, all (*O. E.*, 607)
Alis, *v. pres.*, ails
Alkin, alkyn, all kind of
Allace, alace, *exclam.*, alas !
Allane, *adv.*, alone
Allanerly, *adv.*, only
Allegit to, *v.*, preferred, claimed
Allow, *v.*, have
All quhair, *adv.*, everywhere
All to rent, *v.*, completely torn

277

Almous, *n.*, alms, charity
Almous-deid, *n.*, gift of charity, or
    alms
Almycht, *adj.*, almighty
Als, *adv.*, also
Alsone, *adv.*, immediately, 'pretty
    soon'
Alswa, *adv.*, also
Alterait, *v. pp.*, altered, disfigured
Alyke, *adj.*, the same, like, another
    adv., alike, also
Alyte, *adv.*, a little
Amang, amangis, *prep.*, amongst
Ambassatry, *n.*, diplomacy. *In A*
    'as an ambassador'
Amycabill, *adj.*, amiable, pleasant
Anceane, *adj.*, ancient, aged
Ancestre, *n.*, ancestry, descent
And, *conj.*, if, though
Ane, *adj.*, a, one
    of ane, very, specially
Aneuch, eneuch, anew, etc., *adv.*
    and *adj.*, enough
Angerlie, *adv.*, angrily
Angrie, *adj.*, stern, severe
Anis, anys, *n. pl.*, ones
    adv., once
A per se, *n.*, 'A' by itself, paragon.
    See Note, *T. C.*, 78
Apertly, *adv.*, openly, clearly
Apostata, *n.*, apostate
Apparitour, *n.*, apparitor, officer of
    the Consistory Court
Appetyte, *n.*, appetite, longing
Applicate, *v. pp.*, applied, used
Applidis. *See* Note, *Annunciation*,
    28
Arbeteris, *n. pl.*, arbiteris
Areir, *adv.*, behind, away, gone
Argow, *v.*, argue: *maid a.*, 'held
    argument'
Ark, *n.*, box, chest (cp. Kist)
Armit, *v. past*, protected
Armony. *See* Harmonie

Arrace, *v.*, pluck, wrest
Arrayit, *v.*, arrayed, decorated,
    scattered
As, *n.*, ashes, cinders
    adv., though, as though
Ase, *v.*, ask
Ask, *n.*, ask, newt, eft
Assent, *n.*, aid
    v., consent, agree
Assyis, *n.*, assize (legal)
Astonist, stoneist, *v.*, astonished
Atour, atouir, etc., *prep.*, above,
    across, over, about
Atteichit, *v. pp.*, attached (legal)
Aucht, *v.*, ought
Audiens, *n.*, hearing (legal)
Auster, austryne, *adj.*, stern, grave,
    severe
Autentik, *adj.*, serious, important,
    carrying authority (as opposed
    to fables)
Authoreist, *adj.*, authorised, au-
    thoritative (cp. 'Authorised
    Version')
Availl, *n.*, value, avail
    v., avail, serve, be of use
Aventour, -ure, etc., *n.*, fortune,
    chance, destiny
Avise, *v.*, consider, think over
Avysitlie, *adv.*, advisedly, wisely
Aw, *n.*, awe, fear
Awin, *adj.*, own
Awner, *n.*, owner
Awoik, *v. past*, awoke
Ay, *adv.*, always, ever

B

Bacis, *v. See* Note, *Annuncia-
    tion*, 57
Bacod, *n.*, scrotum
Baid, *n.*, bidding, stay, resting
    v., abode
Baill, *n.*, sorrow, pain, torment

Bair, *n.*, boar
adj., bare, without hope
v. past, bore
Baisit, baissit, *v. pp.*, abased, degraded
Baiss, *adj.*, base (musical)
Bait, *n.*, contention, strife ; food for horses, or halt for rest and food ; halt ; bait (fishing)
Baith, etc., *adj.*, both
Bak, *n.*, bat (animal)
n. back
Bakon. Bauer bakon. *See* Note, *Fables*, 906
Balandis, *n.*, balance
Bald, *adj.*, bold, assured
Balk, bank, *n.*, ridge, furrow
Ballet, *n.*, ballad, poem. *See* Notes
Band, *n.*, bond, tether
v., bound, tied
Bandonit, *v. pp.*, subdued
Bandoun, *n.*, control, durance
Bane, *n.*, bone
Baneis, banis, etc., *v.*, banish
Banestikill, *n.*, stickleback
Bankouris, *n. pl.*, tapestry coverings
Barnage, bernage, *n.*, youth
Barne, berne, etc., *n.*, child
Barret, *n.*, trouble, sorrow
Basare, *n.*, executioner
Bastoun, *n.*, stick, weapon
Bat, *n.*, blow, stroke
Bath, baith, *adj.*, both
Bawdronis, *n.*, familiar name for cat. *See* Note, *Fables*, 329
Bawer, *adj.*, beaver
Bawsie broun, *n.*, name of a dog. *See* Note, *Fables*, 546
Be, *n.*, bee
= by the time that, before, when
= in reference to, concerning
prep., by

Befoir the hand, *adv. phr.*, beforehand
Begouth, begowth, *v. p.*, began
Beid, = be it. *See* Notes
Beik, beke, *n.*, beak
v., warm
Beild, *n.*, shelter, place of safety
Beildit, *v. pp.*, adorned, decorated. *See* Note, *T. C.*, 97
Bein, beinly, *adj.* and *adv.*, comfortable, comfortably
Beir, *n.*, barley
n., bear (animal)
n., funeral bier
n., clamour
v., bear or carry
Beird, *n.*, beard
Beis, *v.*, is, are
Beit, *n.*, bundle, little sheaf
v., beat, strike ; relieve
Bek, *n.*, beck, bow
Bellerophont. *See* Note, *Fables*, 888
Bellie blind, *n.*, blind-man's-buff
Belliflaucht. *See* Note, *Fables*, 2904
Bellox, *n.*, ballocks, testicles
Belyif, etc., *adv.*, belive, straightway
Bene, *v.*, = be
adj. and *adv.*, pleasant, pleasantly
Benedicite, *v.* as *n.* or *exclam.* = bless you
Benis, *n. pl.*, beans
Benit, *v.*, filled, made comfortable
Benk, bink, *n.*, bench
Bent, *n.*, grass, ground, heath
v. pp. and *p.*, bent
Berk, *v.*, bark
Berrie, Burrye, *n.*, name of a dog. See *Fables*, 545, and Note
Bes, *v. imperf.*, be
Beschrew, eschrew, schrew, *v.*, curse : *b. us* = 'plague take us.' *See* Notes

Beseik, *v.*, beseech, pray

Besene, *v. pp.*, adorned, arrayed

Besie, besy, *adj.*, careful, busy

Besoucht, *v. pp.*, sought, sought after : *b. with*, 'a prey to'

Best, *n.*, beast
adj., best

Bestiall, *n.*, animals—esp. domestic cattle

Besyd, *adv.*, astray

Bet, *v. past*, struck, beat

Beteiche, *v.*, deliver, hand over

Bethit, *v. pp.*, ? beaten, stripped

Betill, *n.*, beetle, for beating flax

Betis, *v.*, relieves

Betraisit, *v. pp.*, betrayed

Beuch, buche, etc., *n.*, bough

Bever, *n.*, beaver (animal)

Bigly, *adj.*, pleasant

Bill, *n.*, formal document, 'bull.' *See* Note, *T. C.*, 332

Binge, *n.*, cringe, bow

Bir, *n.*, whirr (onomatopœic)

Bird, *n.*, lady. *See* Note, *Aige and Yowth*, 39

Birkye, *n.*, 'spirited fellow,' name of a dog

Birn, *v.*, burn

Birst, brest, etc., *v.*, burst

Bla, *adj.*, pale, livid, discoloured

Blaberryis, *n. pl.*, blaeberries (S. Eng. bilberries or whortle-berries)

Blaiknit, *v. pp.* and *adj.*, pale (*blake*) or dark (*blac*)

Blait, *adj.*, pale, abashed, dull

Blasit, *v. pp.*, defamed, decried

Bleit, blait, *v.*, bleat

Blenk, *n.*, look, glance
v., look

Blenking, *n.*, look, expression

Blin, blyn, *v.*, cease

Blome, *n.*, bloom

Blunt, *adj. See* Note, *Fables*, 977

Bocht, *v. pp.*, bought, redeemed

Boig, *n.*, bog

Boist, *n.*, threat, brag

Boit, *n.*, boat

Boll, *n.*, pod (of flax plant)

Bolling, bolnyng, *n.*, swelling, pride

Bone, *n.*, bane, woe

Borch. *See* Borrow

Bordourit, *adj.*, bordered

Boreall, *adj.*, northern, cold

Borous toun. *See* Note, *Fables*, 164

Borrow, borch, *n.*, bail, pledge, guarantee

Bosteous, bustious. *See* Note, *Fables*, 8

Bosum, *n.*, womb

Bot, *conj.*, but ; *b. and* = and also ; *b. if* = unless

Boun, *adj.*, ready, prepared

Bourd, *n.*, joke, jest

Bowcher, *n.*, executioner

Bowranbane. *See* Note, *Fables*, 914

Bowsumest, *adj.*, buxomest, blithest

Bowtit, *v. pp.*, 'boltit,' bobbed

Bra, *n.*, brae, hill, hillside

Bracis, *v.*, encloses, contains

Brag, *n.* (of a trumpet), brag, blast

Braid, *n.*, start, quick movement. *See* Abraid, and Notes
n., breadth : *adj.*, broad, wide
adv., broadly, freely, clearly
v. (brade), dart off, hurry, burst into speed, etc.

Brast, *v.*, burst. *See* Birst, etc.

Brats, *n.*, poor clothes. *See* Note, *Fables*, 2945

Breif, *n.*, writing, statement

Breik, *n.*, breech, hinder-parts

Breir, *n.*, brier-bush, thorn, etc.

Breird, *n.*, first shoots. See *Fables*, 10, and Note

Breith, *n.*, breath, fury

Brent, *adj.*, high, smooth (of the forehead)

Bricht, *adj.* as *n.*, lady. *See* Note, *Bludy Serk*, 57

Brod, *v.*, prod, goad

Browderit, *v. pp.* and *adj.*, embroidered

Bruik, *v.*, use, enjoy, have the use of

Brukkill, *adj.*, frail

Brukkilnes, *n.*, frailty

Brutall, etc., *adj.*, irrational

Brybouris, *n. pl.*, beggarly creatures

Brym, *n.*, water, flood

Brymly, *adv.*, loudly, shrilly

Bud, *n.*, bribe

Bugill, *n.*, buffalo, wild ox
n., horn, trumpet

Buik, *n.*, book

Buk, *n.*, buck (animal)

Bukheid, *n.*, hide-and-seek

Bullar, *n.*, bubble

Bur, boir, buir, etc., *v.*, bore, carried, etc.

Burely, burelie, etc., *adj.*, goodly, handsome

Burges, *n.* and *adj.*, burgess

Burion, *v.*, burgeon, bud

Bursin, *v. pp.*, burst

Busk, *n.*, bush

Buste, buist, *n.*, small box or case

Bustious. *See* Bosteous

But, *adv.* and *prep.*, without

But and ben, *n. phr. See* Note, *Fables*, 360

Bute, *n.*, help, comfort

Byit, byte, *n.*, bite

Byle, *n.*, outbreak, boil

C

Cabok, *n.*, cheese

Caill, *n.*, broth, kail

Caip, *n.*, cape or cope

Cair, *n.*, sorrow, care

Cairfull, *n.*, sorrowful, full of care

Cairt (Court), *n.*, cart, carriage

Cais, cace, *n.*, case, chance, example

Calf, *n.*, (animal) calf
n., chaff

Caller, *n.*, driver. *See* Note, *Fables*, 2238

Callour, *adj.*, fresh

Campis, *n. pl.*, whiskers

Can (*with parts*. couth, cowth, culd, etc.), *v.*, do, does, did, etc.

Cannon, *n.*, canon, system

Cant, *adj.*, merry, lively

Cape (*Lat.*) = take, *Recipe* (in prescriptions)

Capill, *n.*, horse

Carage, *n.*, carriage, mien

Carll, churle, *n.*, man, fellow

Carp, *v.*, speak, debate

Casualtie, *n.*, chance, luck

Cautelous, *adj.*, cunning

Cavillatioun, *n.*, trickery

Ceder, *n.*, cider

Cedull, sedull, *n.*, writing, document

Ceis, etc., *v.*, cease

Celsitude, *n.*, high rank, dignity

Chalmer, chaumer, *n.*, chamber, bower

Chalmerglew, *n.*, capacity in love

Chambelate, *n.*, a fine cloth

Chanceliary. *See* Note, *Fables*, 1014

Cheir, *n.*, face, countenance, cheer

Chemeis, *n.*, shirt, robe, loose gown

Cheverit, *v. past*, shivered, shook

Chuff, *n.*, clown, boor

Churle. *See* Carle

Claik, *n.*, clack (of a goose)

Clamp, *v.*, botch, add to

Claucht, *v.*, clutched

Cled, *v.*, clad, covered

Clergie, *n.*, 'clergy,' clerkly learning or skill

Clink, *v.*, twang

Clinschand, *v. p.*, limping, halting
Clippis, *n.*, eclipse
Clippit, clepit, *v. pp.*, called, named
Clout, *n.*, portion, very small piece
Clowtit, *v. pp.* as *adj.*, clumsy
Clud, *n.*, cloud
Cluke, *n.*, claw, talon, grip
Clyng, *v.*, shrink, wither
Codies, *n.*, codes (legal)
Coft, *v. past*, bought
Coif, *n.*, cove, hollow
Colleraige, *n.*, water-pepper
Columbie, *n.*, columbine (flower)
Commoun, *n.*, man of no rank or degree
Communit, *v. pp.*, conversed, communed
Compair, *n.*, equal, compeer
Compeir, *v.*, appear (in court)
Complexioun, *n.*, (*astrol.*) temperament, nature, appearance
Compone, *v.*, compose, make composition (legal)
Con, *n.*, squirrel
Concord, *v.*, agree
Conding, *adj.*, condign, worthy
Confidderit, *adj.* and *n.*, confederate
Conjunctioun, *n.* (used of planets), *O. E.*, 594
Conqueis, *v.*, conquer
Consuetude, *n.*, custom, habit
Contagious, *adj.*, tainted, harmful
Contending, *v. p.*, contesting, striving
Contrair, *adj.*, opposed, unfriendly
Contrairie, *v.*, oppose
Contrait. See Note, *Fables*, 1218
Contrufit, *v. pp.* as *adj.*, contrived, devised
Contumax. See Note, *Fables*, 1004, 1050
Convenient, *adj.*, morally suitable
Convocatioun, *n.*, assembly. See Note, *T. C.*, 346

Corbie Ravin (F. *corbeau*). See Note, *Fables*, 1160
Coronat, *v. pp.*, crowned
Corruptioun, *n.*, bodily disease
Corruscant, *adj.*, bright
Corss, *n.*, cross : *maid a c.* 'crossed myself'
Couchit, *v.*, lay down (of animals)
Count, *n.*, female genitals (of a sow)
Countermaund, *n.*, hindrance, opposition
Courtass, *adj.*, courteous
Courtlie, *adj.*, of law courts, *C. Knax*, 'lawyer's tricks'
Courtyne, *n.*, curtain
Crab, The, sign of the Zodiac
Crabitlie, *adv.*, crabbedly, sourly
Crag, craig, *n.*, neck : crag, hillock
Cragbane, *n.*, neckbone
Craikand, *v. p.*, croaking
Crampand, *adj.*, curly
Cramp, -ing, *v.*, swagger, -ing
Cran, *adj.*, long ('crane')
Crap, *v. past*, crept
Credence, *n.*, belief, credit, consent
Cresch, *v.*, grease ('creesh')
Croip, *n.*, crop ; crest or top of tree
Crous, *adj.*, confident, cheeky
Crownar, *n.*, coroner
Crud, *n.*, curd, excrement
Cruikit, *adj.*, deformed, crooked
Cryme, *n.*, fault, sin
Culcakit. See Note, *Pract. of Med.*, 27
Culome, *n.*, fundament
Cum, *v.*, come, came
  v. (*aph.*), become, suit
Cunning, cunnand, *n.*, knowledge, skill
Cunyng, *n.*, rabbit
Cunnand, *adj.*, learned
Curage, *n.*, courage, heart, spirit
Curageous, *adj.*, spirited, keen, brave

Curcheis, *n.*, kerchief, mutch, cap
Cure, *n.*, care, responsibility
Cursing, *n.*, excommunication
Custom, *n.*, custom, tradition, tax
Cuvating, *n.*, desire

D

Da, *n.*, doe
Daft, *adj.*, foolish
Dail, *n.*, dale ; deal, part
Daill (deill, dele), *v.*, have intercourse
Dais, *n.*, table
Dampnit, *v.*, condemned
Dawing, *n.*, dawn
Debait, *n.*, quarrel, dispute
Decerne, *v.*, judge. *See* Note, *Fables*, 1296
Declerde, = declare it
Decreit, *n.*, decree ; *v.*, decreed
Decretalis, *n. pl.*, decrees
Defame, *n.*, disgrace, slander
Deformait, *v. pp.*, altered, deformed
Degest, *v. pp.* and *adj.*, considered, grave, settled
Degraid, *v.*, diminish, shame
Deid, *n.*, deed, death
  adj., dead
  v. past, died
Deidlie, *adj.*, mortal
Deidlyk, *adj.*, deathly
Deif, *adj.*, deaf
Deificait, *v. pp.*, deified
Deip, *n.*, deep water, deep part of a hole
Deir, *n.*, harm, trouble
  v., hurt, harm, trouble
  adv., dearly
Delectatioun, *n.*, pleasure, delight
Deluge, *v.*, dislodge, remove
Demyng, *n.*, report, judgment, suspicion
Denger, *n.*, disdain, etc. *See* Note, *R. M.*, 21

Denteit, *adj.*, dainty
Denude, *adj.*, naked, bare
Denye, dedene, *v.*, deign. *See* Note, *Fables*, 1401
Depairt, *v.*, part, divide
Depryve, *v.*, debar
Deray, *n.*, disturbance
Derenye, *v.*, challenge, arrest, put on trial
Derne, *n.*, secret, secret place
Devide, *v.*, break in two halves
Devise, *v.*, conceive, state, make
Devyne, *v.*, devise, contrive
  adj., divine
  n., divinity. See *Fables*, 1101
Dia-, = made of (in pharmacy)
Diapenty, *n.*, interval of a fifth
Diatesserone, *n.*, the interval of a fourth
Dicht, *v. pp.*, ornamented, covered, put to death
Digestis, *n.*, digests (legal)
Dill, *v.*, soothe, assuage
Ding, *adj.*, worthy, noble
Dirigie, *n. See* Note, *Fables*, 448
Dirk, *adj.*, dark, obscure
Disagysit, *v. pp.*, disguised
Discens, *n.*, lineal descent
Discrepance, *n.*, division, quarrel
Diseis, *n.*, discomfort, insecurity
  n., disease
Dislug. *See* Deluge
Dispens, *n.*, dispensation, relief
Dispone, *v.*, dispose, settle, arrange
Dissaif, desave, *v.*, deceive
Dissait, desait, *n.*, deceit
Distort, *v.*, turn aside
Do, *v. aux.*, used periphrastically (in all tenses)
  v., perform, act
Doctrine, doctryne, *n.*, opinion, lesson
Document, *n.*, instruction, warning
Doggitlie, *adv.*, cruelly

Doif, *adj.*, dull, slow

Dome, *n.*, judgment, sentence

Donk, *adj.*, moist

Dosinnit, *v. pp.*, dazed

Dosor, *n.*, hanging, curtain

Dottit, *v. pp.*, = *adj.*, foolish, idiotic

Douk, *n.*, duck, duckling, dive (of a duck)

v., duck, plunge

Dour, *adj.*, severe, stern

Dout, *n.*, doubt, scruple, hesitation

Dow, *n.*, pigeon, dove

Draif, *v.*, 'drove,' hurried on

Dre, *v.*, endure, suffer

Dreddour, *n.*, fear

Drekterss, *n.* *See* Note, *Pract. of Med.*, 42

Drift, *n.*, drove, team ; rush, whirl

Drop, *n.*, drop ; village. *See* Note, *Fables*, 411

Drowrie, *n.*, love-token. *See* Note, *Fables*, 497

Drubly, *adj.*, turbid

Drug, *v.*, draw, pull

Dub, *n.*, pool, puddle

Duke, *n.*, duck

Dule, *n.*, sorrow

Dull, *v.*, become slack (of a bow)

Dungering, *n.*, dungeon

Dungin, *v. pp.*, beaten

Duplare, *n.*, double (duple) tone

Dure, *n.*, door

Duschit, *v.*, dashed, leapt

Dyapasone, *n.*, the interval of an octave

Dyss, *n.*, (*musical term*) 'dis' = 'bis' as in 'Dis-diapason'

Dyte, dite, *n.*, writing, poem

v., write ; indict, charge

E

E, ee, *n.*, eye

Effeir, affeir, *v.*, become, befitting, customary, suitable

Effray, *n.*, fear, fright

Eftir, *prep.* and *adv.*, from, according to, in due course

Egeis, *n. pl.* *See* Note, *Pract. of Med.*, 24

Eik, *v.*, add to, increase.

adv., also

Eir, *n.*, ear

v., plough

adv., *lang e.* = erelong

Eird, *n.*, earth

Eirdlie, *adj.*, earthly

Eirnist, eirnistfull, *adj.*

Eit, *v. past* and *pp.*, ate, eaten

Eith, *adj.* and *adv.*, easy, easily

Eld, eild, *n.*, age, time of life

Elevait, *v. pp.*, carried away

Emetricus (*musical term*). *See* Note, *O. E.*, 227

Enchessoun, *n.*, reason, cause

Encres, incres, *n.*, increase

v. increase, grow

Endure, indure, *v.*, endure, continue

Enolius (*musical term*). *See* Note, *O. E.*, 228

Ensure, *v.*, assure

Entres, *n.*, entrance

Eoye (= Eous). *See* Note, *T. C.*, 212

Epoddeus (*musical term*). *See* Note, *O. E.*, 229

Erss, *n.*, fundament

Eschaip, schaip, *v.*, escape

Eschame, schame, *v.*, shame, 'think shame'

Esperus (= Esperance ?). *See* Note, *T. C.*, 48

Ethios (= Aethon). *See* Note, *T. C.*, 213

Everilk, *adj.*, every

Evin, evyn, even, *n.*, even, evening

adj., even, just, balanced

Exceptioun, *n.*, objection to procedure (legal)

Excommunicat, *v. pp.*, cursed
Excusatioun, *n.*, defence (legal)
Exemplair, *n.*, example
Exemplative, *adj.*, yielding example
Exione, Ixion
Expert, expart, *adj.*, knowing, experienced
Expone, *v.*, expound, explain, state
Extasie, *n.*, ecstasy, frenzy, swoon

F

Fa, *n.*, foe (*pl.* fon)
Fachioun, *n.*, falchion, curved blade
Facound, facund, *n.*, eloquence
adj., eloquent
Faculte, -ie, -y, *n.*, profession, occupation, ingenuity, method, authority
Faikin, -yn, *adj.*, false, deceitful
Faill, fall, *n.*, failure, doubt
Faill, failye, *v.* fail
Fair, *n.*, fare, provision
adj., fair, handsome, goodly
v., fare, go
Fairheid, *n.*, beauty
Fairn, farne, *n.*, fern, bracken
Fald, *v.*, fail; turn away (from truth and fair dealing); weaken, collapse
Fall, *n.*, trap, fall
v., happen, come to pass
v., fall
Fallow, *n.*, fellow, friend, companion
v., associate
Falset, *n.*, falsehood
Falt, *n.*, fault, blame; lack, want, default
v., to do wrong, to fail
Fandit, *v. past*, attempted, busied . . . in
Fane, *adj.*, glad, willing, happy
adv., eagerly, willingly
Fang, *n.* and *v.*, catch, capture

Farie, *n.*, dream, vision
Fary, *n.*, fairy-folk
n., condition of tumult
Fasse, *n.*, something of no value
Fasshe. *See* Flasche
Fassoun, *n.*, fashion, manner
Fastnes, *n.*, constancy
Fatherwar, 'Father-worse,' name of a fox
Faw, *adj.*, streaked, bright
Fax, *n.*, hair of the head
Fayest, *adj.* (*superl.* of fay, fey, 'fated to die') used as *n.*
Fe, *n.*, animals, cattle, sheep = 'fee,' *n.*, reward, wage
Fecht, *v.*, fight, struggle
Feid, fede, *n.*, feud, quarrel
v., feed
Feill, *n.*, knowledge
adj., many
v., feel = 'smell'
Feir, *n.*, companion, fear, way, demeanour, appearance
n., space in a field
Feirfull, *adj.*, awe-inspiring, fearsome
Feiritnes, *n.*, terror
Feisik, *n.*, physic, medicine
Feit, fete, *n.*, feat, feet
Feitho, *n.*, fitchew
Fell, fele, *n.*, fell (*firth and f.*)
adj., very great, mighty
adj., severe, dire, terrible
Fellit, *v. pp.*, felled, slain
Felloun, *adj.*, deadly, great, high
adv., desperately, greatly
Felterit, *adj.*, matted, tangled
Fence, *v.* (of a court of law). *See* Note, *Fables*, 948
Fent, *n.*, opening in a garment
Fenyeit, feinyeit, *adj.*, insincere, feigned, untrue, fabulous, treacherous
Ferd(e), *adj.*, fourth

Feriat, *adj.*, in vacation (legal)

Ferles, ferlesse, *n.*, marvels, wonders

Ferlie, ferlye, *adj.*, wonderful, strange

adv., suddenly, strangely

Ferlyis, *v.* ; *me ferlyis*, I wonder, I marvel

Ferslie, *adv.*, fiercely, hotly

Ferther, forder, *adv.*, farther, further

Fervent, *adj.*, hot, fiery ; cold, severe, wintry

Fettillie, *adv.*, featly, skilfully

Fibert, *n.*, beaver

Figurait, *v. pp.*, figured, imagined, dignified, likened

Figurall, *adj.*, shown by figure, or allegory

Figure, *n.*, figure, appearance ; rhetorical figure

Firth, *n.*, coppice, wooded country

Fitch, *n.*, vetch

Flaft, *v. pp.*, puffed

Flaill, *n.*, well-beam

Flane, *n.*, arrow

v. pp., flayed

Flasche, *n.*, sheaf of arrows. *See* Note, *T. C.*, 167

Flaw, *v. past*, flew

Fle, flee, flie, *n.* and *v.*, fly

Flear, *n.*, one in flight

Fleidnes, *n.*, fright

Fleit, *v.*, swim, sail, flow

v. pp., = ? had fled, was withered

Flemit, flemyt, *v. pp.*, banished, exiled, driven away

Flet, *n.*, inner part of a house

Flew, *v. past*, flayed

Flewer, *n.*, 'flavour,' savour, odour

Fleyis, *v.*, divests, frees from

Flicht, *v.*, flock (of birds)

Flit, *n.*, to remove oneself and goods

Flocht, *n.*, state of excitement

Fluke, *n.*, flounder (fish)

Flyrdome, *n.*, bounce, humbug

Flyte, *v.*, scold, quarrel, argue

Fog, *n.*, moss

Foirrun, *v.*, exhausted

Foirspeikar, *n.*, spokesman, chief speaker, chairman

Fold, *n.*, earth

Fon, *n.*, folly

Fontall, *adj.*, original, parent

For, *used occasionally as* in spite of ; notwithstanding

Force, forss, etc., *n.*, strength, force ; *on f.*, of necessity, assuredly

Forcelie, *adv.*, strongly, vigorously

Forcy, *adj.*, strong, powerful

Fforfair, *v.*, spoil (a furrow in ploughing)

Forfault, etc., *n.* and *v.*, forfeit

Forlane, *v. pp.*, forgotten, *passé*

Forlore, forloir, *v. pp.*, lost

Forthink, *v.*, repent

Forthy, *adv.*, for that reason

Fortunait, *v. pp.*, made a victim of fortune

Fowmart, *n.*, polecat

Fra, *used in the sense of* when, from the moment that, etc.

Fraellar, frewollar, *adj.*, more brittle, frailer

Frak, *adj.*, eager, quick

Frank, *adj.*, free, not under bondage

Fraucht, *n.*, freight, passage-money

Frawart, frawert, *adj.*, froward ; strong, bitte

Fray, *n.*, fright

Freir, *n.*, friar

Freit, fret, *v.*, to destroy

Frek, freik, *n.*, man

Fremmit, *v. pp.*, ? exiled

Frivoll, *adj.*, poor, miserable

Fronsit, *adj.*, frounced, wrinkled. *See* Note, *T. C.*, 155

Frosnit. *See entry above*

Fructuous, *adj.*, fruitful, full of good meaning

Fulfair, *adj.*, very fair or beautiful

Fulminate, *v. past*, issue (of legal censure or judgment)

Fundin, *v. pp.*, found

Fur, *n.*, furrow

Fure, *v. past*, fared

Furmage, *n.*, cheese

Furth, *adv.*, forth, away, forthwith

Fyle, *v.*, defile

Fyndar, *n.*, finder, inventor, discoverer

Fyne, *adj.*, artful, subtle ; good, excellent

G

Gadder, *v.*, gather

Gair, *n.*, gore

Gaist, *n.*, spirit, guest

Gait, *n.*, way, road ; goat

Gam, *n.*, amusement, fun

Ganand, *adj.*, suitable, good

Gane, *v.*, win, gain, suit
    v., =go (gang)

Ganecome, *n.*, return

Ganesay, *v.*, unsay, retract

Ganestand, *v.*, oppose

Gansell, *n.*, garlic sauce. *See* Note, *Fables*, 345

Gant, *n.*, yawn

Gar, ger, *v.*, cause

Garneist, *v. pp.*, ornamented

Garnisoun, *n.*, garrison

Garray, *n.*, noise, hubbub

Garth, *n.*, enclosed ground, garden

Gaw, *n.*, gall-bladder

Gay, *adj.* as *n.*, *Annunciation*, 21

Geif, *v.*, give, grant

Geill, *n.*, jelly

Gemilling, gemynyng, *n. See* Note, *O. E.*, 370

Generabill, *adj.*, created, capable of generation

Gent, *adj.*, beautiful, fair

Gentill, *adj.*, well-born, noble, good

Gentilnes, *n.*, noble demeanour, courtesy, good birth

Gentrice, gentrace, *n.*, generosity, honourable action

Gers, gerss, etc., *n.*, grass

Gersum. *See* Gressome

Gest, *n.*; *pl.* gestis, *gesta*
    n., guest

Gib Hunter, familiar name for cat

Gif, gife, *conj.*, if

Gigotlike, *adv.*, wantonly, like a harlot

Gilbert, Tom-cat. Cp. Gib Hunter

Gillet, *n.*, mare

Gilt, *n.*, guilt
    adj. and *pp.*, gilt

Gimpis, *n. pl.*, quirks, tricks

Ginnes, *n. pl.*, devices, ingenuities

Gird, *v. past*, struck
    v., spring down, prepare, get ready, etc.

Girnand, *v. p.* as *adj.*, snarling

Gite. *See* Note, *T. C.*, 164

Glaikit, *adj.*, foolish, senseless

Glar, *v.*, make muddy

Glas, *n.*, glass, window, mirror

Glean, *v. See* Note, *Pract. of Med.*, 42

Glebard. *See* Note, *Fables*, 910

Gled, *n.*, kite (bird)

Gleid, *n.*, ember

Glew, *n.*, merriment, fun

Glose, *n.*, gloss (legal)

Glowmand, *adj.* and *p.*, gloomy

Glowrand, *v. p.* as *adj.*, staring

Goddes, *n.*, goddess

Goikit, *v. past*, stared foolishly

Gole, *n.*, howling, crying

Gorrit, *v. past*, gored, pierced

Govand, *v. p.*, staring, gaping

Gowand, *n.*, gallant

Gowk, *n.*, cuckoo

Gowpene, *n.*, a double handful

Grane, *n.*, colour

Grathit, *v. pp.*, bedecked, equipped

Gravin, *v. pp.*, buried

Gre, *n.*, degree

Greif, *n.*, greive, reeve

   v., grieve, vex

Greit, *n.*, lamentation

—, grit, *adj.*, great

   v., weep, lament

Gressome, *n.*, tenant's fine. *See*

   Note, *Fables*, 2745

Grew, *n.*, Greece, Greek (language)

   v., grew

Grimmit, *v. pp.*, befouled

Gripe, graip, *n.*, vulture, griffin

Grouf, *n.* ; *on g.*, grovelling

Growis, *v. pres.*, trembles

Growme, *n.*, man

Grunching, *n.*, grumbling, grousing

Grutchit, *v. past*, grumbled, complained

Gryce, *n.*, sucking-pig

Guberne, *v.*, govern, control

Gude, *n.* = *gudis*, goods, property

Guk, guk. *See* Gowk

Gukit, *adj.*, stupid, foolish

Guse, *n.*, goose

Gust, *v.*, taste, give relish to

Gyane, *n.*, giant, monster

Gyis, *n.*, guise, method

   n. = *gite*, garment

Gyn, *n.*, contrivance, trick

H

Habirgeoun, *n.*, coat of mail

Hace, hais, *adj.*, hoarse

Haik, *v.*, go, proceed

Haill, *n.*, hail

   adj., whole, full, entire

Haill—*continued*

   adv., wholly, altogether

   v., draw, move up quickly

   —, a form of exclamation, ' Haill,

     yule, haill ! ' *Fables*, 289

Hailsum, *adj.*, wholesome

Hair, *n.*, hare (animal)

   adj., hoar, hoarse, rough, grey,

     etc.

Haising, *v. n.*, hoarseness

Hakkit, *v. past*, hacked, cut

Hald, *v.*, hold, go, stand, rule,

   proceed, support, etc.

Halfheid, *n.*, ' haffet,' cheek

Halk, *n.*, hawk

Hall, *n.*, dining-hall, *T. C.*, 358

Hals, *n.*, neck

Hame, hamewart, *n.* and *adv.*,

   home, homewards

Hankit, *v. pp.*, entangled

Hant, *v.*, frequent, accustom

Harberie, herberie, *n.*, shelter

   lodging

Hardelie, *adv.*, certainly, by all

   means

Harl, *v.*, drag

Harnes, *n.*, harness, armour

Harnis, *n. pl.*, brains

Harsky, *adj.*, ragged, rugous

Hart, hairt, *n.*, hart (animal) ;

   heart

Harvest, *n.*, Autumn

Hate, *n.*, hat

Hattrell, *n.*, crown (of the head)

Having, *n.*, demeanour, comportment

Haw, *adj.*, livid, dull, wan

Hebel hable, *n.*, higgledy-piggledy

Hecht, *n.*, promise, oath, vow.

   v., promise, undertake

   v. pres. and *past*, call, be called ;

   name, be named

Heclit. *See* Hekkillit

Hedit, *v.*, beheaded

Heich, *adj.*, high
v., elevate, raise up
Heid, hede, *n.*, head
n., heed
Heidismen, *n. pl.*, men in authority
Heidit, *v. pp.*, headed, tipped
Heill, *n.*, health, happiness
n., heel
Heillit, *v. pp.*, covered, hidden
Heird, = hear it. *See* Notes
Heit at the hairt, *n. phr.*, heartburn
Hekill, *n.*, hackle (of a bird)
Hekkillit, heklit, etc., hackled, fringed. *See* Note, *T. C.*, 244
Herato, the Muse Erato
Hering, *n. s.* and *pl.*, herring
Hesperous, the Evening Star
Hething, *n.*, mockery, derision
Heuch, huche, *n.*, ravine, glen, gully
Hewmound, *n.*, helmet
Heynd, *adj.*, gentle, gracious
Hicht, *n.*, height
Hie, he, *adj.*, high
v., elevate, raise
Hindir, *adj.*, last, most recent. *See* Note, *Bludy Serk*, 1
Hint, hynt, *v.*, take, catch
Hird, *n.*, herdsman, shepherd
Hire, hyre, *n.*, reward, payment
Hirpland, *v. p.*, 'hirpling,' limping
Hoche, *n.*, hough (of leg)
Hog, hoig, *n.*, a young sheep, not yet shorn for the first time
Holkit, *v. pp.* and *adj.*, hollow, 'dug out'
Holt, *n.*, wood
Holyne, *n.*, holly
Hone, hune, *n.*, delay
Host, -and, *n.*, cough, -ing
Hovit, *v.*, heaved, raised
How, ho, *exclam.*, Ho !
adj., hollow

Huntis up. *See* Note, *Fables*, 2083
Hurcheoun, *n.*, urchin, hedgehog
Hurd(e), *n.*, hoard
Huresone, *n.* and *adj.*, whoreson
Hy, *n.*, haste ; *in hy*, quickly
v., hie, haste
Hynd, *n.*, hind (animal)
Hyne, *adv.*, from this time, till

I

Ice-schoklis, *n. pl.*, icicles
Idole, *n.*, image. *See* Note, *T. C.*, 507
Ilk, *adj.*, each
Ilkane, each one, every one
Imbrace, Imbrass, *v.*, embrace, wear
Impit, ympit, *v. pp.*, grafted, attached
Implicate, *v. pp.*, involved
Importable, *adj.*, unbearable
Incertane, = 'in certane,' certainly
Indorsat, *v. pp.*, endorsed
Indurat, *v. pp.* and *adj.*, hardened, callous
Infect, *v. pp.*, 'infected,' filled
Infild, *v. pp.* and *adj.*, undefiled
Inflat, *v. pp.*, inflated, puffed up
Influence (*astrol.*). *See* Note, *T.C.*, 149
Ingeing, *n.*, ability, skill, genius
Ingyne. *See above entry*
Innes, *n. pl.* as *sing.*, inn, shelter. *See* Note, *Fables*, 262
Insolent, *adj.*, inexperienced
Intermell, *v.*, meddle, interfere
Interply, *v.*, interplead
Interpreit, *v. pp.*, interpreted
Intruse, intruss, *v.*, intrude, urge
Irk, *adj.*, loath, indifferent
Ithand. *See* Ythand

T

J

Janglour, *n.*, gossip, scandal-monger

Jasp, *n.*, precious stone

Jeperdie, etc., *n.*, trick, sleight : *J. of weir*, fortune of war

Jonet, *n.*, jennet, small Spanish horse

Jonit, *v. pp.*, joined

Jowal, jowell, *n.*, jewel

Justifyit, *v.*, given judgment for

Jympis. *See* Gimpis

K

Kaill. *See* Caill

Katche, *n.*, chase

Keikis, *v., pres.*, peeps

Keip, *n.*, care, heed
  v., keep, guard, watch

Keipar, *n.*, keeper, herd

Keitching, *n.*, kitchen

Kemmit, *v. pp.*, combed

Ken, *v.*, know

Kendill, *v.*, kindle

Kennet, *n.*, small hunting dog

Kinbute, *n.*, wergeld, paid by the slayer to his victim's kin

Kinnisman, *n.*, kinsman

Kirk, *n.*, church

Kirtill, *n.*, woman's petticoat or gown

Kist, *n.*, chest

Kith, *n.*, place, district, home
—, kyth, etc., *v.*, show, manifest

Kittok, *n.*, paramour, trollop

Knak, *n.*, snap of the fingers

Knakis, knax, *pl.*, tricks, quibbles, jests

Knap, *v.*, strike

Knet, *v. pp.*, entangled

Knok, *v.*, knock, strike, beat

Kynd(e), *n.*, nature, instinct, kin, species, variety, etc.

L

Lack, lak, *n.*, blame, reproach; lack
  v., want, lack

Lad, *n.*, serving-man : in opposition to 'laird.' *See* Note, *Want of Wyse Men*, 60

Laich, *adj.*, low

Laif, lave, *n.*, the rest, remainder

Laikly, *adj.*, (?) loathsome

Laip, *v.*, lap, drink

Laird, *n.*, landowner, master

Lait, *adj.* and *adv.*, late, once, formerly, recently

Laith, *adj.*, loath, unwilling

Laitis, *n. pl.*, manners, mien

Lans, *v.*, leap, bound, hop

Lap, *v. past* and *pp.*, leapt

Laser, *n.*, leisure

Lat, latt, *v. See* Let

Late, *v.*, search for, seek

Lauch = leuch?, laughed. *See* Note, *T. C.*, 231

Lauchfull, *adj.*, lawful

Laverok, *n.*, lark (bird)

Law, *n.*, law ; hill, mound
  adj., low
  adv., lowly
  v., lower, degrade, reduce

Lawdian, *n.*, Lothian

Lawitnes, *n.*, ignorance

Lawrean, *n.*, laurel

Lawte, lawtie, etc., *n.*, loyalty

Lazarous, *n.*, leper

Le, lye, etc., *n.*, lea, field
  n., safety, security
  n., lie, falsehood
  adj., 'lee' : sheltered
  v., lie, prevaricate

Leiche, *v.*, heal ; *l.-craft*, leechcraft

Leid, *n.*, man, person, folk, people
  n., lead (mineral)
  v., lead, pass, etc.
  v. past, lied, told lies

Leill, *adj.*, true, loyal, honest

Leir, lair, etc., *n.*, learning, teaching
   v., learn, teach, inform
Leit (=let), *v.*, tarry
Lemanrye, *n.*, adultery
Leme, *n.*, ray, gleam
Lemman, *n.*, lover, sweetheart
Lempet, *n.*, limpet
Lend, lind, *n.*, loin, buttock
Lene, lein, etc., *adj.*, lean ; *v.*, lean
Lentring, *n.*, Lent
Lerioun, *n.*, (animal). *See* Note,
   Fables, 914
Lerit, lernit, *adj.*, learned
Lest, -and, *v.* and *adj.*, last, -ing
Lesum, *adj.*, lawful
Lesure, *n.*, hurt
Let, lat, latt, *v.*, allow ; prevent,
   hinder ; think ; make a move
   to ; etc.
   n., hindrance, ceasing
Letter, *n.*, order of court; letter
—, latter, etc., *adj.*, latter
Leuch, *v. past*, laughed
Leve, leif, *v.*, live
Lever, levar, etc., *n.*, liver (of body)
   adv., rather
Lewer, *n.*, louver, on barn-roof
Lib, *v.*, cut, castrate (?)
Licht, lycht, *n.*, light (of day)
   adj., light, nimble
   adv., lightly
   v., alight, rest, dismount
Lichtlie, *adv.*, easily, softly
   v., disparage
Liggand, *v. p.*, lying
Likame, *n.*, body
Liklynace, *n.*, likeness
Ling, *n.*, heather, patch of heather
Linget, *n.*, lint, flax
Lint, *n.*, flax
Lipper, *n.*, leper ; leper-folk
List, *n.*, border, selvedge
Loggerand, *v. p.* as *adj.*, loosely
   hanging

Loif, leif, *v.*, praise, flatter
Lokker, *adj.*, curled
Longis, *n. pl.*, lungs
Lorne, *v. pp.*, lost
Lorum. *See* Note, *Fables*, 2831
Loun, *n.*, fellow
—, (lowne), *adj.*, quiet, unruffled
Lour, *v.*, skulk, lurk, crouch
Lous, lows, etc., *adj.*, free, loose,
   immoral
   v., loosen, relieve, unyoke
Lout, lowt, *v.*, bow, do obeisance
Loving, *n.*, praise
Lowd, *adv.*, openly
Lowe, *n.*, flame, glow
Lowrence, Lowrie, Laurence,
   familiar names for the fox
Lucerne, *n.*, lamp
Lude, *v. pp.*, loved
Ludge, *n.*, lodging, home
   v., lodge, live
Lue, *n.*, love ; *v.*, love
Lufe, luve, luif, etc., *n.*, love
Luffage, *n.*, lovage (plant) : *Levisti-*
   cum officinale
Lug, *n.*, ear
Luif, *n.*, palm of hand
Luik, *n.*, look, expression
   v., look, search for, watch
Luking, *n.*, body. *See* Likame
Lukkin, *adj.*, webbed
Lundin, Lundy or Lundin (Fife)
Lurdane lane, ?animal. *See* Note
   on *Bourabane*, *Fables*, 914
Lure, *v.*, snare (of hawks)
Lusumest, *adj. superl.*, most lovely
Lyart, *adj.*, silvery grey, grey
Lybell, *n.*, document, book, writing
   See Note, *T. C.*, 74
Lyif, lyfe, *n.*, life
Lyking, *n.*, liking, desire, beloved
   v. p., preferring, choosing
Lymmar, etc., *n.*, rogue
Lynage, lenage, *n.*, lineage, descent

Lyne, *n.*, stalk (of flax)
Lyre, *n.*, skin, complexion
Lyte, *n.*, little

M

Ma, mo, *adj.*, more
  v., make
Mache, matche, *n.*, match, equal
  v., match, mate
Maculait, *v. pp.*, spotted
Magnificence, *n.*, high authority,
  majesty
Maill, *n.*, rent
Maill men, mailler, *n.*, tenants,
  tenant, small-farmer
Mailling, *n.*, rented farm
Mailyeis, *n.*, eyelet holes in a laced
  garment
Mais, *n.*, food, meat
Maisterlig. *See* Misterlyk, and
  Note, *Fables*, 198
Maistrie, maistry, *n.*, wrongful force,
  tyranny
Makdome, *n.*, form, appearance,
  comeliness
Malisone, *n.*, curse
Mane, *n.*, moan ; fine bread ; mane
  (of animal) ; force, strength
Manesworne, *adj.*, forsworn
Mangerie, *n.*, feast
Maniss, *v.*, menace, threaten
  n. poss., man's
Mansioun, *n.*, dwelling-house
Manure place, *n.*, manor house
Mark, merk, *n.*, a coin, 13/4d
  (Scots)
  v., go, find one's way ; consider
Marmisset, *n.*, marmoset
Marrow, *n.*, companion, mate
Mart, *n.*, ox, fattened for market
Mast, *n.*, pole
—, maist, *adj. superl.*, most
Mat, *v.*, baffle, nonplus

Maveis, *n.*, thrush
May, *n.*, maid ; (month of) May
Meid, *n.*, reward, bribe, etc. *See*
  Note, *Fables*, 1233
Meir, *n.*, mare
Meit, *n.*, meat, food
  adj. and *adv.*, meet, proper(ly).
  v., meet, encounter
  v., mete, measure
Mekill, mekle, *adj.*, much
Meldrop, *n.*, mucus from the nose
Mell, *v.*, mix, copulate, mate
Memoriall, *n.*, remembrance, keep-
  sake, token
Memour, *n.*, memory
Men. *See* Note, *Fables*, 651
Mend, *v.*, amend, assuage, reform,
  cure
Mene, *v.*, think, ponder
Menye, *n.*, injury, hurt, maiming
—, menyie, *n.*, many, folk, people,
  servants
Mercat, *n.*, market, trade
Merle, merll, *n.*, blackbird
Mertrik, *n.*, marten (animal)
Miching, *n.*, skulking, pilfering
Midding, myddyng, *n.*, midden
Ming, myng, *v.*, mix, mingle
Minorall, *n.*, miner's work
Mirk, merk, *adj.* and *adv.*, dark,
  obscure
Mis, myss, *n.*, error, fault, sin
Misdum, *n.*, misjudgment (?) *See*
  Note, *Yowth and Aige*, 18
Mister, *n.*, need, want
Misterlyk, *adv.*, skilfully, craftily
Mo, *adj.*, more, other
Mocht, *v.*, might, may
Modifie, *v.*, assess. *See* Note,
  T. C., 299
Mold, mow, etc., *n.*, earth, dirt, dust
Mone, *n.*, moon
—, mane, *n.*, moan, lamentation
Monische, *v.*, admonish

Movar, *n.*, Mover, God

Mowdewart, *n.*, mole (animal)

Mowis, *n. pl.*, jests, quibbles

Mude, meid, *n.*, mood, frame of mind

Mure, muir, *n.*, moor

Murne, *v.*, mourn, lament

Murther, murthour, *n.*, murder

Musk, *n.*, civet-cat. *See* Note, *Fables*, 917

Mydred, myddret, *n.*, midriff, diaphragm

Mynnis, *v.*, wane (of the moon)

Mynour, *n.*, miner

Mysdirt, *n.*, excrement of mice

Myte, myt, *n.*, mite, jot, tittle

N

Nanis, *n.*, nonce

Naple. *See* Note, *O. E.*, 282

Nathing, *n.*, nothing, not in the least

Neidis, neidlingis, *adv.*, of necessity

Neip, *n.*, turnip

Neiss, nois, *n.*, nose

Neist, *adv. superl.*, nearest, next

Nekhering, *n.*, a blow on the neck or ear. *See* Note, *Fables*, 2089

Nichtbour, nychtbour, *n.*, neighbour

Nippis, *v.*, clutches, grips

Nois, *n.*, nose

Noit, note, *n.*, note (musical)
 v., note, observe, notice

Nop, *v.*, take a nap or light sleep

Noter, notar, *n.*, notary

Noyes, *n.*, clamour, song (of birds)

Nureis, nurice, *n.*, nurse

Nuttieclyde, *n.*, name of a dog, ' Brown Clyde '

Nyce, nyse, *adj.*, difficult to please, fine, subtle, pretty, pleasant

O

Object, *v.*, adduce reasons against, offer as an instance against

Oblissing, *n.*, obligation, bond

Ochane, *exclam. See* Note, *T. C.*, 541

Ocht, aught, *n.* and *adv.*, anything, at all

Of, off, *prep.*, from, by ; for ; off

Okker, *n.*, usury

Once, *n.*, ounce (animal). *See* Note, *Fables*, 906

Onwarly, *adv.*, unwarily

Operatioun, *n.*, working, action, deed

Opinioun, *n.*, reputation, good name

Oppositioun, *n.* (*of a planet*)

Orature, *n.*, oratory, private chapel

Orloge, *n.*, clock

Ornate, *adj.*, endowed, adorned

Oster, *n.*, ? oyster

Ostlaire, *n.*, innkeeper, host

Oulk, *n.*, week

Oursyld, *v. pp.*, hidden, overcast

Outher, owthir, *adj.*, either

Outred, *v. pp.*, brought to an end

Outthrow, *prep.*, throughout

Outwaill, *n.*, outcast

Outwin, *v.*, get away, escape

Over, ouir, *adv.*, too

Over draif, *v.*, covered, choked

Overheillit, *v.*, covered over laden

Overpas, *v.*, pass over

Overset, *v. pp.*, sunk, overwhelmed

Ovircome, *v.*, recover, come to. *See* Note, *T. C.*, 540

Ovirfret, *v. pp.*, decorated, variegated

Ovirquhelmit, *v. past*, overcast, overwhelmed

P

Pace, pasche, *n.*, Easter
Pad, *n.*, paddock, frog
Paddock, Paddok, *n.*, frog
Paip, *n.*, Pope
Pairt, *n.*, part, example, sample, share
   v., divide, share, break
Pairtles, *adj.*, having no part in, innocent of
Paiss, *n.*, weight, burden of blame, consequences, etc.
   v., weigh, ponder, calm, appease
Palmester, *n.*, palmist
Palpis, papis, paupis, etc., *n. pl.*, paps, breasts
Palyeoun, *n.*, tent, pavilion
Panch, paynch, *n.*, paunch
Pane, *n.* (flower) bed
—, payne, *n.*, punishment, distress, ill-health, penalty
Pansing, *n.*, meditation
Parabole, *n.*, parable, comparison
Paramour, *n.*, lover, love, love-affairs
   adv., amorously
Parpall, perpall. *See* Note, *Fables,* 348
Parralling, *n.*, partition wall
Party-tressoun, *n. See* Note, *Fables,* 1089 *B*
Pary, *v.*, bet, wager
Patelet, *n.*, woman's ruff
Patill, *n.*, plough-staff. *See* Note, *Fables,* 2243
Paynt . . . furth, *v. phr.*, display (a lesson)
Peax, pes, etc., *n.*, peace, salvation
Pedder, *n.*, pedlar
Pegase, *n.*, Pegasus
Peill, *v.*, strip, plunder, skin
Peip, pepe, *n.*, squeak, cheep (cry of a mouse)

Peir, *n.*, peer, equal
Peirrie, *n.*, perry
Peit pot, *n.*, peat-hole
Pellet, *n.*, pelt, skin
Pen, *n.*, feather, quill, wing
Penetryfe, etc., *adj.*, searching, bitter
Penner, *n.*, writing-case
Pennit, *adj.*, quilled
Pennyfull, *adj.*, full and round
Pepill, *n.*, people
Peros. Pyroeis, one of the steeds of the Sun. (*See* Note, *T. C.,* 215)
Perqueir, *adv.*, by heart, thoroughly
Perreist, *v. pp.*, perished
Perrell, peril, etc., *n.*, peril, pains (legal)
Perrie Doig. *See* Note, *Fables,* 1166
Pertok, Partlot, name of a hen. *See* Notes
Pew, *n.*, cry of a bird
Peyntet, *v. pp.*, spotted (referring to panther's skin. *See* Note, *Fables,* 896), decorated
Phary. *See* Fary, *n.*
Philologie. (*See* Note, *T. C.,* 216), Phlegon
Phisnamour, *n.*, physiologist
Phisnomie, *n.*, physiognomy
Picht, *v. past,* planted, pitched (a tent)
Pik, *n.*, pitch, resin
   n., spike (of thorns)
Pill, *v.*, plunder
Pith, pytht, *n.*, strength
Plane, *n.*, valley ; space
   adj., plain, clear, manifest
   adv., plainly, clearly
Plank. *See* Note, *Fables,* 2270
Play, *n.*, game, venture, lesson
—, pley, *n.*, plea ; *v.*, play
Pleid, *n.*, discussion, talk, pleading (legal)

Plenyeit, *v. past,* complained, lamented

Plesaunce, etc., *n.,* pleasure, happiness, enjoyment

Plet, *v.,* embrace ; pleat, weave

Pleuch, *n.,* plough

Pley, *n. See* Play

   v., to plead

Ply, plye, plicht, etc., *n.,* plight, peril, misfortune, condition

Poik, *n.,* ? poke (stomach) ; *or* pock, scab ?

Poleist, *adj.* and *v. pp.,* polished

Poleit. *See* Note, *Fables,* 3

Poll, pollis, *n.,* skull, skulls : *deid pollis,* death's-heads

Pontificall, *n. pl.,* episcopal vestments

Porteouss, *n.,* book. *See* Note, *Fables,* 1273

Portioun, *n. See above entry*

Potestate, *n.,* potentate

Pothecairis, *n. pl.,* apothecaries

Pottingary, *n.,* art of the apothecary, pharmacy.

Pow. *See* Poll

   n., paw

Poysonabill, *adj.,* poisonous, detestable

Practik, prettik, etc., *n.,* practice, evidence, knowledge

Practysis, *n. pl.,* prescriptions (medical)

Prais, prayis, *n.,* reward

Pray, *n.,* prey. *See* Note, *Fables,* 2259

Precelling, *v. p.,* excelling

Preclair, *adj.,* famous

Preiching, etc., *n.,* preaching, lesson

Preif, *v.,* ('pree') make proof of, try, test, sample

Preis, press, *v.,* press, contend, strive, resist ; praise, prize

   n., price. (*See under.*)

Prene, *n.,* pin

Prent, *n.,* evidence, character, print

Pres, *n.,* (clothes)-press

Presonair, *n.,* prisoner

Presume, *n.,* expectation

   v., dare, presume, think, take for granted

Pretend, *v.,* show, venture on, lay claim, bring an action at law

Price, *n.,* price, cost, fee, bribe

   n., honour or praise

Primeros, Prymeros, *n.,* primrose

Princes, *n.,* princess

Privilage, *n.,* respite, exemption

Proceid, *v.,* proceed with a case, or in an action at law

Profixit, *adj.,* previously fixed

Progenetryse, *n.,* ancestress

Progenitour(e), *n.,* ancestor

Prompit, *v. past,* moved, bounced

Pronuncit, *v.,* delivered or pronounced

Propertie, *n.,* possession, quality, attribute

Proplexite, *n.,* perplexity

Propone, *v.,* propose, state a case (legal)

Proportionat, *n.,* proportioned, balanced (musical)

Prostrait, *adj.,* prostrate, submissive, stricken down

   misreading of *Pro* strait. *See* Note, *Fables,* 1218

Provisioun, *n.,* foresight, providence

Provokit, *v. past,* incited, prompted

Pryme, *n.,* Prime (6 A.M., or sunrise) *MS. variant of* Pyme, *q.v., B* 1787

Puddingis, *n. pl.,* forced meat

Pull, *v.,* draw (of flax)

Pungityve, -ive, *adj.,* sharp, stinging

Purches, purcheis, *n.,* chase, concubinage, sharp practice

   v., manage, succeed

Pure, peure, etc., *adj.*, poor; pure, chaste
Purfellit, *v. pp.*, bordered, decorated, embroidered
Purpour, purpure, *adj.*, purple
Purpurate, *adj.*, *literally*, empurpled. *Used actually as a superl. epithet*, the very finest, greatest, etc.
Pursephant, *n.*, pursuivant
Pyip, pype, *n.*, pipe (of wine)
  v., pipe, sing
Pyk, pike, etc., *v.*, pick
  v., steal, pilfer, plunder, etc.
Pykeris, *n. pl.*, pilferers
Pyme, *n.*, cry. *See* Note, *Fables*, 1788
Pynnis, *n. pl.*, pegs (of a harp)
Pypand, *adj.*, clear, 'wet and glossy'

Q

Quadruplait, (musical) quadruple tone
Quailye, *n.*, quail, corncrake
Quair, *n.*, book
Querrell, *n.*, plea, contention, dispute
Quert, *n.*, health; *in q.*, in good health, alive and well
Quha, *pron.*, who
Quhaill, *n.*, whale
Quhair, *adv.*, where
Quhairat, *adv.*, whereat
Quhairthrow, *adv.*, through which, whereby
Quhais, *pron. poss.*, whose
Quhaisill, *n.*, weasel
Quhat, *pron.*, etc., what
Quheill, *n.*, wheel
  v., wheel
Quheit, *n.*, wheat, 'corn'
Quhen, *adv.*, when
Quherland, *adj.* (*v. p.*), ? whirling
Quhether, *adv.*, etc., whither

Quhetting, *v. p.*, whetting
Quhidder, *n.* (of a whale), ? spouting
—, quhether, *adv. conj.*, etc., whether
—, quhither, etc., *adv.*, whither
Quhilis, quhylis, *adv.*, at times
Quhilk, quhylk, *pron.*, who, which
Quhill, *adv.-conj.*, till
  adv., etc., while
Quhirl, -yng, *v.*, whirl, -ing
Quhisling, *v. p.*, whistling
Quhite. *See* Quheit
—, quhyte, *adj.*, white
  n., white (of eye)
Quhitlie, *adj.*, whitish
Quhitret, *n.*, stoat
Quhome, *pron.*, whom
Quhrynand, *adj.*, whining (*A.S.*, hrinan). *See* Note, *Fables*, 911
Quhuirand, *H. variant of above* (? whirring), or perhaps a scribal confusion of the same word
Quhy, *adv.*, why : *for q.*, because, since
Quhyle, *n.*, time, period
Quhylum, *adv.*, whilom, once upon a time
Quhyte, quhite, etc., *adj.*, white, fair
Quietie, *n.*, quiet, peace
Quik, *n.*, the quick, living
Quitclame, *v.*, release, discharge
Quotidiane, cotidiane, *adj.*, daily
Quyte, quit(e), *v.*, requite, repay
  adv., etc., quite, entirely

R

Ra, *n.*, roe (deer)
Rache, *n.*, a hound of scent
Rad, raid, *adj.*, afraid, startled, terrified
Raddour, reddour, *n.*, terror, fright

Radicat, *v. pp.*, implanted, rooted

Raid, *v. past*, rode

Raif, *v.*, rave, be angry

Raik, *v.*, go, wander

Raip, *n.*, rope

Rais, *n.*, race
   n., rose
   v., to raise

Rait, rate, *n.*, style, custom, manner

Raith, *adv.*, soon, quick

Rak, *n.*, and *v.*, reck, care

Raklie, *adv.*, recklessly, impetuously

Ram (*sign of the Zodiac*)

Rampand, *v. p.*, rearing (heraldic use). *See* Note, *Fables*, 999

Rarit, *v. past*, called out, roared

Rattoun, *n.*, rat. *See* Note, *Fables*, 910

Raucht, racht, *v. past*, 'reached,' gave, delivered

Rauk, rawk, *adj.*, raucous, hoarse

Raw, *n.*, row, order

Rax, *v.*, prevail, domineer

Record, *n.*, evidence, statement (legal)

Recure, *n.*, recovery

—, recuir, *v.*, recover, get back

Refet(e), *v.*, recuperate, revive

Refuis, *v.*, refuse, surrender, let go

Regrait, *n.*, complaining, sorrow

Reheirs, *v.*, relate, tell, rehearse

Reid, *n.*, counsel, thought
   n., reed, rush
   adj., red
   v., advise, counsel, tell
   v., read

Reif, *n.*, theft, robbery

Reik, *v.*, grant, extend

Reird, *n.*, loud noise, shout, roar

Rekill, *n.*, heap

Remeid, *n.*, remedy, cure, solace, remission
   v., cure, amend

Remord, *v.*, repent, have remorse

Remufe, *v.*, depart, fail

Rent, *n.*, income, possessions
   v. pp., torn, rent, crucified

Renye, reinye, *v.*, govern, control

Repair, *n.*, association, resort
   v., go, resort

Reprufe, *n.*, shame

—, repruif, etc., *v.*, reprove

Repudie, *n.*, repudiation, divorcement

Reput(e), *v.*, reckon, esteem, hold

Resoll, *v.*, resolve (an argument)

Respite, *n.*, exemption

Responsaill, *n.*, response

Ressaif, etc., *v.*, receive

Ressoning, *n.*, argument, dispute

Rethorike, rethory, *n.*, rhetoric

Retour, *n.* and *v.*, return

Retreit, *v.*, withdraw (a sentence)

Revand, *adj.*, robbing, ravenous

Revar, etc., *n.*, robber

Reule, reull, rewll, *n.*, rule, authority, power
   v., rule

Reulr, *n.*, ruler

Revolve, rewoll, *v.*, turn over, consult (of books)

Rew, rewth, reuth, *n.*, compassion

Rew(e), *v.*, rue, be sorry for, take pity on

Rewert, *v.*, recuperate, recover

Reylock, *n.*, robbery with violence (Sc. law). *See* Note, *Fables*, 486

Rhetorie, etc. *See* Rethorike

Ribband, *v. pp*, trimmed, adorned (as with ribbon)

Riche, *v.*, enrich

Richt, rycht, *n.* and *adj.*, right
   adv., very, quite

Richteouslie, *adv.*, legitimately, in wedlock

Rin, ryn, *v.*, run, go one's own way

Ring, *n.*, ring (on finger)
v., ring (a bell)
v., reign, rule
Rink, renk, etc., *n.*, a man
—, rynk, *n.*, course
Rippillit, *v. past*, removed the seeds from (in flax preparation)
Roche, rotche, etc., *n.*, rock
Rod, *n.*, path
Roif. *See* Rufe
Roising, *adj.*, rosy, rose-like
Rok, *n.*, distaff
v., rock, sway
Roll, rowll, etc., *n.*, writing, document
—, row, *v.*, roll, turn, sway
Ron, rone, *n.*, thicket, brushwood
Rosier, rosere, *n.*, rose-tree
Rouch, *adj.*, rough
as n., rough ground
Roun, round, *v.*, whisper
Roustie, *adj.*, rusty, rusted ; bronze, bronze-colour
Rout, *n.*, blow, stroke
Roy, *n.*, king
Rud(e), *n.*, the Cross
n., complexion
adj., rough, coarse, unpolished
Rufe, roif, *n.*, rest, ease
n., roof
Ruffill, *v.*, bewilder
Rug, *v.*, tear, tug, rend
Ruik, ruke, *n.*, rook (bird)
Rummissing, *v. n.*, bellowing
Runkillit, *pp.* as *adj.*, wrinkled
Ruse, *v.*, extol, praise
Russell, *adj.*, reddish. *See* Note, *Fables*, 1962
Rusticat(e), *v. pp.* and *adj.*, vulgarised, boorish
Rute, *n.*, root, herbage, rough ground
Ryal, royall, etc., *adj.*, royal
Ryallie, *adv.*, triumphantly

Ryaltie, etc., *n.*, state, pomp, ceremony
Ryce, *n.*, twigs, brushwood
Ryip, rype, etc., *adj.*, ripe
v., ripen
v., seek, rummage, search out
Ryt(e), *n.*, custom, habit
Ryve, reif, rife, etc., *v.*, tear, destroy, rob

S

Sa, *adv.*, so
Sabill, *adj.*, sable
Sad, *adj.*, sober, serious, dull, steadfast, reliable
—, sadlie, *adv.*, soberly, seriously
Sagis, *v.*, assails, makes assault on
Sagittarie (*sign of the Zodiac*)
Saif, *v.*, save, preserve
prep. and *conj.*, except
Saik, *n.*, sake
Saikles, *adj.*, innocent
Saipheron, *adj.*, saffron
Sair, *n.*, sore, disease
adj. and *adv.*, sore, sorely ; sorry, sad
Sairnes, *n.*, disease
Sait, *n.*, seat
Salmond, salmound, *n.*, salmon
Sals, *n.*, sauce
Salviour, *n.*, saviour
Salusit, *v. past*, saluted, greeted
Samin, samyn, *adj.*, same
Sample, *n.*, (*aph.*) example. *See* Exampill
Sapheir, *n.*, sapphire ; (*pl.* sapheris)
Sapour, *n.*, flavour, quality
Sarie, *adj.*, sorry, poor, miserable
Sark, serk, *n.*, shirt, shift
Satisfy, satisfie, *v.*, (*legal: of an executor's act*)
Satlingis, *n. pl.*, ?lees or dregs of wine

Sauf, *adj.*, safe, free (of disease)

Saul(e), *n.*, soul

Sauld, *v. pp.*, sold

Saw, *n.*, word, proverb

  n., salve

  v., sow

Sawrand, *adj.*, savoury, pleasant, agreeable

Sayne, sane, *v.*, say

Scaith, skaith, *n.*, hurt, damage, harm

Scant, skant, *adv.*, scarcely, hardly

Scantlie, etc. *See above entry*

Schadow, schaddow, *n.*, shadow, reflection in mirror

Schaip, chaip, *v. See* Eschaip

Schame, *n.*, modesty

  v. See Eschame

Schankis, *n. pl.*, legs

Schaw, *n.*, wood, copse, covert

  v., show, demonstrate

Sched, *v. pp.*, poured, scattered, parted, divided

Scheill, *n.*, cot, hovel, crazy erection

Schell, *n.*, shell

Schene, *adj.*, bright, beautiful

Schent, shent, *v. pp.*, undone, destroyed, ruined, spent, tired

Schill, *adj.*, shrill

Schiref, etc., *n.*, sheriff

Scho, *pron.* and *adj.*, she

Schone, *n. pl.*, shoes

Schore, schoir, *n.*, threat, menace

Schortlie, *adv.*, shortly, immediately

Schot, schoit, etc., *n.*, shot

—(e), schute, *v.*, shoot

Schour, schowr, *n.*, shower

Schow, chow, *n.*, shove, thrust, spring, pounce

Schrew, *n.*, shrew, contrary or perverse person

Schryve, schryif, etc., *v.*, shrive

Schuik, schuke, *v. past*, shook, clattered, broke in pieces

Schuir, *v. past*, cut, sheared

Schulderis, *n. pl.*, shoulders

Schulit, schuillit, *v. pp.*, shovelled, cleared

Schupe, *v. past*, 'shaped,' made to, began

Schyn, schin, etc., *n.*, shin

Scorne, *n.*, laughing-stock, something to be scorned

Screit. *See* Note, *Fables*, 139

Scroll, skrow, *n.*, writing

Sculis, etc., *n. pl.*, schools

Scutchit, *v. past*, scutched

Se, sey, *n.*, sea

—, sy, *v.*, see

Sedull. *See* Cedull

Sege, *n.*, (plant) ? sage, or sedge

Seggis, *n. pl.*, people

Seid, *n.*, seed

  v. = see it

Seik, *adj.*, sick

  v., search, seek

Seill, *n.*, seal

Seinyeis. *See* Senyeis, Sonyeis

Sek, *n.*, sack

Selch(e), *n.*, seal (animal)

Selcouth, *n.*, marvel, strange thing

Seldyn, seldin, *adv.*, seldom, rarely

Sele, *n.*, happiness

Selie, sely, sillie, etc., *adj.*, innocent, foolish, poor, unhappy

Sell, *pron.*, self

Semblie, *n.*, assembly

Sempill, etc., *adj.*, simple

Sen, *adv.*, since

  v., send

Sendill, *adv.*, seldom. *See* Seldyn

Sentence, *n.*, moral, lesson, purpose, opinion ; judgment (of court of law), doom

Senyeis, seinyeis, *n. pl.*, marks, tokens, signs

Senyeour, etc., *n.*, elder man, senior

Serve, *v.*, serve, aid, grant
  v. (*aph.*), deserve
Sessoun, *n.*, season
  n., seasoning
Set, *v.*, normal English uses. Also
  v., become,suit (of a costume) ;
  give, convey, (legal), etc.
Sethe, seith(e), *v.*, boil, cook
Sew(e), sowe, *n.*, pottage, meat-
  broth
  v., sew, stitch
Sic, sik, *adj.*, such, such a one
  adv., so
Sich, sicht, *n.* and *v.*, sigh
Sicht, sycht, *n.*, sight = eyes
Sicker, *adj.* and *adv.*, sure, certain
Speid, *v.*, thrive, speed, save, hurry
Speir, *n.*, spear
—, spheir, spere, *n.*, sphere
—, spere, *v.*, inquire, ask
Speldit, *v. pp.*, skewered, stretched
Spence, *n.*, larder
Spensar, spenser, *n.*, steward
Spill, *v.*, spoil, harm, ruin (*pp.*, spilt)
Spittaill hous, *n.*, lazar-house
Splene, *n.*, spleen, heart
Spoliat(e), *v. pp.* and *adj.*, deprived
Spreit, *n.*, soul, spirit
Spring, spryng, *n.*, merry tune ;
  water-spring
  v., spring, burst, spread
Sprutok, name of a hen. *See*
  Note, *Fables*, 483
Stabil, stable, *adj.*, secure, firm,
  disciplined
Stad, *v. pp.*, beset, bestead
Stair, *n.*, stare, bewildered look
Stall, *v. past*, stole
Stammeris (*MS.* scammeris), *v.*,
  staggers, stumbles
Standfray, (*in adv. and adj. sense*)
  opposed
Stane, *n.*, stone
Stark, *adj.*, stout, strong, stiff

Starnis, *n. pl.*, stars
Stryfe, stryif, *p.*, dispute, contention
Stubbill, *adj.*, stubble
Stude, stuid, *n.*, brood mare
Stule, *n.*, stool, seat
Sturtfull, *adj.*, vexatious
Styll, *n.*, plight
Styme, *n.*, whit, little bit
Subcharge, *n.*, additional course at
  meals
Sucker, *n.*, sugar
Sueitand, *v. p.*, sweating
Suffrage, *n.*, favour, aid
Sugerit, *v. pp.*, sugared
Suith, suth(e), *n.*, truth
—, suyth, etc., *adj.*, true, trustworthy
Sum, *adj.*, some
Sumdeill, *adv.*, somewhat
Summar, *adv.*, shortly, quickly
  (legal)
Sumquhat, *adv.*, somewhat
Superne, *adj.*, celestial, supernal
Superscriptioun, *n.*, description,
  title
Supple, supplie, *n.* and *v.*, aid, help
Suppryis, *n.*, surprise, disappoint-
  ment
  v., surprise, take at a disad-
  vantage
Suspensioun, *n.*, suspension (from
  the sacraments)
Suthfast, *adj.*, honest, reliable
Swak, *n.* and *v.*, swing, heave
Sweir, sueir, *v.*, swear, attest (legal)
Sweit, swete, *n.* and *v.*, sweat
—, sueit, suet, *adj.*, sweet, kindly
Swelly, *v.*, swallow, devour
Swelt, suelt, *v. past*, fainted, died
Swepe, swope, etc., *v.*, sweep
Swerd, etc., *n.*, sword
Swingill, *v.*, scutch
Swyith, swyth, etc., *adv.*, straight-
  way
Swynk, *v.*, labour, work

Syde, syd, *n.*, side
adj., wide
Sydelingis, sidlingis, *adv.*, on one side, sideways
Syis, *n. pl.*, times
Sylet, *v. pp.*, covered, overlaid
Syn, syne, etc., *n.*, sin
Syne, *n.*, sign
adv., then, afterwards
Syropis, *n. pl.*, syrops
Syt(e), *n.*, sorrow, suffering

T

Ta, tay, *n.*, toe
—, tak, *v.*, take
Taid, *n.*, toad
Taikin, takin, taikning, etc., *n.*, token, sign
Tailisman, *n.*, tale-teller
Tailyeis, etc., *n. pl.*, cuts of meat
Tait, *adj.* and *adv.*, playful(ly)
Tak, *n.*, tack, holding
—, ta, *v.*, take
Talia, Thelya, (the Muse Thalia)
Tappok. *See* Note, *Fables*, 483
Tar, tere, *v.*, to handle roughly
Tarage, *n.*, quality, character
Tarie, tary (tarrow), *n.* and *v.*, delay
Tederit, tedderit, *v. pp.*, tethered
Teir, *n.* and *v.*, tear
Teithis, *n. pl.*, teeth
Tendour, *n.*, guide, attender
Tene, teyne, *n.*, anger, fierceness, cruelty
—, teyn, *adj.*, angry, wrathful, cruel
Tent, *n.*, care
Tepat, *n.*, woman's tippet
Term(e), *n.*, term, period, time of repayment
Termigant, *n.*, false god, devil. *See* Note, *Annunciation*, 68
Tersicor, etc. (the Muse Terpsichore)

Teuch, tewch(e), etc., *adj.*, tough
Thairout, *adv. phr.*, in existence
Theolog(e), *n.*, theologian
Theseus, *in error for* Tityus
Thetes, Thetis (sea-nymph)
Thidder, *adv.*, thither
Thift, *n.*, theft
Thig, *v.*, beg
Thik, *adj.*, close
Thir, *pron. pl.*, these
This, *adv.*, thus
Thocht, *n.*, thought
v. past, thought
—, thouch, etc., *adv.* and *conj.*, though
Thole, thoill, etc., *v.*, endure, suffer
Thraf, *adj.*, unleavened
Thrawand, *v. p.*, twisting, wrenching
Thrawart, thrawert, *adj.*, stubborn, crooked, ill-natured
Thrawin, *adj.*, ill-tempered, crooked
v. pp., thrown
Thrift, *n.*, luck
Thrist, *n.*, thirst
Throw, throwch, etc., *prep.*, through, by
Thusgate, etc., *adv.*, in this manner
Tig, *v.*, play with, meddle
Tippit, *v. pp.*, pointed
Tirlit, etc., *v. past*, tugged, pulled
Tirrane, *n.*, tyrant
adj., tyrannical
Tithingis, *n.*, tidings
Titlar, (-is), *n.*, tale-bearer(s)
To, *adv.*, too
= as, for
intensive. Cp. All to rent
-fore, *adv.*, before
Tod, *n.*, fox
Tolter, *adj.*, swinging
Toppok. *See* Tappok
Tothir, tother, *adj.*, other
Toun, *n.*, farmtown, village

Toxicate, *adj.*, poisonous, poisoned
Trace, traiss, *n.*, track, course
Tragedie, *n.*, tragical story
Traist, trest, *v.*, trust, expect, hope
Traistly, trestly, *adv.*, truly, safely
Traitie, *n.*, treatise
Twin, *v.*, part, separate
Twist, *n.*, branch (of a tree)
Twyn, twin, *v.*, twist, destroy
Tyd(e), *n.*, season, time, hour
Tyll, tyl, *prep.*, to
Tyne, *v.*, lose, deprive
Tyt(e), *adv.*, quickly

U

Udir, uthir, *adj.*, other
Unbrynt, *v. pp.*, unburnt
Unce, *n.*, ounce (weight)
Undirta, *v.*, undertake
Uneis, uneith, *adv.*, scarcely, with difficulty
Unfane, *adj.*, displeased, disappointed
Unfute sair, *adj.*, comfortable, at ease
Unhailsum, *adj.*, unhealthy, unlovely
Unlusty, *adj.*, unhealthy, unwholesome
Unlusum, *adj.*, unlovely
Unroikkit, *adj.*, ? excited, vociferant
Unsmart, unsmert, *adj.*, dull (of a bow)
Unsuspect, *adj.*, honest, true (of an assize)
Untill, *prep.*, unto, to
Untment, *n.*, ointment
Unusit, *v. pp.* as *adj.*, not broken in
Unwarly, unwarlie, *adv.*, unwarily, without warning
Unyt. *See* Note, *O. E.*, 224

Uponland, *adj.*, country ; of, or in, the country
Upryse, *v.*, rise up ; *past,* 'uprais'
Upsone, *adv.*, soon up, soon
Uttir, *adj.*, outer

V

Vaill, *n.*, vale
v., avail. *See* Availl
Vailyeit, etc., *v. past. See* Availl
Vaneglore, *n.*, vainglory
Vaneiss, *v.*, disappear, vanish
Veiling, *v. p.*, lowering, taking off
Ver, *n.*, Spring
—, wer, = war (worse)
Verray, *intens. adj.* and *adv.*, very
Vestiment, *n.*, garb
Vilipend, *v.*, dishonour
Vincust, *v. pp.*, vanquished, overcome
Vocatioun, *n.*, calling together, convocation
Voce, woce, *n.*, voice
Volvand, *v. p.*, rolling, tossing
Vult, vilt, *n.*, countenance, expression

W

Wa, *n.*, woe
Wag, *v.*, shake, stir
Waid, *v.*, wade
Waik, *adj.*, weak
Waillit, *v. pp.* as *adj.*, choice
Wailyeit, *v. past,* availed
Wair, *adj.* ? wild, stormy
—, war, *v.*, were
—, ware, *v.*, spend, endure, pass
Wait, wate, wat, etc., *v.*, know
Waith, wacht, *n.*, hunting
Waitskaith. *See* Note, *Fables,* 667
Wald, *v.*, would, wish

Waldyne, waldin, etc., *adj.*, supple, active
Walk, *v.*, walk
— *v.*, watch, wake, awake
Walkrife, walkryfe, *adj.*, vigilant, sleepless, watchful
Wall, *n.*, wall
— *n.*, wave (*pl.*, wallis, wawis)
Wallowit, *v. pp.*, withered
Waltownis, *n. pl.*, walled towns
Wame, wambe, *n.*, belly, stomach, womb
Wammillis, *v.*, rolls, tosses, turns
Wan, *v. past*, won, gained, reached
—, wane, *adj.*, pale, withered
Wane, *n.*, dwelling, abode; purpose
— *v.*, grow less or dull
Wanhope, *n.*, despair
Wanrufe, *adj.*, restless, unhappy
Wappinnis, *n. pl.*, weapons, teeth
Wappit, *v. past*, plunged, dashed down
War, *adj.*, wary, watchful, alert
—, ware, wer, *adj.*, worse
—, wair, etc., *v.*, wear, spend, use up
— *v.*, were
Wardit, *v. pp.*, imprisoned
Warison, waresoun, *n.*, reward
Warldlie, *adj.*, worldly
Warsch(e), *adj.*, sickly in appearance, pallid
Warwolf, *n.*, werewolf
Waryit, *v. pp.*, cursed, execrated
Wawland, *v. p.*, rolling the eyes
Wayting. *See* Waiting (hunting)
Wecht, *n.*, weight
Wedder, weddir, *n.*, weather
— *n.*, wether
Wedlingis streit. *See* Note, *O. E.*, 188
Wedo, wedow, *n.*, widow, widower
Weid, *n.*, weed, withered grass
— *n.*, garment
Weir, *n.*, doubt, fear, apprehension

Weir, wer, *n.*, war, dispute, feud
— *v.*, wear, waste away
— *v.*, ward off
— *v.*, were, would be, was
Weird, werd, *n.*, fate, destiny
Weit, wete, *n.*, wet, rain, sap
— *v.*, wet
Welterand, *v. p.* and *adj.*, weltering, rolling, struggling
Welterit, *v. pp.*, overthrown, reversed
Wendin, *v.*, change (as the moon)
Wene, wein, *n.*, doubt
— *v.*, think, believe, etc.
Werk, wark, *n.*, work
Wery, werie, *adj.*, weary; w. for= weary of
— *v.*, weary, tire
— *adv.*, very
Wesche, *n.*, 'wash,' stale urine
— *v.*, wash
Wex, *v.*, vex, anger
Wicht, wycht, *n.*, wight, man
— *adj.*, strong, sturdy, powerful
Wickit, wicket, *adj.*, wicked, unfortunate
Widderit, *adj.*, withered, stale
Widdinek. *See* Note, *Fables*, 661
Wilfull, *adj.*, deliberate, true; freely undertaken, willing
Will, *adj.*, 'wild,' uncertain, at a loss for
Wilsum, *adj.*, wild, wandering, etc.
Winning, wynning, *n.*, dwelling, abiding
Wirking, *n.*, working, power
Wirrie, *n.*, worry, kill, devour
Wis, wiss, wyss, *n.*, wish, desire
— *v.*, know, be aware of
— *adj.*, wise
Wisk, quhisk, *n.* and *v.*, whisk
Wit, *n.*, wit, brains, reason; *pl.*, 'wittis fyve,' five senses
— *v.*, know

Wit, *prep.*, with, by
Withgang, *n.*, liberty
Withouttin, *prep.*, without
Wod(e), woid, wid, *n.*, wood
—, woude, *adj.*, mad, wild
Wodwyss, *n. See* Note, *Fables*, 902
Woik, woke, wouke, *v.*, lay awake
Woir, *v.*, more ; *out w.*, blew out
Womenting, *n.*, sorrow, bewailing
Wonder, winder, etc., *adv.*, very, wonderfully, etc.
Wonyng, *n.*, ? winning, gain
Worth, wirth, *n.*, worth, value
  v., become, be worth, be
Wow, *n.*, vow, wool
  v., woo
Woweir, *n.*, wooer, suitor
Wraik, *n.*, vengeance, punishment
—, wreik, *v.*, avenge, punish, revenge
Wraith, *n.*, wrath, anger, ferocity
—, wreith, *adj.*, angry
  v., anger
Wrak, *n.*, goods, gear
Wrappit, *v. pp.*, thrown down (*cp.* Wappit), enveloped, overcome
Wrethly, *adv.*, ? quickly (rathely) or angrily. (*Cp.* Wraith)
Wrink, wrynk, *n.*, trick, wile
Wrocht, *v. pp.*, wrought, fashioned
Wryt(e), *v.* write ; *past* wrait, wrett, wrat(e)
Wryth, *v.*, expel, turn away

Wy, *n.*, man, person
Wyn, won, *v.*, dwell
  v., gain, procure, learn, reach, escape, etc.
Wynd, *v.*, guide (of a plough)
Wyrschip, *n.*, worship, honour
Wyse, wyis, etc., *n.*, way, method, style
  adj., wise
Wyte, *n.* and *v.*, blame

Y

Yaip, *adj.*, eager
Yede, yeid, etc., *v. past*, went
Yeild, *v.*, requite
Yett, *n.*, gate
Ying, yowng, *adj.*, young
Yis, yes
Yit, *adv.*, yet ; then, when
Ympit. *See* Impit
Yneuch, ynewe. *See* Aneuch
Yokkit, *v. pp.* as *adj.*, yoked, harnessed
Yone, *adj.*, yon, yonder, that
Youtheid, etc., *n.*, youth
Yow, *n.*, ewe
Ypodorica, *or* Ipotdorica, *n. See* Note, *O. E.*, 369
Yporlerica, *n. See* Note, *O. E.*, 370
Ythand, ithand, *adj.*, busy, constant
Yude. *See* Yeid
Yung. *See* Ying